Phoenix of Drury Lane

*Anthea & Jane
From with love

With best wishes
from Peter Thorogood*

Extract from Thomas Hood's engraving, *The Progress of Cant*, showing the new St. Pancras Church in the centre. Instead of the architect's caryatids, Hood has added three elegantly attired society ladies, possibly actresses, thus drawing a parallel between St. Pancras New Church and the new Theatre Royal, Drury Lane, rebuilt in 1812.
(*By kind permission of Aberdeen University*)

Phoenix of Drury Lane
Theatre Royal London

The Sensational Story of London's Greatest Theatre

Peter Thorogood

Bramber Press

First published in 2022 by
Bramber Press
St. Mary's House
Bramber
West Sussex
BN44 3WE
Email: info@bramberpress.co.uk
www.bramberpress.co.uk

Copyright © Peter Thorogood 2022

The right of Peter Thorogood to be identified as the author of this work has been asserted by him in accordance with the Copyright, Designs and Patents Act 1988.

All rights reserved. No part of this publication may be reproduced, stored in a retrieval system, or transmitted, in any form or by any means, electronic, mechanical, photocopying, recording or otherwise, without the prior written permission of the author.

Phoenix of Drury Lane includes parts of letters transcribed many years ago for research purposes and the furtherance of scholarship. Every effort has been made to trace copyright holders. The Bramber Press will be pleased to correct unattributed inclusions in any future editions.

ISBN 978-1-905206-04-9

Design and formatting by Alan Durden

Printed and bound in the UK

*To
the Memory of Derek Wise
Late Chairman of the Byron Society of London
for many convivial conversations about books;
To Maureen O'Connor
former Director of the Byron Society of London,
for her encouragement of my Byron adventure,
and to Members of the Society
for affording me the honour of addressing them
on the vital role played by Byron
in the sensational reopening of
the new Theatre Royal Drury Lane in 1812*

Publications by Peter Thorogood

A Sent-to-Coventry Carol and Other Verses, or, Men, Women, and Other Beasts. Autolycus Press (1961 OP)
Love, said the Astronomers, and Other Poems. Autolycus Press (1961 OP)
Thomas Hood: The Uncrowned Laureate. Privately printed. (1967 (OP)
Translations and Eloborations from Federico Garcia Lorca. British Council Poets (1970 OP)
Thomas Hood and 'The Progress of Cant': *A Study in Iconography . Papers in Research and Criticism.* Ed. D.Hawes. Polytechnic of Central London (1977 OP)
'Thomas Hood: A Nineteenth Century Author and his Relations with the Book Trade to 1835.' In *Development of the English Book Trade, 1700-1899.* Ed. Robin Myers and Michael Harris. Oxford Polytechnic. (1981. 2nd impression 1982, 3rd impression 1983 OP)
Thomas Hood: Poems Comic and Serious. With an introduction and notes. Bramber Press (1995)
Thomas Hood: A Chronological Table of his Life and Times. Bramber Press (1999)
The Witty and the Tender Hood. Readings for performance, arranged by Peter Thorogood.. Bramber Press (1999)
In These Places ...At These Times: Selected Poems 1950-1975 (Smallprint 1997) With watercolours and pen-and-ink sketches by the author.
St Mary's Bramber: A Sussex House and its Gardens Illustrated. English Life Publications Ltd (1998).
St Mary's Bramber: A Pictorial Souvenir Illustrated. (1998).
The Complete Comic and Curious Verse of Peter Thorogood . (Smallprint) (2006) Illustrated with comic pen-and-ink sketches by the author.
South of the River: A Novel of the Fifties (2005)
Could I Hear That Again, Please?: Views and Reviews of a Well-tuned Listener Articles for the BBC weekly magazine *The Listener* 1966-67 (Bramber Press 2006)

Edited works
Late Flowering: Poems for Aurelia. Diana Dykes. Edited with a foreward by Peter Thorogood. (2002) Aurelia and Sylvia Plath interest.
The Tale of Septmus Jones and *The Tale of Sylvester Doo.* Garnet Durham. Illustrated. For young children. Illustrated by Charles Coleman. Edited by Peter Thorogood. (2005)
Portrait of Village Life: Beeding and Bramber with Botolphs in Sussex (2011) Miniature essays by Sussex local historian Keith Nethercoate Bryant. Collated, edited and illustrated, with a biographical introduction and notes.
Two Hearts that Would be True. Poems by twin sisters Margaret and Brenda Carpenter. With biographical introductions by Peter Thorogood.

About the Author

PETER THOROGOOD was educated at Brentwood School (1937-1945), after which he spent a gap year at the London School of Economics (1946-47), where his tutors were Harold Laski, Chairman of the Labour Party, and distinguished criminologist, Karl Mannheim. He proceeded to Trinity College, Dublin (1948-52), where he read Modern Languages (French and Italian), after which he was appointed Director of Studies at the British School of Milan, being promoted to Vice-Principal in 1957.

In 1960, he became Lecturer in English Studies at the British Council in London and, as a visiting lecturer, went on special academic assignments to Bulgaria and Poland under the Communist regimes. He lectured on summer schools in Germany, Greece and Israel, the latter during the Six-Day War. In 1969, he joined the Polytechnic of Central London (now part of the University of Westminster) as Senior Lecturer in English Language and Literature in charge of evening courses, and was subsequently elected a Member of the Academic Council in 1979.

Peter retired in 1984 to take on the task of rescuing the medieval pilgrim inn, St. Mary's, in Bramber, Sussex, in partnership with the conservator and designer, Roger Linton DesRCA. Together, with the help of teams of local volunteers for over 35 years, they succeeded in bringing the house and gardens back to the splendour they are today and to open to the public during the spring and summer seasons. For ten years Peter was, concurrently, 'Key-Keeper' of Bramber Castle (National Trust) on behalf of Emglish Heritage management. Peter and Roger both received MBEs for conservation and the arts in the Queen's 80th Birthday Honours in 2006.

Peter Thorogood is a Fellow of the Society of Antiquaries and over sixty years a Fellow of the Royal Society of Arts. He is an authority on the life and work of the Victorian poet, Thomas Hood, and has, over the years, collected a fine library of first editions of Hood's works, as well as a collection of his letters, pen-and-ink sketches, water-colours, and other memorabilia.

Acknowledgements

London 1960-1980

I am grateful to the late Professor Roger Sharrock (1919-1990), former Head of English at King's College, London, who recognised the value of my research into the life and work of Thomas Hood and my enthusiasm for my subject. I am also grateful to my former tutor, John Woolford, since then, Professor of Nineteenth Century Literature and Culture at Sheffield University, for his patience and forbearance in accepting a very part-time middle-aged postgraduate student with only one day a week to spare in the pursuit of his chosen subject.

I should not forget my former Head of the Department of Languages at the Polytechnic of Central London (now University of Westminster), the late Professor Peter Newmark (1916-2011), who, though sceptical of my ever finishing my thesis, allowed me my 'Friday off' for research, and trusted that one day I would finally type in the last full stop!

I thank especially the distinguished publisher, the late John 'Jock' Murray (1908-1993) and the late Leslie Marchand (1900-1999), editor of the invaluable *John Murray* edition of Byron's letters (1973-1982), with both of whom I enjoyed pleasant and useful conversations and advice during my Byron researches in the 1970s.

I began my research before computers were made more widely available. Writers and researchers relied heavily on library catalogues, and major resources such as the *Dictionary of National Biography*, the *Oxford Companion to English Literature*, the Bowker two-volume *Books in Print*, and a wide range of specialist reference works.

Sussex 1990-2021

Derek Wise, (1925-2012), Chairman of the Byron Society of London, friend and discerning fellow-bibliophile, had an equal passion for browsing through the shelves of antiquarian bookshops in London and the provinces. It was he who found for me one of the most precious books in my library: Benjamin Dean Wyatt's *Observations on the Principles of a design for a Theatre*, a rare volume which provided me with first-hand information on the rebuilding of the Theatre Royal, Drury Lane, for which Wyatt was the chosen architect.

I have been greatly helped by Robin Myers MBE FSA, friend of some sixty years, former archivist of Stationer's Hall, London, and a luminary in the world of bibliography. Dr. Paul Davis, of Buckingham University, gave me the incalculable benefit of his academic and publishing expertise. Anne Jennings and Elspeth Clarkson kindly gave me their time as research assistants.

I have no words to match the loyalty and industry of my friends, Alan and Diana Durden, for their practical help in seeing my book through to its finished stages – Alan, for months of detailed editing, formatting and final presentation, and Diana, for her patient and meticulous proof-reading. Latterly, useful comments were given, by Emeritus Professor Jackie Bratton, Royal Holloway College, as I at last approached the finishing line.

Contents

List of Colour Illustrations	xi
Preface	xiii
INTRODUCTION: Abbey Garden to 'Old Drewerie'	**1**
CHAPTER ONE: Tennis Court to Temple of the Muses	**11**
1. Davenant and Killigrew: New Beginnings	12
2. Dryden and the New House	15
3. Colley Cibber and the Ruthless Reign of Christopher Rich	21
4. William Collier and the Triumvirate	25
5. Addison's *Cato* and Whig Politics	28
6. The Decline of Cibber and the Decline of Drury	34
7. Revival with Fleetwood and Macklin	36
8. Westminster Tories and the Drury Whigs	37
9. Garrick and the Prima Donnas	43
CHAPTER TWO: Richard Brinsley Sheridan – The Profligate Accountant	**49**
1. Wheelings and Dealings	50
2. Sarah Siddons: 'The Tragic Muse'	53
3. Henry Holland and his 'New Drury'	56
4. Dog Days at Drury!	63
5. 'The Young Roscius' Saves the Day	65
6. Decline and Fall	67
CHAPTER THREE: Prologue and Epilogue	**71**
1. Tradition and Purpose in the Prologues	72
2. Classical to Neo-Classical: Jonson to Johnson	80
3. Monody and Threnody	86
CHAPTER FOUR: Plagiary and Parody	**91**
1. The Spanish Theme	92
2. The Purpose of Parody	99
3. From Travesty to Tragedy	102
CHAPTER FIVE: The Great Literary Competition of 1811	**113**
1. Whitbread, and Wyatt's 'New Drury'	114
2. Rivals in Platitudes: The Genuine Rejected Addresses 1812	123
CHAPTER SIX: A Noble Lord and His Noble Critic	**141**
1. The French Connection: The Holland House Set	142
2. Byron's 'Ferocious Rhapsody'	148
3. Byron: Champion of the Frame-Breakers	153
CHAPTER SEVEN: The Reluctant Poet: Execution or Persecution?	**163**
1. The Making of the Drury Lane 'Address'	164
2. Putting the Final Touches	177
3. A Matter of Urgency	185

CHAPTER EIGHT: Phoenix Triumphant — 191
1. 'In one dread night…' — 192
2. Lord Byron's Real Sir Fretful — 198
3. A Man of Many Parts: Busby the Polymath — 203
4. 'Inspiring Apollo' and 'Lucretian Fire' — 208
5. Battle of Wits: Byron versus Busby — 214
6. The Flickering Flame of Fame — 221
7. 'Mad, bad, and dangerous to know' — 226

CHAPTER NINE: The Rejected Addresses — 235
1. Horace and James Smith: Parody Personified — 236
2. *A Loyal Effusion* by W.T.F. (W.T. Fitzgerald) — 242
3. *The Baby's Début* by W.W. (William Wordsworth) — 245
4. *An Address without a Phoenix* (James Smith) — 252
5. *Cui Bono?* (Byron) — 254
6. *The Hampshire Farmer* (Samuel Whitbread) — 257
7. *The Living Lustres* (Thomas Moore) — 261
8. *The Rebuilding* (Robert Southey) — 264
9. *Drury's Dirge* (Laura Matilda) — 279

CHAPTER TEN: The Shape of Things to Come — 301
1. Edmund Kean: A Tempestuous Spirit — 302
2. Stephen Price: An American Means Business — 303
3. Pride shall have a fall: Alfred Bunn and William Macready — 306
4. Dion Boucicault Saves the Day — 308
5. The Great 'Gussie': Pantomime versus Opera — 310
6. Arthur Collins: From Seedsman to Saviour — 313
7. Nights out for the Working Classes — 315
8. The Monologue: The Comic Genius of Dan Leno — 318
9. Henry Irving: All Bells and No Vampires — 321
10. Curtain Up on a New Era — 325

Appendix A: Anthology of Monologues — 329

Appendix B: Poems, Plays and Prologues mentioned in the text — 346

Appendix C: Published authors of the Genuine Addresses — 348
   Index of first lines in Genuine Rejected Addresses — 351
   Authors Parodied in Rejected Addresses — 354

The Theatre Royal, Drury Lane: A Timeline — 355

Sources and Further Reading:
   Holland House Papers (British Museum) — 357
   Bibliography — 360
   Sources, notes and references — 366

Index of persons — 383

Subject index — 390

List of Colour Illustrations

Frontispiece: Extract from Thomas Hood's cartoon The Progress of Cant, showing the new St. Pancras Church

1. Thomas Killigrew
2. Charles Macklin
3. David Garrick as Richard III
4. Sarah Siddons
5. William Henry Betty (the 'Young Roscius')
6. Portrait of Richard Brinsley Sheridan
7. John Philip Kemble
8. Statue of Dr Samuel Johnson
9. Ambrose Philips
10. Samuel Whitbread
11. View of Drury Lane under construction
12. Façade of architect Henry Holland's Drury Lane 1794
13. View of Drury Lane showing entrance to foyer
14. Old Drury Lane theatre on fire in 1809
15. Contemporary print of Old Drury Lane in flames
16. Whitbread Brewery
17. 'Clearing away the Rubbish of Old Drury' (cartoon)
18. Lady Elizabeth Holland
19. Portrait of Sir Godfrey Webster
20. Portrait of Lord Holland
21. Mary Russell Mitford
22. Robert Elliston
23. Lord Byron in Albanian dress
24. Lady Caroline Lamb
25. The Hon. Augusta Leigh
26. Catherine Gordon, Byron's mother
27. Extract from Hood's *Progress of Cant* cartoon
28. Frederick Howard, 5th Earl of Carlisle
29. Charles Maurice de Talleyrand
30. Bonaparte crossing the Alps on a white stallion
31. Bonaparte crossing the Alps on a mule
32. The King of Brobdingnag and Gulliver (cartoon)
33. Nottingham market place
34. Ned Ludd, leader of the Luddites
35. Frame breakers
36. The Grande Théâtre de Bordeaux
37. Benjamin Wyatt's Theatre Royal
38. Henry Vassall-Fox, 3rd Baron Holland
39. Revd. Gilbert Wakefield

40. Caricature of Lord and Lady Holland
41. Edmund Kean as Richard III
42. William Macready as Macbeth
43. Sir Henry Irving
44. *The Four Mr. Prices* cartoon

Note: Every effort has been made to trace copyright holders and the author will be happy to correct mistakes or omissions in future editions.

Preface

In the summer of 1965, as part of my research into the life and work of the 19th century poet and caricaturist, Thomas Hood, I found myself in the Prints and Drawings Department of the British Museum. It was there that I first set eyes on Thomas Hood's etching *The Progress of Cant*, the study of which would, for some years, lead me away from the main line of my Hood research, into an entirely new area, much beloved by him – the London Theatre.

The Progress of Cant is an intricate design with a complex network of some fifty human figures, each carrying a banner protesting about a contentious issue of the day. At the centre of the etching, in which Hood displays his supreme mastery of the visual pun, is an image of a building under construction (see frontispiece). Ostensibly, it is an image of St. Pancras New Church, over which there was much debate, for it was the most costly enterprise since Wren's St. Paul's Cathedral. Hood points to the controversy surrounding the adoption of neoclassical decoration by architect William Inwood[*] for his new church which was seen by some critics as inappropriate for the changing times. Inwood had boldly introduced a copy of the Erechtheion, with its four supporting caryatids, again a dominant feature of the Parthenon and a major challenge to the anti-classicists.

Inwood's caryatids at St. Pancras New Church   The Caryatid porch of the Erechtheion, Athens

More relevant for our purpose is that Hood's image covertly refers to the controversy over the style of, and costings for, Benjamin Wyatt's new Theatre Royal Drury Lane. Hood adds an opulent frieze of bucrania (or ox skulls), which were to form part of the decoration on the north face of

---

[*] William Inwood (1794-1843). Architect. Designed St. Pancras New Church (1819-1894) in fashionable Greek style, with an Erechtheum on the north side facing the Euston Road.

the Parthenon, and echoes Inwood's Erechtheion by transforming three of the four caryatids into elegantly attired female figures, adorned with priceless pearl necklaces, a possible reference to the three principal mistresses of the Prince Regent: the actress Mary Robinson, Maria Fitzherbert and Frances Villiers, Countess of Jersey.

Hood's version of the new Theatre Royal

The consistent threads of my book are not only about the stage, its actors and managers, but about poetry and the role it played in moulding the thoughts and sensibilities of audiences. If anything, the early 17th century and late 19th century chapters are like bookends between which stand a number of topics, all inter-related, yet existing individually in their own right. The story is like a labyrinth, its twists and turns taking readers through a variety of experiences. At all times, I hope it is an enjoyable if eccentric journey through the why's and wherefore's of theatrical tradition. Traditional prologues and epilogues, for example, would provide the authors of the sensational 'Drury Lane Addresses' with the vital substance for their verses.

My theme then is not primarily about the history of a famous London theatre. Neither is it simply an account of plays or acting. It will also be about the inner life of a specific theatre, and some unusual aspects of its existence – not normally part of an account of the stage and its role in the life of performers and audiences. Sometimes the reader seems to be experiencing the rough-and-tumble of life in the theatre - in the critic's study as he scribbles his reviews, perhaps attending a 'Siddons Night', being present at an interval show-down with the Prince Regent, or getting involved in a riot in 'the gods'. By 'eavesdropping' on the epistolary 'conversations' between Byron and Lord Holland, we can learn something of the detail of their exchanges. We can witness the struggle to create a prologue. We can observe the comical and sometimes vicious wrangles between plagiarists and imitators as they steal scenes and ideas from one another. Meanwhile, the threat of invasion by Napoleon (beloved of Whig extremists such as Lord and Lady Holland, Byron, Thomas Moore and Robert Southey), hung like a shadow over the nation and, countered by copious references to Nelson, Wellington, and other patriotic Britons, made a frequent appearance in the 'Addresses'.

Parody would create vicious rivalries, enough to ridicule authors mercilessly and, in its most devastating form, destroy reputations. Rivalry between playwrights frequently arose from instances of blatant plagiarism, as wittily portrayed in Sheridan's *The Critic* - a cunning satire on the practice.

The framework of *Phoenix of Drury Lane* consists of a number of studies arranged in a sequence and at least ostensibly is about the establishment of an English tradition of drama, from John Dryden to David Garrick and Richard Brinsley Sheridan, to the great days of Henry Irving and Dan Leno - a tale of the highs and lows, triumphs and failures, thrills and scandals of the London stage. At its centre, it tells of the sensational destruction by fire of the Theatre Royal, Drury Lane, in 1809, its rebuilding, and re-opening in 1812, and the extraordinary public protests that followed. It explains the hold Lord Holland had in persuading a reluctant Lord Byron to attempt the composition of an opening 'Address' for the newly-built theatre, and the events that unexpectedly led to the publication by two brothers, Horace and James Smith, of a remarkable collection of poetical parodies. *Rejected Addresses, or, Theatrum Poetarum,* an unpretentious little volume, which would light up the London social scene, become the talk of the literary *cognoscenti* for decades to come, and as such was destined to remain an intriguing part of publishing history.

I had for some years been in search of an annotated volume (1829) of the *Rejected Addresses*, with a useful introduction by Andrew Boyle. I hoped the book would give me a clue as to the whereabouts of the original manuscripts of the 112 genuine Addresses submitted by the aspiring poets for the opening of the new Theatre. Once the book was found, I was disappointed to discover that the editor considered it unnecessary to reveal the manner in which he came into possession of 'this fair sample of the present state of poetry in Britain.' In due course, I acquired a later edition containing the Preface to the Eighteenth Edition (1833), in which it was revealed that Horace's own 'Address' had been at one time sold 'with two volumes of the original Addresses at Mr. Winston's sale Dec 14 1840'.

A chance find - Arthur H. Beavan's 1899 biography of the authors of *Rejected Addresses* - in a corner of Walter Spencer's antiquarian bookshop in Holborn some years later, would lead me to a further discovery. A footnote revealed that the elusive *Genuine Addresses* manuscript had been acquired by the British Museum and lodged with the Department of Manuscripts.

A few weeks after my discovery I was once again sitting at my usual desk in the Print Room reflecting upon the series of events that had led me at last to this particular place at this particular time. The leather-bound albums were finally before me. I opened the first of them to find page after page of neatly pasted-in, hand-written originals of the *Genuine Addresses*. In the following months, my Fridays were spent copying out those parts of each poem (only 21 of the original 112 had been published), adding my thoughts and opinions as I read. These were typed out on my primitive portable Olivetti typewriter at home each evening. There were no computers or laptops in those days!

Scholars and researchers today are largely spared that degree of ingenuity, dexterity and expecially physical energy required to track down over space and time the minutiae of their research. The internet is there to help - an instantaneous resolution to a problem that might have taken weeks or even months to discover in my day. The excitement of discovery after climbing through mountains of research is almost unkown today. At least it avoids that breathless, feverish rush of note-taking necessary to beat the deadline at closing time. But let us to return to the pre-digital age.

The second volume was a revelation. It contained the whole of Lord Holland's correspondence with Lord Byron concerning the writing of Byron's attempt at composing an 'Address', which was to play an important part in the dramatic events that were destined to follow. These letters I interwove with Byron's letters to Lord Holland, thus showing the growth of the poet's mind as he wrestled with the choice of images and metaphors. This had never been attempted before. The poem had long been relegated to the bottom of the pile. It became clear that I had to discover how the friendship between Byron and Lord Holland had come about and what the secret was which made that historic liaison so vital a part of the story.

In 1979, I became heavily involved with committee work at the Polytechnic of Central London, and it seemed inevitable that my Drury Lane project had to be put on hold. There were countless moments when I hoped to return to the *Drury Lane* project. In 2012, by coincidence exactly two hundred years after the opening of Wyatt's new theatre, the opportunity arose to revive and complete my researches. What follows, nine years on, is my testament to the remarkable survival of a great theatre.

Peter Thorogood
Bramber, West Sussex
2 June 2021

INTRODUCTION

Abbey Garden to 'Old Drewerie'

Place of Faith and Place of Fornication

Looking eastwards from the medieval tower of the 'West Mynstre' in 1539, before Henry VIII dissolved the monasteries, it was possible to look over pleasant pastures and peaceful convent gardens, bordered on the north side by a leafy lane known as Long Acre, and on the south side by 'The Strande' (shore), bordering the Thames and stretching from the City of London to the Palace of Whitehall and beyond. The district between adjoined the precinct of Savoy, though the Savoy Palace, once the home of John of Gaunt, had itself fallen into dereliction with the changing political times and had suffered the indignity of being divided up into tenancies, destined to be destroyed by rebels during the Peasants' Revolt.

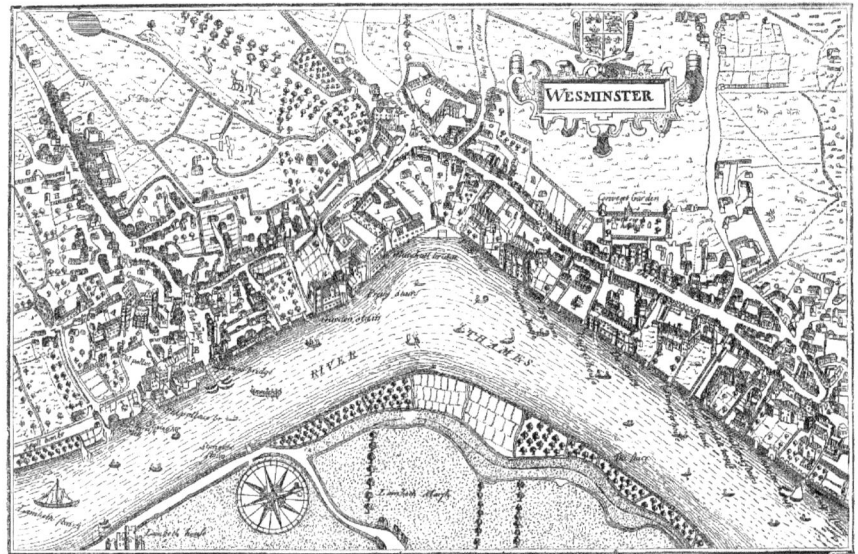

Plan of Westminster (1593) showing Covent Garden, Lincoln's Inn Fields and Drury Lane on the right.

The contrast of the west end of London and the east end must have been a striking one. The juxtaposition of a nunnery next to a street of rowdy inns and taverns presents an image of extremes, more so because the Strand itself was at times a quagmire of 'noxious and foule' mud, discarded offal and horse dung. Boards were laid down for the use of pedestrians, and crossing-sweepers toiled endlessly to keep the ways clear. It was in such squalid conditions that the carriages of the nobility and wealthier classes trundled and rattled their way to theatres and coffee houses in one direction, and out to the more salubrious rural villages of Kensington, Chelsea and Chiswick in the other.

North of the Strand and bordering the river, once lay the great palaces of the nobility: Leicester House, Arundel House, Somerset House and Savoy House. The only palace to survive was Somerset House, formerly the London residence of the Dukes of Somerset, and even that was demolished in the 18th century and replaced by the splendid building we know today.

Sir Richard Drury's large 15th century mansion was situated on the other side of the Strand in Wyche Street, off Old Wyche (Aldwych), in the parish of St. Clement Danes. Drury House, built by Sir William Drury,[*] who held command of the Irish Forces during the reign of Elizabeth, was the house in which the Earl of Essex had plotted the Queen Elizabeth's downfall. Early maps seem to show the existence of a medieval hall with a central lantern. In the course of time, the Drury family broke the estate up by granting leases for the mansion house and its outbuildings, the court and garden, and Drury Stables. Drury House ended its long and distinguished life by being reduced to a drinking establishment called 'The Queen of Bohemia'.

Inevitably, leases became fragmented 'leaving the great aristocratic dwellings...beached like the flotsam of less distinguished neighbours....' By the nineteenth century, the parish of St. Clement Danes had fallen in grace to such a degree that even the tradesman had deserted it, leaving only the poor and destitute to eke out their lives until they were all swept away by street development. The *London Spy*, remarking on the resultant increase in crime and immorality in the area, reported that the Hundred of Drury was made up of several parishes:

> There are reckoned to be one hundred and seven pleasure houses within and about this settlement; and a Roman Catholic priest who has lodged here for many years, assures me that to his knowledge the Societies for the Reformation of Morals have taken as much pains, and expended as large sums to reclaim this new Sodom, as would have fitted out a force sufficient to have conquered the Spanish West Indies.[1]

In Shakespeare's time there were steam-baths, or 'stewes', on the south bank of the Thames, which were the haunt of 'bawds and loose women'. Since no houses of whatever quality possessed bathrooms before the latter part of the 17th century, it was still customary for the middle and upper classes to visit bath-houses, known as 'hummums' or 'bagnios'. In such places, members of the 'oldest profession' were still practising their

---

[*] Sir William Drury (1527-1579). Lord Justice to the Council of Ireland. As a Protestant, he retired from public life on the accession of Queen Mary. Knighted in 1570, he escaped assassination several times.

trade. Many of the grand houses, once owned by Royalists in the locality, had been confiscated during the Civil War and rapidly deteriorated into places of ill-repute. It seems that the word 'drowerie' or 'drewerie' may have existed since the 13th century and stood for a place designated for sexual assignation and recreation. One such place was close to Snow Hill in the neighbourhood of St. Clement Danes. Such favours were offered nightly even under the elegant arches of the newly-built Piazza in Covent Garden.

> The houses were built very high and close together, the upper part projecting over the lower, thus admitting very little light... At the back of this court there stood formerly a block of houses, from four to five storeys in height, which were let out to vagrants, thieves, sharpers, smashers, and other abandoned characters. Throughout the vaults of this dark and dangerous place there existed a continuous communication or passage, so that easy access could be obtained from one to the other, facilitating escape or concealment in the event of pursuit, which, from the nature of the nefarious trafficking, in practice very often occurred.
>
> In the more prosperous middle class district, merchants in the catering and confectionary businesses converted their cellars into ice wells, as did the more well-to-do houses of the new terraces. Newspapers reported that, in the summer months, 4000 tons of ice were consumed every day by the more affluent residents of central London.

After the Great Plague of 1665 and the Great Fire in 1666, when 400 streets were burnt to the ground, homeless city-dwellers, looking out for cheap rooms to rent, caused serious over-crowding in the area around Covent Garden and Drury Lane. Grasping slum landlords charging high rents were a social menace. Since ventilation was discouraged by the State, most builders planned houses with only a few windows on the ground floor, whilst cellars, stairwells and closets were dark, airless and invariably disease-ridden dens of iniquity.

Between Lincoln's Inn Fields almost as far as what was to become Regent Street, stretched a vast slum which, on the south side, bordered the Strand itself. The infamous 'Rookery' near to St. Giles Church was a 'quintessential London horror' where impoverished tenants existed like rats, huddled in attics and on rooftops. No less than 84 sewers polluted the river and 600,000 people had no water supply. All manner of crime and immorality began to thrive in the adjoining streets. Seven Dials, with its seven radial streets, was a place of beggary, trading in illicit wares and cheapjack goods. Marauding gangs of discontented youths threaded their way through pickpockets and prostitutes plying their trades among the sight-seeing crowds. A story is told of the dramatist, John Dryden, who was on his way home to his house in Long Acre on 18 December 1679 when he was assaulted by a crowd of thugs and suffered considerable injury as a result.

Thieving Lane, by J T Smith, 1808

The streets of London were just as threatening in the days of Henry Fielding and Charles Dickens as in former times when James I had been forced to stop the rash of criminality with his Stabbing Act. The Act, repealed in 1828, provided that, should a person be stabbed and die from his wounds, the culprit would suffer the death penalty 'without the benefit of clergy'. If the victim survived more than six months, the sentence was commuted to manslaughter 'with the benefit of clergy'. Lord Ellenborough's 'Malicious Shooting or Stabbing Act' of 1803 sought to clarify the law further by including malicious shooting and 'the murthering of Bastard children', thus introducing a new attitude to abortion, the sentence for which was transportation or the death penalty. In Scotland, the Act was still further extended to include the discharge of fire arms, and cutting, wounding, poisoning, disfiguring or disabling a person.

Following the Great Fire in 1666, one ambitious speculator, quickly took up the challenge. He was Nicholas Barbon, the son of the Puritan 'Praise-God Barebones'. His full birth-name was Nicholas If-Jesus-Christ-Hadst-Not-Died-For-Thee-Thou-Hadst-Been-Damned, a name which turned out to be not much of a compliment in his maturity, yet such a burden did not prevent him from seeing the attractions of a speculative career in property.

As an economist, he was the creator of the idea of the 'free market'. He stepped forward with alacrity to snap up swathes of land and schemed to create a network of squares and streets of terraced houses, which could be rapidly erected to provide refuge to the homeless citizens of the City. Such was the origin of Bloomsbury and its environs. In so doing, he encouraged the idea of connecting up the Cities of London and Westminster. The wily Nicholas always had an eye to the main chance and was soon to invent and collar the mortgage market with his 'National Land Bank'. In spite of his skills he overstretched his funds and died penniless in 1698.

Gradually the extensive selling of parcels of land by greedy speculators altered the social spectrum and gave rise to inappropriate development. The 3rd Duke of Bedford, landlord of the Theatre Royal Drury Lane, sold many such plots when he leased out his land for building. In time, the inns and taverns of the elegant Covent Garden Piazza disappeared in favour of shops and coffee-houses.

The noise, rowdiness, and vulgarity of street life were invariably reflected in the low-grade, even obscene, content of the some of the plays themselves. As to the jostling assemblies of unruly theatregoers, there was little or no control as seats were not numbered – the more energetic ruffians able to dodge from pit to gallery and back again to avoid purchasing a ticket. Noisy orange-sellers drowned out the actors with their calls.

Disorderly conduct broke out not only among the lower orders. The aristocracy and even royal personages could break the bounds of decency, and propriety too. An unfortunate incident occurred in the Crush Room (the Rotunda) at Drury Lane one evening, shortly before the opening of the new theatre, when the old King came face to face with his son, the Prince Regent, and set about him with some violence. He smacked the Prince's face and boxed his ears in full view of the attendant company. The Management, wishing to avoid such a event happening again, decided that there should be a 'King's Side' and a 'Prince's Side', and 'the Rotunda was made a 'no man's land' to the Royal parties, who were tactfully persuaded to keep in future to the territory allotted to them.' [2]

Introduction

One of the beleaguered poets of the *Genuine Addresses* called to task the playwrights and managers for the lewdness of their plays:

> In earlier days, offended Wisdom sigh'd
> At Wit deprav'd and talents misapplied;
> When grossest ribaldry in Charles's reign
> Encourag'd Vice, and gave fair Virtue pain;
> For brightest Wit became its own disgrace,
> That rais'd a blush on Betty's[*] modest face!
> Licentious Plays debauch'd – the Actors too!,
> They copied manners which their Authors drew.

Whilst the upper tiers were reserved for the more elegant, well-behaved aristocratic part of society, there was frequent disruption and mayhem in the pit, where dangerous and explosive arguments and fights could break out at any moment. Actors could not be heard above the tumultuous racket and sometimes had to come forward to plead with their audiences for more calm and consideration.

In spite of some theatres enjoying the dignity and honour of royal patronage, even they might quite conceivably have been closer to houses of questionable repute. Sir Charles Sedley, for example, shared the sexual favours of Nell Gwynne[†] with Lord Buckhurst before the King took on the role. In 1663, these two libertines visited the Cock Tavern in Bow Street and, after imbibing large volumes of drink, were reported to have exhibited themselves on the balcony in indecent postures and gave great discomfiture to those present – Sir Charles going so far as to strip naked. Thus represented, the aristocratic class was not exempt from public condemnation and ridicule. In 1669, the actor, Kynaston, unwise enough to mimic Sedley, was beaten up by a posse of Sedley's men. As we shall see, any young girl intent upon a career on the stage was putting her virtue at great risk unless she could very soon acquire a protector, an actor or manager perhaps who had a heart of gold and the character of a saint. There were, alas, few such persons to be found, and very soon she would become the victim of many sexual encounters with ruthless employers and, inevitably, seductions by predatory actors. It would be many decades

---

[*] William Betty (1791-1874). Known as 'The Young Roscius', after the Roman actor of the same name. Played first *Romeo* at Belfast, and *Hamlet* and *Prince Arthur* in Dublin in 1803. Waterford, Cork, Glasgow, Edinburgh. Played at Covent Garden and Theatre Royal, Drury Lane, in 1805. Returned to the stage in 1812. Retired 1824.

[†] Eleanor Gwyn (1650-1716). Known variously as Gwyn Gwynn or Gwynne. Created Duchess of St. Albans (1684). She was the first actress to wear male costume, thus making 'breeches' parts popular.

before actresses and female playwrights were taken seriously enough to acquire the elusive respect they deserved from their male counterparts. The great David Garrick was a shining example of the generous, principled protector, a genius in the nurturing of young talent, and the father-figure to many aspiring young ladies who yearned for fame and fortune on the London stage.

Elizabeth Barry, who made her first appearance on stage at Dorset Gardens, owed her early success to her protector, the licentious John Wilmot, second Earl of Rochester (1648-80), author of many scurrilous verses, and a profligate rake of the first order. Rochester was attractive both in person and manners and as a favourite of Charles II his many sexual pursuits were conveniently overlooked. Under Wilmot's 'protection', Elizabeth was able to pursue a glittering stage career, creating over a hundred roles, but her additional activity as a 'demi-rep' (a contraction of 'demi-reputable') probably earned her more 'wages' at Court than in the bedrooms of the aristocracy. We can understand why William Hogarth chose Drury Lane for his setting of 'The Harlot's House' series of satirical caricatures. Moll Hackabout, innocent, pretty in her simple country dress, arrives in Cheapside, is accosted by the notorious brothel-keeper, Mother Needham, is lured into service in her establishment, brutally punished in the pillory and stricken down by disease. She is finally abandoned to a cruel death - a moral tale which self-respecting young women did well to ponder.

In the course of time, much of these slum areas were swept away, to be replaced by the crisp neo-classical architecture of the talented Scottish brothers, Robert and James Adam. Along the Strand, overlooking the Thames, they built the elegant Adelphi Terrace, named after 'adelphoi', Greek for 'from the same womb'. Rejecting the Palladian style adopted by Inigo Jones, Adam, like William Inwood, chose to return to classical antiquity for his models.

As yet, architecture had not fully begun to make any significant impact on demographic change in central London, and thus had not produced a new kind of playgoer. The wealthier aristocratic and upper class ranks still occupied the private boxes, whilst the rest were confined to the lower levels. In 1811, an important change took place that enabled architects and speculators to extend development to the north and west; the area stretched from St. James's Square as far as Parliament Hill Fields. The East End became more and more the home for the less privileged parts of society. This would have an important influence on the development of a new kind of theatre in the later part of the century. Property was made more vulnerable through the expiry of leases. The elegant terraces of houses in Spitalfields, for example, deteriorated as the poorer underprivileged class such as emigré Huguenots settled there and

Introduction

set up their weaving industry, and disadvantaged Jews were restricted to the 'rag-trade'. This considerable opportunity for advancement enabled the architect, John Nash (1752-1835) to embark upon a vast development, with the blessing of the Prince Regent, which would eventually include the planning and reconstruction of Regent's Park, Cumberland Terrace, Regent Street, the Carlton House Terraces, and Trafalgar Square (later redesigned by Sir Charles Barry). Thus, a whole new middle-class of London society could be encouraged to frequent the theatres.

The prestigious patented theatres, such as the King's Theatre in the Haymarket, the Theatre Royal, Drury Lane, and Covent Garden Opera House, were virtually places of devotion for play-loving audiences. From lords and ladies in the grand boxes to the hoi-polloi in the pit, playgoers swarmed in through the elegant foyers, gasping at the richly decorated interiors as they took up their places, revelling at the thought of seeing, close-up, the 'stars' of the day such as Sarah Siddons, David Garrick, William Betty, Dorothy Jordan, Edmund Kean, and later in the century, William Macready, Henry Irving and Dan Leno.

For the moment, there remained considerable dangers with which to contend. During the 18th and early 19th centuries, theatre audiences were fortunate to escape with their lives from the countless accidents and conflagrations that they were regularly prey to. Many London theatres had checkered histories: the Royalty Theatre was opened in 1787, burnt down in 1826, re-opened as the Brunswick Theatre on 25th February 1828 and only four days later the walls collapsed under the weight of the heavy iron roof, killing twelve people during a rehearsal of Scott's *Guy Mannering*. The Haymarket Theatre was opened in 1702, rebuilt in 1720 as The Little Theatre, and reconstructed as a royal theatre in 1767. It was the scene of a serious incident, which happened during a royal visit on 3rd February 1794, when sixteen people were trampled to death and many others subsequently died of the injuries they sustained. The English Opera House, later to become famous through the performances of the celebrated *diva*, Madame Vestris,* suffered a similar fate, being burnt down in 1830 and rebuilt four years later. Even Covent Garden did not escape the raging flames of theatrical conflagration in 1808, and was again destroyed by fire in 1856. Incredibly, by 1840 there were no less than seventeen theatres in London, but not one single Georgian interior remained.

---

* Madame Vestris (1797-1856). Actress and singer. Daughter of Gaetano Stefano Bartolozzi, son of the engraver Francesco Bartolozzi See biography by Charles Matthews. She sang in Italian opera and acted in Paris (1816). Appeared frequently at Drury Lane, Covent Garden, and The Haymarket. Married Charles James Matthews (1835).

Phoenix of Drury Lane

CHAPTER ONE

From Tennis Court to Temple of the Muses

1. Davenant and Killigrew: New Beginnings

Sir William Davenant

In 1639, Sir William Davenant[*], whom Charles I had recently appointed Court Poet after the death of Ben Jonson, succeeded in obtaining a Royal Patent to erect a theatre. He acquired, by agreement with the Earl Marshall, the Earl of Arundel and Surrey, a plot of land in Fleet Street. Perhaps because funds dried up or the promised patronage was not forthcoming, he never built his theatre. He was, however, Governor of the Cockpit Theatre (later called 'The Phoenix'), a disreputable small roofed-over construction which had been built on the site of the old cockpit in Drury Lane. It was here that he attempted to appease Cromwell's hatred of the Spanish, as well as the Lord Protector's suspicion of the theatre, by staging, in 1658, an extravaganza of songs, declamations and dancing, entitled *The Cruelty of the Spaniards in Peru.* In the following year Davenant put on *The History of Sir Francis Drake*, a further diatribe against the Spaniard, but Roundhead troopers raided the theatre and the playgoers 'were mulcted [fined] there and then of three pounds, eight shillings and sixpence.'[1] Davenant was arrested and incarcerated in the

---

[*] William Davenant (D'Avenant) (1606-1668) Court Poet (i.e. Poet Laureate) 1638. Wrote masques for the Court. Fled to France for support of Charles I. Virtual founder of English opera.

Chapter 1 – From Tennis Court to Temple of the Muses

Tower of London. On his release, undeterred by fear of official censure, and spurred on by his enthusiasm for the cause of English drama, he negotiated with Thomas Lisle for a lease on his Tennis Court in Portugal Street, Lincoln's Inn Fields, for use as a theatre. Presumably the risk of such a venture proved too great, and he fled to France to join other exiled Royalists. Whilst there, he had the good fortune to become acquainted with the young Thomas Killigrew,[*] who had been a Page of Honour to Charles I, and whose enthusiasm for the stage was hardly less than that of Davenant himself, though his experience was as yet limited. The two men made an admirable partnership – Davenant, the sophisticated courtier and established dramatist, and Killigrew, the younger by ten years and an 'illiterate courtier.'[2] On their return to England, now flourishing in the more relaxed conditions of the reign of Charles II, whose support and patronage they enjoyed, they established a company of players.

In spite of the opposition from the Master of the Revels, Sir Henry Herbert,[†] Killigrew managed to obtain a warrant from the King 'to erect one company of players, which shall be our own company.'[3] They then succeeded in persuading him to grant them a monopoly of London theatres, and thus to build a theatre each, and each to have his own company, Davenant to play at the Cockpit and Killigrew to play at Gibbons's Tennis Court in Vere Street. Davenant still possessed the Royal Patent and, together with Killigrew's 'King's Company of Players', they were the founders of the first Theatre Royal, though not as yet established in the building that was to undergo many changes in the years to come. In 1661, Davenant and Killigrew ended their association by seeking the Royal assent for their own theatres, and on the same day, 25 April, they were each granted the Royal Patent - Davenant for the Duke's House, Lincoln's Inn Fields, and Killigrew for the King's House, Drury Lane. In company with eight of his fellow actors, including John Lacy,[‡] Michael Mohun[§] and Charles Hart (Shakespeare's great-nephew), Killigrew leased from the Duke of Bedford, the Theatre Royal Drury Lane. The Bedford estate covered an area from Euston, Tottenham Court Road, to New Oxford Street and Covent Garden, and a number of planned elegant squares in Bloomsbury.

The 11th Duke began to sell off the estate in the late 1800s. Unlike

---

[*] Thomas Killigrew (1612-1683) Dramatist. Arrested for supporting Charles I. Groom of the Bedchamber to Charles II. Master of the Revels 1679.

[†] Sir Henry Herbert (1595-1673) Brother of poet George Herbert. Friend of John Evelyn. Treated Killigrew ruthlessly.

[‡] John Lacy (d.1681) His acting commended by Pepys and Evelyn. First to play Bayes in *The Rehearsal* (1671)

[§] Michael Mohun (1616?-1684) First performed at the Cockpit. Fought with Royalist army. Brilliant swordsman, which served him well on stage.

the locality depicted in Thomas Hood's etching, *The Progress of Cant*, Drury Lane in Charles II's day was a place of affluence. To begin with, it was the home of the Drury family, who gave it its name. The Marquis of Argyll and the Earl of Anglesey, among other distinguished residents, lived in the vicinity.

The playhouse stood in a field and playgoers approached it by means of a footpath from Drury Lane to Brydges Street (now Catherine Street). The interior consisted of three tiers of boxes and a gallery, whilst below were the cloth-covered benches of the Pit, with its steeply-raked floor. A glazed cupola above let in the light and, as Samuel Pepys confirms, also the rain, for he caught a cold from the drips and the draught. The Green Room[4] was the heart of the theatre, not only a place where players awaited their cues, or gossiped with their friends, but also one in which the pulse of the theatre could be tested, not least by the 'Mr. Dangles' and 'Mr. Puffs' of the critical world, agog for any scrap of scandal that might be dropped by innocent greenhorns of the acting profession.[*]

Old Drury, or the King's House, or the Theatre Royal, Brydges Street, as it was variously called, was not yet the ideal establishment it was intended to be. Nevertheless, the proprietors made the auspicious decision to appoint Charles Hart as their first general manager, or 'Keeper of the House', thus carrying on a family tradition handed down from William Shakespeare, who had been one of the 'Housekeepers' of the Globe Theatre.

Hart was an excellent actor of strikingly handsome appearance and possessed a fine voice suited equally to comedy and tragedy. It was he who took on an illiterate orange-seller, Eleanor Gwyn (popularly known as Nell Gwyn) and trained her in the craft of acting sufficiently well for her to make her first appearance on the stage in 1665 as Cydaria in John Dryden's tragedy, *The Indian Emperor*. Pepys deplored this performance, for on 22 August 1667 he noted in his diary that he 'was most infinitely displeased with her being put to act the Emperor's daughter, which is a great and serious part, which she does most basely.'[5] Pepys later admitted that he preferred her in the character of Florizel in Dryden's *Secret Love, or, The Maiden Queen*, in which Hart played her tutor and lover, Celadon – a part he vigorously played out in real life. But for Hart's patience and assiduity, Nell Gwynn, who, as can be inferred from Pepys's remarks, proved to be more successful in comic parts, might never have risen from the Pit to the Stage of the King's House.

---

[*] Mr. Dangle and Mr. Puff were parodies of critics in Sheridan's *The Critic*, who spread tittle-tattle and gossip picked up in the Green Room.

2. Dryden and the New House

On 25 January 1672, after the play was over and the audience had departed for home, the Drury Lane theatre caught fire. The absence of fire-proofing allowed the flames to spread rapidly and, in order to quench the fire, the old method of igniting gunpowder was adopted. Some 60 houses in the vicinity were emptied and blown up, leaving, amid a chaos of domestic debris, the charred and smoking embers of a ruined theatre. Undeterred, Killigrew set about the business of rebuilding, and the theatre finally re-opened in 1674. Meanwhile, Killigrew sent his company off to Lincoln's Inn Fields (later the Lyceum), where they opened with a performance of Beaumont and Fletcher's comedy, *Wit Without Money*. In the hope of gaining public sympathy, the actors called themselves 'The Shipwrecked Mariners'. Thus, Dryden, in his Prologue, begins:

> So shipwrackt Passengers escape to Land
> So look they, when on the bare Beach they stand,
> Dripping and cold, and their first fear scarce o'er,
> Expecting Famine on a Desart [*sic*] Shore.
> From that hard Climate we must wait for Bread,
> Whence ev'n the Natives, forc'd by hunger, fled.
> Our Stage does humane Chance present to view,
> But ne'er before was seen so sadly true.[6]

John Dryden

Two years after, the architect, Robert Adam, was called in to reconstruct the interior of Drury to make it more spacious. The ceiling was painted to represent blue sky with Cupids sporting among the clouds. It extended over the gallery, the occupants of which were said to be 'among the gods'; sitting in the higher tiers of the auditorium is to be sitting 'up in the gods.' The burning down of Old Drury gave rival companies the chance they had been waiting for. In the previous year, the Duke's House had been rebuilt to grand designs by Sir Christopher Wren, and was now being managed by the brilliant actor-manager, Thomas Betterton.[*] A proportion of the Drury Lane audience had begun to transfer its allegiance to the new Dorset Gardens Theatre, as the Duke's House was now known, even before the fire had forced Killigrew's company into their makeshift premises. Those who remained loyal to Old Drury were bombarded with the canting propaganda of the Puritan Zeal-of-the Land-Busy's, who put it about that the fire was the result of the wrath of God, akin to the destruction of the temples of the ancient world.

> You cherish't it, and now its Fall you mourn,
> Which blind unmanner'd Ze[a]lots make their scorn,
> Who think that Fire a Judgment on the Stage,
> Which spared not Temples in its furious Rage.[7]

The theme of clerical disapproval was still current in 1825, when Thomas Hood was etching *The Progress of Cant*, and dissenting preachers like Rowland Hill[†] and Edward Irving[‡] spoke out with passionate eloquence against the wickedness and immorality of the Stage. Other rivals of a different kind threatened the survival of the Old Drury company, and Dryden, in spite of his admiration for the French dramatist, Pierre Corneille[§], did not forego the opportunity of expressing with some

---

[*] Thomas Betterton (1635?-1710) Had a strong, impressive voice. Bound to Davenant under contract. Played Orestes, Oedipus and King Lear among many leading parts. Sent to Paris by Royal Command to learn about French stagecraft for possible improvements at Drury. He and Colley Cibber were two shining lights in a world of theatrical skulduggery.

[†] Rowland Hill (1744-1833) Itinerant preacher at Surrey Chapel. Conducted Sunday Schools.

[‡] Edward Irving (1792-1834) Founder of the Catholic Apostolic Church. Minister of Hatton Garden Chapel from 1783. A charismatic preacher. Compelled to retire in 1832 for encouraging the practice of 'speaking in tongues'. Features in Hood's *Progress of Cant*.

[§] Pierre Corneille (1606-1684) French dramatist. Best known play *Le Cid*, concerning the exploits of a medieval warrior. He was criticised by the all-powerful Académie Française for ignoring the traditionally inviolable principles

Chapter 1 – From Tennis Court to Temple of the Muses

vehemence his abhorrence of their garish playbills in black and red:

> If all these Ills could not undo us quite,
> A brisk French Troop is grown your dear delight;
> Who with broad bloudy [bloody] Bills call you each day
> To laugh and break your Buttons at their Play;'
> We dare not on your Priviledge intrench,
> Or ask you why you like 'em? They are French.[8]

Killigrew could not hope to rival the architectural splendours of the new Duke's House. With few resources available to him, he was constrained to mortgage the vital Patent (or Charter), which was his one safeguard against the loss of royal patronage. He raised a building fund and commissioned the architect of the rival theatre, Sir Christopher Wren, to draw up the plans, which out of necessity would have to be of the plainest unadorned variety. Colley Cibber[*] describes the interior in his *Apology*. The stage, he wrote, was in the form of a semi-oval which projected forward into the Pit, and side-wings replaced the old stage-boxes, thus removing the audience from the stage itself. The exterior, as seen in contemporary engravings, had a covered porch of five arches, above which two storeys faced with fluted pilasters surmounted by a classical pediment flanked by statues of lion and unicorn.[9] The outside of the theatre, indeed, was more imposing in its simplicity than the - to some of its critics - bare auditorium.

The opening night was fixed for 26th March 1674, and Dryden was quick to point a finger at the shortcomings of the House in his *Prologue*, especially written for the occasion:

> A Plain built House, after so long a stay,
> Will send you half unsatisfi'd away;
> When, fall'n from your expected Pomp, you find
> A bare convenience only is designed.

---

of the Unities of Time (the action must take place within 24 hours), Place (the action must happen in one place/setting), and Action (the plot must concern one single conflict/problem).

[*] Colley Cibber (1671-1757). Actor and dramatist. Known respectfully as 'Mr. Colley'. More popular as a comic actor, being skilled in playing eccentric characters. The gentle Cibber's appointment as Poet Laureate brought derision on his writings, Alexander Pope making him the hero of his biting satire, *The Dunciad* (1742). His *Apology for the Life of Colley Cibber, Comedian* remains an important source of information on the theatre of his time.

The 'mean ungilded Stage' and 'homely' auditorium give no cheer:

> We, broken Banquiers, half-destroy'd by Fire
> With our small Stock to humble Roofs retire;
> As to the rival 'Dukes House':
> Pity our loss, while you their Pomp admire,
> For Fame and Honour we no longer strive;
> We yield in both, and only beg to live;
> Unable to support their vast Expense,
> Who build and treat with such Magnificence. [10]

Two years of enforced exile undoubtedly led Hart to make the ironic choice of Beaumont and Fletcher's *The Beggar's Bush* the opening play. Its vivid portrayal of the hero, Flores, deprived of his birthright and forced to live in exile in a den of thieves and vagabonds, provided ample scope for any criticism of the rival theatre. Such a concern for survival among the Drury Lane company was justified for another reason. Killigrew, nearing the end of his life, reluctantly decided to hand over the Patent to his impetuous son, Charles.

In spite of its new, if simple, home, the King's House began rapidly to decline. Debts began to build up and the best actors and actresses defected to Dorset Gardens, taking with them a proportion of their loyal audiences. There, Thomas Betterton was the attraction, both as an actor of considerable talent, and as a manager who was not only competent and far-seeing but known and respected for his fairness and honesty, rare qualities in days when few entrepreneurs of the theatrical world cared for the comfort and welfare of their invariably underpaid performers.

Thomas Killigrew and Charles Hart had virtually retired, leaving the Theatre Royal to the mercy of Killigrew's two young and extravagant sons. The decision was taken to amalgamate the Duke's House and the King's House, a decision which brought down the former to a place of tight-wire walkers, tumblers and acrobats, with now and again a light opera or two. The King's House, however, possessed the Royal Patent. Thomas Betterton transferred to the Theatre Royal, Drury Lane to become its new manager, and the theatre re-opened on 16 November 1682. In the following year, Killigrew and Hart died and another phase in the history of the King's House was almost at an end. Charles II, an enthusiastic admirer of the drama, lived long enough to see the new Drury Lane 'Phoenix' take wing to heights it had not yet known.

Charles II, if he can be forgiven his inordinate dislike of Shakespeare, was, perhaps, of all royal patrons, the most influential in helping to establish a particular tradition that set the pattern for more than

Chapter 1 – From Tennis Court to Temple of the Muses

two hundred years and was peculiar to Drury Lane alone. His abiding pleasure in 'the Play' and his interest in those who wrote for and acted in his own special theatre can be measured by the abundant generosity he had shown towards Davenant and Killigrew and their companies of actors. His frequent appearances in the Royal Box, especially at times when his private life was the subject of some scandal or intrigue, were hardly of less interest to the inquisitive audience than the play itself. The subsequent death of such a staunch supporter of the theatre would be mourned by actors and audiences alike:

> The Vertues of a Royal Mind,
> Forgiving, bounteous, humble, just and kind:
> His Conversation, Wit, and Parts,
> His Knowledge in the Noblest, useful Arts,
> Were such, Dead Authors cou'd not give;
> But habitudes of those who live;....[11]

Among 'the peaceful Triumphs of his Reign', he revived 'the drooping Arts', encouraged Science, and restored 'Our Isle' after the rebellious years:

> As when the New-born Phoenix takes his way,
> His rich Paternal Regions to Survey....
> So, rising from his Father's Urn,
> So glorious did our Charles return....
> Live then thou great Encourager of the Arts,
> Live ever in our Thankful Hearts;
> Live blest Above, almost invok'd Below;
> Live and receive this Pious Vow,
> Our Patron once, our Guardian Angel now.[12]

Dryden's *Threnody* in memory of Charles II expressed sentiments that were to be revived by some of the writers of the Drury Lane *Addresses* in 1812, for in their view the drama had declined since –

> Dryden, the Jubal of that matchless day,
> Invok'd Cecilia; – heaven attun'd the lay.
> Next Farquhar's Stratagem attracts the sight,
> We glean and stengthen wisdom in delight:
> Then Rowe's Fair Penitent, and Cato's fate,

> Show trial cannot sink the mind that's great.[13]

Even during the subsequent reign of William and Mary, there were always the dissenting voices, decrying the familiar coarseness of the Restoration drama:

> 'Tis true, our English wits in Charles's days,
> Debas'd the Drama, gathering weeds with bays;
> And then the Stage a wanton Court addrest,
> Who lov'd her only in a harlot's vest.
> Illicit Wit, of prurient Folly born,
> Now both the Poet and the Patron scorn
> Like brothers, arm in Modesty's defence,
> And drive mad Comus and his monsters hence.[14]

Plays continued to follow the decadent path despite their Puritan critics. Sexual innuendo and even descents into bald obscenities became a common feature of the popular play as audiences, in an increasingly permissive society, grew more vociferous in their response. Actors, too, became more gross and coarse in their interpretations and were willing to abandon their professionalism to appease the whim of the Pit and the Gallery. Dryden gave a stern warning to his audiences in the Prologue to *The Rivals*, telling them that they only had themselves to blame if prologues were all too often mere excuses for thin plots plumped out with a superfluity of scenes, musical interludes and witless rhymes:

> 'Tis much Desir'd, you Judges of the Town,
> Would pass a Vote to put all *Prologues* down;
> For who can show me, since they first were Writ,
> They e'er Converted one hard-hearted Wit?
> Yet the World's mended well; in former Days
> Good *Prologues* were as scarce, as now good *Plays*
> For the reforming Poets of our Age,
> In this first Charge, spend their Poetique rage;
> Expect no more when once the *Prologue*'s done;
> The Wit is ended ere the *Play*'s begun.
> You now have Habits, Dances, Scenes, and Rhymes;
> High Language often; I [*aye*], and Sense, sometimes:
> As for a clear Contrivance doubt it not;
> They blow out Candles to give Light to th' Plot.
> And for Surprize, two Bloody-minded Men
> Fight till they Dye, then rise and Dance agen:

> Such deep Intrigues wou'd welcome to this Day:
> But blame your Selves, not him who Writ the Play.[15]

Dryden cannot let the argument go without a sharp word or two to the in the Second Prologue:

> For they, like Thieves condemn'd, are Hang-men made,
> To execute the Members of their Trade.
> All that are Writing now he would disown;
> But then he must Except, ev'n all the Town.
> All Chol'rique, losing Gamesters, who in spight
> Will Damn to Day, because they lost last Night.
> All Servants whom their Mistress's scorn upbraids;
> All Maudlin Lovers, and all Slighted Maids:
> All who are out of Humour, or Severe;
> All, that want Wit, or hope to find it here.[16]

3. Colley Cibber and the Ruthless Reign of Christopher Rich

The Theatre Royal, Drury Lane, was now at its lowest ebb, and it was at this point in its history that one of the wiliest of managers, Christopher Rich,* in league with the notorious Sir Thomas Skipwith, acquired a substantial interest in the Theatre.[17] Skipwith, learning of the financial predicament in which Davenant's sons, Charles and Alexander, now found themselves, made an offer for the family share of the Patent, which he secured by means of a loan to assist the reprobate Alexander to pay off his debts. Alexander thus relinquished five-sixths of his interest, and when more ready money was needed urgently he sold the remaining sixth to Christopher Rich.

The reign of Rich at Drury Lane has been described by theatre historians as one of fraudulent dealings, lying, cheating, and arrant suppression of actors' rights. 'He was as sly a tyrant as ever was set at the head of a theatre; for he gave the actors more liberty and fewer days' pay than any of his predecessors....He kept them poor that they might not rebel.'[18] At the same time, he was able to line his pockets with gold, for his principal aim in life was self-aggrandisement through the abuse of power. Thomas Betterton and his fellow-actors appealed to Rich, and

---
* Christopher Rich (d.1714). Avaricious and tyrannical Theatre manager. Purchased a share in Drury Lane in 1688. Controlled three London playhouses – Drury Lane, Dorset Gardens and The Haymarket.

when he ignored their pleas, they petitioned the Lord Chamberlain to settle their grievances.

Towards the end of 1694, Queen Mary suffered a fatal illness and London theatres were closed for a period of mourning. Betterton was able to take advantage of the lull to seek an audience with King William, by whose favour he succeeded in obtaining a special licence to act elsewhere other than Drury Lane. With a group of 'rebels' he opened up on the familiar ground of Lisle's Tennis Court at Lincoln's Inn Fields, with the first production of Congreve's *Love for Love*.

Conditions at Drury Lane continued to deteriorate, Rich frequently stealing the takings and ruthlessly refusing his impoverished actors even as much as a living wage. One of these, a poor youth who at that time was only given walk-on parts, Colley Cibber, was to oust the sly 'tyrant' from his throne. Until that could happen, an internecine feud developed between the factions of Betterton and Rich that reached at times a state of open civil war. Congreve, who preferred Betterton's superior actors, supported the Lincoln's Inn Fields company. Cibber, who was not at that time sufficiently established to do otherwise, decided to support Rich, and was given a ten-shilling rise for his pains, bringing his 'salary' to thirty shillings a week. His task was to comb the provincial theatres for talent, but he had no great success.

Cibber was a true man of the theatre; he was a reliable actor, a competent playwright, popular with his fellow-actors, could produce, direct, and manage when the opportunity arose, and – a facet of his character which Rich was to underestimate – had a keen eye to the main chance, though so far that chance had not presented itself.

Colley Cibber's extremely successful first play was *Love's Last Shift, or, The Fool in Fashion*, the author playing the popular part of Sir Novelty Fashion, which required him to wear a periwig of prodigious proportions. Vanbrugh was delighted, and decided to write its sequel, *The Relapse, or Virtue in Danger*, in which Sir Novelty was raised to the peerage and dubbed Lord Foppington. In 1704, Cibber was encouraged to refashion his play, *The Careless Husband*, and Anne Oldfield, whom the dramatist, George Farquhar had discovered serving in the Mitre Tavern in St. James's Market, scored a success as Lady Betty Modish.

Meanwhile, Congreve had provided a tragedy, *The Mourning Bride*, and a brilliant comedy, *The Way of the World*, whilst Farquhar contributed two comedies, *Love and a Bottle* and *The Constant Couple*. In this way, the fickle (and larger) part of the Drury Lane audiences was lured back from the rival theatres, at least for a time, to laugh at the antics of Sir Novelty Fashion, Lady Betty Modish, Lady Wishfort, and Sir Harry Wildair. Drury Lane at the turn of the century was a place of light comedies and coarse wit well suited to the taste of the age.

Chapter 1 – From Tennis Court to Temple of the Muses

Colley Cibber

Cibber was also known for his own versions of Shakespeare's plays, in which he cut, re-worked, or added lines wherever he felt Shakespeare was at fault. The 17th century fashion for re-writing Shakespeare was encouraged by the new view of the play as a visual performance (even if not always audible), a performance to be given beneath a proscenium arch, and pleasing the eye with all manner of scenery, machinery and other spectacular stage effects. Not only that, in an increasingly sentimental age, dramatists like Nahum Tate, the Poet Laureate, had adapted the plots of such tragedies as *King Lear* to the more superficial aesthetic requirements of the audience. Cordelia, in Tate's version, marries Edgar and lives happily ever after. In the much-quoted version of *Richard the Third*, Colley Cibber included the line: 'Off with his head – so much for Buckingham!' – a line which earned him a place in almost every Dictionary of Quotations, though most modern readers would associate the first part with the Queen of Hearts' ruthless imperative in *Alice in Wonderland*.

Whilst Cibber permitted himself the luxury of tampering with Shakespeare, he nevertheless took exception to anyone else making adjustments to his own work. On one occasion, Rich decided to liven up a play of Cibber's by bringing in some rope-dancers. Cibber, annoyed by such impertinence, stood up in the Pit and addressed the audience, saying that his decision to abandon the stage of Drury Lane was no mark of disrespect to them, but the expression of his distress at the low state to which the legitimate drama had been reduced.

There were marked differences of style and organisation between the two companies, Betterton's at Lincoln's Inn Fields, and Rich's at Drury Lane. After a time, it became noticeable that all was not well at the Tennis Court. Betterton and his associates had set up their company on more democratic principles, so much so that, since they all considered one another to be of equal rank and authority, each took to countermanding the orders of another, thus creating a situation which was largely unmanageable. Disagreements arose as to the running of the company, and the all-embracing management, having started out with such high hopes, now began to crack at the seams. Some of the more distinguished performers began to drift back to Drury Lane, in spite of the poor conditions prevailing there. Rich, 'infamous, thieving, grasping, penny-snatching',[19] still held tightly to the reins and exercised the sort of discipline that could only achieve its purpose through ruthless Machiavellian double-dealing.

One of his schemes ended by turning the Theatre Royal into a rough house. In order to entice a better class of patron to come to the play, he hit upon the idea of giving footmen free access to the upper gallery. This 'Free List' led to more rioting and disturbances than Drury Lane had seen before and, as with the notorious O.P. (*Old Price*) riots at Covent Garden,* the wealthier patrons simply stayed away, or transferred their loyalty to theatres like The Haymarket, where operas, and plays with music, attracted the more genteel of the theatre-going classes. Cibber tells a sinister story in his *Apology*[20] of being taken by Rich on a guided tour of the Drury Lane Theatre on which occasion he revealed 'fifty little back-doors, dark closets, and narrow passages' constructed on his orders during some brick-laying operations. It is one of these 'closets' that was to reveal, in the late 19th century, a gruesome occupant that may provide a clue to the legendary ghost, for 'a wall was taken down revealing a tiny room containing a corpse in the remnants of an early 18th-century costume with a dagger sticking between its ribs.'[21]

---

* O.P. riots (Old Price). On 20 September, The Theatre Royal Covent Garden, with its scenery, costumes, and scripts, was destroyed by fire. Damages amounted to some £250,000. Rebuilt in 1809, the cost of the new theatre was so high that ticket prices had to be raised to pay the bills. Riots ensued, the theatre filled with rowdy protesters carrying banners and shouting slogans. The scene was a gift to caricaturists like Isaac Cruikshank.

Chapter 1 – From Tennis Court to Temple of the Muses

A curious circumstance now arose which would weaken Rich's hold over the company. Vanbrugh did a deal with Rich, through a friend of Cibber's, Owen Swiney, to employ some of the Drury Lane actors at The Haymarket. Rich was only thinking in terms of profit (he would, under the terms of the agreement receive 50% of any profits earned by his actors in the new house).

Meanwhile, whilst legitimate drama went to The Haymarket, Rich kept the Theatre Royal open with trivial harlequinades and circus acts. He reduced the salaries of his remaining actors, and in turn brought the actors to a state of penury. Cibber and Anne Oldfield, his only mainstays in a dire situation, deserted him for Swiney. The actors retaliated by complaining of Rich's oppressive measures to the Lord Chamberlain, who at once sent Rich an order to pay actors their full benefits; these were supplementary performances given by a particular actor or actress who was permitted to retain part of the proceeds by way of compensating for an insufficient salary. Clearly here, Rich was filching a third of all moneys derived from such 'benefits'. He chose to ignore the matter and a Silence Order was placed on the Theatre so that no performances could be given. Colley Cibber had the satisfaction of making an appearance in the Pit while a rehearsal was in progress, and spoke the words that effectively marked the end of the reign of Christopher Rich:

> Sir,
>
> *I have now no more business here, than you have; in half-an-hour, you will neither have actors to command, nor authority to employ them.*[22]

A messenger arrived bringing the Silence Order from the Lord Chamberlain, and a silken cord was fixed across every entrance with the official seal of his Office. Thus on the thirtieth of April, 1709, the Theatre Royal, Drury Lane was closed until a new tenant could be found.

4. William Collier and the Triumvirate

The new manager of the Theatre Royal, Drury Lane, was to be William Collier, who succeeded in persuading The Haymarket rebels to return to the Drury fold. Like Rich, he was a lawyer, with no interest in the theatre beyond what it could do for his pocket. He preferred to remain a sleeping partner, at the same time demanding of his three principal fellow partners, Robert Wilks, Thomas Doggett, and Colley Cibber, the sum of £600 each per annum as well as half of the £200 they had been forced to pay under the Haymarket agreement. All was not so simple at the beginning, however, for Rich refused to vacate the theatre, 'silent' as it was, and defiantly advertised the sale of the scenery and properties:

> That a Magnificent Palace with great Variety of Gardens, statues and Waterworks, may be bought cheap in Drury Lane....several Castles to be disposed of, very delightfully situated, as also Groves, Woods, Forests, Fountains and Country-Seats, with very pleasant prospects on all Sides of them, being the Moveables of Ch--------r R-ch Esq., who is breaking up House-keeping....[23]

On 22 November 1709, Collier 'invaded' the Theatre Royal with a small army of soldiers, whom he had supplied with a goodly amount of liquor. Rich, perhaps on hearing of the projected invasion, had removed everything of value the night before. *The Tatler* gave a wry description of the event. A celebratory bonfire was lit in front of the theatre:

> War immediately ensued upon the peaceful Empire of Wit and the Muses; the Goths and Vandals sacking of Rome did not threaten a more barbarous Devastation of Arts and Sciences. But when they had forced their Entrance, the experienced Divito [i.e. Rich] had detached all his Subjects, and evacuated all his Stores.[24]

The reference to Goths and Vandals is of interest, since the authors of the 1812 Drury Lane *Addresses* echoed in their verses the Augustan abhorrence of artistic vandalism, masquerading under the mask of 'improvement' and denying the old-fashioned canons of taste in favour of a vulgar radicalism. Under such influences, the Muses had fled from Greece and Rome, from Rome to France and, after the French Revolution, to England (Land of the Free), making their natural home in their own Temple of Apollo – where else but the Theatre Royal, Drury Lane:

> At length, by Goth and Vandal overthrown,
> Prostrate they fell beneath the prostrate throne.
> By barb'rous foes then crush'd from age to age,
> Genius and Wit were exiled from the Stage;[25]

> Disgusted at their fall'n Athena's fate,
> They fled, for ever fled the Grecian State;
> Now the last relicts of their glories come,
> And seek on Britain's shores a safer home.[26]

According to *The Tatler*, on the evening before Collier's assault on the Theatre Royal, local inhabitants were witness to an extraordinary spectacle as Rich and his remaining company escaped from the 'silent' building:

> Doorkeepers came out clad like Cardinals, and Scene-drawers like Heathen Gods. Divito himself was wrapped up in one of his black Clouds, and left the Enemy nothing but an empty Stage, full of Trap-doors, known only to himself and his Adherents.[27]

Once established, Collier re-opened the Theatre under the rule of the Triumvirate. Wilks, who had a fiery temper and high artistic standards (not always a happy combination), had little sympathy for Doggett's austere attention to low costing. Doggett did not care for the extravagant trappings of tragedy and sought, when necessary, to economise wherever he could find a way.

The third member of the Triumvirate, Colley Cibber, was an effective mediator and 'steered an uneasy path of compromise between them.' 'I was,' wrote Cibber, 'rather inclin'd to Doggett's way of thinking, yet I was always under the disagreeable restraint of not letting Wilks see it,'[28] - precisely the attitude that MacQueen-Pope refers to in his assessment of Cibber's contribution to the success of the 'Rule of Three':

> Cibber was a great pourer of oil on troubled waters. He would agree with both sides when there was an argument, but not give way to either. He would give some credit to one, and then some to another, with the result that a friendly compromise was always effected.[29]

5. Addison's *Cato* and Whig Politics

Joseph Addison

On 14th April 1713 (according to Cibber) Joseph Addison's *Cato* was given its first performance at Drury Lane. The play is hardly known today and never now performed, but its phenomenal success on the first night requires some explanation. Cibber had first set eyes on four acts of the play in 1703, read them to Sir Richard Steele,* editor of *The Tatler*, who expressed his approval but thought Addison† might not allow it to be performed because of its liberal sentiments. The Whigs were not yet in power and the story of the last stand of the republican, Cato, against the power of Caesar, would not have had the wholehearted applause of a largely Tory audience. With a change of government in 1712 however, renewed attempts were made to persuade Addison to complete the play for Drury Lane. Doggett, a Whig himself, was excited, and as soon as the play was ready, he hurried into production. The theme of succession was also of topical interest. The rivalry between Cato's two sons for the love of Lucia, resolved by the death of one of them, parallelled in some respects the problem of succession that England was facing with the failing health of Queen Anne, who, in spite of her many illegitimate offspring, had not produced a legitimate heir to the throne.

The public enthusiasm for the cause of liberty brought forth scenes of

---

* Steele, Sir Richard, politician, author and dramatist. Acted at Drury Lane.
† Joseph Addison (1672-1719). Whig statesman, essayist, poet, and classical scholar. Dryden admired his Latin poems. Member of Kitcat club. His drama, *Cato*, acted with great success at Drury Lane in 1713. Friendship with Swift and Steele among other writers. Produced with Steele *The Spectator*.

unrestrained emotion on the first night of *Cato*. The hero's opposition to an oppressive dictator highlighted contentious links between contemporary politics and a dramatic episode in classical history. The historical Cato, renowned for his remarkable powers of oratory and his devotion to the Stoic school of philosophy, had made a staunch moral stand against the profligacy of the Roman nobility, and this aspect of his character had enormous appeal for the Whigs in 1713. Furthermore, Cato had vehemently opposed the oppressive measures of Caesar and Pompey, and, on the outbreak of civil war, had joined forces with Scipio in Africa. After Scipio's defeat at Thapsus, the African territories fell to the power of Caesar, and Cato, rather than submit, resolved to die by his own hand, and put an end to his life after spending the greater part of the night reading Plato's *Phaedo* on the immortality of the soul.

Clearly, here was a great champion of freedom under repression, whose tragic self-sacrifice in the cause of liberty had some considerable impact on the audience of the Theatre Royal, Drury Lane on 14 April 1713. It was a time in English history when the new liberal politics were gaining ground. Just as Cato's tragic death had been the inspiration for Cicero's *Cato* (and indirectly Caesar's reply, *Anticato),* so Addison saw the timeliness of his own re-appraisal of the event in modern terms. The portrayal of Cato as the personification of an almost god-like virtue, a phoenix of the liberal spirit, rising from the flames of an outmoded, largely patrician society, took hold of the imagination of the first-night audience at Drury Lane and raised the emotion of the house to a pitch of unparalleled fervour:

> Here tears shall flow from a more gen'rous cause,
> Such tears as Patriots shed for dying Laws;
> He bids your breasts with ancient ardour rise,
> And calls forth Roman drops from British eyes.
> Virtue confess'd in human shape he draws,
> What Plato thought, and godlike Cato was;[30]

He was, in the words of Alexander Pope's *Prologue* to the play: 'a brave man struggling in the storms of fate,' a hero 'in his Country's cause':

> Who sees him act, but envies ev'ry deed?
> Who hears him groan, and does not wish to bleed?[31]

He was, the 'last good man dejected Rome ador'd', and since such plays 'should win a British ear' and warm the 'native rage', the willing audience was raised to a peak of enthusiasm:

> Britons, attend: be worth like this approv'd,
> And show, you have the virtue to be mov'd.'[32]

Though Addison had no intention, originally, to draw political parallels in his play, it was admirable propaganda for the Whig Party. Indeed, the Pope's *Prologue* remains the perfect Augustan expression of the genre, to which the writers of the *Genuine Addresses* could, and did frequently refer:

> To wake the soul by tender strokes of art,
> To raise the genius, and to mend the heart;
> To make mankind in conscious virtue bold,
> Live o'er each scene, and be what they behold:
> For this the Tragic Muse first trod the stage,[1]
> Commanding tears to stream thro' ev'ry age;
> Tyrants no more their savage nature kept,
> And foes to virtue wonder'd how they wept.
> Our author shuns by vulgar springs to move
> The hero's glory, or the virgin's love;
> In pitying Love, we but our weakness show,
> And wild Ambition well deserves its woe.
> Here tears shall flow from a more gen'rous cause,
> Such Tears as Patriots shed for dying Laws:
> He bids your breasts with ancient ardour rise,
> And calls forth Roman drops from British eyes.
> Virtue confess'd in human shape he draws,
> What Plato thought, and godlike Cato was:
> No common object to your sight displays,
> But what with pleasure Heav'n itself surveys,
> A brave man struggling in the storms of fate,
> And greatly falling, with a falling state.
> While Cato gives his little Senate laws,
> What bosom beats no in his Country's cause?
> Who sees him act, but envies ev'ry deed?
> Who hears him groan, but does not wish to bleed
> Ev'n when proud Caesar 'midst triumphal cars,
> The spoils of nations, and the pomp of wars,

Chapter 1 – From Tennis Court to Temple of the Muses

Ignobly vain and impotently great,
Show'd Rome her Cato's figure drawn in state;
As her dead Father's rev'rend image past,
The pomp was darke'd , and the day o'ercast;
The Triumph ceas'd, tears gush'ed from ev'ry eye;
The World's great Victor pass'd unheeded by;
Her last good man dejected Rome ador'd,
And honour'd Caesar less than Cato's sword.
    Britons, attend; be worth like this approv'd,
And show, you have the virtue to be mov'd.
With honest scorn the first fam'd Cato view'd
Rome learning arts frin Greece, whom she subdu'd;
You scene precariously subsists too long,
On French translation, and Italian song,
Dare to have sense yourselves; assert the stage,
Be justly warm'd with your own native rage:
Such Plays alone should win a British ear,
As Cato's self had not disdain'd to hear.[33]

    British patriotism had reached new heights with the signing of the Treaty of Utrecht, which secured the Protestant succession in England, separated the French and Spanish crowns, and enlarged the British colonies and plantations in America. As well as this, the hero of Blenheim, the Duke of Marlborough, disgraced by the Tory ministry on a charge of peculation (embezzlement) and dismissed from all his offices, went over to the Whigs, amidst much jubilation. He asked to be made Commander-in-Chief, a request which Tories such as Harley[*] and Bolingbroke[†] considered tantamount to a bid for dictatorship. They called upon Barton Booth,[‡] who had once played the Ghost to Wilk's Hamlet, to now play the part of Cato. Booth was virtually bribed with contributions collected from the Tory boxes in recognition of Cato's 'honest opposition

---

  [*] Edward Harley, 2nd Earl of Oxford (1689-1741), was a book collector and friend of Pope and Swift.
  [†] Robert Bolingbroke, Earl of Oxford (1678-1751). Supported Harley and Tory party. With his philosophy of 'democratic Toryism', he was critical of Walpole's policies
  [‡] Barton Booth (1681-1733). Educated Westminster School. Appeared at Smock Alley Theatre, Dublin, 1698. Engaged by Betterton for Lincoln's Inn Fields (1700-4). Gave outstanding performances as Pyrrhus in *The Distressed Mother* by Ambrose Philips.

to a perpetual dictator, and his dying so bravely in the cause of liberty.'[34] Booth did rather well out of this for, not to be outdone by the opposition, Doggett and his two colleagues matched the sum with a further fifty guineas on behalf of the Whigs. The matter went to Booth's head. He conceived it, in the terminology of the Tennis Court, as an 'advantage'.

Educated at Westminster, Booth was a man of some sophistication, with friends in high places, and succeeded in obtaining from the Lord Chamberlain an order admitting him as a partner, thus breaking the Whig Triumvirate and leading to a rash of law-suits in which Doggett sued for a share of Booth's £600 contribution to the partnership.

Within a few years, the bond of the 'Rule of Three' began to weaken. Wilks became ill and Cibber handed over his share of the Patent to his ambitious son, Theophilus Cibber, a tolerably good actor who, in spite of his personal excesses, was to turn out to be an effective leader of men and assistant manager to the ailing Wilks. Booth sold half his share for £2,500, weakening the partnership even further and paving the way for yet another sensational power struggle.

With the death of Queen Anne and the accession of George I, it seemed probable that the Whigs, who had aligned themselves with the Protestant succession, would gain the upper hand at the Theatre Royal, and Tories like Collier and Booth would be even more unpopular than they were already. Cibber the Younger and Wilks managed to oust Collier and replace him with the influential Sir Richard Steele, a strong Whig supporter. Steele succeeded in obtaining a new Patent, which demanded, among other requirements, the exclusion of 'abusive and scurrilous representations of the clergy', a proviso that would have satisfied Horace, the virtuous dramatist, rather more than the Triumvirate themselves, for audiences continued to call for coarseness as well as sublimity in Drury Lane productions. Whilst he had had his uses in obtaining the Patent, Steele, whose interests lay more in the drama of politics than the politics of drama, spent more time with the business of Parliament than the business of running a thriving theatre. Through his incompetence, debts began to pile up again.

Troubles rarely came singly to the Theatre Royal, Drury Lane. John Rich,[*] who had inherited the theatrical interests of his father, Christopher Rich, had opened up a rival house at Lincoln's Inn Fields, under the old Davenant Patent. Rich became one of the foremost pantomimists and attracted enthusiastic audiences. Cibber and Wilks retaliated by putting on their own pantomimes with all kinds of mechanical effects to surprise

---

[*] John Rich (1692-1761). Actor and theatre manager. Produced pantomimes from 1717 to 1760, and played the character Harlequin. Opened New Theatre at Lincoln's Inn Fields (1714). Opened Theatre Royal, Covent Garden in 1732.

Chapter 1 – From Tennis Court to Temple of the Muses

the superficial part of the spectators. Gradually a tradition arose for even the most sublime of tragedies to be followed by the most trivial of afterpieces. Booth's support of the custom was entirely a practical one at a time when audiences were being spirited away by rival companies. His remark that 'there were many more Spectators than Men of Taste and Judgement,'[35] though it had an overtone of cynicism, was an accurate assessment of the average audience in the eighteenth century. Rich's greatest success was John Gay's *The Beggar's Opera* in 1728, a brilliant production that was said to have made 'Gay rich and Rich gay'.[36]

John Rich (c.1750)   Barton Booth (c.1770)

In 1732, Rich raised a subscription with the purpose of building a new playhouse in Bow Street, Covent Garden, the original footprint of the present Royal Opera House. A further threat to the Theatre Royal, Drury Lane, were the unlicensed theatres beyond the boundaries of the City such as the Goodman's Fields Theatre. An actor at Drury Lane, John Palmer, defied the Patent monopoly and opened his Royalty Theatre in 1787 with a production of *As You like It*, but with no official licence, he was arrested and the theatre forced to close. As if these rivalries were not enough, a mysterious rumour began to circulate that the structure of the Drury Lane Theatre was unsafe and that it was in danger of collapsing at any moment. Cibber called in the State surveyor, Sir Thomas Hewat, who reported the building to be safe, and, after advertisements to that effect appeared in the newspapers, the loyal part of the audience returned. As to the identity of the instigator of this unfortunate rumour, little is known, though it was suggested that it was, in fact, John Rich, and it is tempting to believe it.

6. The Decline of Cibber and the Decline of Drury

Colley Cibber's remarkable resilience amid the cut and thrust of the theatrical management of his day is a testimony to his integrity. His amiable nature and his genuine regard for things theatrical did not always assist him, for even he, with all his brilliance, had his enemies. He had married the daughter of a trumpet major, raised a large family on a salary of one pound a week, at least at the beginning of his career, but he was always a gambler and lost more money and friends than he gained. He was one of the great peacemakers, never a popular species with their counterparts, the troublemakers. It is hard to see the gentle Cibber as the subject for a satire on dullness such as Pope made in *The Dunciad*.

Colley Cibber's connection with the Theatre Royal, Drury Lane lasted for over fifty years, during which time he brought an element of civility and sophistication to an atmosphere of cant and domestic wrangling that otherwise prevailed there. His father, Caius Gabriel Cibert, a sculptor from Holstein, had, among other works, sculpted the phoenix over the door of St. Paul's Cathedral,[37] and this mythical bird was to have some significance for the authors of the Drury Lane *Addresses* in years to come. Colley Cibber's background thus provided him with a standard of excellence that was a pillar of strength in times of crisis, and a yardstick by which his fellow-actors and partners could judge their own conduct and be found wanting, as they all too frequently were.

As Poet Laureate he was a failure. His verses were viciously attacked by Pope, Gay and Fielding, not only for their poetasting banalities but for the obsequious pandering to the Royal Favour and the House of Hanover, with such extravagances as *'Hail! Royal Caesar! Hail!'*, and the unfortunate lines:

> Around the royal table spread,
> See how beauteous branches shine!
> Sprung from the fertile genial bed
> Of glorious GEORGE and CAROLINE.[38]

Pope sees him as the 'Fool of Quality' singing his Royal Birthday Ode to the accompaniment of choirs:

> Thou, Cibber! thou, his Laurel shall support,
> Folly, my son, has still a friend at Court.
> Lift up your Gates, ye Princes, see him come!
> Sound, sound, ye Viols; be the Cat-call dumb![39]

The choir and orchestra of the Chapel Royal sing and sound their praises to their King of Dunces:

> ...Then swells the Chapel-royal throat:
> 'God save King Cibber! mounts in ev'ry note.
> Familiar White's, 'God save King Colley!' cries;
> 'God save King Colley! Drury-lane replies.[40]

While Pope points to the more vulnerable aspects of Cibber's verse, it cannot be denied that in the theatre Cibber was above reproach, in spite of the attack on his plays in the First Book of *The Dunciad*. The play, *Love's Last Shift*, was said to have been translated into French as *La Dernière Chemise de l'Amour*, though there is no record as to what French audiences might have made of it. *The Non-Juror*, one of his most successful plays, was based on Molière's *Tartuffe,* and vastly superior to Medbourne's[*] travesty. The theme of a Popish priest masquerading as a Church of England cleric greatly appealed to the Protestant loyalists, though it was attacked by the Jacobites, and, it is said, even by the Pope. The brilliant cast included Cibber, Booth, and Anne Oldfield, and the play ran for eighteen consecutive performances, which for a repertory theatre was a mark of its success. King George was delighted and made Cibber a present of £200, but the Jacobites plagued Cibber with protests at almost every subsequent performance of his plays.

In 1733, Cibber retired from the stage, though he made occasional appearances until 1745, having handed over his share to his son. Booth fell ill and died in 1728, Anne Oldfield in 1730, and Wilks in 1732. Thus Cibber was left alone to watch the decline of Drury Lane from one of its greatest peaks of success. With his retirement, only the squabbling inheritors remained to plague him with regrets, and he died on 11 December 1757.

During those last years, Cibber was to witness the arrival of one of the greatest actors of all time, David Garrick, whose performances were to change styles of acting out of all recognition, and above everything to forge a new and vital tradition of dramatic production that was to last for over half a century. Before that could happen, there was to be another struggle for power among the Patentees that would all but ruin the Theatre Royal, Drury Lane.

---

[*] Matthew Medbourne (died 1680) was an English stage actor and occasional playwright of the Restoration era. He wrote a version of *Tartuffe* in 1670 which was staged at the Theatre Royal, Drury Lane.

7. Revival with Fleetwood and Macklin

In July 1732, the ailing Triumvirate had succeeded in obtaining a new twenty-one year Patent and, given their poor state of health and wealth, and the familiar scheming venality exercised by the management, it was obvious to observers that the new Patentees intended to sell their shares. After Wilks died, his widow sold out to John Highmore and Cibber rented his share to his son, Theophilus. Highmore, a gentleman of some means; had regrettable pretensions to acting and, after a bet at White's, was allowed to play Lothario and Hotspur, much to the dismay and discontent of the audience. Theophilus Cibber resented Highmore's intrusion into the affairs of Drury Lane. Highmore, whilst amateurish in his thespian ambitions, was by no means so when it came to matters of business. He brazenly offered Colley Cibber £3000 for his share of the Patent and, surprisingly in the circumstances, Cibber agreed to the deal. Theophilus was given his notice to leave by the end of the season. What Highmore did not bargain for was the manner in which Theophilus Cibber would react. Banding together his fellow actors into a kind of rudimentary trade union, Cibber persuaded the shareholders of the building to sub-lease it to them for a period of 15 years. Highmore was thus left holding most of the Patent with no complete control over the theatre itself. Cibber and his 'union' ordered Highmore to keep out of the way of the management and he was bribed with 200 guineas a year to remain a sleeping partner. Highmore responded with force. He hired a gang of armed thugs to break into the theatre and throw out the actors. Theophilus sued Highmore for a Writ of Ejectment, and after a series of court appearances, succeeded in expelling Highmore, who cut his losses by selling his share to another of means, Charles Fleetwood, distinguished mainly for his employment of Charles Macklin,[*] the Irish actor, and the 'Roscius'[†] of the English Stage, David Garrick. Cibber fell out with Fleetwood too, and left Drury Lane to devote himself to play-writing. He died in 1758, only one year after his father. Thus ended the great 'actor rebellion' of 1733.

Macklin pioneered an entirely new school of acting at Drury Lane. He deplored the slow, mechanical mannerisms of the old style employed by his predecessors, and even some of his contemporaries such as James

---

[*] Macklin, Charles, actor and stage-manager. Played at Lincoln's Inn fields 1730 and Drury Lane 1733-48, and made his name in the part of Shylock. Appeared in Dublin for Sheridan and latterly at Covent Garden, variably between 1750 and 1789 when he retired from the stage.

[†] Roscius was a celebrated comic actor in Roman times, greatly admired by Cicero, and considered to have reached the height of his profession. The name came to be used for any male actor of distinction.

Quin,* whose rolling lines were drawing enthusiastic audiences to Rich's theatre at Lincoln's Inn Fields. Macklin adopted a more realistic approach, speaking the lines as naturally as he could and punctuating them by a series of carefully-timed pauses, his so-called 'short', 'middle' and 'Grand' pauses. He once struck the prompter, who dared to interrupt him in the middle of one of his Grand Pauses, for Macklin was a man given to violent fits of rage. On 10 May 1735, in the Green Room at Drury Lane, he quarrelled with an actor, Thomas Hallam, over the possession of a wig, and struck him with the end of his stick, piercing Hallam's eye. Hallam fell to the ground and died within a few hours. It is entirely praiseworthy that, in the moments before death, the offended young actor absolved Macklin of any blame in the matter.

Macklin was said to have lived to be 107 years of age. During his career, audiences had flocked to see his performances (no more sensational on the stage than off) and George II, who was little given to praise plays or playwrights, was 'frightened out of his life by the grim, tragic, stark intensity'[41] of Macklin's new portrayal of Shylock. Macklin had gone out into the coffee-houses to study Jewish mannerisms at first hand, and, armed with accurate observation of detail and with all the poison and gall he could draw from his own experience of life, he roused his audience to respond with cheer upon cheer at almost every scene. His remarkable performance as Shylock not only restored Macklin to public favour (in spite of the accusation against him of manslaughter), but also made theatrical history.

8. Westminster Tories and Drury Whigs

London in the reign of George II was a bustling metropolis with a thriving theatre, but saddled with a king who had no feeling or respect for 'blaze and boetry'. The 1730s were the years of Walpole and Whig politics, of Wesleyan Methodism, of the new Covent Garden Opera House, of Alexander Pope's *Essay on Man*, Handel's *Xerxes*, Hogarth's *Rake's Progress*, and the execution of Dick Turpin.

The Theatre Royal, Drury Lane, was now to turn its back on its humble origins and look towards a new vital period. Early in 1737, Samuel Johnson, after the failure of his Edial House school venture, set out for London from Lichfield, accompanied by one of his former pupils, David Garrick. Garrick was 20 years of age and eager to make a career

---

* Quin, James (1693-1766) actor. First appeared at Drury Lane (from Dublin) in 1714 and soon achieved a notable performance as Bajazet in *Tamerlane*. Took leading parts in tragedy at Lincoln's Inn Fields 1717-32.

for himself as a professional actor. In the process, he brought about a change in the lifestyle of the Theatre and its occupants, a greater degree of sophistication in the techniques of acting and of stage plays that would make the Theatre Royal, Drury Lane one of the finest theatres in Europe.

Once Garrick was established in London he spent much of his time at Whitechapel, studying and observing what he could of the Goodman's Fields performances. Eventually, with his portrayal of Richard III, Garrick completed what Macklin had begun – the revitalisation of legitimate drama in London. No exaggerated gesticulation, no bombast, no ranting and raving, no rolling syllables such as Quin had used, marred his style of acting. As his exciting and original performances became more widely known, the roads between Temple Bar and Whitechapel were regularly blocked with coaches. He was the new 'theatrical Newton';[42] he was London's 'Roscius'; everyone wanted to see him, willingly deserting the powerful Patent theatres, Drury Lane and Covent Garden, to travel the precarious route through the narrow streets of the crowded City to Goodman's Fields, which today would be described as a 'fringe' theatre.

Quin thought and hoped that Garrick's success was little more than a temporary aberration of the sensation-loving audiences. 'Garrick is the new religion', he said. 'Whitefield* was followed for a time; but they'll all come to church again.'[43] Quin was wrong. Garrick's congregation of dissenting admirers from the Patent Theatres continued to flock to Goodman's Fields, much to the annoyance of the wily Patentees – Rich at Covent Garden and Fleetwood at Drury Lane. They hit upon the idea of enlisting the support of Sir Robert Walpole, who was known to have been greatly displeased at Henry Fielding's unflattering portrait of him in the satirical comedy, *Pasquin*, produced at the King's Theatre in the Haymarket in 1736. Fielding was not popular with other theatrical cliques and côteries either, for in 1730 he had mercilessly burlesqued his fellow playwrights in *Tom Thumb*, and in 1733 had actively supported the revolt of the distressed actors of Drury Lane under the leadership of Theophilus Cibber.

The Tragedy of Tragedies: or, The Life and Death of Tom Thumb the Great, as the play was renamed in the year following its first performance in 1730, was an entertaining satire on the kind of bombastic tragedy popular since the days of Dryden and Davenant, and forms an interesting,

---

* Rev. George Whitefield (1714-1770). Leader of the Calvinistic Methodists. Undertook a missionary journey to Georgia USA. Engaged in evangelical preaching. Founded Moorfields Tabernacle, London. Excluded from churches in Scotland. Opened chapel in Tottenham Court Road in 1756. Opened Countess of Huntingdon chapels at Bath. Returned to America in 1769. Depicted in Hood's *Progress of Cant*. See Pope *Works* p385

even essential, link between the Duke of Buckingham's *The Rehearsal* (1671) and Sheridan's *The Critic* (1779). Tom Thumb, 'a little hero with a great soul', as he is described in the 'Dramatis Personae', is in love with the Princess Huncamunca, the daughter of the delightfully tipsy Queen Dollalolla, who is in turn in love with Tom Thumb, though she is married to the passionate King Arthur, who is in love with the captive Queen of the Giants, Glumdalca. The insatiably amorous Huncamunca is also in love with the choleric champion of liberty, Lord Grizzle, and as she would willingly settle for two husbands rather than one, has designs on His Lordship and Tom Thumb as well. Noodle, Foodle and Doodle represent the political parties of the day and are by no means flattering portraits of the Tories and Whigs. In the last scenes, everybody kills everybody else and tragedy runs riot with such hilarious dialogue as when Grizzle and Glumdalca fight to the death:

>Glumdalca: Have at thy heart then! (*thrusts at, but misses him*)
>Grizzle: Rampant queen of sluts!
>Now have at thine. (*strikes*)
>Glumdalca: You've run me through the guts.[44]

At which point, Tom Thumb rushes in and strikes Grizzle in the place Glumdalca missed. The Queen kills Noodle, the lover of Huncamunca's lady-in-waiting, Frizoletta, who in turn kills the Queen. 'Kill my mamma!' cries Huncamunca, who kills Frizoletta, whereupon Doodle, out of revenge for Noodle's untimely demise, kills Huncamunca, whose loyal servant Plumante kills Doodle. The King, in a fit of passion, kills Plumante and stabs himself. Thus, the farce ends in the fashion of some ludicrous parody of *Gorbuduc*,* with no one left alive to reign over an impoverished land. Miraculously, Merlin appears and brings everybody back to life, and all join in the final chorus:

> Let discord cease,
> Let all in peace
> Go home and kiss their spouses;
> Join hat and cap
> In one loud clap
> And wish us crowded houses.[45]

---

* Gorboduc, the legendary king of the Britons as recounted by Geoffrey of Monmouth, was the subject of a play by Thomas Norton and Thomas Sackville, the earliest English play in tragic verse, first performed in 1561.

Like *The Rehearsal* and *The Critic*, *The Life and Death of Tom Thumb* is a clever satire on the heroic style of tragedy perpetuated by Davenant and Cumberland. 'The love-scenes, rage, marriage, battle, and catastrophe, are such forcible imitations of the rules observed by the tragic writers of that time, that the satire conveyed in them cannot escape the observation of anyone conversant with the tragic writers of the last century.' [46] Fielding's *Pasquin*, on the other hand, was a more biting political satire which concerned the rehearsal of two plays, a comedy entitled *The Election* and a tragedy, *The Life and Death of Common-Sense*. Walpole's anger expressed itself in his wholehearted support of Fleetwood and Rich and led to the iniquitous Licensing Act of 1737, which virtually closed down all the unlicensed theatres, including Henry Giffard's theatre at Goodman's Fields. Garrick now was left effectively without a theatre to play in. Fleetwood was delighted (though not for long) and thus succeeded in coercing Garrick into acting exclusively at his Patent Theatre.

Charles Fleetwood was a gambler. He and Macklin had spent many a midnight hour gambling away their fortunes and, in Fleetwood's case, the fortunes of the Theatre Royal, Drury Lane. Bailiffs came periodically and carried away props and scenery when loans could not be met. Fleetwood continued to borrow at an alarming rate and his eventual bankruptcy was nearer than ever. Worst of all, he could not pay the actors their agreed salaries. Debts piled up once more as in the bad old days of Christopher Rich. Arrears of salaries brought real hardship to the already poorly-remunerated actors. The brokers came in again. Something had to be done.

The Theatre re-opened on 20 September with Buckingham's farcical comedy, *The Rehearsal*, Garrick playing the part of Bayes, the poetasting tragedian whose play is to be rehearsed. The piece is more of a subtle parody than Fielding's *Tom Thumb*, and sets out to ridicule the heroic tragedies of the day, such as Dryden's *The Conquest of Grenada* and *The Indian Emperour*. The plot concerns a poet, Bayes (Dryden), and his two friends Smith and Johnson (Dryden's brothers-in-law, Edward and Robert Howard), whom Bayes takes to see his play in rehearsal. The play is an absurd conglomeration of disparate elements, some of them plagiarised in open parodic style, Bayes interrupting the proceedings with ridiculous remarks mocking the failings of the performers by mimicking their actions and speech, and informing them of their misconceptions of his masterpiece and their negligence in interpreting it. 'You dance worse than the Angels in *Henry Eight'*.

Garrick's performance was, if not a triumph, a considerable success, which is all the more remarkable because little or nothing of it could be heard. Macklin, embittered by Fleetwood's rejection, turned up at the theatre with a band of rowdy followers. Loud hissing and booing greeted Garrick's first entry. Fleetwood, who had got wind of the riot, had taken the precaution of gathering up from the gutters of Hockley Hole and the Bear Garden, places of ill fame as Pope confirms in *The Dunciad*,[47] the toughest bunch of ruffians he could find, and spreading them out over various parts of the theatre. They came armed with sticks and bludgeons, and together with an excessive application of fisticuffs, dealt with Macklin's supporters. Clearly, this was the nadir of the Garrick-Macklin friendship, fallen into decline from former days when they had shared a house together, with the Irish actress, Peg Woffington.*

More riots came in the following year when Fleetwood attempted to put up prices. Tired of the opposition of both actors and audience, he sold his interest in the Patent to two City bankers by the unusual names of Green and Amber. Unlike Fleetwood's impetuous flouting of the rules, their policy in terms of speed was 'go, but with caution!' Unwilling, in their ignorance of theatrical affairs, to take part in the running of the theatre, they offered to Rich's assistant at Covent Garden, James Lacy,† the task of day-to-day management. Lacy offered Garrick a complete partnership, each to draw £500 a year as joint-manager, and Garrick to receive an equal sum as principal actor in the company. In the late summer of 1743, Garrick called a meeting with some of his fellow actors who at that time included Macklin himself, and a remarkable bevy of actresses, including Kitty Clive, Elizabeth Barry,‡ and Hannah Pritchard. The purpose of this was to withdraw their support of Fleetwood by refusing to enter into any negotiation whatsoever without the agreement of the group as a whole. To their utter dismay, he refused to consider their pleas. The suggestion was to follow the example of Betterton before them and appeal to the Lord Chamberlain, at that time the Duke of Grafton. A document was drawn up, signed by the protesters, and the petition was presented to the Duke. Faced now with the displeasure of Fleetwood, they were forced to break ranks and fend for themselves. Garrick, it must be admitted, weakly agreed new but less favourable terms with Fleetwood, and together with his companions, returned to Drury Lane. Macklin remained out in the cold, for Fleetwood refused to take him back on any terms.

The Theatre came under the new management on 15 September 1747

---

* Peg Woffington (1714?-1760), was at Drury Lane from 1741. Played Cordelia to Garrick's Lear.

† James Lacy (1696-1774). Joined John Rich's company at the Lincoln's Inn Fields Theatre in 1724. Appeared in the premiere of John Gay's *The Beggar's Opera*.

‡ Elizabeth Barry (1658-1713). Her patron was the Earl of Rochester. She created more than 100 roles.

with a fresh production of *The Merchant of Venice*, and the customary Prologue was composed by Samuel Johnson, who began with fulsome praise, only to vilify him in a vicious harangue:

> When Learning's Triumph o'er her barb'rous Foes
> First rear'd the Stage, immortal SHAKESPEARE rise;
> Each change of many-colour'd Life he drew,
> Exhausted Worlds, and then imagin'd new;
> Existence saw him spurn her bounded Reign,
> And panting Time toil'd after him in vain:[2]
> His pow'rful Strokes presiding Truth impress;d,
> And unresisted Passion storm'd the Breast.
>   Then JOHNSON [i.e. Jonson] came, instructed from the School,
> To please in Method, and invent by Rule;
> His studious Patience, and laborious Art,
> By regular Approach essay'd theHeart;
> Cold Approbation gave the ling'ring Bays,
> For those who durst not censure, scarce cou'd praise,
> A Mortal born he met a general Doom,
> But left, like *Egypt*'s Kings, a lasting Tomb,
> The Wits of *Charles* found easier Ways to Fame,
> Nor wish'd for JOHNSON's Art, or SHAKESPEARE's Flame;
> Themselves they studied. As they felt they writ,
> Intrigue was Plot, Obscenity was Wit.[7]
> Vice always found a sympathetick Friend;
> They pleas'd their Age, and did not aim to mend.
> Yet Bards like these aspir'd to lasting Praise,
> And proudly hop'd to pimp in future Days.
> Their Cause was gen'ral, their Supports were strong,
> Their Slaves were willing, and their Reign was long;
> Till shame regain'd the Post that Sense betray'd,
> And Virtue call'd Oblivion to her Aid.[8]
>   Then crush'd by Rules, and weaken'd as refin'd,
> For Years the Pow'r of dignity declin'd;
> From Bard, to Bard, the frigid Caution crept,
> Till Declamation roar'd, while Passion slept.

Yet still did Virtue deign the Stage to tread,
Philosophy remain'd, though Nature fled.
But forc'd at length her antient Reign to quit,
She saw great *Faustus* lay the Ghost of Wit:[9]
Exulting Folly hail'd the joyful Day,[10]
And Pantomime, and Song, confirm'd her Sway.[11]

But who the coming Changes can presage,
And mark the future Periods of the Stage? —
Perhaps if Skill could distant Times explore,
New *Behns*, new *Durfeys*, yet remain in Store.[12]
Perhaps where *Lear* has rav'd and *Hamlet* dy'd,
On flying Cars new sorcerers may ride.
Perhaps, for who can guess th' Effects of Chance?
Here *Hunt* may box, or *Mahomet* may dance.[14]

Hard is his lot, that here by Fortune plac'd,
Must watch the wild Vicissitudes of Taste;
With ev'ry Meteor of Caprice must play,
And chase the new-blown Bubbles of the Day.
Ah! let not Censure term our Fate our Choice,
The Stage but echoes back the publick Voice.
The Drama's Laws the Drama's Patrons give,
For we that live to please, must please to live.[15]

Then prompt no more the Follies you decry,
As Tyrants doom their Tools of Guilt to die;
'Tis yours this Night to bid the Reign commence
Of rescu'd Nature, and reviving Sense;
To chase the Charms of sound, the Pomp of Show,
For useful Mirth, and salutary Woe;
Bid scenic Virtue form the rising Age,
And Truth diffuse her Radiance from the Stage.

9. Garrick and the Prima Donnas

The system of understudies was unknown in Garrick's time. However, his first opportunity to act on the London stage arose when the actor, Richard

Yates,[*] was taken ill at Goodman's Fields. The play was a 'Harlequin', or pantomime, and Garrick, having 'understudied' Yates's role by learning by heart every line and gesture, took over the part and made a success of it. His subsequent performance as Macbeth sealed that success, and in his brilliant career he went on to play many Shakespearean roles including Falconbridge and Iago at Dublin (where he had gone to join Thomas Sheridan during the Jacobite rebellion of 1745).

Garrick's attitude to Shakespeare was ambivalent. When Lacy introduced a rope-dancer in 1752, Garrick was shocked at bringing such 'defilement and abomination into the house of William Shakespeare'[48] yet he persisted in his own versions and adaptations, travesties of their originals which pandered dutifully (and sometimes tastelessly) to the demands of 18th century audiences. Garrick's *Hamlet* has no Osric, nor even gravediggers, and because Laertes' dying speech received too little applause too regularly, his lines were given to Hamlet, that is, to Garrick. Though his *Macbeth*, he claimed, was 'as written by Shakespeare', his version of *The Winter's Tale,* entitled *Florizel and Perdita,* was another ludicrous treatment of the original. Mary Robinson,[†] Garrick's 'Juliet' and mistress of the Prince Regent, acquired the sobriquet of 'Perdita', for the Prince's passionate letters to her were signed 'Florizel', and the liaison was mercilessly caricatured in the prints of the day. Just as in Lyly's *Endymion, the Man in the Moon* explored the love between Cynthia (Queen Elizabeth) and Endymion (the Earl of Leicester), so Garrick's version of the love-scenes between Perdita and Florizel, because of the topical allusion, became the object of coarse merriment in the gallery.

Though Garrick's audience might not have been too worried about the infidelity of his adaptions of Shakespeare's plays, they relished them for what must be admitted were all the wrong reasons. Well into the next century, the true spirit of Shakespeare was increasingly sacrificed to extravagance and eccentricity. The play was not the thing, becoming more and more a vehicle for the actor himself, who was the focus of attention, especially if he had the good fortune to be the centre of intrigue or scandal.

Audiences tended to care less and less about plays themselves and more and more about principal actors. The first great actor to establish this trend was Garrick, to be followed in later years by such 'star' actors as Kemble and Kean, Macready and Irving. Just as Macklin had gone out into the coffee-houses to find his prototype of Shylock, so Garrick

---

[*] Richard Yates (1706-1796). Played at Goodman's Fields and Drury Lane. Best at comedy.

[†] Mary Robinson (1758-1800), Actress and author. Pension from Fox. Took part, it is said, in Della Cruscan literature under a variety of signatures.

Chapter 1 – From Tennis Court to Temple of the Muses

frequently based his interpretations on his own observations of incidents from life. When he came to rehearsing the mad-scenes from *Lear*, he was reminded of something he had seen at Goodman's Fields some years before. A man was leaning out of a window with a baby in his arms. Accidentally, he dropped the child and it was killed. The man became demented and was removed to Bedlam. The compassion that Garrick felt at this appalling circumstance illustrates something of the warmer part of his nature. From time to time he visited the man in the asylum. It was this very warmth that made him vulnerable in any emotional situation that arose behind the scenes and might be considered as contributory to many a feud among the ladies of the company. His amorous liaison with Peg Woffington had deteriorated into a bickering and nagging relationship that inevitably ended in separation. She could be hot-tempered and sharp-tongued when roused, and on one occasion came to blows with Kitty Clive in the Green Room. On another occasion, in a fit of jealousy or pique, she chased the actress, George Anne Bellamy,* through the theatre brandishing a dagger. Garrick's company also included Susannah Maria Arne (1714-56), sister of Thomas Arne, the composer. She possessed a fine singing voice which so impressed Handel that he wrote the contralto arias in *Messiah* especially for her, as well as the part of Galatea in *Acis and Galatea*. She married Theophilus Cibber but the marriage broke up and, after Cibber's bankruptcy and subsequent flight to France to escape his creditors, she settled for a more reliable companion called Sloper, though her letters to Garrick reveal an affection for the great actor that goes beyond the bounds of merely professional association.

The 'prima donnas' of Drury Lane were eventually to be Garrick's downfall. Hannah Pritchard was the greatest Lady Macbeth of her day, but her advancing years and expanding girth discouraged Garrick from giving her the younger parts she most desired. The more troublesome Frances Abington,† daughter of a private in the Guards, began life as a flower-seller, working her way from street-seller to actress by a tortuous route. One of her employers was the comedian, Robert Baddeley, to whom she was cook-maid at the time when he was cook to Samuel Foote.‡

---

* George Anne Bellamy (1731?-1788). Played Juliet to Garrick's Romeo. Published her *Apology* 1785. A rival of Mrs Cibber and Elizabeth Barry.
† Frances Abington (1737-1815). Flower-seller and cook-maid. First appeared at Haymarket in 1855. Had great success in Dublin. Returned to Drury Lane at Garrick's invitation.
‡ Samuel Foote (1720-1777). Actor and dramatist. Played comedy parts in imitation of Cibber 1745. Devised an amusing entertainment mimicking leading actors and actresses. Wrote a play ridiculing the Methodists. Sent for trial for sexual offences. Died a year afterwards from natural causes. See Mr. *Foote's Other Leg.* Ian Kelly Picador 2012.

According to Garrick, she was 'treacherous', 'the worst of bad women',[49] a view shared perhaps by her husband, a trumpeter in the King's Service, who disappeared soon after their marriage. Garrick's troubles were further exacerbated by Jane Pope,[*] who had been with the company since her childhood, and Elizabeth Younge,[†] who made her debut as Imogen, and married the namesake of the poet, an actor and painter of miniatures called Alexander Pope. It seems, however, that whilst Frances Abington had the most devastating effect on Garrick's morale, all these actresses, in their own blunt or subtle ways, in the end brought him to his knees. It certainly was not all his own doing, though his sensitivity to their plaguings and protestations was undoubtedly a contributory factor in his ultimate downfall. Nor were their antics to rest there, for they would reappear with ever-increasing frenzy to pester the life out of Sheridan at the disorderly rehearsals of *The School for Scandal.*

Garrick's retirement from the stage came as a surprise to those who knew him well, but it shocked his public, who came flocking to the crowded theatre for his farewell performance as Don Felix in Mrs. Centlivre's *The Wonder*.[‡] The audience were in no mood for an 'After-Piece' as they watched him bow respectfully to gallery, boxes and Pit, and with slow and deliberate pace, walk from the stage of the Theatre Royal, Drury Lane, never to return. In the thirty-six years of his association with the theatre, he had brought to it an atmosphere of dedication and respect, as well as dignity and decorum to the craft of acting. He had begun by removing audiences from the stage, employing great scenic artists like the German painter and Royal Academician, Philip James Loutherbourg,[§] with whose help he was able to dress plays with greater historical accuracy. He brought a sense of professionalism into the theatre by his insistence on punctuality at rehearsals, and the practice of rehearsing as if the audience were present in the auditorium. As to Shakespeare's texts, in spite of his popular adaptations, it should be said that he did much to restore the original dialogue, no doubt encouraged by Samuel Johnson, whose edition of the plays had appeared in 1765. What Garrick had done for the English Stage was inestimable, but insofar as it could be assessed, the sheer power of his acting, the magnitude of his conception, the range

---

[*] Jane Pope (1742-1818). At Drury Lane 1756 and remained there until she retired in 1808. Praised by Lamb, Hazlitt and Leigh Hunt.

[†] Elizabeth Pope (nee Younge). (1744?-1797). First wife of Alexander Pope.

[‡] Mrs Susannah Centlivre (1667?-1723). Married Joseph Centlivre, cook to Queen Anne. She was author of 18 plays. Acted in provinces

[§] Philippe-Jacques Loutherbourg, (1740-1812). Born in Germany. Royal Academician. Studied under Canova in Paris. Assisted Garrick as designer of scenery and costume.

Chapter 1 – From Tennis Court to Temple of the Muses

of his styles, both in comedy and tragedy, and above all his passionate enthusiasm for the thespian ideal, earned him the right to be considered as the greatest English actor who had ever lived.

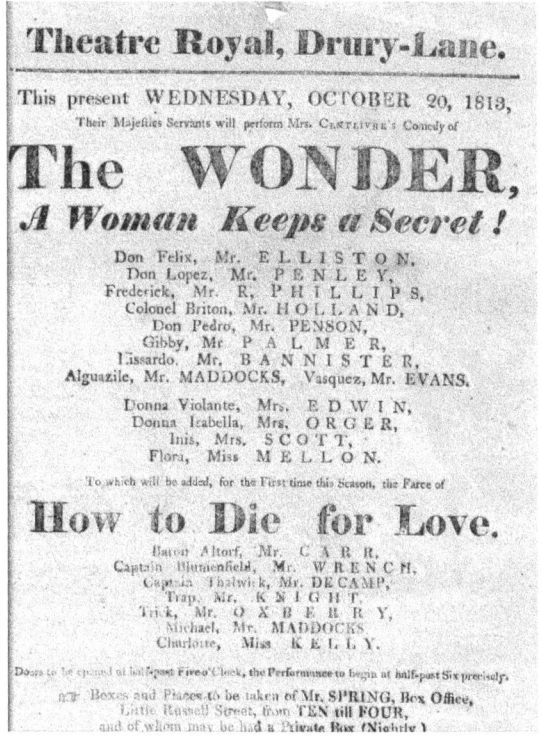

Playbill for Mrs Centlivre's comedy *The Wonder*

In the Epilogue to Garrick's play, *The Clandestine Marriage*, written in collaboration with George Colman,* he refers to the transitory nature of the actor's condition when compared to that of the painter who leaves behind the permanent records of his talents and skills:

> The painter's dead, yet still he charms the eye,
> While England lives his fame can never die;
> But he who struts his hour upon the stage
> Can scarce protract his fame through half an age;
> Nor pen, nor pencil can the actor save;
> The art and artist have one common grave.[50]

---

* George Colman, the Younger (1762-1836). Nephew of William Pulteney, Earl of Bath. Manager of The Haymarket. Published coarse comic poems.

Never did Garrick's words apply less to anyone than himself, for he remained in the memories of many admirers of his genius well into the next century, and his name and fame have permanently established themselves in the annals of theatrical history and beyond. For Sheridan he was 'matchless Garrick', and never was an epithet so aptly applied to him. In *Verse to the Memory of Garrick, spoken as a Monody*, Sheridan echoed the very fears Garrick had himself expressed:

> Ev'n matchless GARRICK's Art to heav'n resign'd,
> No fix'd Effect, no Model leaves behind;
> The GRACE of ACTION — the adapted MIEN
> Faithful as Nature to the varied Scene;
> Th'EXPRESSIVE GLANCE — whose subtle Comment draws
> Entranc'd Attention, and a mute Applause;
> GESTURE that marks, with Force and Feeling fraught,
> A Sense in Silence, and a Will in Thought;
> HARMONIOUS SPEECH, whose pure and liquid Tone
>   Gives Verse a Music, scarce confess'd its own;
> As Light from Gems, assumes a brighter Ray
> And cloathed with Orient Hues, transcends the Day! —
> PASSION's wild Break — and FROWN that awes the Sense,
> And every CHARM of gentler ELOQUENCE —
> All perishable!...

The grace of action, the expressive glance, the liquid tones of his speech, the passion and eloquence remained only in the memory of those who were still alive to remember him; three years after his death, Sheridan had to remind his audience, as they listened to the recitation of his *Monody*:

> By the hush'd Wonder that his Accents drew!
> By his last parting Tear repaid by you!
> By all those Thoughts, which many a distant Night,
> Shall mark his memory with a sad Delight! —
> Still in your Hearts' dear Record bear his Name;
> Cherish the keen Regret that lifts his Fame.[51]

CHAPTER TWO

Richard Brinsley Sheridan: The Profligate Accountant

1. Wheelings and Dealings

The fortunes of the Theatre Royal, Drury Lane, had suffered a serious setback with the bankruptcy of Green and Amber, a result of the run on the banks during the Jacobite rebellion of 1745. James Lacy had struggled on until 1778, when Sheridan bought his share for £31,500. With the help of his father-in-law, Thomas Linley, and a physician, Dr. James Ford, he had also purchased Garrick's share of the Patent and the leases for £35,000. Mortgaging part of his interest, he then purchased, for a further £18,000, Dr. Ford's share. Thus, with only about £1000 of his own money he had managed to raise about £80,000 from shareholders. This was no mean achievement but it says more for his Irish charm than his common sense. Unfortunately he was no great financier and proved within a few years that he was incapable of managing the affairs of a large theatrical venture. Sheridan was by nature, as his riotous youth had indicated, erratic in his judgements, which were invariably clouded by emotional outbursts or fits of panic. It is all the more surprising therefore that he appointed himself business manager as well as having the tenure of the already-established positions of Lessee and Patentee.

Under Garrick's management the Theatre Royal had been transformed into a magnificent 'Temple of the Muses', where great plays performed by fine (and in Garrick's case, great) actors and actresses could be regularly seen. This home of the 'Scenic Muse' extolled by the authors of the future 'Drury Lane Addresses', did not enjoy as spectacular an opening as might have been expected. Sheridan rewrote Vanbrugh's *The Relapse,* under the title *A Trip to Scarborough.* It was not a success. Garrick had told Sheridan to write more plays, but this feeble adaptation did little to convince audiences that the Muses had actually taken up residence as yet.

The popular taste for 'Harlequins', or pantomimes, continued to preoccupy Sheridan, as it had done his predecessors. *Harlequin Fortunatus, or, The Wishing Cap* was to include a new interlude by Sheridan; the interlude was based closely on dispatches from the Spanish War: a 'British Tar' scales the ramparts of the Spanish fort and, having by chance two cutlasses, offers one of them to a Spanish officer because his British principle will not allow him to cut down an unarmed man. After a struggle, he beats the Spaniard and spares his life.[1]

Sheridan had no self-discipline when it came to writing. His mercurial nature led him rapidly from one thing to another, so that nothing was ever finished on time, with the result that the cast for the forthcoming production of *The School for Scandal* received the play page by page as the author scribbled it down. His most vociferous critics were Frances Abington, who was to play Lady Teazle, with Jane Pope in the part of Mrs. Candour. Fortunately for Sheridan, this was a time when Garrick was still alive and active in the theatre, and could agree to take some of the burden from his shoulders by assuming responsibility for the supervision of rehearsals, for as yet there was no concept of what we would today call 'production'.

The success of the play lay in the way in which Sheridan was able to visualise the actor or actress play the role as part and parcel of the creative process. He could hear the voice of Frances Abington, visualise her gestures and movements, and bring to life the dialogue and character of Lady Teazle. The comic discovery of Lady Teazle hiding behind the screen brought such a roar from the audience at the first performance that a passing journalist fled, believing the building was about to fall in.[2]

The rumour of the imminent collapse of Theatre Royal, Drury Lane, already circulated by John Rich some years before, did not die as quickly as the management of the Theatre would have wished. That part of the audience which defected to Covent Garden had to be wooed back, and this could only be done by brilliant plays and brilliant actors. As long as Covent Garden continued to put on drama and pantomime, Drury Lane had to fight for its audiences. The rivalry sometimes led to the performance of the same play on the same night in the two theatres.

In 1750 Spranger Barry* and Mrs. Cibber played *Romeo and Juliet* at Covent Garden on the same night as Garrick and George Anne Bellamy at Drury Lane. The contest was still going on in 1798 when Covent Garden was suffering a decline as a result of the phenomenal success of Sarah Siddons† at Drury Lane. Ann Crawford‡ (whose husband, Spranger Barry, had died in the previous year), was persuaded to come out of retirement to play the part she had made famous – Lady Randolph in Home's *Douglas*.§ Mrs. Siddons successfully beat her at her own game by scoring such a success in the part that Mrs. Crawford thought it better to return to her former state of idleness and never appeared on the stage again. Some years before at Covent Garden, Mary Ann Yates,** one of the greatest English tragic actresses of her day, had some success as Calista in Rowe's adaption of Massinger and Field's *The Fatal Dowry*, retitled *The Fair Penitent* at Drury Lane. Mrs. Siddons re-interpreted the part, even revolutionised it, and triumphed brilliantly over her rival.

The genius of Garrick and Mrs. Siddons could not be equalled anywhere on the London Stage, and during their reign Drury Lane was secure in the loyalty of its audiences. So it was also with Sheridan's plays, if those who depended on him for their livelihood could ever persuade him to exercise more self-discipline in the writing of them. In the case of *The Critic*, Sheridan, who was supposedly completing the play

---

* Spranger Barry (1719-1777). Bankrupt Dublin silversmith who turned to acting. Successfully played Lear, Henry V, and Hotspur. Joined Drury Lane under Garrick and Lacey (1746). Played Romeo to Mrs. Cibber's Juliet.

† Sarah Siddons ((1755-1831) Married actor William Siddons after opposition from her parents. Engaged by Garrick at Drury Lane but unsuccessfully played Portia (1755). Went off to Manchester under Tate Wilkinson, then to Bath and Bristol, returning to Drury to triumphant applause as Belvidera, Zara in *The Mourning Bride*, and Isabella in Garrick's version of *The Fatal Marriage*. Gave her farewell performance at Covent Garden in 1812. Gave readings at Windsor Castle. Her statue by Chantrey can be seen in Westminster Abbey.

‡ Ann Crawford (1734-1801). Played Cordelia to Barry's Lear. Made her reputation as Juliet and Desdemona. Acted mainly at The Haymarket.

§ *Douglas*. Successful play by John Home (1722-1808). His play, performed first in Edinburgh, was rejected by Garrick but produced by Rich in 1757. Edmund Kean made his debut as the hero, Young Norval. Sarah Siddons made the part of Lady Randolph famous. Home's play, *Alfred (1778)* failed. Formerly tutor to the Prince of Wales.

** Mary Ann Yates (I1728-1787). Played mainly at Drury Lane 1755-67. Made her name with Cleopatra, Rosalind, Desdemona, Cordelia, and Perdita. She played the original Berinthia in Sheridan's *A Trip to Scarborough*. Though hardly remembered today, she was one of the finest English tragic actresses to play at Drury Lane.

at home, was enticed into the theatre by his fellow lessees, Thomas King and John Lacy, and locked in the Green Room with a supply of claret and anchovy sandwiches to sustain him until he had completed the play.

2. Sarah Siddons: 'The Tragic Muse'

Sarah Siddons was to become the mainstay of Drury Lane during her years there, and when she left for Covent Garden the shadow of ruin began to darken Sheridan's life. Reynolds painted her as 'The Tragic Muse', and there is no doubt that she was one of the greatest English tragic actresses who ever lived. Her first appearance for Sheridan was in October 1782 as Isabella in Southerne's *The Fatal Marriage*, a play which admirably suited her gift for portraying grief and dementia in scenes of harrowing intensity that reduced her audiences to tears. Her carefully studied 'dying falls' possessed the magic of excellence that made her greatest role as Belvidera in Otway's *Venice Preserv'd* [3] almost unendurable in the magnitude of its portrayal of human suffering. The audience went wild. Fights broke out at the pit entrances and casualties were caused by the continuous press and throng of the crowds anxious to gain admission. In another notable performance, the King and Queen wept, together with their subjects in the pit and gallery, and were moved to offer Sarah the post of Preceptress to the Princesses in recognition of her triumph. Her second season was even more triumphant, for the King and Queen ordered a Command Performance:

> The front of the Royal Box was built out for this occasion, so that His Majesty's subjects might have a chance of feasting.... on the glory of Royalty. A canopy.... of crimson velvet [was] adorned with carved and gilded decorations, and the draping valances were also enriched with cords of gold. The Monarch.... wore a plain quaker-coloured suit, although it had gold buttons; but the Queen.... gleamed in white satin and diamonds. One Princess wore a blue and white and the other a rose and white dress of figured silk. They had a canopy of their own, of blue satin. His Royal Highness, the Prince of Wales.... sat in solitary state under a canopy of blue velvet trimmed with silver....[4]

Something of the atmosphere of a 'Siddons Night' is given in a description of undignified scenes both outside and inside the theatre:

> ....five hundred to a thousand people.... would shove and

> push and battle outside the pit entrance for an hour before the doors opened. Men used their weight and their fists. Weak men and women went to the wall or underfoot. Often the force with which those first at the doors were shot into the theatre was so great that many hurled past the boxes and so got in for nothing. Seats went to the most muscular of the first comers, and they held them by brute force. The acoustics were bad. Unless the audience was quiet it was difficult to hear the actors and there never was silence save when some great actor or actress compelled it.[5]

Rioting and rough behaviour had always been a fact of life at Drury Lane, as were various forms of violence and protest. No wonder religious figures throughout this period were deeply committed to closing the theatres. During a performance by Spranger Barry in 1746, for example, a man in the gallery threw an apple at the stagehand which 'by mistake struck 'a lady of quality' in the face.' On other occasions, disapproval expressed itself by showers of peas being flung at the stage if performances did not meet the dubious standards of the Gallery and the Pit. Sometimes stones and nails were thrown at the offending actor or actress. Even Drury Lane's greatest performers suffered these indignities.

Another eruption happened when Garrick, who for years had wished to abolish the system of half-price admission for any member of the audience arriving at the theatre after the third act of a play, hoped to establish full prices, but the mob would not have it. A protest was staged for a night when a new version of *The Two Gentlemen of Verona* was to be put on. Whilst the ringleader, Fitzpatrick, had wanted an orderly expression of disapproval, the matter ended by Garrick being howled from the stage, the actors threatened, the benches broken up and the inside of the theatre largely wrecked.

Public anger waxed even more when Garrick announced his intention in 1755 of staging Jean Noverre's Paris production of *Les Fêtes Chinoises*. As England was at war with France, the rabble were in no mood to stomach imported performances by the enemy. In spite of the outcry, the King came to support Garrick on the noisy first night, and for the following five nights a battle of some ferocity was fought in the pit; benches were ripped out, women screamed as swords were drawn and blood spilled. The mob went to Garrick's house, hurled stones at his windows, and threatened to burn the house to the ground. A xenophobic antipathy was shown towards Garrick after his marriage to the Austrian dancer, 'Violette', who was known to be resented by Quin and Macklin, Barry and Mrs. Cibber. After the 'Full Price' riots of 1763, Garrick and his wife went to France and met Diderot, Beaumarchais and Marivaux,

Chapter 2 – Richard Brinsley Sheridan: the Profligate Accountant

but his French sympathies did not endear him to that more militantly patriotic part of his audiences.

Even Mrs. Siddons suffered the humiliation of defeat on occasion. Whilst in Dublin, she collapsed under the pressure of continual performance and was accused of 'false pretences' by Richard Daly,[*] the Patentee of the Theatre Royal, Dublin. The rumour spread rapidly to London, and together with other untruths circulated about her by the vicious Daly, helped to create an unpleasant atmosphere of animosity among the Drury Lane audience assembled to hear her return performance on 5 October 1784. The crowd were angry. They booed and hissed, and shouted at her to get off the stage. She tried to speak but was again shouted down. Her brother, John Philip Kemble,[†] whom she had introduced into Sheridan's Drury Lane, led her, distraught, into the wings, where she fainted from the shock of her reception. Sheridan and Kemble struggled to revive her. At last she found sufficient courage to go on again. The rabble, under the illusion that they had driven her from the stage forever, were astonished to see, on the raising of the curtain, the defiant Mrs. Siddons silently gazing at them. They responded with complete silence. After some moments she stepped forward and spoke:

> Ladies and Gentleman, the kind and flattering partiality which I have uniformly experienced in this place would make the present interruption distressing to me indeed were I, in the slightest degree, conscious of having deserved your censure. I feel no such consciousness. The stories which have been circulated against me are calumnies. When they shall be proved true my aspersers will be justified. But, till then, my respect for the public leads me to be confident that I shall be protected from unmerited insults.[6]

---

[*] Richard Daly (d. 1813). Fellow-commoner, Trinity College, Dublin. Opened the Smock Alley Theatre, Dublin (1781). Patentee for a Theatre Royal at Dublin but surrendered his claim. He was a bitter enemy of Mrs Siddons, and all but ruined her.

[†] John Philip Kemble (1757-1823). Brother of Mrs. Siddons. Child actor in his father's company. Gained great success in Dublin before his appearances at Drury Lane (1783-1802), where he played over 120 characters. Manager of Drury Lane (from 1788), dressed actors unconventionally. Acted Coriolanus, Romeo, Petruchio, but failed as Charles Surface. Made adaptations to Shakespeare's plays. In 1794, re-opened the 'New Drury' After troubles with Sheridan, moved to Covent Garden with Mrs. Siddons until the Theatre burned down in 1808. Re-opened to O.P. riots due to higher prices. Went abroad for his health and died at Lausanne. Introduced the declamatory style of acting adopted by Henry Irving later in the century.

She was allowed to continue her performance though not entirely without interruptions from the more intransigent rabble-rousers.

Mrs. Siddons was not the only actress to suffer the machinations of the iniquitous Daly. He had recently taken under his wing a young actress named Dorothea Bland and, as with other unfortunate actresses, he lent her money and then planned to seduce her. Resisting his forceful attentions for a time, she was abducted by him, and according to her own story, he raped her in a lonely Dublin house. Whatever the truth of her story, after giving birth to his child, she crossed to England, under the name of Mrs. Jordan. Eventually she became the mistress of the Duke of Clarence (later William IV) and bore him ten children, all transparently named Fitzclarence. She was especially popular in 'breeches parts', as they were known in the profession, and was successful as Viola in *Twelfth Night*, though she was equally at home with Rosalind and Hypolita. She was a very real threat to Mrs. Siddons, whose departure for the rival theatre at Covent Garden had been hastened by indecorous squabbling between these two powerful 'prima donnas'.

When it was realised that George IV would not produce an heir to the throne, the relationship between Dorothy Jordan and the Duke of Clarence was permanently severed and, unable to remain in England, she was quietly exiled to France, where she died in poverty, and was buried at St. Cloud in 1816.

3. Henry Holland and his 'New Drury'

The partnership between Sheridan, Linley and Ford at Drury Lane broke up after a few years and it was left to Mrs. Siddons' brother, John Philip Kemble, to pick up the pieces. Sheridan showed himself to be increasingly incapable of running a thriving theatre (thriving at least as far as his public were concerned). The mortgage became an intolerable burden to him and his interests now began to be directed towards activities at the House of Commons. Wren's theatre, which had stood on the site for over a century, had suffered the 'brutalising' of its fabric by countless audiences in Gallery and Pit, as well as the vandalising of its furniture and decoration in mob-riots and other violent upheavals, and all this was in addition to the normal wear and tear of a popular place of public assembly. One by one, the actors and actresses who had been the mainstay of the Theatre Royal, unable to survive on the meagre emoluments Sheridan could afford, drifted away to Covent Garden and the Haymarket, and within a few years he was to lose his two principal performers to a rival Patentee. The final blow came when rumours arose yet again, questioning the safety of the building. A survey found it in a

Chapter 2 – Richard Brinsley Sheridan: the Profligate Accountant

serious condition of dilapidation. Structural deficiencies were discovered, curious proof indeed, confirming former tales-about-town to that effect, and in 1791 the building was condemned.

Sheridan immediately set about finding a suitable architect. He commissioned Henry Holland,* designer of the Prince Regent's Pavilion at Brighton, to devise a building of grandiose proportions, with a magnificent interior unparalleled in the history of Drury Lane, all at an estimated cost of £150,000. The capital for this ambitious venture was raised by offering three hundred shares of £500 each. Incredibly, Sheridan committed himself to granting each subscriber free admission and an additional emolument of two shillings and sixpence for every night on which a performance took place, thus increasing his annual indebtedness by the alarming sum of £7,500. A new ground lease had to be secured from the Duke of Bedford. This proved to be a complicated negotiation because Sheridan found out after his interview with the Duke that he would not for long be the possessor of the Patent since Garrick and Lacy's joint agreement would expire only a year after the new theatre was due to open. Sheridan's 'Renters' would certainly not agree to putting up funds for the building work unless he could show them the vital Patent and confirm its grant of tenure for an agreed term of a hundred years, sufficient to satisfy the financial obligation. Sheridan hit upon the idea of purchasing the old Killigrew Patent granted by Charles II and formerly suspended by the malfeasance of Christopher Rich. This Patent was still in the hands of the Rich family, but due to the complicated system of parcelling of shares, it now rested with Thomas Harris and a man called White. The share of the document had been divided into sixtieths, Harris retaining forty-six and White fourteen. White was offered £5,000 to sell out to Sheridan but he refused. Harris, however, agreed to sell his share for £11,667 in 1793. Although a carpenters' strike held up the work, Sheridan persuaded the strikers to go back to their labours by promising them a free barrel of ale. Thomas Hood etched a protesting carpenter into the design of *The Progress of Cant* in 1825.

The new building, larger in scale, was completed in 1794. The successors to White did not sell their share until 1813, when it fetched the sum of £9,561 19s. 8d. To this day the Patent remains undivided and rests with the Theatre Royal, Drury Lane Ltd. Sheridan secured the ground lease from the Duke of Bedford on condition that the Duke and his descendants could have a private box, a small concession considering the enormous scale of expenditure. Sheridan still possessed the licence from

---

* Henry Holland (1745-1806). Architect to the English nobility. Designed Claremont House, Battersea Bridge, Brighton Pavilion (1787), enlarged Carlton House (1788), and laid out Sloane Street and Sloane Square, Chelsea.

Queen Anne, and now he had to secure the Patent and the funds for rebuilding.

The boxes, eight of them on the stage, accommodated a total of 1,828 people, the pit held 800, the two-shilling gallery 675, and the upper gallery 308, making a total capacity of 3,611. Four tiers of boxes rose to the lofty ceiling. As to the exterior, a long colonnade stretched the whole length of Russell Street, above which were three storeys lit by long lines of barrack-like windows. Towering over the central lantern was the enormous statue of Apollo with his lyre, a proof to all those who came to gaze at the newly-erected theatre that, from its lowly beginnings at Killigrew's Tennis Court, it had, as we have seen, indeed risen in its grandeur to become London's 'Temple of the Muses'. At last, on 12 March 1794, the new Theatre Royal was opened. As it was Lent, no theatrical performances were permissible, so a concert of sacred music was arranged beneath the grand setting of a Gothic cathedral to delight the eyes and ears of the elegant and admiring audience.

On 21 April 1794, the Theatre Royal opened for its first play, with Mrs. Siddons as Lady Macbeth. George Colman the Younger,[*] was commissioned to write a Prologue in which he refers to a new iron curtain that would be lowered, in the event of fire, between the stage and the audience. In fact, this turned out to have the disadvantage of trapping the performers between the flaring footlights and a red-hot wall of iron should they ever have the misfortune to be the victims of such a conflagration as the one of 1672.

---

[*] George Colman, the Younger (1762-1836). Dramatist. Author of the popular comedy, *The Heir at Law* (1787). Wrote and published risqué poetry. Also autobiography, *Random Records* (1830).

Chapter 2 – Richard Brinsley Sheridan: the Profligate Accountant

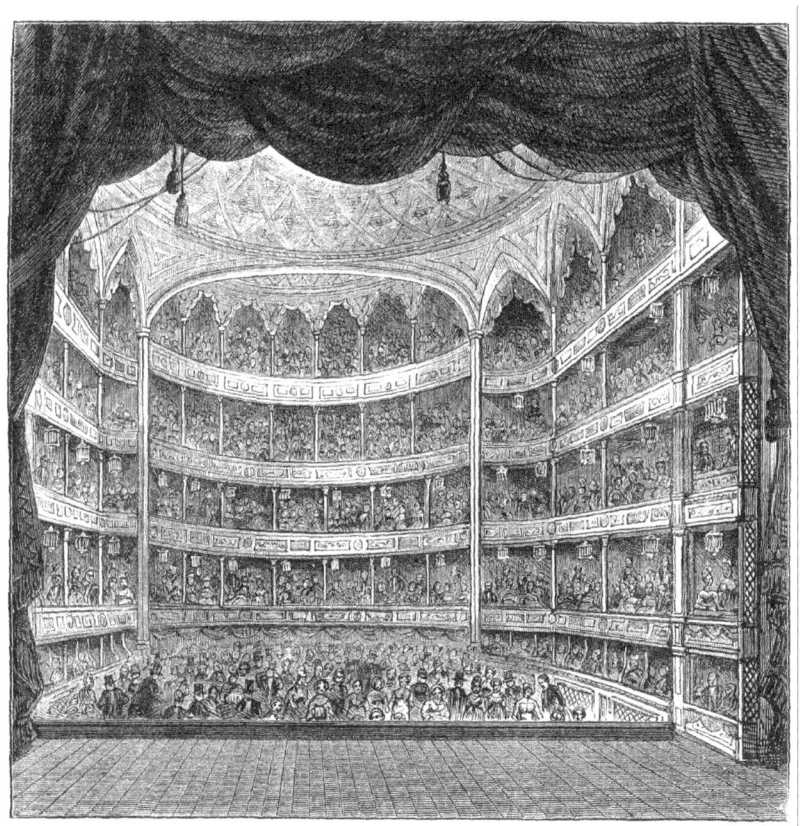

Henry Holland's auditorium, 1794.
The stage was too far from the main body of the audience so that,
from some parts of the theatre, the actors could not be heard.

Colman's Prologue was spoken by Elizabeth Farren,* whom Hazlitt had commended for her 'fine-lady airs and graces'. She was, in 1797, to marry the Earl of Derby. In an attempt to reassure the apprehensive spectators, she added, with some degree of truth:

> No! we assure our generous benefactors
> 'Twill only burn the scenery and the actors![7]

– a sentiment echoed in 1812 by George Terry, one of the authors of the 'Drury Lane Addresses':

> Let no alarm while here your minds invade;
> All is secure, and for your safety made;

---

* Elizabeth Farren (1759?-1829), Countess of Derby. Acted at The Haymarket (1777). Played the original Nancy Lovel in Colman's *Suicide (*1778).

The whole combin'd your persons to protect:
Then weak and idle fears we pray reject.[8]

George Colman the Younger
(Engraving by Ridley & Blood from the *European Magazine*)

As Elizabeth's Prologue ended, the audience was amazed to see the iron safety-curtain slowly lowered. A stage-hand came on and struck it with a hammer to prove its sturdiness, and a great clangour vibrated through the theatre. Then the curtain was raised to reveal cascades of water from the special fire-precautionary tanks in the roof 'rushing, roaring, dashing, splashing, tumbling over artificial rocks.' The water flowed into a tank in the form of an artificial lake on which a man rowed about in a small boat. In spite of all these elaborate precautions the Theatre Royal, Drury Lane, was to suffer serious damage from fire in less than twenty years from its opening.

The disaster that was to befall Henry Holland's magnificent building was typical of the misfortunes that were the ruin of many London theatres in the eighteenth and nineteenth centuries. Audiences and actors were fortunate to escape with their lives from countless accidents and conflagrations. The Royalty Theatre, opened in 1787, burnt down in 1826, reopened as the Brunswick Theatre on 25 February 1828, and was (only four days later) to become the scene of an appalling accident when the walls collapsed under the weight of its heavy iron roof, killing twelve people during a rehearsal of Sir Walter Scott's *Guy Mannering*. The Haymarket Theatre was opened in 1702, rebuilt in 1720 as The Little

Chapter 2 – Richard Brinsley Sheridan: the Profligate Accountant

Theatre, reconstructed as a Royal theatre in 1767, and was the scene of a serious incident which occurred during a royal visit on 3 February 1794 when sixteen people were trampled to death and many others died from their injuries. The English Opera House, later to become famous through the performances of its celebrated 'diva', Madame Vestris, was burnt down in 1830 and rebuilt four years later. Even Covent Garden did not escape the raging flames of a theatrical conflagration in 1808 and was rebuilt only to be burnt down again in 1856. Before the coming of gaslight and electrical illumination, theatres were lit by hundreds of candles, the fumes and heat distressing to both performers and audience. By 1840, there were no less than seventeen theatres in London and not one Georgian interior remained.

In 1802, during Mrs. Siddons' performance as Hermione in *A Winter's Tale* at Drury Lane, a draught blew the filmy material of her costume over some lamps burning at the back of the stage, and within seconds she was enveloped in flames. A stage-hand rushed forward just in time to save her from serious injury, quenching the fire with his bare hands. It was not only a timely warning that went unheeded by a neglectful management, it also marked the end of Sarah Siddons' reign at the Theatre Royal, Drury Lane. Worn out and discouraged by internecine feuding among the cast (involving among others the tempestuous Dorothy Jordan), Mrs. Siddons, together with her brilliant and capable brother, John Philip Kemble, who had presented over one hundred and twenty characters in his nineteen years there, left the stage of Drury Lane for the more reliable establishment at Covent Garden, though, as we have seen, that theatre too was to burn down in 1808. Thomas Hood, remarking on the ossifying effects of age and the changing nature of the times, remembered with regret the old-style performances of the great tragedienne in her famous roles as Belvidera in Thomas Otway's *Venice Preserved* [*] and as Mrs Waller in Kotzebue's *The Stranger*,[†] a portrayal of the repentant adultress that attracted huge audiences at Drury Lane:

---

[*] Thomas Otway (1652-1685). Dramatist. His tragedy *Aicibiades* acted at Dorset Garden Theatre. Caricatured Shaftesbury as Antonio in his internationally *Venice Preserved*(1682), with versions of the play performed in French, German, Dutch, Italian and Russian. Wrote prologues and epilogues.

[†] Kotzebue, August von, (1761-1819). German dramatist and novelist. Author of over 200 plays, including two popular melodramas, *Misanthropy and Repentance* (*Menschen und Reue*), entitled *The Stranger* in England. Anne Plumptre (1769-1838), one of the first translators in London to popularise German plays, including those by Kotzebue. She was an ardent supporter of Napoleon because he would destroy the aristocracy and establish a more egalitarian government.

The Drama once could shake and thrill
My nerves, and set my tears a stealing,
The Siddons then could turn at will
Each plug upon the main of feeling;
At Belvidera now I smile,
And laugh with Mrs. Haller's crying;
'Tis odd, so great a change of style —
I fear my heart is ossifying![9]

Caricature of Joseph Grimaldi and stage companions

With the departure of Sarah Siddons and Dorothy Jordan, two of the Theatre Royal's principal attractions, Sheridan had to resort to more popular entertainment, and it was left to one of the greatest clowns in the history of English pantomime, Joseph Grimaldi, to hold the stage and keep the audiences coming to fill the benches. His popularity with the lower order of theatregoers was phenomenal and, even among London's more sophisticated audiences, he had numerous admirers of his comical antics. The 'essence of his humour was a dynamic energy' punctuated with hilarious moments of 'silent' humour that brought the house down. Thomas Hood, who was to write Grimaldi's farewell speech for his benefit at Drury Lane in 1828, had admired these whimsical tricks for many years. In a letter from Ostend, towards the end of his long exile abroad, Hood described to his wife Jane, the effects of sudden cramps:

'It was CRUEL suffering but I could not describe them

without laughing....I was pirouetting about on one leg & and the other drawn up in such a twist, as only Grimaldi used to effect.'

4. Dog Days at Drury!

The realities of theatrical finance had forced Betterton to introduce stage-effects, and Garrick to rely on the whimsy of pantomime and farce, Sheridan is principally remembered for his performing horses and dogs. One such animated animal was 'Carlo the Dog', whose antics upstaged all human rivals. His principal feat was to perform an act of mercy by saving the life of a child in Frederick Reynolds' *The Caravan.** Sheridan's venal devotion to the creature led him to rush backstage, when the house was packed with excited dog-lovers, for fear some mishap may have occurred to the 'star' of the evening. 'Where is my preserver?' he cried. 'I am here,' said the author of the play. 'No,' said Sheridan, 'I mean the dog!'[10]

Frederick Reynolds, drawn by G H Harlow (1814)

James Gillray, the indefatigable persecutor of cant in any form, accused Sheridan of not only defrauding his shareholders but demeaning

---

* Frederic Reynolds(1764-1841). Dramatist. Composed nearly 100 tragedies and comedies. Adopted contemporary themes in his plays, his most popular *being The Caravan, or, The Driver and His Dog*, when he introduced a live dog trained to save a child from drowning by leaping from a rock and plunging into real water. From 1814 to1822 Reynolds was at Covent Garden but later assisted Elliston at Drury Lane.

the hard-won reputation of a great theatre by pandering to the more philistine element in his audience. It seemed that the splendour of the dramatic word had been replaced by little else but 'barking and neighing'.

One of the authors of the *Genuine Addresses* sent in a second version of his poem 'at which time the mania for equestrian exhibitions was at its height' and might be 'too *pointedly allusive* to a rival concern at Covent Garden and thereby secure its own defeat.' He clearly intended it to be read all the same, and took the opportunity to air his views of the Drury Lane stage, where once was 'sense' and 'wit', and now was a place of 'outraged Reason' and mere 'novelty':

> Quick! Let some fresh experiment be tried;
> With speed, let every Actor learn to ride.
> Brutes fill the parts too long usurp'd by men,
> And what is now a Stage, be made a Den.

Another, echoing lines in Samuel Johnson's *Prologue*, warns the Opening Night audience:

> No horses here shall leap o'er Nature's fence…
> The Drama's best support is Common-sense.[11]

A Cambridge competitor of the 'dog-days' of Old Drury, after Kemble and Mrs Siddons had left for Covent Garden, had stepped in to save the declining Theatre Royal from further ruination:

> Say — Judges, Guides, Supporters, Patrons, say,
> ('Tis yours to fix the fashion of the day)
> Shall quadrupeds or bipeds fill our Stage?
> Shall horses prance, or tragic heroes rage?
> Shall scenic charms with human grace unite?
> Or pond'rous elephants appal the sight?
> Nay, at your mandate, ev'n our lives we'll risk,
> And conquer'd tigers shall be taught to frisk!
> Or gladiators, more ferocious still,
> Our scene illume with pugilistic skill;
> Our Theatre to an arena fit,
> While boxing amateurs control our Pit: —
> Forbid it SHAKESPEARE, Nature, Reason, Wit!
>   No! — from our Stage be such intruders chas'd;

Chapter 2 – Richard Brinsley Sheridan: the Profligate Accountant

Too long perverting genuine British taste![12]

George Frederick Busby, who, only a short time after the opening of the future Theatre Royal in 1812, was himself fated to become the 'motley Fool' on the night of a notorious protest; he made an untimely attack on Grimaldi and his fellow entertainers which the audience would not perhaps have appreciated. It was too near to the truth:

> The giddy Harlequin and senseless Clown,
> Rush'd forth; and bore all opposition down —
> Rush'd grinning Pantaloon, and motley Fool
> Drove sense away, and sway'd with mad mis-rule:
> Burlesque and Melo-drame usurp'd the Stage,
> And wild monstrosity was all the rage!
> Against those rude invaders now we make
> A firm decisive stand for Britain's sake —
> For Britain's sake — for shall the land that gave
> A SHAKESPEARE birth, become the Drama's grave?[13]

5. 'The Young Roscius' Saves the Day

Sheridan was now deserted by his best actors, and even the lesser fry began to drift away. The promise of Holland's grandiose scheme for a new Theatre Royal had not been fulfilled, for it appears that the building was never completed, more than likely due to lack of funds. Audiences began to defect to Covent Garden, where Siddons and Kemble were now playing to packed houses. Even 'Carlo the Dog' had gone to rest. Joe Grimaldi had departed for Sadler's Wells, though Kemble's successor continued to lure into the theatre whatever public he could with his horses and harlequinades. But in the midst of all the dwindling classic performances and the slapstick, a violent incident threatened the comparative peace of the Theatre Royal, Drury Lane.

On Thursday 15 May 1800, an assassination attempt was made on George III, who had commanded a performance of Colley Cibber's comedy, *She Would and She Wouldn't*. As the King and Queen entered the Royal Box to the enthusiastic applause of the audience, a pistol shot was fired from the pit and a bullet embedded itself in a pillar only a foot from the King's head, shattering the plaster and causing consternation among the playgoers. Amidst the scuffling and confusion, a man was set upon, overpowered, and dragged below stage to the music room. He was

James Hadfield, a soldier and formerly an orderly to the Duke of York, but now discharged. During his trial he showed signs of a mental disorder; the Judge, Lord Kenyon, stopped the proceedings, and Hadfield was committed to Bedlam, where he died. To the long list of crimes of assault and battery, seduction and rape, mutilation and murder that were connected with the history of the Theatre Royal could now be added the crime of attempted regicide. The Church continued to call for more draconian measures to bring about a stricter control of management and the content of plays. A special medal was struck to commemorate the saving of the King's life and Sheridan quickly set down an additional verse to the National Anthem to be sung by the audience there and then:

> From every latent foe
> From every assassin's blow,
> God save the King!
> O'er him thy arm extend
> O Lord our God defend
> Our Father, Prince, and Friend,
> God save the King.[14]

As yet, Sheridan's nemesis had not struck him down. Disaster was momentarily avoided by the arrival in London of a child-actor called William Betty. Born in Shrewsbury, he spent his infancy in Dublin, where his acting talents were mercilessly exploited by his father. At the age of twelve, he played Hamlet and Romeo, and in the next year (1804) he arrived at Drury Lane, following sensational performances in Cork, Glasgow, Edinburgh, and Birmingham. His handsome appearance, his beautiful voice, and above all, his considerable talents as a tragic actor (he added *Richard the Third* and *Macbeth* to his repertoire in 1805), brought the fickle audiences back to Drury Lane in their thousands. The hysteria that surrounded his performances was one of the strangest phenomena in the history of drama. The absurdity of a thirteen-year-old Macbeth does not encourage any serious consideration of Betty's interpretation of the part, at least in the context of this work, but 'Bettymania', as it was called, (like the 'Beatlemania' of the 1960s) took London by storm. Here was 'Roscius' Garrick reborn. Behold 'The Infant Roscius'. Such is the judgement of the age, that Betty's performances commanded more money at the pay-boxes than Sarah Siddons had attracted herself. His manager extorted enormous fees for Betty's appearances at both Drury Lane and Covent Garden, especially in the part of Young Norval in Home's popular tragedy, *Douglas*. His death scene reduced the house to tears as he whispered his dying word, 'Mother!' But 'The Young Roscius' never became 'The Old Roscius', nor even 'The Middle-aged Roscius', for his talent died with his youth. On his return to the stage in 1812, when he had just turned twenty, 'The Young Roscius' could no longer claim the privileged attention fitting to an infant prodigy. Byron went to see the aging idol perform at Covent Garden and reported to Lord Holland on 10 September 1812:

> His figure is fat, his features flat, his voice unmanageable, his action ungraceful.... I was very sorry to see him in the character of 'elephant on the slack rope' for when I saw him I was in raptures with his performance, but then I was sixteen....[15]

To Lady Melbourne, on the same day, Byron penned a wickedly playful comment:

> Betty is performing here, I fear, very ill, his figure is that of a hippopotamus, his face like the Bull and mouth on the pannels [sic] of a heavy coach, his arms are fins fattened out of shape, his voice the gargling of an Alderman with the quinsy, and his acting altogether ought to be natural, for it certainly is like nothing that Art has ever exhibited on the stage.[16]

Betty retired in 1824 with fifty years of life still ahead of him. During his brief period at Drury Lane, he could rival any actor of mature years, and brought in more money than any other performer, but his rapid rise to fame and fortune was all too soon to be followed by a slow gradual descent into mediocrity. Once adored by Pitt and Fox, Lady Caroline Lamb and the Prince of Wales, he was to be forgotten within a few years of his prime, and 'Bettymania' was relegated to the dusty shelves of Drury.

6. Decline and Fall

Sheridan's financial success with *Pizarro*, and his remarkable piece of luck in discovering such a lucrative source of income as 'The Infant Roscius', gave him the chance of redeeming his past extravagances, paying off at least some of his debts, settling the unpaid wages bill and securing funds for new ventures. Instead of leaping at this opportunity, he drew out more and more money from the coffers of the Drury Lane treasury to subsidise his parliamentary activities. From 1780, when, as a supporter of Fox, he had been returned as Member for Stafford, he had shown himself to be a skilled orator as well as an inexhaustible one. He gave his greatest speech in moving the adoption of the Oude (or Oudh) in North India, a vice-royalty, seized by the vizier, Sujah-ud-Dowlah. Following the Battle of Buxar in 1764, the king's ineptitude had lead to insurrection and misgovernment, and the dependency was finally annexed to the North West Provinces in 1856. The subsequent sensational trial against Warren Hastings lasted six hours. As for Sheridan, his past political successes failed to help. Time did not sit comfortably on the shoulders of a man who persistently failed to meet the demands made on him in respect of his financial obligations. In the end, his Drury Lane interests, in hopeless disarray, brought him to the brink of bankruptcy. Overwork and the strain of meeting responsibilities in two demanding careers at once, led to a serious decline in his health. Alcoholism and brain disease did the rest.

Few of Sheridan's friends were more tolerant of his shortcomings than Byron, who, though he could drink as well as any man, watched with dismay the dramatist's decline and fall.. After a bout of imbibing, Byron recorded his impressions of the incident, hazy as it may have been:

> Poor fellow! he got drunk thoroughly and very soon. It occasionally fell to my lot to convey him home – no sinecure, for he was so tipsy that I obliged to put on his cock'd hat for him; to be sure it tumbled off again, and I was not myself so sober as to be able to pick it up again.[17]

Sheridan experienced feelings almost akin to grief and when told of Byron's praise for his dual talents of oratory and drama, he burst into tears in the midst of a gathering at Holland House. It was 'the voiceless thought that would not speak but weep'[18]:

> When last the sunshine of expiring day
> In summer's twilight weeps itself away,
> Who hath not felt the softness of the hour
> Sink on the heart, as dew along the flower?
> With a pure feeling which absorbs and awes
> While Nature makes that melancholy pause,
> Her breathing moment on the bridge where Time
> Of light and darkness forms an arch sublime,
> Who hath not shared that calm, so still and deep,
> The voiceless thought which would not speak but weep,
> A holy concord, and a bright regret,
> A glorious sympathy with suns that set?[19]
> Hard is his fate on whom the public gaze

> Is fix'd forever to detract or praise;
> Repose denies her requiem to his name,
> And Folly loves the martyrdom of Fame.
> The secret enemy whose sleepless eye
> Stands sentinel, accuser, judge, and spy,
> The foe, the fool, the jealous, and the vain,
> The envious who but breathe in others' pain,
> Behold the host! delighting to deprave,
> Who track the steps of Glory to the grave,
> Watch every fault that daring Genius owes
> Half to the ardour which its birth bestows,
> Distort the truth, accumulate the lie,
> And pile the pyramid of Calumny![20]

If 'gaunt poverty', 'deep Disease', 'indignity' and 'sordid Rage' are added to the poet's portion, how can he find strength to 'wrestle with Disgrace' and 'faithlessness'?

> If such may be the ills which men assail,
> What marvel if at last the mightiest fall?[21]

Sheridan's sublime talent for wit and farcical situations has set him among the very best of British dramatists, his comedies a permanent memorial to one of the rarest of humourists with a keen eye for the twists and foibles of human nature. His gift for parody, so brilliantly displayed in *The Critic*, has rarely been equalled and has set a standard hard to follow in later attempts at the *genre*. He eschewed the earlier bawdy humour of Vanbrugh and Jonson in favour of a more subtle interplay of farce and witty dialogue closer to Congreve that did not fail to set his more sophisticated audiences in stitches. His plays have without doubt remained a popular part of our national tradition:

> Long shall we seek his likeness, long in vain,
> And turn to all of him which may remain,
> Sighing that nature form'd but such a man
> And broke the die – in moulding Sheridan.[22]

On the eve of 24 February 1809, a new age in the history of the English theatre was about to begin, but in what manner the change would manifest itself, no one could have possibly foreseen.

Phoenix of Drury Lane

CHAPTER THREE

Prologue and Epilogue

1. Tradition and Purpose in the Prologues

As a defence against unwelcome criticism.

The tradition of introducing a play with a Prologue established itself at the Theatre Royal, Drury Lane, at the very beginning of the theatre's existence. Thomas Killigrew introduced the practice of beginning the evening's performance with music. The 'First Music' was usually a rustic air, the 'Second Music' a minuet, and the third *a coranto*. The principal actor or actress would then come forward to speak the Prologue. The curious and, to the modern sensibility, slightly distasteful tradition persisted of concluding with a bathetic and sometimes facetious Epilogue, even if the play had ended with the most harrowing of scenes. Dryden's *Tyrannic Love, or, The Royal Martyr*, published in 1669, is a case in point. The plot concerns the passionate love of the Roman Emperor, Maximin, for Catherine, the Christian princess of Alexandria, who finds herself unable to return his love.[*] In the course of Dryden's tragedy, Catherine succeeds in converting Empress Berenice to Christianity, and for this they are ordered to be executed. One of Maximin's officers, Placidus, out of love for Berenice, stabs the Emperor. The catharsis is complete.

Whilst the play contains some fine passages it also includes stylistic absurdities which were among those to be mercilessly ridiculed in Buckingham's *The Rehearsal*, a parody of the 'heroic' kind of drama so popular with Restoration audiences. Dryden uses his Prologue as a defence of the Poet against unwelcome criticism, an attempt to beguile his audience into thinking they, not the critics, will ultimately be the best arbiters of his plays:

> Self-love (which never rightly understood)
> Makes Poets still conclude their Plays are good:
> And Malice in all Criticks reigns so high,
> That for small Errors, they whole Plays decry;
> So that to see this fondness, and that spite,
> You'd think that none but mad men judge or write
> Therefore our Poet, as he thinks not fit
> T'impose upon you, what he writes for Wit,

---

[*] A version of the tragedy, *Bérénice,* was produced by Jean Racine (1639-99) in 1670 and another rival, *Tite et Bérénice*, by Pierre Corneille (1606-1684) in the same year at the same time but in different theatres.

Chapter 3 – Prologue and Epilogue

> So hopes that leaving you your censures free,
> You equal Judges of the whole will be:
> They judge but half who only faults will see.[1]

Recommending poets to be, like lovers, bold and daring, he advises against creeping after sense, and favours instead a freer pursuit of 'Excellence', a view entirely in keeping with the aims of these extravagant tragedies:

> Hence this our Poet in his conjuring,
> Allow'd his Fancy the full scope and swing,
> But when a Tyrant for his Theme he had
> He loos'd the Reins, and bid his Muse run mad;
> And though he stumbles in a full career,
> Yet rashness is a better fault than fear.[2]

As an appeal or justification to the critics.

The Prologue and Epilogue were not only vehicles for modest apology. They could also be the instrument, as we have seen, for patriotic appeals, personal vituperation, scandalous accusation, and immoral suggestiveness. Not least were they a convenient means of attacking the Dangles and Sneers of the critical world. Dryden's Prologue to *The Indian Emperour* begins:

> Almighty Critiques [i.e. critics]! whom our Indians here
> Worship, just as they do the Devil for fear,
> In reverence to your pow'r I come this day
> To give you timely warning of our Play.
> The Scenes are old, the Habits are the same.
> We wore last year, before the Spaniards came.
> Now if you stay, the blood that shall be shed
> From this poor Play, be all upon your head.[3]

The Poet in the second Prologue to *Secret Love* bows to every 'great and noble wit':

> But to the little Hectors of the Pit
> Our Poet's sturdy, and will not submit
> He'll be before-hand with 'em, and not stay

> To see each peevish Critick stab his Play:
> Each puny Censor, who his skill to boast,
> Is cheaply witty at the Poets cost.
> No Criticks verdict, should, of right, stand good,
> They are excepted all as men of blood;
> And the same Law should shield him from their fury
> Which had excluded Butchers from a Jury.[4]

In the Prologue to the second part of *The Conquest of Granada*, Dryden reminds the Critics that, since the play is only halfway through, they have no right to pre-judge it, and in the Epilogue to *The Indian Queen*, he blatantly suggests that the naked Indians would rather be subjected to the cruel domination of the Spaniards than the cruel domination of the Critics. Dryden's bitterest outcry is in the opening to his Prologue to *All For Love*:

> What Flocks of Criticks hover here to day,
> As Vultures wait on Armies for their Prey!
> All gaping for the carcass of a Play!
> With Croaking notes they bode some dire event;
> And follow dying Poets by the scent.

Prologues, nevertheless, still had their critics and came under fire from a number of quarters. Pope, who had after all composed a model of the genre (the Prologue to Addison's *Cato*[5]) to serve for several of the poets of the Drury Lane *Addresses* (including Byron himself), recognised the form as a prosaic expression of haphazard ideas, no more in fact than an annotated Preface by 'the Magna Mater of Dullness':

> Here to her Chosen all her works she shows;
> Prose swell'd to verse, verse loit'ring into prose:d
> How random thoughts now meaning chance to find,
> Now leave all memory of sense behind;
> How Prologues into Prefaces decay,
> And those to notes are fritter'd quite away.[6]

Dryden, however, in his Prologue to *The Assignation: or, Love in a Nunnery*, set the balance in a neat couplet:

> Prologues, like Bells to Churches, toul [toll] you in

Chapter 3 – Prologue and Epilogue

With Chiming Verse; till the dull Playes begin.[7]

The function of the prologue had, in principle at least, remained consistent in spite of changes in style and structure within the play itself. It had something in common with its forbear, the Greek chorus, in that it sought to address the audience directly, to present a statement or declaration on the characters and incidents to be portrayed upon the stage. The Prologue, therefore, was an effective means of drawing the attention of boisterous and, more often than not, unruly members of the lower orders of the audience.

As an apology for shortcomings in the play, the production, or the acting.

Shakespeare's Chorus, at the beginning of *Henry V* asks the audience to imagine events of grander significance than could be encompassed within the 'wooden O' of the Globe Theatre:

> Piece out our imperfections with your thoughts;
> Into a thousand parts divide one man,
> And make imaginary puissance;
> Think, when we talk of horses, that you see them
> Printing their proud hoofs i' the receiving earth;
> For 'tis your thoughts that now must deck our kings;
> Carry them here and there, jumping o'er times,
> Turning the accomplishment of many years
> Into an hour-glass: for the which supply
> Admit me Chorus to this history:
> Who prologue-like, your humble patience pray,
> Gently to hear, kindly to judge, our play.[8]

Dryden, in his earliest Prologue to *The Rival Ladies* (1661), follows a similar vein of apology for his failure and ineptitude, asking for forgiveness and tolerance of his shortcomings:

> 'Tis much Desir'd, you Judges of the Town
> Would pass a Vote to put all Prologues down;
> For who can show me, since they first were Writ,
> They e'er Converted one hard-hearted Wit?
> Yet the World's mended well; in former Days

> Good Prologues were as scarce, as now good Plays.[9]

In two of his Prologues Dryden apologises for the condition of the theatres in which the players and spectators are assembled, making thus a common bond between the two sides of the footlights. But mostly his concern is for the success of the play.

The convention that the Prologue-writer (the dramatist did not always write his own prologues) should clothe himself in a cloak of false modesty, necessitated the adoption of a particular tone and attitude which was designed to win over the reluctant part of the audience prior to the commencement of the action:

> Is it not strange, to hear a Poet say,
> He comes to ask you, how you like the play?
> You have not seen it yet? alas 'tis true,
> But now your Love and Hatred judge, not you.[10]

The apology is continued in the Epilogue to the same play:

> The Wild Gallant had quite playd out his game;
> He's marry'd now. And that will make him tame;
> Or if you think Marriage will not reclaim him,
> The Critiques swear they'll damn him, but they'll tame him.
> Yet though our Poet's threat'n'd most of these,
> They are the only People he can please:
> For he to humour them, has shown to day,
> That which they only like, a wretched Play:
> But though the Play be ill, here have been shown
> The greatest Wits and Beauties of the Town.
> And his Occasion having brought you here
> You are too grateful to become severe.
> There is not any Person here so mean,
> But he may freely judge each Act and Scene:
> But if you bid him choose his Judges then,
> He boldly names true English Gentlemen.[11]

As a sermon on morality, a eulogy, or a protest.

The Prologue was a vehicle for praise, but it could equally be a vehicle for moral condemnation. From the Restoration on, Thalia and Melpomene were compelled to take up arms against the philistines who, forcing their way into the Temple, threw out Learning and Virtue in favour of Folly, Obscenity, and Vice:

> Themselves they studied, as they felt they writ,
> Intrigue was plot, Obscenity was Wit.
> Vice always found a sympathetick Friend.

In the medieval morality play, *Everyman*, the Messenger, in his Prologue, begs his audience to treat with reverence the matter of his 'morall playe', for it is wondrously precious. He then goes on to outline the plot that is shortly to unfold before them. A century later, the authors of the travesty, *Gorboduc*, used the 'chorus' (one actor) to mould the thoughts of their particular audience and, on the principle that 'coming events cast their shadows before'[12], to establish the moral viewpoint by warning not only of the dangers but of the wrongness of conspiracy and civil strife.

As an expression of national pride, Englishness, patriotism.

Such sentiments were popular among the Drury Lane audiences, and dramatic expediency was occasionally assisted by political necessity in times of national crisis. The Prologue of *The Wild Gallant* proclaims:

> This play is English, and the growth your own;
> As such it yields to English Plays alone.
> He could have wish'd it better for your sakes;
> But that in Plays he finds your love mistakes;
> Besides he thought it was in vain to mend
> What you are bound in honour to defend,
> That English Wit (how e'er despis'd by some)
> Like English valour still may overcome.[13]

Dryden was generally critical of the vogue for anglicising French plots, and nowhere does he speak more plainly than in his Prologue spoken at the opening of the new Drury Lane Theatre on 26 March 1694:

> 'Twere Folly now a stately Pile to raise
> To build a Play-house while You throw down Plays,
> Whilst Scenes, Machines, and empty Opera's reign,
> And for the Pencil You the Pen disdain.

> While Troops of famisht Frenchman hither drive,
> And laugh at those upon whose Alms they live;
> Old English Authors vanish, and give place
> To these new Conqu'rors of the Norman Race'
> You'r new grown Vassals to 'em in your wit:
> Mark, when they Play, how our fine Fops advance
> The mighty Merits of these Men of France,
> Keep Time, cry Ben, and humour the Cadence
> Well French Machines have ne'er done England good.[14]

The tone of the patriotic speeches in *Richard II* and *Henry V* were echoed in many speeches in the 'heroic' plays, but the authors of the 1812 Drury Lane Addresses looked more to the Prologues of Dryden, Pope and Johnson to provide ideas for their verses, for they could find little that was original in themselves. The form and substance of the traditional prologue was to lend itself admirably to the *Addresses*, since both were in essence theatrical recitations, like the Chorus, though they could be in a sense undramatic:

> Whether the device of the Chorus is by its nature undramatic depend entirely upon one's definition of drama; but no one could claim that the Choruses are untheatrical. That David Garrick....chose to play the Chorus should be sufficient testimony to the role's attractions for an actor.[15]

As a intrinsic part of the play

Both the actor playing the Chorus and the actor reciting the Prologue were characters in their own right, speaking on an empty stage and, it is hoped, receiving the complete attention of the audience. Though the Prologue was an aspect of Shakespeare's work that Johnson disliked, the effect of the Chorus, as of the Prologue, was to dispel the feeling of distance between the performers and the spectators. For the dramatisation on Mme. de La Fayette's romance, *The Princess of Clèves*,[16] Dryden composed both Prologue and Epilogue, in which the 'We and You' distinction provides an admirable example of this process at work. The plot concerns the passionate love of the Duke de Nemours for the virtuous wife of the Prince de Clèves, who, on hearing his wife's confession of her love for the Duke, dies of a broken heart, the Princess ending her days, like Malory's Guinevere, in a convent. The tragic plot is flanked, as might be expected, by facetious Prologue and Epilogue. The Prologue begins:

> Ladies! (I hope there's one behind to hear,)
> I long to whisper something in your Ear;
> A Secret, which does much my Mind perplex,
> There's Treason in the Play against our Sex.
> A Man tha's false to Love, that Vows and cheats,
> And kisses every living thing he meets!

Such words might satisfy the female part of the audience. The Epilogue is addressed to the other part:

> A Qualm of Conscience brings me back agen
> To make amends to you bespattered Men!
> We women Love like Cats, that hide their Joys,
> By growling, squaling, and a hideous noise.

The whole is summed up in these astonishing lines:

> We show'd a Princess in the Play, 'tis true,
> Who gave her Caesar more than all his due.
> Told her own Faults, but I shou'd much abhor,
> To choose a Husband for my Confessor.
> To see what Fate follow'd the Saint-like Fool,
> For telling Tales from out the Nuptial School,
> Our Play a merry comedy had prov'd,
> Had she confess'd as much to him she lov'd,
> True Presbyterian-Wives, the means wou'd try,
> But damn'd Confessing is flat Popery.

As a bridge between actors and audience

Such familiarity lent a strength to the prologue-reciter's role as sole performer, breaking of necessity Johnson's classical rule that there must be a functional distance between performer and spectator. Prologues not only provided the audience with vital information and emotional direction, thus playing an important part in the process of dramatic orientation, they were also addressed primarily to the audience, and took on the function of a public address. From the medieval Devil, haranguing his largely illiterate audience between the scenes of a Mystery Play, the Messenger in *Everyman* and the Chorus in *Henry V* to the Restoration Prologues by

Dryden, Vanbrugh, and Congreve is not such a very large step to take, and by comparison the step from Prologue to public Address is even shorter. In time, the Address would leave the theatre and go into the street, to be used as a popular vehicle of political and social discontent, but until that time came, the Prologue delivered under the proscenium arch could serve just as well, as a typical medium of protest.

2. Classical to Neo-Classical: Jonson to Johnson

It is demonstrably the case that the writers of the 1812 Drury Lane Addresses turned to the Prologues for inspiration. An analysis of the *Genuine Addresses* reveals an abundance of references to the theatre in its function as 'Temple of the Muses' to the institution of the Stage, to Poetry, Music, Art, and Learning, and to Virtue, Vice and Morality. They provided an impression of the prevailing ethos, adapted perforce from an earlier time. The old hatred of the Spanish was now aimed at the French, with suitable incitements to patriotic fervour at the mention of national heroes such as Marlborough, Nelson and Wellington. These preoccupations obsessed the writers of the *Addresses* and in their passionate response to the challenge, helped to inject the dramatic scene with new life. Comparisons were constantly made between the superior genius of ancient Greece and Rome, and the steadily declining values and morality of the English Stage from the Restoration onwards. They had only to turn to Dryden to compare the aesthetic discipline of the classical canon with the reckless permissiveness of the contemporary theatre:

> When Athens all the Grecian State did guide,
> And Greece gave Laws to all the World beside,
> Then Sophocles with Socrates did sit,
> Supreme in Wisdom one, and one in Wit:
> And wit from Wisdom differ'd not in those,
> But as 'twas sung in verse, or said in Prose.
> Then, Oedipus, on Crowded Theaters,
> Drew all admiring Eyes and listening Ears;
> The pleas'd Spectator shouted every Line,
> The noblest, manliest, and the best Design![17]

The contrast is shown in Dryden's Prologue to Thomas Southerne's *The Disappointment: or, The Mother in Fashion*, in which the progress of the rakish Fop is seen in all its squalor:

> Your Nurses, we presume, in such a Case,
> Your Father chose, because he lik'd the Face;
> And, often, they supply'd your Mother's place.
> The Dry Nurse was your Mothers ancient Maid,
> Who knew some former Slip she ne'er betray'd.
> Betweixt 'em both, for Milk and Sugar Candy,
> Your sucking Bottles were well stor'd with Brandy.
> Your Father to initiate your Discourse
> Meant to have taught you first to swear and curse;
> But was prevented by each careful Nurse.
> For, leaving Dad and Mam, as Names too common,
> They taught you certain parts of Man and Woman.[18]

At School the 'rakish fop' learnt the Latin names for those certain parts. At College, instead of the 'Art of Thinking', he learnt all the Moods and Figures of good Drinking. In Town he got to know 'the Vertues of the High Dice, and the Low'. And finally, hiring a homely room, 'Love's Fruits to gather', he 'Garret-high, rebels against his Father.' Unlike him:

> Some Marry first, and then they fall to Scoring,
> Which is, refining Marriage into Whoring.

Others looked to Drury's Galleries for their 'punks' (a cant term for prostitute):

> Last, some there are, who take their first Degrees
> Of Lewdness, is our Middle Galleries:
> The Doughty BULLIES enter Bloody Drunk,
> Invade and grubble one another's PUNK;
> They Caterwaul, and make a dismal Rout,
> Call SONS of WHORES, and strike, but ne'er lugg-out:
> Thus while for Paultry Lane they roar and stickle,
> They make it Bawdier than a CONVENTICLE.*

Dryden bemoans the decline of Wit, Satire, Humour and Comedy, at the opening of the Prologue to *The Kind Keeper*:

---

* Conventicle: Clandestine religious meeting, usually Nonconformist or Dissenters

> True wit has seen its best days long ago,
> It ne'e look'd up, since we were dipt in Show:
> When Sense in dogrel [sic] Rhymes and Clouds was lost,
> And Dulness flourish'd at the Actor's cost.
> Nor stopt it here, when Tragedy was done,
> Satyre and Humour the same Fate have run;
> And Comedy is sunk to Trick and Pun.
> Now our Machining Lumber will not sell,
> And you no longer care for Heav'n or Hell;
> What Stuff will please you next, the Lord can tell.[19]

In the Prologue to *The Loyal General*, a play by Nahum Tate,[*] Dryden accused his audience of forsaking their solemn vows to the Muse - in his view an act of apostasy:

> 'Remove your benches your apostate Pitt.' [†]
> And take Above, twelve penny-worth or Wit;
> Go back to your dear Dancing on the Rope,
> Or see what's worse the Devil or the Pope!
> The Plays that take on our Corrupted Stage
> Methinks resemble the distracted Age;
> Noise, Madness, all unreasonable Things,
> That strike at Sense, as Rebels do at Kings![20]

As advice to choose Shakespeare and Johnson as the arbiters of taste

Only Shakespeare, Pope and Johnson remained shining lights in an age of declining stadards of elegance. Their works remained a yardstick by which the seventeenth and eighteenth century actor-dramatists were able to measure their own work:

---

[*] Nahum Tate (1652-1715). Educated Trinity College, Dublin. Rewrote *King Lear* in which Cordelia survives and marries Edgar. Appointed Poet Laureate 1692. Published new version of the Psalms. Christmas carol 'While shepherds watched their flocks by night,' said to have been written by him.

[†] William Pitt (1759-1806). England's youngest Prime Minister, aged 25. Reformed taxation to relieve the national debt by introducing income tax and establishing a sinking fund. Had a phenomenal lack of support in Parliament yet survived numerous political perils. Engaged Whig support for his policies, particularly that of Charles James Fox (1749-1806).

Chapter 3 – Prologue and Epilogue

> How's this, you cry? An actor write? - we know it;
> But Shakspear [sic] was an Actor, and a Poet.
> Has not Great Johnson's [i.e. Jonson] learning, often fail'd?
> But Shakspear's greater Genius, still prevail'd.
> Have not some writing Actors, in this Age,
> Deserv'd and found Success upon the Stage?[21]

Dryden's most effective comparison of the dramatic merits of Shakespeare and Jonson is to be found in the Prologue to *Julius Caesar*:

> Such artless beauty lies in Shakespeare's wit,
> 'Twas well in spight [sic] of him whate'er he writ.
> His Excellencies came and were not sought,
> His words like casual Atoms made a thought:....
> Those then that tax his Learning are to blame,
> Great Johnson [i.e. Jonson] did that Ignorance adore,
> And though he envi'd much, admir'd him more;
> The faultless Johnson equally writ well,
> Shakespeare made faults; but then did more excel.[22]

Similar thoughts occurred to Samuel Johnson in composing his own Prologue for the opening of Garrick's new Drury Lane Theatre in September 1747:

> When Learning's Triumph o'er her barb'rous Foes
> First rear'd the Stage, immortal SHAKESPEARE rose;
> Each change of many-colour'd Life he drew,
> Exhausted Worlds, and then imagin'd new;
> Existence saw him spurn her bounded Reign,
> And panting Time toil'd after him in vain:
> His pow'rful Strokes presiding Truth impress;d,
> And unresisted Passion storm'd the Breast.
>   Then JOHNSON [i.e. Ben Jonson] came, instructed from the School,
> To please in Method, and invent by Rule;
> His studious Patience, and laborious Art,
> By regular Approach essay'd the Heart;
> Cold Approbation gave the ling'ring Bays,

For those who durst not censure, scarce cou'd praise,
A Mortal born he met a general Doom,
But left, like *Egypt*'s Kings, a lasting Tomb,
The Wits of *Charles* found easier Ways to Fame,
Nor wish'd for JOHNSON's Art, or SHAKESPEARE's
   Flame;
Themselves they studied. As they felt they writ,
Intrigue was Plot, Obscenity was Wit.
Vice always found a sympathetick Friend;
Tthey pleas'd their Age, and did not aim to mend.
Yet Bards like these aspir'd to lasting Praise,
And proudly hop'd to pimp in future Days.
Their Cause was gen'ral, their Supports were strong,
Their Slaves were willing, and their Reign was long;
Till shame regain'd the Post that Sense betray'd,
And Virtue call'd Oblivion to her Aid.

   Then crush'd by Rules, and weaken'd as refin'd,
For Years the Pow'r of dignity declin'd;
From Bard, to Bard, the frigid Caution crept,
Till Declamation roar'd, while Passion slept.
Yet still did Virtue deign the Stage to tread,
Philosophy remain'd, though Nature fled.
But forc'd at length her antient Reign to quit,
She saw great *Faustus* lay the Ghost of Wit:
Exulting Folly hail'd the joyful Day,
And Pantomime, and Song, confirm'd her Sway.

   But who the coming Changes can presage,
And mark the future Periods of the Stage? —
Perhaps if Skill could distant Times explore,
New *Behns*, new *Durfeys*, yet remain in Store.
Perhaps where *Lear* has rav'd and *Hamlet* dy'd,
On flying Cars new sorcerers may ride.
Perhaps, for who can guess th' Effects of Chance?
Here *Hunt* may box, or *Mahomet* may dance.

   Hard is his lot, that here by Fortune plac'd,
Must watch the wild Vicissitudes of Taste;
With ev'ry Meteor of Caprice must play,

> And chase the new-blown Bubbles of the Day.
> Ah! let not Censure term our Fate our Choice,
> The Stage but echoes back the publick Voice.
> The Drama's Laws the Drama's Patrons give,
> For we that live to please, must please to live.
>
> Then prompt no more the Follies you decry,
> As Tyrants doom their Tools of Guilt to die;
> 'Tis yours this Night to bid the Reign commence
> Of rescu'd Nature, and reviving Sense;
> To chase the Charms of sound, the Pomp of Show,
> For useful Mirth, and salutary Woe;
> Bid scenic Virtue form the rising Age,
> And Truth diffuse her Radiance from the Stage.

Such lines as these represent the ideal neo-classical approach. By drawing a comparison between the genius of the past, with all its attention to rule and method, and the moral and stylistic freedom of the contemporary drama, Dryden, Pope and Johnson established the fundamental principles to which future writers of prologues and addresses could turn for the substance of their verses. Starting with the dramatic genius of ancient Greece and Rome, reference could be made to Apollo and the Muses, who, after the decimation of the old world by Goth and Vandal, fled to France and thence to England, where they made their home in their own Temple in Drury Lane. There, they could be at one with Nature and Truth in the works of Shakespeare and Jonson. This gave the prologue-writers scope for expressions of pride in the lineage of the English genius, for tributes to Thespis and the Scenic Muse, to dramatists like Webster, Otway, Rowe, Vanbrugh, Farquhar, Congreve and Sheridan, and actors such as Garrick, Siddons, Kemble and Kean.

Johnson's Prologue for Drury Lane, as much as Dryden's Prologues before him, Pope's Prologue to *Cato* and his indispensable guide to 18th century literary taste, the *Essay on Criticism*, would provide a matrix for the authors of the Drury Lane Addresses which would be invaluable in the desperate search for striking images. In what measure such excesses succeeded in introducing the English Stage, and in particular the Theatre Royal, Drury Lane, from the exalted position of 'Temple of the Muses' to that of a common-or-garden place of entertainment may be seen in the increasing numbers of harlequinades, pantomimes and quasi-circus acts presented to the eager public during these years. The venal pandering by self-seeking managers like Rich and Collier to the lowest common denominator of play-going taste reached its nadir by the end of the 18th century.

Dr. Johnson had wished for a sense of order and proportion in the conduct of the Stage, tempered by Reason and a taste for Learning. The 'Truth of Shakespeare's grand design' he held to be the high point of English drama which the authors of the Drury Lane Addresses were not slow to appreciate in their search for an advocate from the past, distinguished enough to give sufficient weight to the substance of their poetical effusions. Johnson's *Prologue* formed part of the stuff (and sometimes in their case at least, the nonsense) of versifying that the creators of the 1812 *Addresses* could comfortably grasp. Some of them were unashamedly imitative of the *Prologue*. Others, being either inappropriately facetious or poetically inept, may have been the first and possibly the only conscious or unconscious parodies of it in existence.

3. Monody and Threnody

As oratory. The declamatory style.

As a 'Temple', the Theatre Royal Drury Lane was not only a place for the celebration of dramatic genius but also for national rejoicing and mourning. Party politics and national crises played their part in the life of the theatre. The Whig supremacy encouraged ideas of freedom in dramatic expression and performance, while a Tory administration tended to impose dogmatic restrictions unpalatable to both managers and dramatists. The views and tastes of the reigning monarch had also to be considered in the choice and presentation of plays. Prologues and epilogues provided a convenient means of praising or criticising the matters of the day, just as satire and parody played their role in ridiculing contemporary personalities and topical issues. *The Dunciad* gave birth to a number of satirical progeny including *The Rolliad*, *The Lousiad* (Walcot's mock-heroic satire on George III, in which a louse from the head of a palace servant falls into the King's dish of peas), *The Baviad* and *The Maeviad* by William Gifford (both parodied by Horace Smith in *The Rejected Addresses*[*]).

In the case of the *Monody on His Late Majesty George the Third* by the translator of Lucretius, Dr. Thomas Busby, the stylistic weaknesses common to occasional verse are all too obvious:

>   On Albion's loss, what mind unmoved can dwell —
>   What British heart — and not with sorrow swell?

---

[*] See chapter 9.

> Though long the radiant course our Monarch run,
> Too soon, alas! We viewed his sinking sun!

In spite of the bathetic 'sinking sun', Busby pursues the patriotic theme undeterred, for in George's reign Nelson and Wellington were victorious and Britannia ruled the waves, Britons were loyal and the Sovereign bestowed grace upon his people:

> Benign as pious — Patriotic — Husband — Sire —
> In all things lov'd — that reason can admire.
> The Saint combining with the kingly part,
> God and a faithful people shared his heart.

The banalities of these verses owe much to the prologues for their tone and subject-matter. Sarah West (1790-1876), a leading tragedian at Drury Lane from 1818 to 1828; was chosen to recite this paltry stuff. In a theatre which provided a happy hunting ground for the Prince Regent, had not 'Florizel carried off Mary Robinson after her enchanting performance as Perdita, it would have seemed politic to include some unfashionable words of praise for the new King:

> The Star of Brunswick still in glory reign
> Still a loved George its shining course maintain.
> The Son, enkindled by the Parent fire,
> Shall emulate the honours of his sire.

As a tribute to the dead.

The monody, like the threnody, took the irregular form of a Pindaric ode. Named after the Greek lyric poet, Pindar, this form of ode is in the nature of a 'poetic address', spoken or sung. The number of 'feet' or 'steps' in a line vary in number, giving a prose-like effect to the texture, tempered by deftly placed occasional rhymes. Introduced into England by Abraham Cowley,[*] the form was later adopted by Dryden and Pope, and imitated in

---

[*] Abraham Cowley ((1618-67). At age of ten, composed romance, *Pyramus and Thisbe*. Scholar and Fellow of Trinity College, Cambridge. Directed comedy against the Puritans and was ejected as a result of the Civil War. Secretary to Queen Henrietta Maria. Royalist spy in England. Odes on the Restoration and against Cromwell. Created fashion for rhetorical odes in irregular

mock-heroic style by 'Peter Pindar'* and Thomas Hood.

In essence, the monody is a poem in which one person laments another's death. The threnody was a lamentation or funeral dirge, as with Dryden's *Threnodia Augustalis, a funeral-pindarique sacred to the happy memory of King Charles II,* and could be spoken by more than one person (as with the Greek 'Chorus') and largely supplanted other forms of public address. The straightjacket of the rhyming couplet concomitant with the poetical form of the prologues could be abandoned and a looser sequence of paragraphs in iambic lines of irregular length could be adopted, giving the poet more latitude to express a loftier, lyrical passion.

As elegy.

Byron would, in 1816, encapsulate his thoughts and emotions in his moving *Monody on the Death of Sheridan*. With his Drury Lane Address four years before, Byron felt self-conscious at the thought that his verses would be read before a Drury Lane audience. Writing in the first period of his long exile, rejected by his own country, he would see in Sheridan that same sorrow, that same sense of dejection and isolation that assailed him at the Villa Deodati. It was 'the voiceless thought that would not speak but weep'[23]:

> When last the sunshine of expiring day
> In summer's twilight weeps itself away,
> Who hath not felt the softness of the hour
> Sink on the heart, as dew along the flower?
> With a pure feeling which absorbs and awes
> While Nature makes that melancholy pause,
> Her breathing moment on the bridge where Time
> Of light and darkness forms an arch sublime,
> Who hath not shared that calm, so still and deep,
> The voiceless thought which would not speak but weep,
> A holy concord, and a bright regret,
> A glorious sympathy with suns that set?
> Hard is his fate on whom the public gaze

---

verse imitated by Dryden and others. Cf. the prologue.

* 'Peter Pindar'. Pseudonym for John Wolcot (1738-1819). Physican to Governor of Jamaica. Took holy orders. Helped John Opie, the painter. Composed mock-heroic poem, *The Lusiad* (1785) and satires on George III. Attacked by William Giffard in *The Anti-Jacobin*. Criticised for his 'vulgarity of thought and inelegance of style.' (OCEL).

> Is fix'd forever to detract or praise;
> Repose denies her requiem to his name,
> And Folly loves the martyrdom of Fame.
> The secret enemy whose sleepless eye
> Stands sentinel, accuser, judge, and spy,
> The foe, the fool, the jealous, and the vain,
> The envious who but breathe in others' pain,
> Behold the host! delighting to deprave,
> Who track the steps of Glory to the grave,
> Watch every fault that daring Genius owes
> Half to the ardour which its birth bestows,
> Distort the truth, accumulate the lie,
> And pile the pyramid of Calumny![24]

If 'gaunt poverty', 'deep Disease', 'indignity' and 'sordid Rage' are added to Sheridan's portion, how can he find strength to 'wrestle with Disgrace' and 'faithlessness'?

> If such may be the ills which men assail,
> What marvel if at last the mightiest fall.[25]

1. Thomas Killigrew by Sir Anthony Van Dyck

2. Charles Macklin by John Opie, c1792

3. David Garrick as Richard III, painted by William Hogarth

4. Sarah Siddons, by Thomas Gainsborough (1785)

5. William Henry West Betty (the 'Young Roscius') by John Opie

6. Portrait of Richard Brinsley Sheridan by Sir Joshua Reynolds (1789)

7. John Philip Kemble (1757-1823), brother of Sarah Siddons. He made his name as an actor at Drury Lane, before becoming manager there in 1788.

8. Statue of Dr Samuel Johnson, outside his birthplace in Lichfield (*photo: Alan Durden*)

9. Ambrose Philips of Garendon, by Rosalba Carriera

10. Samuel Whitbread, by Joshua Reynolds. He made his fortune from brewing and was able to save the theatre from financial ruin.

11. View of Drury Lane under construction showing the covered entrance to the stage door and the colossal statue of Apollo, god of poetry, towering above the theatre. Engraved by W J White from a drawing by J Capon.

12. Façade of architect Henry Holland's Drury Lane 1794.
Five tiers of galleries supported by iron columns enclosed the huge auditorium (25m wide by 28m deep). Sarah Siddons called it "a wilderness of a place" and decamped in protest to the Theatre Royal, Covent Garden. Productions at Drury became more like spectacles at the expense of the spoken word.

13. View of Henry Holland's Drury Lane, showing the entrance to the foyer.

14. Old Drury Lane theatre on fire in 1809, painting by Abraham Pether

15. Old Drury Lane in flames 1809.
A Contemporary print showing the fire engine and ranks of firemen in action.
Printed by J. Pitts, printseller of Seven Dials, London.

16. A painted engraving of Whitbread Brewery in Chiswell Street London in 1792. Young Samuel is seen here as an apprentice and wears his brewer's apron. *Painted by G. Garrard and engraved by W. Ward.*

17. Clearing away the Rubbish of Old Drury. Samuel Whitbread wheels away a drunken Sheridan. Th of the old Management Committee follow in barrows. An Irish navvy comments: "By Jasus, you've a ra there, to be sure enough some of the ould Foundation." Empty tankards marked 'Whitbread's Entire' are disc by a heap of rubble. *Printed on 10th October 1810 by Walker & Knight, Cornhill, London. Private collection*

18. Lady Elizabeth Holland, painting by Louis Gauffier, 1794

19. Portrait of Sir Godfrey Webster, 4th Baronet, by Louis Gauffier, 1796

20. Portrait of Lord Holland (Henry Vassall-Fox, 3rd Baron Holland) by François-Xavier Fabre, 1795

21. Mary Russell Mitford, c.1836
Contributor to the *Genuine Addresses*

22. Robert William Elliston (1774-1831). Lessee and manager of Drury Lane 1819-26. He delivered the address written by Byron on the opening night of the rebuilt Theatre Royal, 10 October 1812.

CHAPTER FOUR

Plagiary and Parody

1. The Spanish Theme

Whilst the authors of the 1812 *Genuine Addresses* openly admitted their debt to Johnson, others took what they could as slyly as they could in order not to be accused of arrant plagiarism. It is ironic, therefore, that some should turn for secondary inspiration to a work which has, as one of its central characters, a conceited poetaster* whose commonplace book is nothing but 'pilfered witticisms....kept with as much method as the ledger *of the lost-and-found office.'*

Sheridan's *The Critic, or, The Tragedy Rehearsed*, was produced at Drury Lane on 30 September 1779, and was acted no less than forty-eight times in the season. Apart from *Pizarro*, which was an adaptation from Kotzebue, *The Critic* was Sheridan's last comedy and last original piece. Given the theme and content of the play, with the added interest that it was one of the most popular in the repertoire at Drury Lane, it was natural for the poets of the Addresses, severely pressed for time as they were, to supplement what they could not find in Johnson's Prologue (and those of Dryden and Pope) with ideas culled from the back-biting conversations of the canting critics, Sneer and Dangle, and the unscrupulous literary advertiser, Mr. Puff. Besides which many poets were heavily engaged in the practice of plagiarism from the start.

The Critic derives principally from three events, one political and two theatrical, which Sheridan employed to great effect in order to satirise the current fashion for sentimental drama and the canting kind of criticism that was the bane of the theatrical profession of his day.

An exact parallel in 1812 explains the interest of the poets of *Genuine Addresses* in similar themes. England declared war on Spain in 1762-3 and again in 1796, and in the following year defeated the Spanish fleet at the battle of Cape St. Vincent. After the capture of the Spanish Treasury in 1804, Spain and France declared war against England, but were totally defeated at the battle of Trafalgar. In 1807, on 4 December, Napoleon entered Madrid, and the Spanish royal family was imprisoned the following day. On 16 January 1808, the Spanish were defeated at Corunna. Wellington, after several victories, successfully stormed Badajos, won a victory at Salamanca and occupied Madrid, totally defeating the French at the battle of Vittoria on 21 June 1813. In the following September, Wellington entered France. This sensational sequence of events caught the imaginations of not only poets and

---

* Poetaster – a derogatory term applied to bad or inferior poets. The word was coined in Latin by Erasmus in 1521 and used by Ben Jonson as the title of his 1601 play *Poetaster*.

dramatists, but of countless audiences night after night, ever seeking confirmation that Britannia still ruled the waves. These bellicose events ensured the success of *The Critic*, whose frequent productions served to satisfy the powerful public need for topical works which praised British heroes and ridiculed the enemy.

With the re-opening of the Theatre Royal, Drury Lane, in 1812, the bosoms of the Muses throbbed 'on venerated earth', 'like Britons, — proud to owe to Britain birth.' Nelson was dead; Moore and Abercromby were gone, yet:

> E'en while she [*Britain*] thus each valiant name deplores,
> Still has she Heroes left to guard her shores:
> The rights of Spain are now Britannia's care,
> The cause is just — and WELLINGTON is there!

One young contributor to the Drury Lane Addresses wrote some timely lines to rouse the patriotic sentiments of her audience:

> Soon as Mars' crimson standard was unfurl'd,
> He fought — the wonder of the gazing world!
> And whilst each Briton feels his soul on fire,
> Our new-born Phoenix rises to admire.
> Once more our fabric rears its lofty head,
> Tho' long it slumber'd with the silent dead.
> Should WELLINGTON e'er grace our new-rais'd dome,
> How will we welcome the brave Hero home![1]

Byron could not have written better, indeed did not do better lines in the circumstances, though he did not care for composing occasional verse under pressure, and his Address, competent though it proved to be, did not show the measure nor the genius of the recently published first cantos of *Childe Harold's Pilgrimage*.

A young poetess among the Drury Lane Addresses was only following the vogue for patriotic utterances in her panegyric of the Iron Duke, and asks his forgiveness lest Britons should ever forget their debt to him:

> Remember still th'immortal Poet's line:
> "To err, is human – to forgive, divine!"[2]

For another competitor, the 'barbed shafts of Vertue' were once more to be found in the house of Apollo and the 'Sun of Joy gleams bright' in

> An age where War in giant form appears
> And stalks destructive o'er the toil of years[3].

The examples quoted here are sufficient to show how, through feelings of national pride and an enthusiasm for the cause of Liberty at home and abroad, the authors of the Addresses sought to rouse their prospective (and hoped-for) audience. Indeed, the idea of Freedom, whether under the ever-present threat of bellicose Spanish aggression or at the mercy of Napoleon's armies was, as we have seen, a constant preoccupation with dramatists and poets as well as composers of operas (grand and light) and the concocters of nonsensical farces.

The Spanish theme, so popular with Tudor and Jacobean tragedians, as well as those of the Restoration period, was admirably parodied, but never so well as in Sheridan's *The Critic*, a parody of Buckingham's farce, *The Rehearsal*,[4] in which Tilburin, daughter of the Governor of Tilbury Fort, falls in love with her father's captive enemy, the absurdly heroic Don Whiskerandos, whose death-scene is one of the most laughable things in the whole of English theatre. The subject of Mr. Puff's play deals with preparations that have been made for war with Spain. In come Sir Walter Raleigh and Sir Christopher Hatton, who commence their lines with ludicrous interpolations from the three onlookers in the box, hypocritical Mr. Puff, malicious Mr. Dangle, and his fellow-critic, the supercilious Sneer. After some discussion concerning the assembled army, mustered on the plain below Tilbury Fort, Leicester enters and, in bombastic lines parodying Shakespeare's (and Cumberland's) 'high style', reprimands his two countrymen for their doubts about the outcome of the war.

Mr. Dangle is discussing the state of the London theatre scene with his fellow-critic, Sneer, when the conceited poetaster Sir Fretful Plagiary is announced. Sneer despises Sir Fretful, for whenever his plays are rejected he becomes petulant and arrogant in the face of criticism. Dangle has received Sir Fretful's tragedy the day before and when the playwright enters, both Dangle and Sneer praise him and his play to the skies. Sir Fretful is flattered by such unbounded admiration, but in an aside, refers to Sneer as 'a damned double-faced fellow', whilst at the same time calls him 'a man of taste and sincerity' to his face. Sir Fretful refuses help from Dangle in sending the play to a manager, for he is proud to confirm that he has that very morning sent it to the Covent Garden Theatre manager. He would never, he says, send a play to Drury Lane, to a manager that writes himself, for there is 'not a passion so strongly rooted in the human heart as envy', and it is not safe to leave a play in such

Chapter 4 – Plagiary and Parody

hands. The conversation proceeds in the following manner:

Sneer: What, they may steal from them, hey my dear Plagiary?

Sir Fretful: Steal! — to be sure they say; and, 'egad, serve your best thoughts as gypsies do stolen children, disfigure them to make 'em pass for their own.

Sneer: But your present work is a sacrifice to Melpomene, and he, you know, never —

Sir Fretful: That's no security. — A dexterous plagiarist may do any thing — Why, Sir, for aught I know, he might take out some of the best things in my tragedy, and put them into his own comedy.

After this exchange of views on the craft of plagiary, Sir Fretful asks the assembled company if they like his new tragedy. 'Wonderfully,' replies the vicious Sneer, whereupon Sir Fretful unwisely presses them for any faults they may have found. Dangle hypocritically remonstrates that it would be 'ungracious' to do so, but Sir Fretful plays into his hands by insisting: '....I am never so well-pleased as when a judicious critic points out any defect to me.' Sneer acquiesces. There is 'one small objection,' he says. 'It lacks incident.' The conceited Sir Fretful, greatly surprised that anyone should consider his masterpiece to be anything other than faultless, protests that the play is crowded with incident. Dangle agrees with him, but Sir Fretful's self-satisfaction is short-lived when Dangle adds that the first four acts are the best he ever read, but interest 'rather falls off in the fifth.'

Sir Fretful: Rises, I believe you mean, Sir.

Dangle: No, I don't, upon my word.

Sir Fretful: Yes, yes, you do, upon my soul! – it certainly don't fall off, I assure you.

A final judgment is sought of Mrs. Dangle, who declares she did not see any fault in the play from beginning to end, but it was 'a little too long.'

Sir Fretful: Pray, Madam, do you speak as to duration of time; or do you mean that the story is tediously spun out?

Mrs. Dangle: O lud! no, — I speak only with reference to the usual length of plays.

As to newspaper criticisms, they are, says Sir Fretful. 'the most villainous – licentious – abominable – infernal – Not that I ever read them – No – I make it a rule never to read a newspaper.' However, mention is made of an ill-natured attack in Thursday's paper, and Sir Fretful's egotism leads him on to discover the content. Apparently, according to Sneer, who appears to have written the article, there is not the slightest invention or original genius, and its author is 'the greatest traducer of all other authors living.' He has, in comedy, not one idea of his own, and has 'not even the skill to steal with taste: — But that you glean from the refuse of obscure volumes where more judicious plagiarists have been before you; so that the body of your work is a composition of dregs and sediments – like a bad tavern's worst wine.' Finally, as to the serious part of his writing, the critic complains that:

> .... your bombast would be less tolerable, if the thoughts were ever suited to the expression; but the homeliness of the sentiment stares through the fantastic encumbrance of its fine language, like a clown in one of the new uniforms....that your occasional tropes and flowers suit the general coarseness of your style.....while your imitations of Shakespeare resemble the mimicry of Falstaff's page, and are about as near the standard of the original.....In short the finest passages you steal are of no service to you; for the poverty of your own language prevents their assimilating; so that they lie on the surface like lumps of marl on a barren moor, encumbering what is not in their power to fertilise.

Recollections of Sir Fretful Plagiary must have been very much in the minds of the readers appointed to judge the 112 *Addresses* for the opening night of the new Drury Lane theatre on 10 October 1812. Imitations in the style of Shakespeare, Dryden, Pope and Johnson, aptly (though more often than not, as we have suggested, ineptly) adapted quotations from their works, and audaciously unattributed plagiarisms abounded in poetical effusions of the less accomplished poets, and were even to be found in verses of some of the more established authors who unwisely chose to send in contributions.

Sneer's remarks about Sir Fretful Plagiary's style might well be applied to some of the authors of the Drury Lane *Addresses*: '....the finest passages you steal are of no service to you....encumbering what is not in their power to fertilise.' One among many such encumbrances was exemplified in the numerous references to 'sister Muses', Melpomene (Tragedy) and Thalia (Comedy and Pastoral poetry) and Calliope (Epic poetry) respectively, as represented by Richard Fitzpatrick[*] in his Prologue to *The Critic*:

> The Sister Muses, whom these realms obey,
> Who o'er the Drama hold divided sway,
> Sometimes, by evil counsellors, 'tis said
> Like earth-born potentates have been misled;
> In these gay days of wickedness and wit,
> When Villiers criticiz'd what Dryden writ,
> The Tragick Queen, to please a tasteless crowd,
> Had learn'd to bellow, rant, and roar so loud,
> That frighten'd Nature, her best friend before,
> The blust'ring beldam's company foreswore.
> Her comic Sister, who had wit 'tis true,
> With all her merits, had her failings too;
> And would sometimes in mirthful moments use
> A style too flippant for a well-bred Muse.
> Then female modesty abash'd began
> To seek the friendly refuge of the fan,
> Awhile behind that slight entrenchment stood,
> 'Till driv'n from thence, she left the stage for good.
> In our more pious, and far chaster times!
> These sure no longer are the Muse's crimes!

Some of the rejected poets complain that the reformation of the stage has gone too far, bemoaning the loss of the 'frantic hero's wild delirium'. Bombast has given way to insipidity and boredom. Recalling the mood of *The Dunciad*:

> Here dullness seems her drowsy court to keep,
> And we, are scarce awake, whilst you are fast asleep.
> Thalia, once so ill behav'd and rude,
> Reform'd; is now become an arrant prude,
> Retailing nightly to the yawning pit;
> The purest morals, undefil'd by wit!

---

[*] Richard Fitzpatrick (1747-1813). One of the authors of the satirical diatribe, *The Rolliad*, which took its name from John Rolle, a supporter of Pitt, and ridiculed the Tories.

> Our Author offers in these motley scenes,
> A slight remonstrance to the Drama's queens,
> Nor let the goddesses be over nice;
> Free spoken subjects give the best advice.

As we have seen, the Theatre Royal, Drury Lane, had always been a place of scandal and intrigue, and in a more sensational sense had been a witness to fraud, violence, manslaughter, murder, attempted regicide, and all manner of foul play. Yet it had also remained hallowed ground in which the English drama could put down roots and send forth the flowering of the national genius:

> Yes; — where a GARRICK's energy and fire
> Were wont resistless transports to inspire;
> Where matchless SIDDONS charm'd a later age,
> Reflecting Nature's image from our Stage: —
> Still shall Britannia's ancient fame increase,
> And emulate the classic lore of Greece!
> Warm'd by your smile, and foster'd by your hand,
> The bud of native genius may expand,
> And future SHAKESPEARES, future GARRICKS rise
> To earn immortal fame — their glorious prize!

London was not only the thriving capital of a patriotic nation, it was the new 'Athens', it was 'Ithaca' itself. In lines by one of the authors of the Addresses, the Drury Lane Theatre is depicted as a great ship sailing through the storms of time, the 'crew, depriv'd of all', now 'uprais'd', their sails at the full:

> With ardour o'er the world our keel shall roam,
> And bear for you, the brightest treasure home;
> Our polar star shall blaze, the wish to please;
> And should a new-found land attract our sight,
> As wide we plough the regions of delight,
> Here shall the produce of the coast be shown
> We navigate for you — the risk your own;
> And tho' our hopes are high, the bulk to store,
> With pearls and diamonds from the sparkling shore,
> Enraptur'd oft we'll touch on Avon's coast,

> Melpomene's delight, and Thalia's boast,
> Lur'd by the jewels, with effulgent glare,
> The grand and unexhausted mine is there.
> Propitious pow'rs! Our helm instructing steer;
> Nor Sylla [*sic*] touch, nor sail Charybdis near;
> Let Sirens' charms nor Circe's arts detain
> Our course to Ithaca — your Drury Lane.

The rivalry between Cumberland and Sheridan had resulted in one of the most brilliant of parodies, a cunning satire on the practice of plagiarism. A parallel situation arose between Byron and the translator of Lucretius, Dr. Thomas Busby, which became a *cause célèbre* following the opening of the new Theatre Royal, Drury Lane.

2. The Purpose of Parody

Parody has been a part of European literature since Greek and Roman times. It is usually an ironic or satirical interpretation of its original, lying parallel to it, in 'equal' measure (*par*), in the form of a song or poem (*ode*). If it is a good parody it accurately mimics the style, measure, and mood of its original and, if not raising a laugh, brings a smile to the face of the listener, or in the case of the reader, a feeling of satisfaction and enjoyment at a well-crafted piece. In *Divine Songs for Children*, the Nonconformist poet, Isaac Watts, composed beguiling little poems just waiting to be parodied by later writers. In 'Against Idleness and Mischief', for example, lines beloved of 18th century parents, held a gentle warning for lazy children:

> How doth the little busy bee
> Improve each shining hour,
> And gather honey all the day
> From every opening flower!
>
> In work of labour or of skill
> I would be busy too,
> For Satan finds some mischief still
> For idle hands to do.[5]

Lewis Carroll composed the perfect parody in *Alice in Wonderland*:

> How doth the little crocodile
> Improve his shining tail
> And pour the waters of the Nile
> On every golden scale!
>
> How cheerfully he seems to grin
> How neatly spreads his claws
> And welcomes little fishes in
> With gently smiling jaws![6]

In the Watts poem, the bee points to the positive, life-enhancing benefits of an industrious life and a dedication to daily tasks; in Lewis Carroll's interpretation, the crocodile represents the negative attributes of deception and exploitation of one's fellow human beings.

In some cases the parody became in the course of time inseparable from its original as in the case of Christopher Marlowe's *The Passionate Shepherd to his Love*:

> Come live with me and be my love,
> And we will all the pleasures prove,
> That valleys, groves, hill, and fields,
> Woods, or steepy mountain yields…
>
> The Shepherd's Swains shall dance and sing
> For thy delight each May morning:
> If these delights thy mind may move,
> Then live with me, and be my love.

and Sir Walter Raleigh's *The Nymph's Reply to the Shepherd:*

> If all the world and love were young,
> And truth in every Shepherd's tongue,
> These pretty pleasures might me move,
> To live with thee and be thy love…
>
> But could youth last, and love still breed,
> Had joys no date, nor age no need,
> Then these delights my mind might move
> To live with thee, and be thy love.

Some notable parodies have become 'classics' in their own right: Dryden's political parody in the style of Ben Jonson, *Absalom and Achitophel*,[7] David Garrick's parody of Shakespeare's 'Seven Ages of Man' from *As You Like It*, Thomas Chatterton's *Rowley Poems*, Jane Austen's *Northanger Abbey*, Henry Fielding's, *Shamela* (a parody of Samuel Richardson's epistolary novel, *Pamela)*, and, as we have seen, Sheridan's parody, *The Critic*, deriding Buckingham's play, *The Rehearsal*.

Over the next two centuries, thousands more parodies helped to establish a sophisticated, informed and often entertaining commentary on their vulnerable originals. Parody continued to amuse in the pages of the popular *Punch* magazine through two centuries, and for the last hundred years or so more, in the puzzle pages of *The Times* daily newspaper.

When the Management Committee of the new Theatre Royal, Drury Lane, advertised for a suitable 'Address' to be spoken at the opening in 1812, they could not have imagined the risk they were taking in the unconscious encouragement of wearisome imitation, and its livelier companions, parody and travesty.

Whilst imitation is a direct re-creation of its original, travesty is an extreme parody, as in this chapter we shall prove, is more perverse, debasing the original work almost out of recognition; it is malicious and devastatingly destructive, highlighting the glaring faults and deficiencies of its model. Freud makes the distinction in his analysis of humour, *Der Witz:* 'Parody and travesty achieve the degradation of something exalted in another way: by destroying the unity that exists between people's characters as we know them and their actions and speeches, by replacing either the exalted figures or their utterances by inferior ones.' In this context could be included major political and social satires such as Cervantes' *Don Quixote*, Voltaire's *Candide* and Swift's *Gulliver's Travels*.

A liberal number of parodies are represented in almost every volume of light verse, for light verse is what parody frequently becomes in the transformation of style and content from the serious intent of the original. Parody can take off as much into flights of fancy as of fury.[8] In its destructive form it can be outrageous and cruel, yet in gentler form can ridicule its original without destroying the original. Ceaselessly inventive, imitation and parody occur frequently down the ages when new words are written to old songs.[9]

As a form of criticism, parody enjoyed increasing popularity in the literary and social periodicals of the 18th century - *The Idler,* with contributions by Dr. Johnson, *The Rambler, The Cambridge Tart* and Thomas Warton's *Oxford Sausage,* and countless other satirical imitations of well-known authors became a popular means of amusement. Equally, parody could be an exposé of a current political or social issue. The thought of bringing several authors under one heading – such was Isaac Hawkins Browne's *A Pipe of Tobacco* – lead to one of the most popular publications of the age, *Probationary Odes,* being a collection of feeble poems by the Poet Laureate, Thomas Warton, submitted to the Lord Chamberlain's office in competition for the vacant post. Although the volume was successful for a time, it was not until the 19th century, with the Smith brothers' *Rejected Addresses*, that writers with a strong individuality of style and manner provided the band of eager parodists with their models.

Francis Jeffrey, Editor of *The Edinburgh Review*, contributed the most informative comment on the technique:

> To copy his peculiar phrases or turns of expression – to borrow the grammatical structure of his sentences, or the metrical balance of his lines – or to crowd and string together all the pedantic or affected words which he has become remarkable for using – applying or misapplying all these without the least regard to the character of his genius, or the spirit of his compositions, is to imitate an author as a monkey might imitate a man.... It is another matter, however, to be able to borrow the diction and manner of a celebrated writer to express sentiments like his own – to write as he would have written on the subject proposed to the imitator – to think his thoughts in short, as well as to use his words – and to make the revival of his style appear a natural consequence of the strong conception of his peculiar ideas. To do this in all the perfection of which it is capable, requires the talents, perhaps, not inferior to those of the original on whom they are employed – together with a faculty of observation, and a dexterity of application, which the original might not always possess, and should not only afford nearly as much pleasure to the reader, as a piece of composition – but may teach him some lessons, or open up to him some views, which could not have been otherwise disclosed. [10]

3. From Travesty to Tragedy

Throughout the 17th century, a wearisome series of debilitating wars with Spain, Ireland, France, Holland, Denmark and the America Colonies, sapped the creative energies of the English nation, not only radically changing political and economic conditions, but seriously affecting the world of the arts. The Reformation under Henry VIII had destroyed the abbeys and monasteries and stolen their wealth; the English Civil War under Cromwell had divested religious buildings and aristocratic houses of their treasures. Other influences came about through historical and political circumstance.

George I's personal identification with the Roman Emperor Augustus had a revitalising effect on the prevailing English culture of the time. He recognised the part Augustus had played in stabilising Roman society after years of warring, establishing a Roman peace, *Pax romana*, through a more autocratic, monarchic regime, and re-inventing a Christian patriotism attractive to the educated public. He sought to bring something of his more eclectic European background to a freer more empirical English society. Latin authors like Virgil, Livy and Horace remained the bench-marks of excellence in a culture with little in the way of rules and guide-lines.

The central philosophical debate in 18th century English Augustan literature was about whether the individual or society took precedence as a subject of verse. Poets reacted with and against each other, sometimes in imitation, sometimes with parody. The traditional literary forms such as the lyric, song, ballad, ode and elegy were transformed to suit the new Augustan style, giving a fresh new impetus to the early romantic poets later in the century. A love poem was not only about love but about the lover. Imitation, parody and satire flourished, giving rise to fierce rivalries and recriminations.

While all the cut-and-thrust of management was going on at Drury, a vicious plot took place involving one of the 'composers in residence' at the Theatre Royal, Henry Carey, whose presence was very much in evidence between 1723 and 1733 and yet whose name has today fallen into obscurity. A few scholars have found in him an intriguing subject for study since his origins appear to be elusive, and reason for speculation and rumour. He was said to have been the illegitimate son of George Saville, the 1st Marquess of Halifax. He made no effort to conceal the fact when he gave the name 'Savile' to his three sons. Further suspicion was abroad, as was reported in the *Gentleman's Magazine*, that he was in receipt of an annuity from the Savile family, but no one really knew the truth. That he took the name of his mother, Mary Carey, a school teacher, suggests there was some mystery over the identity of the father, who it was said, rather than being a Savile was much more likely to have been a school-teacher. The scandalous literary plot of which Carey became an unwitting victim made sure that his name would carry a shameful sobriquet for years to come.

At first Henry worked in the sleazy world of Grub Street, placing his work wherever he could, but then moved up the literary scale, writing for a more literate female readership, churning out numerous stories of romance – in other words, inadvertently becoming a pioneer in women's journalism for a more educated, intelligent, middle class readership. His first volume, *Poems on Several Occasions*, came out in 1710.

In the meantime, we hear of Carey as a singer of Italian and English songs at the Theatre Royal, Drury Lane. A confusion has arisen over the identity of his songs as he chose to write them anonymously with the intention of selling them to would-be composers to pass off as their own, but we do know that he was a prolific composer of some 250 songs and ballads, some of them achieving fame and longevity, such as 'Sally in Our Alley'. At first, he busied himself with composing incidental dances and other *entr'acte* pieces and such dances and farcical pieces as were required to embellish the total effect of a performance, for all of which he made sure he was paid good money.[11] In 1723, he composed the music for *Harlequin Dr. Faustus* to a pathetic libretto scrambled together by Barton Booth, and he began to take a more active role in organizing and conducting the music for the entertainments such as pantomimes and spectacles.

Drury was a hotbed of 'Whiggery' and had been since its inception in Davenant's day. With the death of Queen Anne, the Tory government fell, and Robert Walpole saved the day for the Whigs to take power. This event suited the left-wing element at Drury Lane and Carey was happy to join Cibber, Wilks, and Barton Booth, all of whom were under the influence of Joseph Addison, as we have seen, and were consequently enthusiastic promoters of patriotic drama like *Cato*.

Carey, like Fielding, was a powerful despoiler of reputations. Robert Walpole was in the direct line of fire for his curbing of the traditional freedoms enjoyed by dramatists, actors and managers since the carefree days of Charles II's reign. Walpole's mission was to rid the theatres of low humour and plots with sexual content. The Master of the Revels, who had had control over political and religious themes from Elizabethan times, was now superseded by the Lord Chamberlain, who also had the power to approve or censor any play before it was staged, a privilege he retained as defender of public morals until his services were no longer required when the Theatres Act of 1968 became law. Carey vehemently opposed Walpole, whom he came to attack by means of an extraordinary parody. There is no doubt Carey's motive in the parody was political, the main purpose of which was to satirise Walpole and the Tories. As things turned out, it was a risky gesture which was destined to backfire in an unexpected manner, leaving not only his own name in disgrace but those of his famous contemporary, Alexander Pope, and the lesser known Ambrose Philips.

Chapter 4 – Plagiary and Parody

Pope developed a quite specific view of poetry in which he could discourse in a matchless form of 'heroic poetry' – lines of poetry in iambic pentameters, made up of five trochees, composed of two syllables, one short, one long, (as in 'ex<u>pect</u>', 'for<u>get</u>',) a metre Shakespeare used in his sonnets. Pope adopted the trope in his *Essay on Criticism*:

> But where's the man, who counsel can bestow,
> Still pleas'd to teach, and yet not proud to know? [*etc.*]
> Unbias'd, or by favour, or by spite;
> Not dully prepossess'd, nor blindly right;
> Tho' learn'd, well-bred, and tho' well-bred, sincere;
> Modestly bold, and humanly severe;
> Who to a friend his faults can freely show,
> And gladly praise the merit of a foe?
> Blest with a taste exact, yet unconfin'd;
> A knowledge both of books and human kind;
> Gen'rous converse; a soul exempt from pride;
> And love to praise, with reason on his side?
>   Such once were Critics; such a happy few,
> Athens and Rome in better ages knew.[12]

Or more famously in *Essay on Man*:

> Know then thyself, presume not God to scan;
> The proper study of Mankind is Man.[13]

As the outspoken critic of the age Pope had more enemies than he had rivals. If only he could have followed his own set of rules. In his biting satire *The Dunciad*, the ink sizzled on the paper when he wrote of his enemies ('Dunces'). On this occasion, he had been irritated by favourable reviews in *The Guardian* praising the rustic qualities of Ambrose Philips's poetry, which he considered sickeningly sentimental.

Phoenix of Drury Lane

Alexander Pope (engraving by J.Posselwhite)

To be fair, Philips's poems, especially his pastoral verses have a simple, quirky charm, quite undeserving of the attack made on them by jealous contemporaries. Some lines from Philips's epistolary verses describing the environs of Copenhagen in winter (composed while he was secretary to the British Envoy to Denmark), entitled *Epistle to the Earl of Dorset,* must suffice to show his simple, restrained style:

> The hoary winter here conceals from sight
> All pleasing objects which to verse invite,
> The hills and dales, and the delightful woods,
> The flow'ry plains, and silver-streaming floods,
> By snow disguis'd, in bright confusion lie,
> And with one dazzling waste fatigue the eye.
> No gentle breathing breeze prepares the spring,
> No birds within the desert region sing.[14]

Continuing in the simpler vein of some future Blake or Southey, he spins a convincing web of winter chill and desolation:

> The starving wolves along the main sea prowl,
> And to the moon in icy valleys howl.
> O'er many a shining league the level main
> Here spreads itself into a glassy plain:
> There solid billows of enormous size,
> *Alps* of green ice, in wild disorder rise.[15]

Chapter 4 – Plagiary and Parody

These lines have the gentle tone of his earlier *Pastorals*, praised by the reviewer, Thomas Tickell, a member of Addison's 'Little Senate' at Button's Coffee House. Pope's *Pastorals* were printed last in the same volume.[16] Angered by such an insult, though unintended, Pope replied in an article for *The Guardian,* making sure to ridicule Philips by quoting his worst lines as if they were his best. Philips threatened to beat Pope with a staff the next time he came across him at Button's Coffee House, Addison's 'Little Senate'. Pope accused Philips of being sentimental about shepherds in his pastorals, claiming they could only be truthfully depicted in the classical terms of The Golden Age. In a sense, Philips was adapting the pastoral style of Virgil to the new age, breaking its ties with antiquity and taking as his model, the *Eclogues* of Spenser. The archness of creating a quasi-sophisticated dialogue between two simple shepherds with names like Lobbin and Colinet would soon go out of fashion in any case. All the same, Addison joined in the fray in *The Spectator* by praising the simplicity of Philips's lines, unencumbered as they were by remote references to classical mythology. A Dorset shepherd boy, Lobbin, suffers the pangs of unrequited love:

> Fond Love no Cure will have; seeks no Repose;
> Delights in Grief; nor any Measure knows.
> And now the Moon begins the Clouds to rise;
> The twinkling Stars are lighted in the Skies;
> The Winds are hush'd; the Dews distil; and sleep
> With soft Embrade has seized my weary Sheep.
> I only with the prouling [*sic*] Wolf, constrain'd
> All night to wake. With hunger is he pain'd,
> And I with Love. His hunger he may tame:
> But who in Love can stop the growling Flame?[17]

Pope flew into a jealous rage and persuaded his friend, the author of *The Beggar's Opera*, John Gay, to compose some satirical verses mocking Philip's style and introducing us to the country-wise Cloddipole and the witless country bumpkins Cuddy, Lobbin and Clout, and their romps in the hay with shepherdesses, Blouzelinda and Buxoma;

> LOBBIN CLOUT
> From Cloddipole we learnt to read the skies,
> To know when hail will fall, or winds arise.
> He taught us erst the heifer's tail to view,
> When stuck aloft, that show'rs would straight ensue;

> He first that useful secret did explain,
> That pricking corns foretold the gath'ring rain.
>
> LOBBIN
> As with Buxoma once I work'd at hay.
> E'en noon-tide labour seem'd a holiday;
> And holidays, if haply she were gone,
> Like worky-days I wish'd would soon be done.
> Eftsoons, O sweet-heart kind, I love repay,
> And all the year shall be a holiday.
>
> CUDDY
> As Blouzelinda in a gamesome mood,
> Behind the haycock loudly laughing stood.
> I silly ran, and snatch'd a hasty kiss,
> She wip'd her lips, nor took it much amiss.
> Believe me, Cuddy, while I'm bold to say,
> Her breath was sweeter than the ripen'd hay.
>
> LOBBIN
> As my Buxoma in a morning fair,
> With gentle finger strok'd her milky care,
> I quaintly stole a kiss, at first, 'tis true,
> She frown'd, yet after granted one or two.
> Lobbin, I swear, believe who will my vows,
> Her breath by far excell'd the breathing cows.

As it happened, Gay's verses were too deft, too close to the pastoral tradition, and were, ironically, admired for their charm and simplicity. But Philips was not to escape unutterable ridicule. Henry Carey's hatred of Walpole persisted and the thought came to him of writing a parody of Philips's babyish style of expression in his verses, especially those composed for the infant children of Lord Carteret: *To Miss Charlotte Pulteney, in Her Mother's Arms*:

> Timely blossom, infant fair,
> Fondling of a happy pair...
> Little gossip, blithe and hale,
> Tattling many a broken tale,

Chapter 4 – Plagiary and Parody

> Singing many a tuneless song,
> Lavish to a heedless tongue.
> Simple maiden, void of art,
> Babbling out the very heart.[18]

Some might say the poem has a ring of truth about it, a sentimental moment common to any parent with a newly-born child. The sweetness of the verses, when transformed into a political squib, has a bitter centre to it, because it is not after all about an adored baby, but has the fawning pleading of an ambitious man in search of preferment by ingratiating himself with Lord Carteret, who was, at the time, Lord Lieutenant of Ireland. Carey took as his epigraph a popular nursery rhyme:

> Nauty Pauty Jack-a-Dandy
> Stole a Piece of Sugar-Candy,
> From the Grocer's Shoppy-Shop,
> And away did hoppy-hop

Carey was merciless in his parody of Philips' 'baby' style:

> Now the venal Poet sings, [*i.e.Philips*]
> Baby Clouts [*clothes*], and Baby Things
> Baby Dolls, and Baby Houses,
> Little Misses, Little Spouses,
> Little Play-Things, little Toys,
> Little Girls, and little Boys.
> As an Actor does his Part
> So the Nurses get by Heart
> *Namby Pamby*'s Little Rhymes,
> Little Jingle, Little Chimes,
> To repeat to Little Miss,
> Piddling Ponds of Pissy-Piss,
> Cacking-packing like a Lady,
> Or Bye-bying in the Crady [*cradle*].
> Namby Pamby ne'er will die
> While the Nurse sings *Lullabye*... [19]

Carey, in the person of Walpole, opens his verses with a snide recital of the Augustan rules for the 'New Versification' to be adopted by

Drury's rebellious playwrights:

> All ye Poets of the Age!
> All ye Witlings of the Stage!
> Learn your Jingles to reform!
> Crop your Numbers and Conform:
> Let your little Verses flow
> Gently, Sweetly, Row by Row:
> Let the Verse the Subject fit;
> Little, subject, Little Wit.
> *Namby-Pamby* is your Guide;
> [*advice to replace vulgar wit and innuendo with sentiment and sweetness*]
> Albion's Joy, Hibernia's Pride. [*sarcastic reference to Philips*]
> Namby-Pamby Pilly-Piss, [*baby peeing in her pillow*]
> Rhimy pim'd on Missy-Miss; [*nonsense rhyme*]
> *Tartaretta, Tartaree*,
> [*reference to prostitution of talents*]
> From the Navel to the Knee;
> That her Father's Gracy-Grace [*Lord Cartaret*]
> Might give him a Placy-Place. [ll 1-16]
> [*Philips' hope of employment*]

Even though not its author, this extravagance piece of nonsense brought opprobrium and ridicule to Ambrose Philips and to today's wider readership his name means little or nothing, his poetry now largely forgotten. His fall from grace was perpetrated by the unconscionable hatred and contempt shown by his arch enemy, Alexander Pope. The sheer brilliance of Henry Carey's travesty made sure that 'namby-pamby' would become synonymous with flaccid and sentimental writing. No one can ever speak of the epithet without a tinge of contempt in the voice. Its aura hangs about in the air, an uncomfortable reminder of the fragility of fame. Nevertheless, the poetry of Philips had a genuine feeling for nature, a gentleness redolent of an earlier age, to be found in his collection of *Old Ballads*, and his popular plays *Robin Hood* and *Children in the Wood*. His poems were published in 1749, the year before he died.

Namby Pamby was described in its title as 'A Panegyric on the New Versification', meaning poetry composed in the Augustan style. Following the practice of Greek and Roman times, when it was the custom to speak or read a eulogy or encomium in praise of a respected personage, the opening lines of 'Namby-Pamby' are in the form of an 'Address' to an assembled company of rebellious playwrights. Instead of a paean of praise, Carey turns the whole poem inside-out and transforms it into a scathing satire on the Augustan requirements of sentiment and simplicity. The imagery of the poem, liberally plagiarised from traditional nursery rhymes, is broken up and transmuted into a bewildering variety of tropes, each adding to a confusion of conceits, leading the reader (or listener) into a topsy-turvy world such as Lewis Carroll would one day create in *Alice Through the Looking Glass*.

A condition of the panegyric was to praise, even to the point of flattery, the achievements of an important individual, as in Dryden's 'Addresses' to the Stuart Kings, Samuel Daniel's *A Panegyrike Congratulationarie delivered to the King's most excellent majestie*, and, bordering on the obsequious, Edmund Waller's piece addressed to Cromwell: *A Panegyric To My Lord Protector Of the Present Greatness, And Joint Interests, Of His Highness, And this Nation*. However, by Boswell's day, the panegyric, far from being flattering, had become, as its classical ancestor did, a piece of facetious, even vicious and licentious mockery at the victim's expense. With *Namby-Pamby*, the cruel absurdity of its inside-out logic and the blatant spitefulness of its sneering parody gives rise to hollow, uncomfortable laughter:

> *Namby Pamby*'s double mild,
> Once a Man, and twice a Child;
> To his Hanging-Sleeves restor'd, [*his tutor's gown*]
> Now he foots it like a Lord.
> Now he pumps his little Wits;
> Sh[*itt*]-ing Writes and Writing Sh[i]-ts.[20]

Ambrose Philips lost his name to a cruel sobriquet and his poetry to the dust of ages, but fate would have its revenge. Destiny did not allow his tormentor Carey to escape, for he too was ever to be remembered as 'Namby-Pamby Carey'. The manner of Carey's end was unexpectedly tragic and macabre. After the premature death of his beloved son, Charles, Carey fell into a deep depression and hanged himself.

Phoenix of Drury Lane

CHAPTER FIVE

The Great Literary Competition of 1811

1. Whitbread, and Wyatt's 'New Drury'

On Friday 24 February 1809, the Theatre Royal, Drury Lane, burnt to the ground. As it was a Friday in Lent, there were no performances or rehearsals permitted, and consequently Richard Brinsley Sheridan, the patent-holder, was taking some refreshment nearby in the Piazza at Covent Garden. A friend was greatly surprised at Sheridan's imperturbable manner at a time when only a short distance away his theatre was in flames. With remarkable coolness, Sheridan replied: 'May not a man be allowed to drink a glass of wine by his own fireside?'

Byron watched the fire from a rooftop nearby and then hastened down to Westminster Bridge to look at the flames reflected in the waters of the Thames. The blaze lit up the whole of London and could be seen from miles around the city, a scene which gave him the idea for the inspired opening lines of his Address delivered on the opening night of the rebuilt theatre:

> In one dread night, our City saw and sighed
> Bowed to the dust the Drama's tower of pride.
> In one short hour beheld the blazing fane[*],
> Apollo sink & Shakespeare cease to reign.
> Ye, who beheld, & sure there are to night
> Who feared, admired & ah! deplored the sight,
> Through sulphurous clouds the massy fragments riven,
> In fiery pillars chase the night from heaven,
> Saw the long Column of revolving flames
> Shake his red shadow o'er the startled Thames
> As flashed the volumed blaze and ghastly shone
> The skies with lightning, awful as their own,
> While crowds, collected round the burning dome,
> Shrank back appalled, and trembled for their home
> Till all was whelmed beneath the lurid wave
> And blackening ashes make the Muse's grave.[1]

'It was a calamity of the first magnitude; not merely the burning of a theatre but of *the* Theatre, the oldest in the town in tradition and glory, the original holder of the title Theatre Royal.'[2] Sheridan faced absolute ruin.

---

[*] fane = poetic form for 'temple'

The House of Commons proposed to adjourn out of sympathy but he declined with his accustomed conscientiousness towards the business of the House, and remained to debate the Spanish War until three o'clock in the morning:

> His was the thunder, his the avenging rod,
> The wrath — the delegated voice of God!
> Which shook the nations through his lips, and blazed
> Till vanquished senates trembled as they praised.[3]

It is true that Sheridan had always been able to talk himself out of any tricky situation, but no amount of oratory could save him now. It was very soon after this that he sought the assistance of Samuel Whitbread,[*] who had shown some interest in joining the rebuilding committee. In the circumstances Sheridan had little choice. He had insured the theatre, which had cost £150,000 to build, for a mere £35,000, and the loss was crippling. Whitbread, a relation of the playwright's second wife, might have been expected to show some consideration for Sheridan's plight if only on the grounds of family connection, but it soon became clear to Sheridan that he was not to be asked to join the committee, and was deeply hurt when Whitbread excluded him from the management. This was not surprising on two counts. First, the two men were incompatible. Though they belonged to the same party (the Whigs), their political differences in some ways paralleled their personal differences over the running of the theatre. Sheridan's casual methods of accountancy were unpalatable to the son of a successful brewer, and Whitbread could take no chances. Secondly, the discovery of debts on the theatre amounting to £436,971 convinced Whitbread that nothing short of the most rigorous control of expenditure would restore the balance and, in some measure at least, ensure the survival of the national theatre, for no other theatre was capable of replacing it; no other had such a distinguished (if chequered) history.

Whitbread's first task was to deal with Sheridan's creditors, who, knowing of the playwright's erratic accounting, sent in bills for more than the amounts owed, seeking their pound of flesh while the going was good. They descended on him like a plague of locusts. Sheridan's career in the theatre was effectively destroyed, and the few years of life left to him eventually led him to the degradation of the debtors' prison, from which Whitbread was constrained to secure his release. It seems at this time that

---

[*] Samuel Whitbread (1758-1815). Whig politician. Close ally of Charles James Fox. Established a brewery in 1742 which by the end of the century had become London's largest producer of beer.

he experienced feelings almost akin to grief at the lost domains of achievement of which he had once been the possessor.

Meanwhile, the settlement of Drury Lane's debts had to be faced. Whitbread set about persuading the creditors to waive their claims. Many did so, whilst others accepted reduced settlements rather than lose everything by holding out for the whole amount – perhaps an indication that their claims were exaggerated in the first place. Sheridan received £24,000 for his share, half of which was withheld by Whitbread to offset some of the debt. With the help of Lord Holland and Lord Byron, two Royal dukes, two members of the House of Commons, and a representative from the City of London, all of whom were persuaded to join the committee, Whitbread, who now saw himself as the champion of British drama and the saviour of Drury Lane, set about raising funds for the rebuilding of the theatre.[4] He managed to persuade one hundred and thirty-four friends and acquaintances to buy shares of £100 each. The success of these complex and delicate financial dealings was entirely due to the industry, determination, and zeal of Samuel Whitbread alone. Had it not been for his enthusiasm and devotion to the cause of British drama, the Theatre Royal, Drury Lane, would have sunk without trace.

In the year following the fire, an Act of Parliament was passed enabling the Proprietors to form a Joint Stock Company for the purpose of rebuilding on the old site. The first meeting was held in March 1811. Considerable financial problems had to be solved before the building work could begin, but through the intervention of Whitbread, obstacles were overcome and the necessary resources found. 'No language can do justice to the promptitude, discrimination, and perseverance which were displayed by Mr. Whitbread, throughout every stage of this most arduous undertaking.'* In the Smith brothers' *Rejected Addresses*, Whitbread is seen by the Hampshire Farmer (in the style of his own speeches in Parliament) as the great benefactor, chasing the audience out of their rat-hole (the old theatre) and perching them in a palace. He is 'Veeshnu', the Great Preserver, since:

> He treats with men of all conditions
> Poets and players, tradesmen and musicians.[5]

His popular appeal was undeniable, even legendary. To the ordinary man in the street, he was 'our great Commoner', the convivial son of a brewer:

> And since he has saved all the fat from the fire,

---

* *The Tatler*

Chapter 5 – The Great Literary Competition of 1811

I move that the house be call'd Whitbread's Entire*.[6]

In May 1811, the newly-assembled Committee organised a competition to encourage architects to send in designs for a new building. In October, the plans of Benjamin Wyatt[7] were adopted and the first stone was laid on 29 October and, remarkably, the new theatre opened to the public just within the year, on 10 October 1812. The rebuilding of the Theatre Royal, Drury Lane, marked the beginning of a new age in the history of the English theatre, though Wyatt had no great opinion of current attitudes to theatre architecture at the time:

> Architecture, as applied to Theatres, not having been often the subject of public discussion in this Country, and no description ever having been published of the principles on which either of the former Theatres of this Metropolis has been constructed, the Author is induced to submit to the Public the following explanation of the leading considerations which guided him, in the formation of his Plan for Drury Lane.[8]

Throughout its history the Theatre Royal, Drury Lane, had been the centre of scandal and intrigue, involving both actors and managers. Now its architect was also to become the subject of controversy. One newspaper suggested[9] that the adopted designs had been 'borrowed' from designs made by George Wyatt. Admittedly, there appeared to be 'some coincidence' between the two plans, and Benjamin Wyatt was forced to reissue his designs, with a Preface, in 1813, in an attempt to protect his integrity as an architect. His argument was that he had shown his designs to members of the Royal Family and 'other persons of distinction' as early as February 1810 and that he never set eyes on George Wyatt's plans until their publication in 1812. If this is so, then we must accept that Benjamin Wyatt's designs for the Theatre Royal, Drury Lane, originally published in 1811, were unquestionably authentic, and his defence, published in 1813, must be allowed to stand as his testament.

---

* Whitbread's stout was a popular drink consisting of ale with added malt.

Benjamin Dean Wyatt. (Engraving by T Blood, 1812)

Benjamin Wyatt's *Observations*, or proposed plans, were based on four principles: size or capacity of the theatre, its form or shape, ingress and egress, and 'Decorum among the several Orders and Classes of the Visitants to the Theatre'. There were to be boxes, grand staircases, a rotunda, private boxes for the King and the Prince Regent with their own water-closets, a music copyist's room, dressing-rooms for actors separate from those for actresses, a Committee Room, a Manager's Room, fruit store, a carpenter's store-room, a master-tailor's room, hat and feather rooms, a property-maker's room, and wardrobes for male and female costumes.[10] Wyatt's model was the theatre at Bordeaux, considered then to be the finest in Europe. It had been designed by Victor Louis (173-1800) in classical style with a portico supported by 12 Corinthian columns, displaying 12 statues, including the nine Muses.

The exterior of his building was to be embellished with ornate classical decoration, but this was never completed, giving a disappointingly plain and aggressive appearance, saved only by Nash's portico, reassembled from Regent Street, and Samuel Beazley's[*] classical colonnade added some years later.[11] Much of the available space had been given over to the foyer with its grand staircases and public rooms, with little consideration for the comfort of actors and musicians, thus giving

---

[*] Samuel Beazley (1786-1851), architect and playwright. Designed several London theatres and wrote a number of dramatic pieces.

Chapter 5 – The Great Literary Competition of 1811

substance to that perennial grudge of the acting profession against designers and architects whose priorities invariably favour spacious auditoria and grand staircases rather than the simplest backstage amenities.

On 8 August 1812, an advertisement appeared in the *Morning Herald*, and on 14 August in all the principal daily papers:

Rebuilding of Drury Lane Theatre

The Committee are desirous of promoting a free and fair competition for an Address to be spoken upon the opening of the Theatre, which will take place on 10 October next. They have, therefore, thought fit to announce to the public, that they will be glad to receive any such compositions, addressed to their Secretary at the Treasury-Office, Drury Lane, on or before 10 September, sealed up with a distinguishing word, number or motto on the cover corresponding with the inscription on a separate sealed paper, containing the name of the author, which will not be opened unless containing the name of the successful candidate.

As the *Quarterly Review* commented: 'With due modesty, and, in the true spirit of tradesmen, they advertised.....'[12]. Lewis Goldsmith* reported on 20 September:

> A new era in dramatic annals is about to commence by the opening of Drury Lane Theatre, which has again been committed to rear its head and present itself to the eye in a substantial and tenantable form, after having been, for several years, nothing but an unsightly heap of useless ruins.
>
> The first act of its Board of Management has excited some sensation throughout literary circles. It declares that there will be a fair and free competition for an occasional address to be spoken on the opening of the newly-erected theatre; a vast number of writers have consequently tried

---

* Lewis Goldsmith (1763?-1846). Political writer and journalist. Outspoken editor of *The Antigallican Monitor and Anti-Corsican Chronicle*. By arrangement with Napoleon Bonaparte, he published in Paris *The Argus, or London Reviewed in Paris* in 1802, but was imprisoned in 1803 for refusing to print articles against the English Royal Family. Escaped to England in 1809. His anti-French weekly advocated tyrannicide. Died in Paris.

their talents on the subject....[13]

Goldsmith considered what effect such a competition would have on the state of poetic composition in England and warned that, since the Committee had raised a theatre as a 'tribute to the Muses', the address would be required to reflect the views and opinions of the Committee:

> This substantiates the opinion that it will not be the beauty or brilliancy of the sentiments and allusions which will guide the decision of the judges, but their applicability to, and concordance with, the ideas which the committee have formed in regard to the management of their new establishment – How erroneous, therefore, is it to regard this competition as a trial of poetic skill; or to imagine that its result will throw any considerable light on the state of poetic composition at the present period.[14]

He suggested that if Campbell, Crabbe, Southey or Scott 'had consented to curb and chasten the wild exuberances of their genius for the occasion – all their productions would very probably been laid aside and the effusions of some minor pen accepted.' Goldsmith's fears were justified, as was his disapprobation of 'any public trial of poetic merit' on the ground that it was 'by no means beneficial to the cause of literature'. The Committee, he wrote, had 'invited all the *coupleteers* in England to turn over their rhyming dictionaries and had begged 'the very paddlers in the waters of Helicon* to pump up the forgotten fragments of their *prosing poetics*' for the occasion. If only a poet of known talent could be approached, the lesser fry would be prevented from sending their ridiculous poetastings, for now there was a Party man, Samuel Whitbread, son of a brewer, who had set himself up as 'the presiding judge of that formidable junta, who are to decide upon the respective merits of all the poetasters in the United Kingdom.'[15]

Another bone of contention for Lewis Goldsmith was the favourable view taken by the Drury Lane Committee of Napoleon Bonaparte, whom they claimed to be a 'noble' creature not to be vilified upon the stage by any of the competitors, who should eschew those 'slip-shod compositions which have been the disgrace of the stage, especially for the last twenty years – disgustingly panegyrical of ourselves, and as disgustingly slanderous of our enemies.'[16] Goldsmith vehemently argued that mixing Theatre and Party politics was repugnant to everyone who upheld the high principles of drama:

---

* Helicon, home of the Muses, a part of Parnassus. Gray's 'harmonious springs' is an allusion to the fount of poetic inspiration.

> It is, with extreme regret that we have been obliged, in writing on this subject, to connect the Stage with politics – we should have refrained too from these observations, under other circumstances, from a feeling of respect, for one greatly interested in the success of the new Theatre, Mr. Sheridan – Had he continued to share in the management of this establishment, we should have been freed from the effects of the political bias complained of, for no man ever held our enemy in more fervent detestation; and the eloquent speech which he has inserted in the Play of *Pizarro*, will be an everlasting monument of his praiseworthy endeavours to rouse the national spirit, by dwelling on the value of our homes, and by raising the strongest feelings of abhorrence against any enemy who should invade them.[17]

Goldsmith, in the fervour of his feelings of antagonism towards Napoleon, was blindly supporting a lost cause in speaking up on Sheridan's behalf. Admittedly, *Pizarro* had been a phenomenal success. Indeed, it was said that all London saw it, 'from the King and Queen to the crossing-sweepers.'[18] But patriotism was not enough to save Sheridan, or his theatre. All that was in the past. A phoenix had risen triumphantly from the flames, and continued to do so with predictable regularity, as Lewis Goldsmith had warned, from the pens of almost every versifier and poetaster in the land who saw a chance of an overnight rise to fame and fortune. Even Goldsmith himself could not resist the temptation; reporting on the long-awaited First Night, he followed the fashion in describing the theatre as a 'newly-erected Temple of the Muses' rising, phoenix-like, from the ashes'[19]:

> Its exterior....is not calculated to give rise to very high anticipations; but its interior gains greatly by this circumstance....The entrance is superb in the extreme, and the flight of steps, which leads to the boxes, strike the spectator at once with grand and imposing conceptions of the other parts of the house. The plan of the boxes is more circular than that of any other Theatre and better calculated for a view of the stage. They are embellished with the most splendid and tastefully variegated decorations. The proscenium is most beautiful, being bounded on either side by a superb Corinthian pillar, in imitation marble; before which a pedestal, sustaining a tripod Grecian lamp. Upon the whole, this part of the new Theatre, considered abstractedly, stands unrivalled, in this

or any other country, for beauty and elegance of design. Its pre-eminent splendour and magnificence, however, detracts from the appearance of the Stage, which is in consequence thrown back too far from the audience part of the House, and greatly confined on each side. This prevents the actors from being distinctly seen and heard as at the former Theatre, which is so important a defect that we trust some means will be found of remedying it before the next season....The Saloon is particularly elegant, and the dress circle is kept distinct from the other boxes, which relieves its frequenters from a nuisance hitherto universally felt and complained of.[20]

The first manager was Samuel James Arnold,[*] who was under the control of a committee which included Lord Holland (leader of the Moderate Whigs in the House of Commons), William Adam, Lord Byron, Samuel Whitbread, and others of less note. Arnold, however, was the only professional man of the theatre among them. Whilst the theatre was nothing short of magnificent, the company the best possible in the circumstances (all the finest actors and actresses had departed during Sheridan's disastrous reign), the management, in spite of Arnold's worthy attempts to resist the futile squabblings of the committee, was pathetically amateurish. Byron found some five hundred plays on the shelves awaiting production, and all of them too inferior to be considered. As to the committee, who were constantly at variance, Byron found them irritating, especially the despair of Cavendish Bradshaw[†] and the constant complaints of Samuel Whitbread. '....Bradshaw wants to light the theatre with gas, which may perhaps (if the vulgar believed) poison half the audience and all the *dramatis personae*....To crown all, Robins, the auctioneer, has the impudence to be displeased because he has no dividend.'[21]

Byron was not aware that Whitbread was already a sick man. Wyatt's 1813 edition of his *Observations* was dedicated to Whitbread: 'A Memorial of his characteristic Energies, displayed in the Restoration of

---

[*] Samuel James Arnold (1774-1852) dramatist. Produced many original musical plays at The Haymarket Theatre, Drury Lane and the English Opera House. Married the daughter of Henry James Pye (1745-1802), the Poet Laureate. Arnold was the son of composer of operas and oratorios, Samuel Arnold, organist at Westminster Abbey.

[†] Augustus Cavendish Bradshaw, educated Repton & Trinity College, Cambridge. MP for Carlow in the Parliament of Ireland, 1790-1796. MP for Honiton, Devon, 1805-1812. Groom of the Bedchamber in the service of the Prince Regent.

the Drury Lane Theatre,' and it was the uncontrolled use of those characteristic energies that brought about his tragic end. While the new theatre was set on the path to recovery, the principal protagonists in the act of its revival and survival were themselves on the downward path to self-destruction. The Drury Lane Theatre could look forward to the excellence of former times with the future lessee Robert William Elliston[*], and managers, Stephen Price and Alfred Bunn. Yet the extraordinary advent of a new theatrical era, made more magnificent by the rise to fame of the tempestuous actor Edmund Kean,[22] did little to release Whitbread from the stress and strain brought on by his dogged pursuance of his public works.

2. Rivals in Platitudes: The Genuine Rejected Addresses 1812

The history of the Theatre Royal, Drury Lane, and the actors, managers, politicians and financiers connected with it, both before and subsequent to the fire in 1809, provides a useful and interesting background to the confusion that surrounded the Literary Competition itself. The advertisement appeared in the London daily papers on 14 August 1812 and, as we have seen, the opening was planned for 10 October. Owing to an error in the publication dates of some of the advertisements, intending competitors were allowed to submit their poetic effusions by 10 September instead of 31 August. Thus they were given one calendar month instead of the original two weeks in which to invoke the Muse, set down their 'skimble-skamble stuff', as one critic described it,[23] give it a quick polish, and send it off post-haste to the unsuspecting committee who, according to Byron, eventually had to cope with some five hundred entries.[24] Sadly, only one hundred and fourteen remain.[25] Secrecy was paramount. Only the Committee would know the name of the successful competitor. The rest were to be locked away and eventually destroyed. In fact they were preserved.

The Management Committee were dismayed when they saw the massive response to their appeal for an Opening Address, but how much more so when they began to read the pile of entries. Some of its members began to wish they had entrusted the task of writing the address to Walter Scott, or the Poet Laureate, Robert Southey, who, even if he was 'so

---

[*] Robert William Elliston ((1774-1831), actor. First London appearances at the Haymarket Theatre and Covent Garden. Appeared as *Hamlet* at the opening night of the Theatre Royal, Drury Lane. Lessee and manager of Drury Lane 1819-26. Introduced spectacular scenery. Bankrupt 1826.

quaint and mouthey', could be expected to produce an 'occasional' piece of tolerable quality.[26] The Committee were not only confounded by the great number of addresses through which they had to wade so laboriously, but they were also utterly perplexed by their own debates as to the relative merits of the individual entries, even though there appeared to be only 'two or three persons' who had 'some share of taste or genius'.[27] The *Quarterly Review* reported:

> No such confusion of tongues had accompanied any erection since the building of Babel; nor could such matters have been set to rights (unless by a miracle), if the convenient though not very candid plan of rejecting *all* the addresses had not occurred....in which the whole committee might safely agree; and the Addresses were rejected accordingly. We do not think that they deserved, in true poetical justice, a better fate; not one was excellent, two or three only were tolerable, and the rest so execrable that we wonder this committee of *taste* did not agree upon one of them.[28]

The Committee was in a state of uproar, if not of panic, further aggravated by the unwished-for submission of over a hundred spectacles, melodramas, operas, and pantomimes. Lord Holland wrote an urgent letter to Byron asking him to save the situation by writing the Address himself, as a member of the Committee. On 10 September 1812, Byron wrote to Lady Melbourne:

> Today I have had a letter from Lord Holland, wishing me to write for the opening theatre, but as all Grub Street seems to be engaged in the contest, I have no ambition to enter the lists, and have thrown my few ideas into the fire. I never risk <u>rivalry</u> in anything, You see the very <u>lowest</u>, as in this case, discourages me, from a sort of mixed feeling, I don't know if it be <u>pride</u>, but <u>you</u> will say it certainly is not <u>modesty</u>. I suppose your friend Twiss[*] will be <u>one</u>. I hear there are five hundred, and I wish him success. I really think he would do it well, but few men who have any character to lose, would risk it in an anonymous scramble, for the sake of their own feelings.

A number of earnest (but desperate) competitors were still sending in

---

[*] Horace Twiss (1787-1849). Politician, wit and 'squib-writer' (ie, a writer of short satirical pieces). Strongly opposed reform. He sent his Address to the Committee on 8th September, just meeting the Committee's deadline of 10th.

Chapter 5 – The Great Literary Competition of 1811

their poetical attempts days after the closing date of 10 September. One competitor, Edmund Bellchambers, informed the Committee that in spite of not having seen the advertisement, he had written his Address on the previous Thursday and delivered it on the following Tuesday, too late to qualify for consideration. Ironically, it contained the phrase 'The Muse too soon', altered to 'Too soon the Muse', but no amount of alteration was able to convince the judges of its merit, and it was marked 'After the time, but read.' Not only did his Address arrive late; Bellchambers, in company with a number of other competitors, no doubt upset at being rejected, wrote in to ask for the return of his manuscript, 'as I have some business with Mr. T. Dibdin,* which will bring me to the Stage-door in the course of to-morrow forenoon.' Another competitor sent in his Address too late, but perhaps hoping he would be forgiven, signed himself 'Humilitas', but to no avail.

Besides late arrivals, there were also a number of repeated arrivals, sometimes in duplicate or triplicate: 'I trust the Committee will, in my premature Essays of the 14th and 17th Inst, only recognise my alacrity to meet their wishes; and in the present my zeal to fulfil them.'[29] The attached motto was 'Speratum et completum' (hoped for and fulfilled)!

Another entrant, John Gorton, sent in a duplicate Address with correction, since the first verses 'were not properly arrang'd.' A postscript gave the Committee permission to correct 'Any little Impropriety which you might discover.'[30] George Terry sent in three copies of his Address over a period of days, each copy corrected in ink barely allowed to dry in the haste and flurry of delivery.

All the sealed papers were opened and attached to the various contributions. The consternation of the appointed readers can only be imagined, though there is proof enough to show that their reactions were ones of aesthetic revulsion, rapidly followed by critical dismissal. However, it was an act of faith on the part of the Committee, publicly avowed, that all the sealed papers containing the real names of the competitors, except that of the winning entry, would remain unopened. Had it not been for the breaking of these seals, the names of the competitors would never have been known to us. Among them we find several members of the Sheridan family: Sheridan's son, Charles, brother-in-law William Linley, and sister, Alicia Lefanu. We find also Joseph Hume†, the radical politician, who at this time had just been elected Tory

---

* Thomas John Dibdin (1771-1841). Actor and dramatist. Composer of popular song 'The Snug Little Island' (1797). Composed 'The Month of the Nile' in honour of Nelson. Prompter and pantomime writer at Drury Lane, when the theatre re-opened after the fire. Wrote nearly 2000 songs and 200 operas and plays.

† Joseph Hume (1777-1855). Main concern was public expenditure.

M.P. for Weymouth. Hume's Address is a poor piece of work, scrappily put together, probably in haste and was possibly a first and only draft. His verses include some inferior Skeltonic doggerel entirely unsuited to the dignity of the occasion:

> Hurrying ran
> The crimson Ban:
> While many a fane [temple]
> Gives Thames a stain,
> Which Thames discharges on its banks again.[31]

Some members of the Committee itself had 'entered the lists', for we discover the name of the Hon. George Lamb.[*] Even Samuel Whitbread is there, though his Address is nowhere to be found, presumably secretly withdrawn or destroyed by arrangement with the Secretary of the Committee, Charles Ward, to avoid any unfavourable publicity. Charles Lamb, poet and essayist friend of Thomas Hood and other contributors of the *London Magazine*, is also thought to have competed, but no evidence can be found that he did so. Perhaps his Address and sealed paper were also destroyed like those of Whitbread.

It might be expected to find more illustrious names among the competitors: poets Samuel Rogers and Thomas Campbell, for example, or, as were previously mooted, the names of Walter Scott and Robert Southey; instead, we suffer the poetical outpourings of a host of minor poetasters, each with an unfailing belief in his own neglected genius, soon, it was hoped, to be brought to light by this most fortuitous of events:

> Whether the greater Bards disdained competition; or whether a subject so obvious led the Writers into [equally] obvious thoughts; or, lastly, whether the Minor Poets were too feeble to hit the giant expectations of the Committee, cannot be decided; but certainly that Learned Body pronounced, on reading, or not reading them, that for some reason or other, <u>all</u> the Addresses presented were objectionable...[32]

Byron's reservations on the matter were reported in the press:

> It was not until the plebeian swarm of Candidates had

Promoted policy of retrenchment. Tory member for Weymouth (1812).

[*] George Lamb (1784-1834). Son of 1st Viscount Melbourne and brother-in-law of Lady Caroline Lamb. Wrote plays and opera. Translator of Catullus (1821). Successful MP and Government Minister.

been brushed aside, that his Lordship could be induced to bask in the full sunshine of Encouragement. The 'Noble Childe'* disdained to enter the lists with unknown Knights. Perhaps this was an error of judgment.[33]

A selection of 'Elegant Extracts' composed by this 'plebeian swarm' provides an interesting insight into the problems that faced the doughty band of readers. One contributor, William Burton, a house-painter and glazier, helped in his way to assist the reader by writing in such an illegible hand that precious time did not have to be wasted in deciphering it, and the words, 'A Prose Address in so bad a hand I have not attempted to read it,' were scribbled across it. The original Address in the British Library shows that the judgment was unfair since his handwriting was by no means the illegible scrawl it was made out to be. It may be assumed, from a reading of his Address, that he was a young man with pride in his work, that he may after all have been employed at Drury Lane (indeed almost certainly was, for his knowledge of the interior is faultless) during the final stages of the rebuilding. He seemed to know a great deal about the architectural intention that lay behind the design of the separate parts of the theatre, and his naïve assessment of its qualities, and enthusiastic response to the splendours of its auditorium show a degree of sensibility approaching, even occasionally excelling, that of his more sophisticated and erudite rivals. Unfortunately, no one had told him that it was customary to compose an Address in rhyming couplets, and it is just as well he did not try. It is tempting to imagine him, during his lunch break, sitting perched at the top of his ladder, surveying his handiwork with that kind of satisfaction that derives from a job well done, and labouring to emulate the style of speech-making he perhaps had heard many times before at official openings of buildings he had worked on:

> Ladies and Gentlemen – The Proprietors of this Theatre, beg leave to congratulate the Publick on the Completion of this House, which has been built under the direction of Mr. Wyatt, a gentleman on whose well know[n] abilities any encomium would be superfluous, for if this Audience and the Publick are as well pleased with this Theatre as the Committee nothing short of compleat Satisfaction will be the result – several arrangements and improvements have been made in this Theatre peculiar to itself, particularly respecting the Boxes and the Apartments

---

* 'Noble Childe' is a reference to *Childe Harold*, a long poem in Spenserian stanzas (written between 1809 and 1818) describing Byron's travels through Europe.

> leading thereto, in which it is hoped that elegance and convenience have been united. It has also been deemed necessary to finish the external part of this Theatre in a style of simplicity and neatness that the more might be expended on internal decorations which will be found (we trust) to exhibit an exuberance of ornament, splendor and magnificence, that has never perhaps been surpassed in Europe, & the construction of the Theatre is on Philosophical principles, that give the greatest possible accession to the Auditory of the Audience, etc.[34]

Is that not written with a touching sincerity? However, had the Committee bothered to read the Address, they would not have been impressed by the following unexpected inclusion:

> It is not the intention of this Address, Ladies and Gentlemen, to say that all Theatrical Eccellence [sic] is confined to Drury Lane exclusively, each Theatre in this Metropolis has its attractions and its Merit & the Proprietors of this Theatre recommend to the Public to visit each, and give the Preference where Preference is due.[35]

He was right to choose as his motto: 'I wish to please but dare not hope', as well might the rest of the competitors have done, though others contrived to use mottos which not only revealed a lack of confidence in the exercise but also served as armour against hurt pride. Such literary prescriptions as 'Modesty offered', 'Prend moy tel que je suis', 'Je vive en espoir', 'To be or not to be', and 'Fate must determine whether it can be named', are indicative of the crisis of confidence that spread like a virus through the veins of the anxious poets. One contestant adapted lines from Dryden's translation of Juvenal and unwittingly summed up the general feeling of the Committee:

> For, since the world with writing is possest,
> In spite, I'll do my best,
> And make as much waste paper as the rest.[36]

Eugenius Roche (or Roach) wisely entitled his verses 'Address, To be, or not to be, spoken at the opening of Drury Lane.' They were *not* to be, and suffered the same fate as the prose Address by the glazier, William Burton, which was modestly 'intended to be spoken' at the opening of Drury Lane.

Paucity of talent and undue haste were the principle causes of the

Chapter 5 – The Great Literary Competition of 1811

neurotic crisis that overwhelmed a large number of the competitors. Not all however suffered from modesty, rather the lack of it, sending all manner of covering letters justifying their verses to the despairing Committee. Joseph Hamilton ('Josephus') went so far as to have his Address printed privately, including a highly pedantic preamble thus:

> The author, aware that the number of his rivals must preclude the possibility of the committee perusing each address, obeys the advice of friends possessing established critical judgment by placing this effort in a fair and conspicuous shape before the judges for which purpose and to facilitate its correct perusal he presents a printed copy.[37]

Whilst no refusal of the address could be allowed on the grounds of illegibility, the reason for its rejection might suggest a considerable degree of unreadability.

Some indication of the subject matter that preoccupied the ruminating authors may be seen in the references to architecture, music, Greek mythology, and other predictable metaphorical peculiarities contained in the address by J. Wade (whose literary reputation has, not surprisingly, sunk without trace), we are asked to believe 'the Builders sweet! belov'd! divine!' and:

> E'en our Skill'd Wyatt must the contest yield
> And Conquerors own them in the Building Field.[38]

The 'magic sweet' is still to be found at Drury, and thus:

> The Youth and Sage the Dame in Clusters sweep —
> The Blooming Lass, all, at Drury, have — a Peep![39]

Wade's Address was accompanied by a series of notes not only to the actor, who would, in the event of success in the competition recite the verses, but to various members of the Committee to ensure that they fully understood the motives that lay behind his decision to enter the fray. He had included some rather coarse lines, more in keeping with the prologue to a Restoration Comedy than an elegant opening night at a shining new theatre. To the actor, he thought it best to explain his intention more clearly:

> 'N.B. – I insert these [lines] with inverted commas, to show that they may be omitted (or spoken) in the Representation. Tho', by the bye, Shakespeare himself

has sometimes broader Phrases!'[40]

To the Secretary of the Committee, Charles Ward, he composed an extraordinary piece of toadying sycophancy:

> Most Worthy Sir, – Conformable to your very laudable Advert, I enclose the New Address. Trusting in your accustomed, Impartial, and very Gentlemanlike manner, you will be pleased to lay it before the Gentlemen of the Committee for Impartial Investigation. Should I or should I not prove the successful Candidate, it shall in nowise lessen the unalterable Gratitude, Well-wishing, and Esteem I shall ever bear – Yrs sincerely, J. Wade.[41]

To Samuel Whitbread, he dispatched a copy of his Address with an accompanying letter beginning: 'Hon. Sir, – The Enclosed Addressed is submitted for your graphic and superior opinion....'[42]

For fear of an impostor claiming the authorship of his verses, he carefully quoted the first two and the last two lines for the attention of his recipients. Nothing came of it, in spite of all his efforts to win the coveted accolade. It was not surprising, for even after all this, he found it necessary to add a postscript and a note to avoid any misunderstanding on the appointed reader's part:

> P.S. Pray excuse me in my haste not having time to send for the wax. [He used black wax instead of red]
>
> N.B. You are at free Liberty to curtail or alter what you please.[43]

The reader chose not to permit himself such a liberty and promptly rejected the Address.

Of the 112 Addresses, some twenty have no name appended and thus the identities of their authors remain unknown. Some Competitors ignored the Committee's request for a pseudonym and wrote in under their real names. Some pseudonyms are lost or erased. Thus sometimes we know the pseudonym and not the real name, sometimes the real name only, and occasionally neither.

The fashion for signing off with a Latin name in journals and periodicals of the day encouraged the authors of the Addresses to hide behind such tongue-in-cheek names as 'Marcus Junius Brutus', 'Varius', 'Incognitus', 'Pragmaticus', 'Histrionicus', 'Immerito', 'Veritas', 'Humilitas' and 'Modestas'. One contributor, David Lee Steel, concealed his identity more thinly by adopting the anagrammatical pseudonym, 'Levet Desdaile'. Others used initials, some contrived and enigmatic, such as:

Chapter 5 – The Great Literary Competition of 1811

'Z', 'BCY2', 'T. J .Z .Z.' and 'w^w_w w'.

Another vain attempt arrived with the following quaint letter of introduction penned by a young Quaker poetess:

Respected Friend,

> The spirit hath moved me to compose an Address for the opening of the new Play house in Bridge Street which I presume will more properly be called Drury Lane Theatre. I have therefore [MS. torn here] the same to thee trusting thou wilt do me the kindness to lay this my first Theatrical production before the Board of Criticks for their perusal observing that I shall be very much surprized [*sic*] indeed if out of the number of Addresses which may be forthcoming upon this Momentous occasion they should in their superior wisdom select mine – wishing thee the fair fruits of thy laudable zeal in the Publick service

I remain thine assured Friend.

Anne Page[44]

Two other female contributors, one then little known and one never to be heard of again, were foolhardy enough to try their pens. Mary Mackay, who hopefully described herself as 'The Poetess of Nature', we can confidently dismiss. The other, whose poetical attempt was 'scarcely calculated to impress the Committee'[45] chose to trace the drama from its earliest days up to the evening of 10 October 1812 when, she suggested, it had reached its height. Her thoughts on the 'Drama Primitive' conclude with the lines:

> Such was the Drama, when its course began;
> So impotent! So rude! For such was man.[46]

It is inconceivable that such lines could come from the pen of the author of *Our Village*. She may have wished to seek a means of bringing herself to the notice of the Committee, for she had some pretensions towards the drama, but Mary Russell Mitford's[*] successes in that direction did not come until some years later when she was already an established writer.[47] Her rejected Address began with the lines that would have

---

[*] Mary Russell Mitford (1787-1855) Novelist and dramatist. As well as *Our Village* she wrote sketches of country life for *The Lady's Magazine*. *Recollections of a Literary Life* (1852). Much admired by John Ruskin.

seemed to an excited first night audience an absurd irrelevance:

> Of Genius with a savage Nature sprung
> The Drama rose when Man and Mind were young.
> Rose, such as now, o'er-canopied by trees,
> And lighted by the Sun, the Indian Seas.

The Address ends with the peculiar lines:

> Secure that all flames you may defy,
> Except th'unburning flames of Woman's eye.[48]

Some credit at least must be afforded her for her melodramatic lines on the fire itself:

> It was a night
> Of pain and anguish, horror and affright.
> To aid or mourn the assembled Senate sped;
> E'en the dull peasant, starting from his bed,
> Cried, 'London is in flames!' as blazed the Dome,
> And blessed the God who gave his village home.
> The artisan his shrieking infant grasped;
> The wife more fondly her sick husband clasped;
> Needless to them the taper's feeble ray,
> A light was there which mocked the garish day.[49]

It soon became clear that some of the competitors were themselves actors or dramatists, or were in some other way connected with the theatre. George Daniel, an eminent theatrical antiquary and book-collector, as well as a concocter of squibs on royal scandals, wrote certainly two farces for Drury Lane. Francis Godolphin Waldron, who had acted in London from 1769, brought out fairly feeble comedies and adaptations from 1773 to 1804, and was the first actor to play the part of Sir Christopher Hatton in Sheridan's *The Critic* in 1779. He called himself 'Immerito' in the modest hope of being accorded even some small merit by the Committee, but his Address, beginning 'Hail splendid pile – thou newly risen sun', did not impress them one iota. As for the mysterious 'Juba', he composed his Address in the form of a parody of *The Critic* 'To be spoken by a Poor Author and a Fat Cook. In Character.' Since an actor was to recite the Address, he was presumably to act both parts:

Chapter 5 – The Great Literary Competition of 1811

>   Author: New Drury – competition – let me see –
>   Poh! 'tis some hoax – I'm sure it cannot be,
>   This way of Puffing must be done away,
>   For who will write, without the hope of pay?
>   Cook: Honor will be your reward —
>   Author: What do I get while with the Muse I sing,
>   Will Honor, a poor Poet's dinner bring?
>   Cook: You'll get Notoriety. Fame —
>   Perchance be class'd next the Lesbian Dame[*];
>   With that fair Maid you'll coupled be, I say.
>   Author: Will that the calls of piercing hunger stay?[50]

At one point, a fire engine was supposed to be dragged onto the stage (presumably by horses) and firemen were to rush on with their hoses at the ready, to introduce the lines:

> Why Ladies in the Boxes drown the Players
> And with their Engines play – stentorian airs;[51]

George Brewer, who left the Swedish navy to become an attorney in London, and wrote a number of dramas, also sent in a dramatised dialogue, this time between John Bull and a 'North Briton' (a Scot), followed by a Welshman, and an Irishman, expressed in such lines as: 'We'll do the Huse, Sir, aw the gude we can.'[52] This too was rejected.

The best known of this group of contributors was Sheridan's brother-in-law, William Linley,[†] who had worked with the East India Company in Madras and returned to London, where he wrote several farces for Drury Lane, including *Harlequin Captive; or, The Magic Fire*, one of countless farces and pantomimes of the Harlequin theme. Linley suffered a number of failures in the theatre, to one of which Sheridan contributed some deliberately second-rate dialogue in order to secure its unsuccess. Being placed in a position of having to defend himself, Sheridan replied: 'Bill Linley has a good situation in the Company's service – why does he not go back to India? If his damned farce had succeeded, we should have had him here for the rest of his life, scratching his head in a garret, or

---

[*] Sappho, 7th century Greek poet, born on the island of Lesbos.
[†] William Linley (1771-1835) Composer. Produced the comic opera, *The Honeymoon*. Collected Shakespeare's dramatic lyrics, with music by various composers, in two volumes. Wrote novels and verses.

twiddling his thumbs in the green-room, instead of saving rupees enough to come back and loll in his carriage.' Linley wished to propitiate the Committee and to that end inserted into his Address lines praising them to the skies, but the general tenor of his poetical efforts can be seen in the oddly-composed lines:

> No longer, now shall would-be Garricks feel
> The Morning tortures of a cooling Heel;
> Catch longing peeps at the bright Kendal coals,
> The Urn hot smoking and the buttered Rolls.[53]

Looked at in a modern light, these lines have freshness and a ring to them that is lacking in the pedestrian scribblings of many of the Drury Lane poets, but it was sadly dated. With the re-opening of the new Theatre Royal, impoverished actors no longer had to tramp the wintry London streets, wistfully gazing at the street sellers with their hot tea and rolls:

> No longer now shall Authors leave their plays
> To rot in Bags of Managerial Baize.[54]

The critics and the orange-sellers were back in business again. Artfully, Linley makes a sly dig at the politics of Pitt and Peel's Irish policies (his nick-name was 'Orange' Peel), for critics are:

> But Critics of the Pit, and you on high
> Whose Peels of Orange thunder thro' the Sky[55]

A recurring theme that ran reckless and unimpeded through the multitude of Addresses was the irresistible shibboleth of 'Shakespeare'. One, Philip Martineau, begins his Address:

> Yes it is past — the gloomy day is o'er.
> And we can say thank Heav'n we breathe once more.[56]

The lines are not promising. After mentioning Congreve[*], Belvidera (a role made famous by Mrs. Siddons), and several of Shakespeare's plays, he ends by hoping the spark of Genius will be fanned to a flame:

---

[*] William Congreve (1617-1729). Irish playwright. Plays include *Love for Love* (1695) and *The Way of the World* (1700).

Chapter 5 – The Great Literary Competition of 1811

> Thus may new Shakespeares gild some future age
> New Garricks tread where Garrick trod the stage.⁵⁷

This Address is the only one to be marked 'Rejected Addresses', which suggests it was at the top of a pile of unsuccessful entries on Whitbread's desk. The name of W. Patterson should be included in the long line of self-parodists, for he began his Address with the unconsciously comical lines:

> Shakespeare exclaims, Oh, for a Muse of Fire!
> But had he seen the conflagration dire,
> That drown'd Old Drury, sure he'd ne'er have sought her,
> But cried as loudly for a Muse of Water!⁵⁸

In such a case, there is no room for parody, for the original is already a parody of itself. A more eccentric piece of flummery was an Address in the style of a sort of 'Rowley poem'⁵⁹ beginning:

> Some Poems writting by THOMAS NEAVILLE
> On the Abilitys of WILLIAM SHAKSPEARE.
>
> When Shakespeare rained in this our Native shore,
> Fame stampt his vairse as in the Days of yore.

The whole is inscribed in an erratic scrawl that would have shamed Chatterton* and definitely deterred the most diligent of readers.

A sense of dread may well have assaulted the reader of the verses sent in by 'Incognitus', who went to great pains to conceal his identity, confusing the Committee by signing himself with his pseudonym even in his sealed paper which was supposed to bear his real name. His Address was of the utmost banality. Once he had shed 'eternal wreaths,.,.o'er Valour's brow', and scattered 'glory round the Patriot's head', he goes into a lengthy account of the history of the Stage up to the time when 'your Shakespear warbled' – after which anything was possible.⁶⁰

Outshining the flabby inspiration of the 'Bard', as the contestants frequently called Shakespeare, there was the ever-recurring image of the

---

* Thomas Chatterton (1752-1770). Poet. Presented his 'antique' verses as genuine medieval poems under a borrowed name, the *Rowley Poems*. Lodged in London, where he suffered extreme poverty and took his own life by taking arsenic. His collected works appeared in 1803. Hood cleverly parodied Chatterton's style.

'Phoenix'. Hardly had it ascended from the blazing ruins of Old Drury in one Address than it was recalled to the flames and was taking flight again in the next. A certain Samuel Grigg, whose manuscript was endorsed by the despairing reader, 'Read – this one is very unfit,' commenced his lucubration:

> Lo in Majestic Pride behold sublimely rise!
> Erst like the plum'd Phoenix, or in her flames she dies.[61]

He added insult to injury by forgetting to pay the postage on his packet. Samuel Whitbread is said to have made so much of the Phoenix image in his Address (further proof that he wrote one) that Sheridan described the work as that of a 'rhapsodising poulterer'[62] though this remark has been described as 'a flight of humour' on Sheridan's part.[63] Nevertheless, 'every Reader will be on the look-out for the Phoenix, and assuredly he will not be disappointed! That rare bird has deigned to appear *frequently* in honour of the New Theatre.'[64]

A certain John Neville of Dublin included some laughable lines in his Address (which he calls an 'Occasional Prologue', thus linking it with the long tradition of Prologues delivered on the stage of Drury Lane):

> Long in a heap of rubbish has it laid
> Till by our Friends and by our country's aid
> Again it lifts its columns to the skies
> See a new Phoenix from her ashes rise
> Outstripping all done heretofore by far,
> 'Tis not a Frigate — but a man of War[65]

Drury is fitted out for sailing, with its officers at their stations under command of Captain Bobadil*.

The ubiquitous bird persisted, in spite of such flights of fancy, in many of the Addresses, though some of the poets, wishing to avoid the fashion, thankfully replaced it with a volcano:

> When first Vesuvius with tremendous ire
> Burst in a deluge of destructive fire...[66]

This was very much the kind of approach the poets took if they felt any compulsion to describe the blazing shell of Drury. But to most, the image

---

* Captain Bobadil, character in Jonson's *Everyman in His Humour*: an old soldier, boastful and cowardly.

of the Phoenix was irresistible, as in the Address by a Mr. Paul ('Esperanza'): 'To be spoken in the character of the Comic Muse', with the Stage directions: 'Curtains rising, discover Thalia binding a garland round the Brows of the Statue of Shakespeare':

> 'Sweets to the sweet'[*] — and be this Classic shrine.
> Dear to the Muse immortal. Shakespeare thine![67]

After Drury's 'never dying name' rises 'a Phoenix from the flame', and in the confusion of epithets, the bewildered bird is asked to aid 'the good ship Drury in distress.'

One extraordinary entry, by a Mr. Field, attempts to draw an analogy in which the deluge of water used to extinguish the fire is seen as the Flood, with Drury as the Ark. He might just as well have turned Whitbread into a pantomime Noah and Sheridan into Dame Noah, such was the extravagance of the comparison.

In spite of indications that the Committee were largely against the inclusion of panegyrical outbursts about British military might and British military and naval heroes, many competitors seized the opportunity to throw in, where they could, references to Marlborough, Nelson and Wellington:

> Whatever a conflagration may suggest, particularly of a Play-house, it is not easy to find exact propriety in political allusions. Yet the temptation to be applauded is so strong and there fortunately topics so secure, that he who expected a Phoenix may not be surprised to find a WELLINGTON.[68]

Moreover, a Wellington, who, in the bombast of certain of the Addresses, returns home to 'the virtuous applause of a liberal and grateful People!' One of the competitors, a Thomas Adam of Cheapside, fell into this way of thinking when, after giving the stage-direction, 'Applauses', then expected the actor (in this case, the distinguished Robert William Elliston) to walk forward to the footlights and recite the peculiar lines:

> What sounds, what joys, now greet my pensive ears,
> Calls to past memory some grateful tears.

If 'pensive ears' unnerved the Reader, how much more so did the lines that followed:

---

[*] 'Sweets to the sweet, Farewell' – *Hamlet* Act V, Scene I

> Of wonders in the world there's seven straight,
> May Drury's fame renown'd yet form the eight,
> That England may with pride her name resound,
> Therein record'd one Wonder more be found,
> WELLINGTON and VICT'RY IN COURSE OF TIME,
> Will make thyself Great England Number Nine.[69]

The reader endorsed the manuscript 'This one is very unfit indeed,' – a sentence that might have been passed on a very large majority of the Addresses, which only confirms Walter Jerrold's judgment that they were an 'undistinguished medley of skimble-skamble stuff.'

In the end, it is scarcely surprising that none of the Addresses was considered to be suitable for such an elegant and august occasion. With very few exceptions, they failed to reach the standards of poetic skill and inspiration required by the Committee – hardly surprising in the brief time allowed for the competitors to raise the reluctant Phoenix from its nest in the flames. The entries were either too short or too long, too flippant or too pedantic, too naïve or too learned, and, like the proverbial curate's egg, 'only good in parts'. The Committee had no alternative but to abandon their original scheme and, with only days to go before the grand opening of the theatre, look round for some other solution which, *faute de mieux*, would fill the embarrassing gap in the programme caused by the absence of the already much-publicised Address.

It was at this point that one member of the Committee (Lord Holland) wrote to another member of the Committee (Lord Byron) begging him to supply the much-needed verses. It might be supposed that the Committee could have approached Sir Walter Scott, Samuel Rogers, William Wordsworth, Samuel Taylor Coleridge, or even the Poet Laureate Robert Southey – all eventually parodied in *The Rejected Addresses* by Horace and James Smith. However, such an invitation would have been unwise, for the Committee could not discount the reactions of the host of competitors whose frenzied scribblings had been rejected. The hopeful applicants awaited with excitement, some even with a passion, the expected announcement that one of their number had been awarded the coveted laurels of Drury. They would not have tolerated an outsider, however august a personage. Byron, being a member of the Committee, would have been in more of a position to stand his ground should there be any serious opposition.

As it was, a theatrical sensation resulted, which gave the Sneers and Dangles* of the London press a field-day. Meanwhile, the long-suffering,

---

* Characters in Sheridan's *The Critic*.

gently persuasive Lord Holland set about the business of encouraging the reluctant Byron in his task of providing the urgently-needed Address. The reasons for Byron's unwillingness and subsequent acquiescence require some explanation, for they not only shed light on a neglected corner of Byron studies but help to bring to life again a long-forgotten episode in the history of a great theatre.

Phoenix of Drury Lane

CHAPTER SIX

A Noble Lord and His Noble Critic

1. The French Connection: The Holland House Set

The relationship between an author and his critic is invariably of absorbing interest to scholars and readers alike and, when the critic happens to be a remarkable man in his own right, we cannot resist the temptation to delve more deeply. But for the intervention of the third Lord Holland in the life of the sixth Lord Byron on 13 September 1812, there might never have been an Address for the opening of the new Theatre Royal, Drury Lane at all. Lord Holland was the leader of his Party in Parliament and married to one of the most celebrated hostesses in Europe; Byron was one of the most universally admired poets of his time, adored by women of all ranks from serving-maids to countesses, author of an audacious satire on his contemporaries and recognisably a genius.

Henry Richard Vassall-Fox, third Lord Holland, was well acquainted with fire, since he had been miraculously saved by his mother in his first year of life from a great conflagration that consumed the family home, Winterslow House in Wiltshire, in 1774. He inherited the title at the age of one, and on the death of his mother when he was only five years old, he was left to the care and tutelage of his uncles, the Earl of Upper Ossory[*] and Charles James Fox[†]. He was then sent to Eton and Christ Church, Oxford, where he became a friend of George Canning[‡], the nephew of a Whig banker, and since the liberal politics of the Whig Party were popular with Oxford undergraduates of the day, such friendships undoubtedly helped to establish his own political leanings for the future. Fox travelled widely in Europe, meeting Napoleon in Paris in 1802 and Murat in Naples in 1814, and later disagreed with Napoleon being made a prisoner-of-war.

During his last year at Oxford, Lord Holland visited Paris, where he met Talleyrand[§] and Lafayette[*]. It is difficult to see what the youthful,

---

[*] Earl of Upper Ossory (Richard Fitzpatrick 1747-1813). Politician and wit. Lifelong friendship with Charles James Fox. One of the chief writers of *The Rolliad*.

[†] Charles James Fox (1749-1806). Prominent Whig statesman whose parliamentary career spanned 38 years of the late 18th and early 19th centuries. Over-indulged by his doting father. Made himself unpopular through speeches against the liberty of the press. Interviewed Bonaparte in 1802. As Foreign Secretary under Grenville, revealed plot to assassinate Napoleon and open negotiations with France.

[‡] George Canning (1770-1827). Statesman. Deplored French Revolution. Supported William Pitt. Planned seizure of Danish fleet (1807). Fought duel with Castlereagh. Refused office under Spencer Percival. Resigned as favouring Queen Caroline. Shielded Greece from the Turks. Friend of Sir Walter Scott.

[§] Charles Maurice de Talleyrand, French bishop and politician. Foreign Minister. Distrusted by those who served under him, but Napoleon found him

Chapter 6 – A Noble Lord and his Noble Critic

liberty-loving lord could possibly have in common with 'a sly, cunning, and malicious man' like Talleyrand, who, 'thrust into Orders against his will, had at the age of thirty-five just acquired a bishopric as a reward for his wit, his social gifts, and his unblushing careerism.'[1] But the friendship was to flourish in later years at a time when France had found some degree of political stability. When Talleyrand wished to read his memoirs at Holland House one evening in January 1832, Lord Holland, ever a sensitive and sympathetic critic, listened and admired:

> 20 January. Remained at home. Talleyrand in the evening read the early part of his memoirs, beautifully written, full of wit and feeling. He was shy and nervous in reading them! They spoke of great taste and delicacy but with deep and natural feeling of the conduct of his parents, and mother in particular, who neglected and slighted him in his childhood and forced him into the Church when grown up, from an indulgence of their passions of family pride and wounded vanity on his becoming lame from an accident during his infancy. He sat up till three. I could have sat up till sunrise and from thence to sunset to hear these memoirs.[2]

Whilst it is tempting to look still further into the reasons that brought these two remarkable men together in an atmosphere of mutual respect and esteem, a friendship which endured for many years after their first meeting in 1791, such a venture, fascinating in itself, would be outside the scope and purpose of this book. The personal relationship between the future leader of the Moderate Whigs in the British Parliament and the man who would be responsible for the restoration of the French monarchy under Louis XVIII is no less interesting than their political association. The parallel with Byron is also apposite since both he and Talleyrand had suffered lameness from infancy, with its resulting shyness, and both had to contend with difficult relationships with their mothers. Perhaps Byron saw too much of himself in Talleyrand to feel comfortable with his ideas and political stance, for when John Cam Hobhouse[†] returned from Paris to

---

useful. His name is synonymous with crafty, cynical diplomacy. Opposed Napoleon's wars with Austria, Prussia and Russia (1805-6).

[*] Lafayette, Marquis de (1757-1834). French aristocrat. Fought for United States in America Revolution. Close friend of George Washington and Thomas Jefferson. Prominent in French Revolution. Refused to participate in Napoleon's government. Supported Louis-Philippe.

[†] John Cam Hobhouse (1786-1869). Travelled with Byron through Greece and Turkey. Wrote personal observations of Bonapartist account of The Hundred Days. Imprisoned in Newgate for breach of privilege 1819. Byron's executor.

report on the situation there, and Byron learned of the strength of the support of the English Tories for the French king-maker and his new King, he wrote down some vicious paragraphs, perhaps intended for a newspaper but never published in his lifetime, describing Talleyrand as the 'living record of all that public treason, private Treachery, and moral Infamy can accumulate in the person of one degraded being.'[3]

Lord Holland's acquaintance with General Lafayette was less subtle than his friendship with Talleyrand. Lafayette's enthusiasm for the cause of liberty had great popular appeal among the citizens of Paris. Quixotic and gallant as he was, he had given up his life to 'the destruction of despotism and the liberty of mankind,' and 'complacently expected a gradual and peaceful change from feudalism to social equality, from absolutism to limited monarchy, and from the rule of privilege to representative government.'[4] All these views could be held in varying degrees by both English Whigs and French 'Girondistes.'[*] 'Louis Philippe,' wrote Lord Holland, 'owed his crown to Lafayette, the republican.'[5] At a festival to mark the anniversary of the fall of the Bastille, Lafayette swore to support the Constitution, but as Queen Marie-Antoinette remarked: 'I clearly see that Monsieur de Lafayette wishes to save us, but who will save us from Monsieur de Lafayette?' To the young undergraduate from Oxford, however, he was the champion of liberty and the idol of the people, and however vague the deeper aspects of those attributes appeared to Lord Holland at the time, the more emotional and superficial impressions of his first meeting with the French General were satisfying to his Whiggish sympathies at home.

Furthermore, the year 1791 was a crucial turning point in the process of revolution. Unemployment was never worse, causing great bitterness among the lower orders of French society. Many people no longer voted. In March, Mirabeau died,[†] 'shocked at the idea that he had contributed only to a vast demolition.' Worst of all, the King, no longer free to act according to his own conscience, fled from Paris, was recognised, arrested and brought back to the howling Parisian mobs. Only months later, in June, the Jacobins, angry at Lafayette's moderate sympathies, condemned him as 'a rascal, a traitor, and an enemy of the Fatherland.'

In such rapidly changing, dangerous and volatile times, the young

---

Advised destruction of Byron's Memoirs.

[*] Girondistes. Group of moderate Republican party members in the French Legislative Assembly (1791-2), led by deputies from the Gironde district near Bordeaux, who tried to restrain Robespierre and his followers.

[†] Comte de Mirabeau (1715-1789). French economist, who played an important part in the early days of the Revolution. President of the Constituent Assembly. Author of *Testament Politique* (1747). 'He was a man of fiery eloquence and a cool politician' (OCEL).

Chapter 6 – A Noble Lord and his Noble Critic

Lord Holland continued his Grand Tour of Northern Europe through Denmark and Prussia. After a short spell in England, he set off for Spain and Italy. While on a visit to Naples, he made the acquaintance of the fascinating Elizabeth Vassall, Lady Webster.

Elizabeth Vassall was the daughter of Richard Vassall, a wealthy planter in Jamaica, who had brought his family to England before the American Revolution. When she was sixteen years of age, she married Sir Godfrey Webster of Battle Abbey in Sussex, a man twenty-three years her senior. After a chance encounter with Lord Holland, who was then midway through a three-year sojourn in Florence, she spent much of her time in his company. Suspicious of their patent intimacy, Sir Godfrey sought to dissolve the marriage on the ground of adultery by her with Lord Holland. The news created a great scandal, for not only did the matter necessitate a number of parliamentary enquiries, the whole business was extremely costly to her, and the fact that she had already given birth to an illegitimate son, Charles Richard Fox, made the affair a major *cause célèbre* of 1797. Three days after her marriage was dissolved, she married Lord Holland, such was her passion and her pride, for she would not only become the most celebrated Lady Holland of all, but she would one day reign over what was to be one of the most famous salons in Europe, the haunt and venue of statesmen, men of letters and wits. Holland House had just been restored and refurbished. Here, she would one day become Carlyle's 'proud old dame', welcoming men of promise in political and literary circles, so long as they reached her exacting standards of wit and worldly knowledge. She possessed the great gift of 'making her guests display themselves to the best advantage. Traits in her character that were by no means attractive rendered her power of fascination the more extraordinary.'[6] Cyrus Redding[*] thought her polite, cold, haughty, and offensive to those to whom she took a dislike. Thomas Moore,[†] whose verses she described as 'vulgar' and whose *Life of Sheridan* she referred to as a tasteless romance, remarked that poets 'inclined to a plethora of vanity would find a dose of Lady Holland now and then very good for their complaint.'[7] On one occasion, Matthew Gregory Lewis[‡] bemoaned the fact that he was parodied in

---

[*] Cyrus Redding (1785-1870). Published an autobiography, reminiscences, a history of wine-making and books on county history.

[†] Thomas Moore (1779-1852) Educ. Trinity College, Dublin. Considered as Ireland's national poet. Known more widely in Europe for his *Lalla Rookh* (1817), his life of Byron, and for editing Byron's *Letters and Journals*. Burnt Byron's *Memoirs* on orders from family. Supported 'United Irishmen' movement.

[‡] Matthew Gregory Lewis (1775-1818), known as 'Monk Lewis' for his lurid Gothic novel *The Monk*. His poetry was a great influence on the earlier poetry of Walter Scott.

Rejected Addresses as a writer of burlesque, a literary form he never attempted in his life, to which Lady Holland replied: 'You don't know your own talent.'[8]

Lady Holland's manner at table was amiable to some and daunting to others of her guests, but she always kept a tight control on the drift of conversation, never allowing any one of her 'subjects' (not even her husband!) to rule in her own kingdom, never permitting any one topic to dominate too much or too long. She was known to have cut Lord Macaulay short several times in a single conversation, once sending a young page to him to ask him to stop talking as she was waiting to hear Lord Aberdeen, who could not get a word in. 'Elle est toute assertion,' said Talleyrand, whose only explanation for her insistence on dining at the unreasonably early hour of six or six-thirty was merely 'pour gêner les autres'.[9]

No account of this remarkable woman would be complete without some reference to her unbounded admiration for Napoleon, whom she had met at Malmaison in 1802, when he was First Consul. His boundless energy, powerful political vision, and heroic greatness as Emperor of France, earned him the undying respect and admiration of Lady Holland. Such attributes as these were hardly less to be admired in some of the more liberty-loving côteries of British politics as well as among men of letters. Napoleon captivated the ebullient Lady Holland. At Elba, he received a message of respect and sympathy from her. Infatuated beyond salvation, she later sent him parcels of books and Neapolitan sweetmeats during his exile on St. Helena. In return, as a mark of gratitude for her attentions, he bequeathed her a gold snuff-box given to him by Pope Pius VI. Intensely moved by his gesture, she managed to procure as relics Napoleon's ring and cross of the Legion of Honour and, oddly, a sock he had worn at his death.

Lady Holland's admiration for Napoleon was infectious, influencing Lord Holland not least among those of her circle, and was undoubtedly a view with which Byron willingly concurred on his visits to Holland House. In *Ode on the Star of 'The Legion of Honour'*, Byron conjures up a tricolour rainbow, radiant in the storm-laden skies of Europe, where there is little hope of freedom for a deposed Emperor and a bereft people:

> Star of the brave! thy ray is pale,
> And darkness must again prevail!
> But, oh thou Rainbow of the free!
> Our tears and blood must flow for thee.
> When thy bright promise fades away,
> Our life is but a load of clay.

> And Freedom hallows with her tread
> The silent cities of the dead;
> For beautiful in death are they
> Who proudly fall in her array;
> And soon, oh Goddess! may we be
> For evermore with them or thee![10]

Byron's deep-seated wish for self-dramatisation so evident in the early Cantos of *Childe Harold's Pilgrimage* undoubtedly engendered in him an attitude of mind towards the Napoleonic ideal that was entirely in keeping with his radical thinking. In *From the French*, a poem whose title might suggest a wish on his part to obviate any criticism from the more patriotic supporters of British interests in Europe, a French soldier, who has survived the carnage of the battlefield, mourns the exile of his Emperor in terms which Lord and Lady Holland would have heartily approved:

> Must thou go, my glorious Chief,
>   Sever'd from thy faithful few?
> Who can tell thy warrior's grief,
>   Maddening o'er that long adieu?
> Woman's love, and friendship's zeal,
>   Dear as both have been to me —
> What are they to all I feel,
>   With a soldier's faith for thee?[11]

Such sentiments were prevalent among the more extreme radical element of British society, a few of whom saw Napoleon as a kind of perverse saviour who would rid them of all their political and social ills:

> My chief, my king, my friend, adieu!
>   Never did I droop before;
> Never to my sovereign sue,
>   As his foes I now implore:
> All I ask is to divide
>   Every peril he must brave;
> Sharing by the hero's side
>   His fall, his exile, and his grave.[12]

For Byron, Napoleon was a 'fatally-flawed Prometheus;' he was Nietzsche's 'Fallen Titon.' In some ways, Byron's own fall from grace parallelled Napoleon's. In mythological terms, the doomed Emperor was 'the wounded god' as Byron himself would be, when the scandal surrounding the dissolution of his marriage drove him from England forever.

2. Byron's 'Ferocious Rhapsody'

Byron was able to derive much solace and encouragement from the amiable *bonhomie* that was his for the asking at Holland House. Not surprisingly, his unkind references to Lady Holland's dinner-parties (to which he had not then been invited) in *English Bards and Scotch Reviewers*, were not appreciated by the Hollands:

> Illustrious Holland! Hard would be his lot,
> His hirelings mention'd, and himself forgot!
> Holland, with Henry Petty at his back,[*]
> The whipper-in and huntsman of the pack.
> Blest be the banquets spread at Holland house,
> Where Scotchmen feed, and critics may carouse!
> Long, long beneath that hospitable roof
> Shall Grub-street[†] dine, while duns[‡] are kept aloof.
> See honest Hallam lay aside his fork,[§]
> Resume his pen, review his Lordship's work,
> And, grateful for the dainties on his plate,
> Declare his landlord can at least translate!
> Dunedin![**] View thy children with delight,

---

[*] Sir Henry Petty-Fitzmaurice, 5th Marquess of Lansdowne (1780-1863), frequently stayed with Lord Holland. He was a moderate Whig, Chancellor of the Exchequer in 1806, and supported abolition of the slave trade - 'the best hope of the Whig party'. Mentioned in the Holland Papers.

[†] Grub Street in London was the haunt of cheapjack scribblers and hack writers.

[‡] Dun, debt-collector, derives from Joe Dun, ruthless bailiff of Lincoln in Henry VII's time.

[§] Hallam, Henry (1777-1859) Historian. Vice-President of the Society of antiquaries. Contributed to *Edinburgh Review*. See Byron *Works* p864.

[**] From 'edina', an obscure poetical form.

> They write for food — and feed because they write:
> At last, when heated with the unusual grace,
> Some glowing thoughts should to the press escape,
> And tinge with red the female reader's cheek.
> My lady skims the cream of each critique;
> Breathes o'er the page her purity of soul,
> Reforms each error, and refines the whole.[13]

Some years later, when the friendship had matured, the Hollands let it be known to Byron, who was then preparing the fifth edition of *English Bards* for the press, that they wished him to withdraw the work from circulation. Lord Holland later recalled the incident:

> That extraordinary young man had satirised and ridiculed me, in common with many others, in his English Bards and Scotch Reviewers, under a very erroneous impression that I had written or caused to be written the criticism on his first publication in the Edinburgh Review; whereas it was from that printed Review that I first learnt of the existence of the poems, or indeed of the author, whose title I had thought was extinct. My friend, Mr. Rogers,* knew this circumstance; he asked if I objected to his repeating it to Lord Byron, I answered: 'Far from it, provided he repeated as he had heard it from me, a fact related in accidental conversation, and not a message or explanation sent from me to Lord Byron.' Mr Rogers soon afterwards informed me that Lord Byron wished to speak in Parliament against the Frame-breaking Bill, and that he was anxious to learn forms and to consult some peer in Opposition. Mr. Rogers asked me if I would allow him to introduce the young poet. I willingly and warmly acquiesced, gave him what assistance I could, and received from him a very handsome and well-written letter.[14]

It seems, at least from reading between the lines of Byron's letters, that Lord Holland aroused some feeling of remorse in the now older and wiser poet, for Byron attempted to make amends with those contemporaries he had criticised wherever and whenever he could. Once, for example, ridiculing Coleridge for his verses *To a Young Ass* (as the Smith brothers were similarly to pillory Wordsworth in their *Rejected*

---

* Samuel Rogers (1763-1855) Poet. Offered but declined poet-laureateship.

Addresses) Byron had written some scathing lines:

> Shall gentle Coleridge pass unnoticed here,
> To turgid ode and tumid stanza dear?
> Though themes of innocence amuse him best,
> Yet still obscurity's a welcome guest.
> If Inspiration should her aid refuse
> To him who takes a pixy for a muse,
> Yet none in lofty numbers can surpass
> The bard who soars to elegise an ass.
> So well the subject suits his noble mind,
> He brays* the laureat of the long-ear'd kind.[15]

All seems to have been forgiven, when Coleridge wrote to Byron asking him to use his influence to find a publisher for a volume of his poems. Byron went out of his way to persuade Murray to publish *Christabel* and *Kubla Khan* in 1816. As a member of the Drury Lane Committee he had, in 1813, pressed Coleridge to write a tragedy, ironically (considering Byron's insult to Coleridge) entitled *Remorse*. A postscript in a letter to Coleridge reveals Byron's deep regret for his youthful pillorying of his contemporaries in English Bards:

> ....it was written when I was very young and very angry, and has been a thorn in my side ever since; more particularly as almost all the persons animadverted upon became subsequently my acquaintances, and some of them my friends.... although I have long done every thing in my power to suppress the circulation of the whole thing, I shall always regret the wantonness or generality of many of its attacks.[16]

Not long after this he wrote to Leigh Hunt:

> ....I was angry – & determined to be witty – & fighting in a crowd dealt about my blows all alike without distinction or discernment. – When I came home from the East – among other new acquaintances & friends – politics & the Notts rioters† – (of which county I am a landholder – & Ld. Holland Recorder of the town) led me by the good offices of Mr. Rogers into the society of Ld. Holland –

---

* brays = 'praises'
† Frame breakers

who with Lady H were particularly kind to me:– about March 1812 – this introduction took place – when I made my first speech on the Frame Bill – in the same debate in which Ld. H spoke. – Soon after this I was correcting the 5th. En. of E. B.* for the press – when Rogers represented to me that he knew Ld. & Lady H would not be sorry if I suppressed any further publication of that poem – and I immediately acquiesced: & with great pleasure– for I had attacked them on a fancied and false provocation with many others – & neither was nor am sorry to have done what I could to stifle that ferocious rhapsody. – This was subsequent to my acquaintance with Lord H & was neither expressed nor understood as a condition of that acquaintance....[17]

As for Byron's hasty reaction to the sarcastic piece in the Edinburgh Review that followed the publication of his undergraduate poems *The Hours of Idleness*, and which aroused his anger and bitterness, it became only too plain to him that he had blundered. He had mistaken one lord for another. Lord Holland was too civilised a creature to criticise with such devastating acuity the gentle, poetical meanderings of a young poet. In any case, the second edition of the work was dedicated to Frederick, Earl of Carlisle,† Byron's guardian and Lord Holland's respected colleague in the Whig Party. The offending review had in fact been written by Henry Brougham,‡ who was to play such an important role in the defence of Queen Caroline in 1820, and whose identity as reviewer was still unknown to Byron even in 1813, eight years after the first publication of his 'Juvenilia'.§ Not even Carlisle, a contributor among other distinctions to Canning's *Anti-Jacobin*,[18] and who had ignored Byron's request to act as his sponsor in the House of Lords, managed to escape the fury of his wild young ward:

> No muse will cheer, with renovating smile,
> The paralytic puling of Carlyle [*sic*].

---

* i.e, Edition of *English Bards and Scotch Reviewers*
† Frederick, Earl of Carlisle (1748-1825) British diplomat. Mother was great-aunt to Lord Byron. A man of pleasure in his youth but in more sombre times he was given the vice-royalty of Ireland in 1780. Supported the dismembering the Ottoman Empire.
‡ Henry, Lord Brougham (1778-1868). Lord Chancellor. Defended Queen Caroline at her trial in 1820. Critical and historical writings published in 11 volumes 1855-61.
§ First title of *Hours of Idleness* (1807).

> The puny schoolboy and his early lay
> Men pardon, if his follies pass away;
> But who forgives the senior's ceaseless verse,
> Whose hairs grow hoary as his rhymes grow worse?
> What heterogeneous honours deck the peer!
> Lord, rhymester, petit-maitre, and pamphleteer!
> So dull in youth, so drivelling in his age
> His scenes alone had damn'd our sinking stage;
> But managers for once cried, 'Hold, enough!'
> Nor drugg'd their audience with the tragic stuff.[19]

The lines were a further reason for Lord Holland's wishing the work to be withdrawn in later years, but in a note to the poem, Byron clearly remains unrepentant:

> It may be asked, why I have censured the Earl of Carlisle, my guardian and relative, to whom I dedicated a volume of puerile poems a few years ago? – The guardianship was nominal, at least as far as I have been able to discover; the relationship I cannot help, and am very sorry for it; but as his lordship seemed to forget it on a very essential occasion to me, I shall not burden my memory with the recollection....I have heard that some persons conceive me to be under obligations to Lord Carlisle: if so, I shall be most particularly happy to learn what they are...[20]

If Byron found himself unable to tolerate Lord Carlisle in the role of *paterfamilias*, it seemed natural that he should turn to someone who could serve as his literary and political guide and mentor through the troubled years before his fatal marriage, someone who could offer advice and encouragement, and occasionally when required, a gentle reprimand. Lord Holland was Byron's senior by fifteen years, Lady Holland by eighteen years. Between them, they provided to a certain degree a stable emotional and critical centre for the 'Noble Childe'[21] that could fill the gap a brash, hysterical mother and the memory of a drunken, debauched father had miserably failed to do. The deep respect and courteous regard which Byron showed towards the Hollands possessed that happy combination of polite distance and genuine affection commonly found in the context of the nineteenth-century patrician family, a position that placed them *in loco parentis*, at a time when Byron was finding fame among the literary and political *beau monde* of London. Indeed, 1812 was to be one of the most remarkable years in his whole life.

Chapter 6 – A Noble Lord and his Noble Critic

Not only did Byron enter the society of Holland House, with all its conviviality and its gastronomic and literary satisfactions, he was soon to be invited to the London home of Lord and Lady Melbourne at Whitehall. There, the young and vivacious Caroline Lamb,[*] daughter of the Earl of Bessborough and niece of the Duchess of Devonshire, was presented with a copy of the *Childe Harold* cantos. From that moment she was eager for a meeting, and it was Lady Holland who finally introduced them. The tempestuous and romantic affair that followed, and Byron's subsequent marriage to Annabella Milbanke, the niece of Lady Melbourne, is a story that can be found elsewhere,[22] but it is worth noting here that throughout the anguished times that followed, Byron was able to find a strength and support in the society of Lady Melbourne. She was over sixty when he met her, and through their meetings and correspondence, Byron was able to open his heart in a way that would have been quite impossible with Lady Holland. Writing to Annabella in 1814, he remarked of Lady Melbourne (underlining the significant words): 'I do love that woman (filially or fraternally) better than any being on earth....'[23] Byron did not 'love' Lady Holland; he was able only to admire her, as he admired and respected her husband, and in the light of coming events at the Theatre Royal, Drury Lane, that was infinitely more important.

3. Byron: Champion of the Frame-Breakers

Having established the common ground which Byron shared with Lord and Lady Holland, it is easier to see why Byron's earlier expressions of unadulterated spleen were later transformed into expressions of loyalty and gratitude. Leaving aside the formidable hostess of Holland House, who now took on the role of *eminence rose* rather than *eminence grise* in whatever discussions she may have had with her husband on the matter of Byron's political education, a plea from Lord Holland for an Address to be performed on the opening of the new Theatre Royal, Drury Lane, filled Byron with dismay. His natural distaste for writing to order, and with so little time available to him, coupled with the guilt of refusal to the one man he respected above all others, brought upon him a sudden crisis of conscience and reminded him of his obligations to Lord Holland, whose assistance he had sought in the preparation of his maiden speech in the House of Lords.

Politically, Lord Holland was a moderate, and wisely exercised some

---

[*] Lady Caroline Lamb (1785-1828). Novelist. Daughter of 3rd Earl of Bessborough. Married William Lamb, later Viscount Melbourne, in 1805. They separated in 1825.

caution in the face of Byron's more extravagant radicalism. Lord Holland's uncle, Charles James Fox, had been the champion of liberty, and was remembered for his toast to 'Our sovereign, the people' in 1798, for which his name was erased from the Privy Council. He had been a supporter of the liberty of the press, Catholic emancipation, the removal of dissenters' disabilities, and the abolition of the slave trade, all of which his nephew gladly accepted as part of his own political creed.

By the 1790s, the Foxites had inherited the appellation of Whigs, and 'Holland's consciousness of his role as a repository of Fox's political principles,'[24] led him to consider the concept of liberty to be concomitant with that of absolute good. 'His politics in opposition acquired a consistency in his vigorous dissent from governmental measures which he deemed detrimental to liberty.'[25] His opposition to Sidmouth's* attempt to restrict the licensing of Methodist ministers was typical of the broad application of his belief, insisting that 'the right to preach was not contingent upon governmental sufferance.'[26] In 1813, he pleaded for the Jews, insisting they should be granted equal political rights with other races and denominations. 'Fox had converted his nephew to faith in party, comprised of educated and propertied aristocracy, as the proper guardian of such liberty and watchdog against encroachments of arbitrary power by crown or ministers.'[27] Such a view led to demands for conciliation in all areas of political life. Coalition with the radicals, as proposed by Samuel Whitbread, on the basis of political reform, though frowned upon by some who distrusted an affiliation with the followers of Sir Francis Burdett,† became an increasingly desirable aim.

Holland himself was suspicious of impracticable visionaries who proposed impracticable schemes that would, in his view, destroy the very institutions that sustained them.[28] In short, 'His enthusiasm for the Revolution was tempered by his own libertarianism.'[29] His view of Napoleon, in spite of Lady Holland's infatuation, was restrained. Whilst considering the Emperor an absolutist, and thus and opponent of true liberty, he praised him for his establishment of equality and justice. 'Holland was a more faithful child of the Enlightenment than was Napoleon of the Revolution. Cosmopolitan, urbane, ardent defender of liberty, and opponent of arbitrary power, reverent of the classics and fashionably anti-clerical, he exemplified the Enlightenment's secular-

---

* Henry Addington, 1st Viscount Sidmouth (1757-1844). Speaker of the House of Commons. Harsh treatment of Luddites. Checked liberty of the Press, leading to the Manchester massacre.

† Sir Francis Burdett ((1776-1844). Politician. Married Sophia Coutts in 1793. Denounced the war with France. Denounced corruption in Parliament, advocating reform. Imprisoned in 1810 and 1820 on political charges.

Chapter 6 – A Noble Lord and his Noble Critic

humanist ethos.'[30] Sidney Smith[*] remarked that 'there never existed in any human being a better heart, or one more purified from all the bad passions, more abounding in charity and compassion, and which seemed to be so created as a refuge to the helpless and the oppressed.'[31] Such was the man from whom Byron was moved to seek advice when he came to begin composing his first political speech.

Byron's short-lived interest in speech-making seems to have asserted itself in infancy, for soon after he had inherited the title, a visitor told him that she hoped one day to read his speeches in the House of Commons. He is said to have replied: 'I hope not; if you read any speeches of mine, it will be in the House of Lords.' Indeed years, during his schooldays at Harrow, he had haunted the galleries of the House of Commons, listening with a keen ear to the debates, holding in his mind the oratory of Burke and Sheridan. After his Speech Day oration, he had the notion that he would turn out 'an Orator, from my fluency, my turbulence, my voice, my copiousness of declamation, and my action.'[32]

Up at Cambridge, Byron had been attracted by the liberal ideas of the Whig Club and the Juvenalian satires of John Cam Hobhouse, the fellow-undergraduate who was to play such an important part in Byron's life during the time of the Greek Committee, and who also figures in Hood's *Progress of Cant* etching. Hobhouse's earlier discovery of the poetry of Alexander Pope was deepened through his growing friendship with Francis Hodgson, also like Hobhouse a translator of Juvenal, and an admirer of Dryden and Pope. Hodgson's father had been a friend of William Gifford,[†] the former editor of *The Anti-Jacobin*, and author of two satires, *The Maeviad* and *The Baviad*, which Byron imitated in his *British Bards* (later to be retitled *English Bards and Scotch Reviewers*), Byron's attempt at a *Dunciad* of his own.

---

[*] Sidney Smith (1771-1845). Canon of St. Paul's Cathedral. He joined Sir Francis Jeffrey and Brougham with others in starting the *Edinburgh Review* in 1802. Supporter of Catholic Emancipation. Noted for his 'exuberant drollery and wit'.

[†] Gifford, William (1756-1826). First editor of the *Quarterly Review*. The satires *The Baviad* (1794) and The *Maeviad* (1795) attack the Della Cruscans. Adversely criticised Keats's poetry.

John Cam Hobhouse

On leaving Cambridge in 1808, Byron prepared himself to take his seat in the House of Lords by temporarily abandoning his reading of poetry in favour of history and political memoirs. He wrote of his intention to his guardian, Earl Carlisle, hoping it would be possible to escape the tedious business of proving his title by being presented to the House as a near relation. Carlisle refused. Byron was deeply hurt at being snubbed, though he was certainly aware that his guardian did not hold his young ward in very high regard. The resulting delays irritated Byron to such an extent that, on the day of the ceremony, he could barely bring himself to take the welcoming hand of Chancellor Eldon as he stepped down from the Woolsack to congratulate the newly-installed Member of the House. Such a beginning was not auspicious for the success of Byron's parliamentary career, and after a waspish reply to put the Chancellor in his place, he turned his thoughts to the isles of Greece.

It is not inappropriate here to digress a little and refer to Byron's first visit to Greece, and in particular to the Acropolis of Athens, for the image is to occur in visual terms in Thomas Hood's *Cant* etching. On 8 January 1810, in the company of Hobhouse and a Neapolitan painter, Giovanni Battista Lusieri, commissioned by Lord Elgin[*] to execute drawings of the ruins (later likened to the ruins of Old Drury), Byron climbed the hill to the Parthenon and the Erechtheion. Elgin had already begun to remove the marble friezes and statues, the first consignment having been exhibited to the British public in 1807 in Park Lane, and which Byron had by no

---

[*] Lord Elgin (1766-141), 7th Earl of Elgin. Arranged for conveyance of Parthenon frieze to England in 1803-12. Employed artists to make drawings of sculptures at Athens.

means neglected to mention in *English Bards*:

> Let Aberdeen* and Elgin still pursue
> The shade of fame through regions of virtù;
> Waste useless thousands on their Phidian† freaks,
> Misshapen monuments and maim'd antiques;
> And make their grand saloons a general mart
> For all the mutilated blocks of art.³³

But now he saw the marvellous stones *in situ*. They were no longer 'mutilated blocks of art' but splendid relics of an ancient past, as it seemed to him, vandalised by British hands. Elgin (the vandal) he immortalised in *Childe Harold*:

> Dull is the eye that will not weep to see
> Thy walls defaced, thy mouldering shrines removed
> By British hands, which it had best behoved
> To guard those relics ne'er to be restored.³⁴

A similar view he expressed in his first letter to Bowles‡: 'I opposed, and will ever oppose, the robbery of ruins from Athens, to instruct the English in sculpture (who are as capable of sculpture as the Egyptians are of skating.)'³⁵ Hobhouse saw the matter in a different light, suggesting that the London exhibition of the marbles would open up new vistas for 'an infinitely greater number of rising architects and sculptors,'³⁶ which proved to be a surprisingly accurate prophecy, as *The Progress of Cant* reveals.

Whilst on his travels, Byron's predilection for self-dramatisation began to show itself in his growing identification with the cause of Greece, a country still struggling for its freedom from the Turkish yoke. The thrilling thought began to take shape in his mind that he might become a part of that revolutionary process, but first he decided he had to 'cut all my dissolute acquaintance, leave off wine and carnal company, and betake myself to politics and decorum.'³⁷ It was easier to do this in

---

* George Hamilton Gordon, 4ᵗʰ Earl of Aberdeen (1784-1860). Travelled in Greece and founded the Athenian society. Served in Wellington's and Peel's ministries. Wanted peace with France though policy of non-intervention.

† Phidias, architect of the Parthenon and superintendent of all works of art in Athens. Accused of embezzlement and wasting money on statuary.

‡ Bowles, William Lisle, (1762-1850). Poet and antiquary. Chaplain to the Prince Regent (1818). Wrote graceful sonnets.

London for the moment, and he accordingly returned there on 14 July 1811. English politics seemed to him too parochial, compared to the grandeur of the Greek cause and the hoped-for revival of that proud spirit that characterised the heroes of old. But something happened to change his mind.

In the following November, a band of Nottingham stocking weavers rioted and began breaking up their frames in the manner of Ned Ludd, who had done the same some years before in a fit of frenzy and frustration. The Luddites, as they came to be called, provided Byron with a theme which, though localised in its incidence, could serve as an illustration of the machinations of Tory politics and the suppression of the right to legitimate protest. In Byron's mind, the affair was symptomatic of larger issues concerning liberty and justice, both now well-established causes among the liberal-thinking Whigs, the moderates of whom Lord Holland was the undoubted leader. The Tory Cabinet had put together a bill which would impose the death penalty for acts of frame-breaking. A serious skirmish with the military occurred on the 29 January 1812. Through the intervention of Samuel Rogers, Byron approached Lord Holland on the possibility of using the forthcoming debate in Parliament as an opportunity of making his maiden speech. Early in February, Lord Holland dispatched to Byron some correspondence he had received on the matter, but Byron did not avail himself of it, explaining that the viewpoint of the writer did not coincide with his own:

> – For my own part, I consider the manufacturers [i.e. factory-workers] as a much injured body of men sacrificed to ye. [the] views of certain individuals who have enriched themselves by those practices which have deprived the frame workers of employment.[38]

It was all a matter of one man and a machine being able to do the work of seven men, six thus being put out of work: 'We must not allow mankind,' he wrote, 'to be sacrificed to improvements in Mechanism,'[39] for the maintenance and well-being of the 'industrious poor is an object of greater consequence' to the community than the 'enrichment of a few monopolists':

> I have seen the state of these miserable men, & it is a disgrace to a civilised country,[40] your Lordship docs not coincide with me entirely on this subject, & most cheerfully & sincerely shall I submit to your superior judgment & experience & take some other line of argument against ye. [the] bill, or be silent altogether, should you deem it more advisable. – Condemning, as every one must condemn the conduct of these wretches, I

believe in ye. existence of grievances which call rather for pity than punishment. – I have ye honour to be with great respect, my Lord, yr. Lordship's most obedt. & obliged Servt.

BYRON

P. P. – I am a little apprehensive that your Lordship will think me too lenient towards these men, & half a framebreaker myself.[41]

Byron clearly had much in common with the more radical elements in Parliament, but the dignity of his lineage held him aloof from extreme attitudes and led him in the direction of conciliatory politics. The debate on the second reading of the Bill took place on 27 February. 'With rhetorical questions and balanced sentences, with rolling periods and reasoned arguments as well as ironic contrasts, he appealed to the feelings and the humanity of his audience.'[42] Whilst Pitt, Burke and Sheridan had provided him with his blueprint, his principle weakness lay in his theatricality:

> You call these men a mob, desperate, dangerous, and ignorant;....But even a mob may be better reduced by a mixture of conciliation and firmness, than by additional irritation and redoubled penalties. Are we aware of our obligations to a mob? It is the mob that labour in your fields and serve in your houses, – that man your navy, and recruit your army, – that have enabled you to defy all the world, and can also defy you when neglect and calamity have driven them to despair! You may call the people a mob; but do not forget, that a mob too often speaks the sentiments of the people.[43]

Such words surprised and discomforted the Lords, but were a delight to Sir Francis Burdett, the leader of the Radicals in the Commons, who described it as 'the best speech by a Lord since the Lord knows when.' Lord Grenville[*] remarked that the construction of the periods was very like Burke's. As to Byron's assessment of his own performance, he wrote of it to Hodgson on 5 March: 'I spoke very violent sentences with a sort of modest impudence, abused every thing and every body, & put the Ld. Chancellor very much out of humour, & if I may believe what I hear, have not lost any character by the experiment. As to my delivery, loud and

---

[*] Grenville, William Wyndham (1759-1834). Member of 'All the Talents', which abolished the slave trade (1807). Resigned on Catholic question. Supported continuance of the war with Napoleon in 1815.

fluent enough, perhaps a little theatrical.'[44] The accuracy of this self-appraisal is borne out in the more archly rhetorical passages of his speech:

> Setting aside the palpable injustice and the certain inefficiency of the bill, are there not capital punishments sufficient in your statutes? Is there not blood enough upon your penal code that more must be poured forth to ascend to Heaven and testify against you? How will you carry the bill into effect? Can you commit a whole county to their own prisons? Will you erect a gibbet in every field, and hang up men like scarecrows?....Will the famished wretch who has braved your bayonets be appalled by your gibbets?....Will that which cannot be effected by your grenadiers, be accomplished by your executioners?[45]

In recalling Byron's performance, Lord Holland spoke as frankly as he could:

> His speech was full of fancy, wit, and invective, but not at all suited to our common notions of Parliamentary eloquence. His fastidious and artificial taste and his over-irritable temper would, I think, have prevented him from ever excelling in Parliament.[46]

Byron's 'Frame-breakers' speech enamoured neither Lords Tory nor Lords Whig, and did little to enhance his image in political circles. Nevertheless, he continued to solicit the good opinion of Lord Holland, whose respect and encouragement he so greatly valued. On the same day that he wrote to Hodgson on 5 March 1812, he sent a whimsical letter to Lord Holland enclosing a presentation copy of the newly-published cantos of *Childe Harold's Pilgrimage*, and quoting Dryden's line from *The Conquest of Granada*: 'Forgiveness to the injured doth belong'. Byron was again attempting to make amends for his 'boyish rashness'[47] in Lord Holland's earlier criticism of him in *English Bards and Scotch Reviewers*, and begging forgiveness for all his other buffooneries. Apart from a facetious letter of cheer, goodwill, and whimsical sympathy for his Lordship's gout, there seems to have been little or no official communication between the noble poet and his noble critic until September 1812, when Lord Holland had written to Byron to ask him to write an Address for the opening of the new Theatre Royal, Drury Lane. After all that had gone between them, how could Byron refuse? Burdened by the debt of gratitude, he reluctantly agreed.

Chapter 6 – A Noble Lord and his Noble Critic

Holland House, Kensington, London

The library at Holland House where Byron and Lord Holland frequently conversed.

CHAPTER SEVEN

The Reluctant Poet: Execution or Persecution?

1. The Making of the Drury Lane 'Address'

Following the scandalous behaviour of Lady Caroline Lamb[*] in August 1812, her long-suffering husband, William Lamb, heir to Lord Melbourne, lost his seat in Parliament over the Catholic Emancipation issue. It was a convenient moment to leave for Ireland with his mother-in-law, Lady Bessborough, accompanied by his recalcitrant wife, who was now in a state of collapse over the failure of her affair with Byron. Weary from the emotional strain of it, Byron was happy to accept an invitation to Cheltenham, where he could indulge himself in the peaceful pleasures of a fashionable watering-place, and pass away the time in the amiable company of the Melbournes, the Jerseys and the Hollands.

Lord Holland had become deeply involved in the plans for the grand re-opening of the Theatre Royal, Drury Lane. Seeing the hopelessness of the situation regarding the selection of an Address from among the 112 submitted to the Committee, he continued to work on Byron's good nature, hoping to receive a positive response to his appeal. However, a few days later, on 10 September 1812, Lord Holland received the following reply from Cheltenham:

> My dear Lord – The lines which I have hatched off on your hint are still or rather were in an unfinished state for I have just committed them to a flame more decisive than that of Drury, – – Under all the circumstances I should hardly wish a contest with Philo-drama – Philo-drury – Asbestos[1] Horace Twiss – and all the anonymous and synonymous[2] of the Committee candidates. – Seriously, I think you have a chance of something much better, for prologuising is not my forte, & at all events either my pride or my modesty won't let me incur the hazard of having my rhymes buried in next month's magazine under essays on the murder of Mr. Percival[†]....I am still sufficiently interested to wish to hear the successful Candidate – & amongst so many – I have no doubt – some will be excellent, particularly in an age when writing verse is the easiest of all attainments....[at Cheltenham]

---

[*] Lady Caroline Lamb (1785-1828). Her first novel, *Glenarvon*, contains a caricature portrait of Byron.

[†] Spencer Perceval (1762-1812). Opposed by Pitt, Fox and Wyndham in the Commons. Prime Minister between 1809 and 1812, when he was assassinated in the lobby of the Houses of Parliament by John Bellingham, a bankrupt who had a grievance against government fiscal policies.

Chapter 7 – The Reluctant Poet: Execution or Persecution?

> they said sing us a song of Drury Lane &c. – but I am dumb & dreary...³

Lord Holland seems to have seen some kind of 'first' attempt, and replied:

> My dear Lord, I am really concerned to find that you have burnt your address – such verses ought not to have been sacrificed to the flames which they described so well – but I am not quite disinterested in my regret as I am convinced we shall not have any address so good as yours even in the unfinished state in which I saw it – Indeed I must confess our terms of proceeding are not favourable to the production of good poetry – it is very rare that a contest for prizes produces any verses fit to be read & I believe no first rate poem had ever been written for such a purpose which considering the numerous opportunities in all countries is really extraordinary. How do you account for this? London is a desert & has not produced any news these six or seven days. We Drury Lane proprietors hope that the rage for shooting will have subsided somewhat by the 10th of next month on which day we shall certainly open our theatre — ....⁴

On the same day that he refused Lord Holland's request, Byron confirmed to Lady Melbourne 'as all Grub Street seems engaged in the Contest, I have no ambition to enter the lists, & have thrown my few ideas into the fire.... I have written to Ld. H. to thank him & decline the chance.'⁵ That might well have been the end of the matter, but Lord Holland meanwhile, together with other readers appointed by the Committee, was spending his time in reading with some degree of alarm the regular flow of Addresses that were now arriving daily at the portals of Drury Lane. What had been expected as a trickle had now become a flood. In desperation, and in spite of having now set eyes on Byron's first poetical fumblings, he wrote a flattering letter to the reluctant poet again:

> My dear Lord – If the sound of your excellent verses rung in my ears even before I read those who were 'responsive' to the Advertisement & who I assure you answered it in the same strain, how much more must I [make excuses?] for them after wading through the trash which it was allotted to me to pursue – I must & indeed I am authorised by the Committee to speak to you confidentially on the subject – the fact is we have found

none of nearly 100 competitors that will do – Some have a little merit but none were even good enough to be spoken....In this difficulty I own I have been vain & foolhardy enough to undertake to apply to your friendship to extricate us – to tell you that the verses which you shewed me or that any which you have made or may make must be better than anything we have rejected would be no great compliment & I can assure you that I can with equal sincerity say that those you shewed me especially the striking & poetical description of the fire would be received with universal applause – & calculated to silence by their merit alone the cavils even of disappointed bards....You are in fact the only person who can extricate us from our difficulties – You can do so by the excellence of your verses & even if it were possible to find a tolerable prologue elsewhere we should not escape censure without a poetical name great as your own to justify us. Pray let me contract you in the name of Drury Lane & her committee, of Thalia & Melpomene[*], to take pity on us. There is no objection to the compliment to Mrs. Siddons or the slap at the Young Roscius – I own notwithstanding all his faults moral & political, I am such an admirer of Genius that I should like to see a couplet in compliment to Sheridan – He was you know our manager & so was Garrick – The first actor & first Comick writer of the Country have managed Drury Lane. I write in a desperate hurry.....[6]

Lord Holland was the only member of the Committee who possessed the advantage of actually having seen and read Byron's first attempt at an Address before it had been consigned to the flames. His anxiety may have urged him, in praising Byron's genius, to err on the side of excess by giving himself up to a few subtle tricks of flattery. But he was a desperate man among desperate men, and gambling on the merest chance, he played his trump card – friendship. A few days later, on 22 September, he received the following reply:

> My dear Lord – In a day or two I will send you something which you will still have the liberty to reject if you dislike it. I should like to have had more time but will do my best, but too happy if I can oblige you though I

---

[*] Thalia and Melpomene were two of the Nine Muses representing Comedy and Tragedy respectively.

Chapter 7 – The Reluctant Poet: Execution or Persecution?

> may offend 100 Scribblers, & the discerning public.
>
> Best respects to Ly. H. Keep my name a secret – or I shall be beset by all the rejected, & perhaps damned by a party.[7]

A fever of activity assailed Byron overnight and the next day, from Lord Holland's house in Cheltenham, he dispatched the first draft of the Address together with a frenetic accompanying letter:

> My dear Lord – Ecco![8]   – I have marked some passages with double readings – chuse between them – cut – add – reject – or destroy – do with it as you will – I leave it to you – & the Committee – you cannot say so called – a "non committendo["] – what will they do (& I do) with the hundred & one rejected troubadours? – "With trumpets – yea – & with shawms"[9] – will you be assailed in the most diabolical doggerel – I wish my name not to transpire till the day is decided – I shall not be in town so it won't much matter – but let us have a good deliverer – I think Elliston should be the man – a Pope* – not Raymond† I implore you by the Love of Rhythmus‡! The passages with words marked thus ----- ----- above and below are for you to chuse between epithets & such like poetical furnitures. Pray write me a line & believe me ever yrs. B.
>
> My best remembrances to Ly. H. Will you be good enough to decide between the various readings marked & erase the others – or our Deliverer will be as puzzled as the Commentator, & belike repeat both – . If these versicles wont do – I will hammer out some more endecasyllables. —
>
> Tell Ly. H. I have had sad work to keep out the Phenix [*sic*] – I mean the fire-office of that name – it has insured the theatre & why not the address! — — .[10]

At last, Lord Holland could see the completed verses, though they were far from being the final version. Byron was uncertain of their

---

* Alexander Pope (1763-1835)   Irish actor and painter. Exhibited 59 miniatures at Royal Academy between 1787 and 182, but principally made impression as actor at Covent Garden in tragic parts.
† George Raymond. Prompter at Drury Lane. He played the Ghost in *Hamlet* at re-opening of Drury.
‡ Rhythmus, i.e., the flow of lines in performance.

quality from the very beginning, and time was extremely short. It was already the last week of September and the opening was planned for the 10th of the following month. The whole piece had to be ready and rehearsed in little more than a fortnight. What Lord Holland now read pleased him, though he expressed his reservations about some parts of the Address, which had arrived in its unpolished state, with all the blunt edges still to be honed. He underlined his alternatives (shown here in italics), hoping for comment from a no doubt exhausted but loyal critic:

> *In one* dread *night* —
> ~~Bowed to the dust~~ — our City saw & sighed
> Bowed to the dust the Drama's tower of Pride,
> In one short hour beheld the blazing fane —
> Apollo sink — & Shakespeare cease to reign. —
>
> Ye who beheld — & those there are tonight,   5
> Who feared — admired and ah! deplored the sight —
> Through sulphurous clouds the massy fragments riven
> In fiery pillars chase the Night from Heaven,
> Saw the long column of revolving flames
> *Fling*
> <u>Shake</u> his red shadow o'er the startled Thames,   10
> *Dart*
> While crowds collected round the burning dome
> Shrank back appalled, & trembled for their home,
>
> Till all was whelmed beneath the livid wave,
> And blackening Ashes marked the Muse's grave:
> Say, shall this humbler, yet, aspiring Pile,   15
> Reared, where once rose the mightiest in our Isle,
> Know the same favour which the former knew —
> A Shrine for Shakespeare, worthy him and — You?
>
> Yes — it shall be — the Magic of that name,
> Though thousand Piles should sink in future flame,   20
> On the same spot shall consecrate the scene,
> And bid the Drama be, where she hath been,
> Though long in vain Melpomene deplore,
> And weep <u>for her with</u> whom she weeps no more,

Chapter 7 – The Reluctant Poet: Execution or Persecution?

Yet Hope shall strive to banish Memory's fear, 25
Till Time mature a second Siddons here;
Though fled the Queen — our Monarchs still remain
Yes — here "old Lear shall be king again."
  whom   *rule*
You — <u>who</u> no tyrants <u>brook</u> but on the stage,
Will here endure Macbeth's & Richard's rage. 30
Here too when tragic tears forget to flow
    chase the
The vein of Wit shall <u>rise for</u> sounds of Woe.
And varied oft as varying Taste allures
Thalia's smile be well repaid by Yours.
Whate'er our fate — howe'er our parts be cast, 35
Oh might we draw our Omens from the past,
Some future day should bid our Drury boast
    hallowed once
Such names as <u>hollow</u> <u>still</u> the Dome we lost.
On Drury first your Siddons' searching Art
O'erwhelmed the gentlest — stormed the sternest Heart, 40
On Drury Garrick's latest laurels grew,
Here Britain's Roscius your last teardrops drew,
Sighed his last thanks, & wept his last Adieu.
And here — could living Wit unenvied share
     fire
The Praise, which cannot <u>wake</u> the Wits that were, 45
With garlands deck your own Menander's[*] head,

Now hoard your honours idly for the Dead,
Him Drury claimed — & claims – nor you refuse
To join her tribute to his matchless Muse
  are   *here*
Such <u>were</u> the names that <u>once</u> your plaudits sought, 50
When Garrick acted & when Brinsley wrote
 do *not* *by comparison*
Oh <u>should then Memory lead you to</u> condemn —

---

[*] Menander (c.342-292BC). Athenian dramatic poet, his realistic story-telling influenced Renaissance writers.

Reflect
<u>Yet</u> — how hard the task to rival them!

Friends of the Stage — for whom our voice we raise   55
And sue in turn for pardon or for praise,
Yours is the choice, as you decide — direct
The ample power to punish, or protect,
The same indulgence which your fathers gave
In the same scenes is all your Servants crave,   60
On the same spot we scarce can plead in vain
      resume their reign
That Sense & Shakespeare may <u>resume the Strain.</u>
      renew
The Pye[*] of Taste prophetically just
Shall guide & guard us faithful to our trust,
The Voice of Wit alike shall check or cheer   65
The heartfelt efforts of our new Career.
But know — our triumph thus alone secures
That judging voice & eye must first be yours.
Ours to obey your will or right or wrong,
To soar in Sentiment, or creep in Song,   70
[interlined] *Nay lower still — the Drama yet deplores*
   That late she deigned to crawl upon "all fours"
When Richard roars on Bosworth for a horse
If <u>you</u> <u>command</u> — the <u>Steed</u> must come in course,
 decree — the Stage must condescend   75
If you ~~demand our intellectual feast~~ —
      we
To soothe the sickly taste ~~*she*~~ *dare not mend* [interlined]
~~*Must furnish at — alike of Men or Beast*~~ [interlined]
Blame not our   *should*   [interlined]
<u>Blush for such</u> judgment <u>while</u> we acquiesce
And gratify you more by showing less. —
Oh! since your Fiat stamps the Drama's laws,   80

---

[*] Henry James Pye (1745-1813). Poetaster and Poet Laureate. Much to his detriment, he chose a political stance in his poetical works and was frequently lampooned for his sycophantic verses.

Chapter 7 – The Reluctant Poet: Execution or Persecution?

> Forbear to mock us with misplaced applause,
> That public praise be never more disgraced —
> From babes & brutes redeem a Nation's taste,
> Then Pride shall doubly serve the Actor's powers
> When Reason's voice is echoed back by ours,   85
> *shall lend it straight to*
> *homage*
> This greeting oer, this previous <u>duty</u> paid,
> *Our Virgin   Drama*
> <u>The Drama's offering</u> be no more delayed!
> *told in*
> This humble welcome, <u>& this</u> faltering tone,
> Springs from our hearts & fain must win your own,
> The Curtain rises — may our Stage unfold   90
> Scenes not unworthy Drury's days of Old,
> *Britons*
> ~~You for~~ our Judges, Nature for our Guide,
> <u>Still</u> <u>may we</u> ple<u>a</u>se — long long m<u>ay</u> <u>you</u> preside![11]
> *Houses*

Few poets can have stood before their judges with such naked art as Byron did, here before Lord Holland. The uncut diamond was in danger of being taken by the unpractised, or in this case, unfamiliar eye to be the finished object. The noble critic had only glimpsed some preliminary lines which the noble poet had petulantly jettisoned in the flames. Now Lord Holland was faced with an imperfect poem which required considerable revision before it could be handed to Robert Elliston for rehearsal. Would it not have been preferable to have selected one of the more worthy Addresses already in the possession of the Committee? Some were certainly more acceptable in their finished state than Byron's first draft. With a little cooperation from the rejected author, some judicious cuts and one or two additional lines, a suitable Address could have been 'concocted' that would have passed muster, and face would have been saved. But it was too late. Lord Holland could not withdraw his request even if he wished to do so. Byron had been under some degree of duress, having composed his lines in only a few days, correcting as he went along. In a postscript to the Address, he suggested that Lord Holland might have it recopied, especially if the opportunity were to present itself of delivering the manuscript to John Murray, with a view to publication. But first, Byron took care to remind his complaisant critic of his task of deciding between various 'underlinings'. He was concerned that 'stormed' [l. 40] might be thought to be too strong in describing the effect of 'Siddons' searching Art', and, anxious to win prompt approval, he consciously or unconsciously misquoted a line from Johnson's 1747 Prologue: 'And unresisted Passion stormed the heart', in support of his choice of image. (Johnson had used 'breast').

In a state of creative agitation, Byron sent three letters to Lord Holland in the course of the following day:

> My dear Lord – I send a recast of the four first lines of the concluding paragraph [ll. 86-9]
>
>> "This greeting o'er — the ancient rule obeyed,
>> "The Drama's homage by her Herald paid,
>> "Receive our Welcome too, whose even tone
>>   *win*
>> "Springs from our hearts, & fain would — your own,
>> "The Curtain rises &c, &c.
>
> And do forgive all the trouble; – see what it is to have do even with the genteelest of us!
>
>   ever yrs.
>   B.[12]

This missive was rapidly followed by another:

> My dear Lord – I must bore you still further with alterations as they rise – Perhaps these couplets —
>
>> "Here too when tragic tears forget to flow
>> "The vein of wit shall chase the sounds of woe [ll. 31-2]
>
> had better run thus —
>
>> "Shall Congreve's Wit succeed to Otway's[*] Woe
>
> and another
>
>> "Friends of the Stage – for whom our voice we raise [l. 55]
>
> had better be —
>
>> "Friends of the Stage – to whom both play'rs &

---

[*] Thomas Otway (1652-1685).

Chapter 7 – The Reluctant Poet: Execution or Persecution?

> plays
>
> "Must sue in turn for pardon or for praise.
>
> Churchill* has Player as a monosyllable frequently – Propound – pronounce, & excuse all this, which will show you that I am anxious to do the little I can as desirably as Time & the Cheltenham waters will allow – to say nothing of my want of practice in this line of rhyming —
>
> ever yrs.
>
> B.
>
> "Livid wave" [l. 13] may be "glowing wave" burning [l. 11] – Blazing [l. 3] – fiery [l. 8] – oh Lord – even "sulphurous" [l.7] are all bespoke "purple" "crimson" are too feeble – if you think some hugeous epithet – in with it instead. [13]

Deferential but persistent, Byron dispatched a third letter before the day was out:

> My dear Lord – I believe this is the third scrawl since yesterday all about epithets. I think the epithet "intellectual"[14] won't convey the meaning I intend & though I hate compounds for the present I will try (col permesso†) the word – "Genius-gifted patriarchs of our line" instead – Johnson has our "many-coloured life" a compound but they are always best avoided – however it is the only one in 90 lines, but will be happy to give way to a better. – I am ashamed to intrude any more remembrances on Ly. H. or letters upon you; but you are fortunately for me gifted with patience already too often tried by your obliged & sincere St. [servant.]
>
> BYRON[15]

The following day, 25 September, Lord Holland sent words of encouragement to Byron, and passed on the news that Samuel Whitbread had taken the verses to the country and was well pleased with what he had

---

* Charles Churchill (1731-1764). Author of *The Rosciad*, a satire on contemporary actors (1761)

† *col permesso* - Italian for 'with your permission'. The interpolation is of interest since Byron is anxious to seek the approval of Lord Holland and would not want to go against his wishes.

read so far. Whilst Whitbread was concerned that the reference to 'future flame' [1. 20] might prove an unfortunate tempting of Providence, Lord Holland deliberated on the poetical infelicity of 'livid wave' [1. 13]:

> My dear Lord – Your verses are better & better every time I read them & you [we] may set the poetasters at defiance – Whitbread who was here this morning was delighted with them though he had not such a horror of the "Phoenix" as you & Ldy Holland for a reason which will divert you when I see you – he has taken your copy to Southill & I shall not have it till Monday morning which will account to you for my silence on verbal criticisms of which however you shall have plenty (if you like them) next week – you give one a large choice of good Epithets & sometimes one has an embarras de richesse – Do you like fling or shake – his shadow on the startled Thames? [1. 10] the verses on Garrick [ll.41-49] & Sheridan [l.51] are admirably executed & make me quite vain of having hinted their names to you – Whitbread has some apprehensions of hinting the possibility of future flame – the Ladies he says will call for their carriages. The verses on the bad taste of the times [ll. 71-83] are very good too & I should not like to alter but there is a feeling in our Committee of liberality to our Sister Theatre & in the Character of Manager not of Critick. I [sense?] Whitbread is inclined to curtail that part of the address – Elliston or Miss Smith[*] – which would you prefer – You have a clear right to chuse your speaker – Both your alterations seem to me improvements [l.55] – players are more than once monosyllables.
>
> "The players & I are luckily no friend" & I believe it is the leaning or as the parliamentary phrase has it the bias of Heroick verse to contract & the Bath guide anapaestic measure to open syllables – You have given an abundance of epithets for "livid", all I think better than it – the fact is I do not know what "Livid" is – is it a pale colour or the colour of a bruise – some say it is the colour of black lead – others say that it is no colour but the state of a colour –

---

[*] Miss Smith (formerly Sarah Bartley) 1783-1850). Appeared at Drury Lane. On retirement of Mrs Siddons, Miss Smith made many appearances, including playing leading lady to Edmund Kean in *Romeo and Juliet* and other plays.

Chapter 7 – The Reluctant Poet: Execution or Persecution?

> Now all this I do not understand but to my ear livid & wave don't go well together. I think some participle epithet a la Gray[*] would do best – signifying set on fire – you have the idea of affrighted in "startled" Thames [1.10]. But I must write a canvassing letter or two. I will write again on Monday. Pray write and receive my most hearty & sincere thanks for your very great good nature – All the poetical return I can make is the old distich
>
> > The friend in need
> > is a friend in deed
>
> & you have really been so to us & ours – I only wish you would come up & assist at [the] opening.[16]

Though there appears to be no proof of Lady Holland's role as *dea ex machina* in the little drama that was now being enacted behind the scenes, judging from inferences in the letters being passed ever more urgently to and fro between London and Cheltenham, Byron's affection and regard for her had its own part to play as the climax approached. Conversation at Holland House had its topical excitements as well as the higher and sometimes heady altitudes of intellect. The urgency of the Drury Lane Address and the many other matters to be dealt with in connection with the opening of Wyatt's new theatre was an obsession with Lord Holland, and undoubtedly attracted the lively mind of his formidable consort. Her earlier romantic and illicit attachment to him, her brilliant stage-management of the conversation at her celebrated dinner-parties, her extraordinary infatuation with Napoleon, and the curious paradox in her nature of being an aristocrat and a Jacobin rolled into one, were characteristics that attracted Byron, who rarely omitted to send her his respectful and sometimes even affectionate remembrances whenever he communicated with her husband. As for Lord Holland, he continued to exercise the greatest tact, patience, and above all enthusiasm for the matter in hand – the completion of the Drury Lane Address. On the same day as the previous letter, he wrote to Byron reassuringly:

> As I perceive you are inclined to be diligent in correction – the moment I get your verses back I will sit down in the spirit of Hypercriticism & find any possible fault with every line – line by line – but then you must recollect that in doing so I am a real and sincere admirer of the whole address & even if not one word more is altered, I

---

[*] Thomas Gray (1761-1771). Author of *Elegy in a Country Churchyard* and in particular his Pindaric ode, *The Progress of Poesy*.

think it among the very best compositions of the mind I ever read – Johnson's & even Pope's prologues are by no means free from botches & imperfections....

Byron, ever anxious to avoid overtaxing his Critic's patience, began to see himself in the guise of an importunate Sir Fretful Plagiary[*]. Post-haste to London, passing on the road Lord Holland's letter to him, Byron dispatched yet another letter on arrival in London, together with a fresh draft of the Address with some omissions and one addition, 'but I fear still too long'[17]:

> Cheltenham Sept. 25th 1812
>
> My dear Lord, Still "more matter for a May morning" having hatched the middle & end of the address I send one more complete for a part of the beginning – which if not too turgid you will have the goodness to add. – After that flagrant image of the Thames [l. 10] I hope no unlucky wag will say of it I have set it on fire, then Dryden in his Annus Mirabilis[18] & Churchill in his "Times" did it before me. I mean to insert this [after l. 10] "As flashing far the new Volcano shone
>
> *Meteors*
>
> "And swept the skies with Lightnings not their own,
> "Which thousands thronged around the burning dome
> &c &c.
>
> I think "thousands" less flat than "crowds collected" [l. 11] but don't let me plunge into Bathos, or rise into Nat Lee's bedlam metaphors.[†]
>
> By the bye, the best view of the said fire which I myself saw from a House-top in C. Garden, was at W[estminster] Bridge from the reflection on the Thames, – Perhaps the present couplet had better come in after "trembled for their home" [l. 12], the two lines being after, as otherwise the image certainly sinks & it will seem just as well. –

---

[*] In Sheridan's *The Critic* Sir Fretful Plagiary is the playwright who blatantly steals from other writers' works.

[†] Nathaniel Lee (c.1653-1692). Dramatist. His plots are drawn mainly from classical history. Author of two popular rhyming plays, *Gloriana* and *Sophonisba* (1676). He lost his reason in 1684 through intemperance and spent five years in Bedlam.

The lines Themselves perhaps may be better thus – chuse or refuse – but please yourself & don't mind "Sir Fretful"
—

> *flashed* *blaze* *sadly guise*
> "As <u>burnt</u> the volumed <u>flames</u>, and <u>fear</u> or shone
> *ghastly*
> "The skies with lightnings aweful as their own,

The last runs smoothest– & I think best, but you know better than best. "Lurid" is also a less indistinct epithet than "livid wave" & if you think so – a dash of the pen will do – I expected one line this morning – in the meantime I shall model & condense & if I do not hear from you shall send another copy. —

I am ever yr. obliged & sincere B. [19]

2. Putting the Final Touches

Letters now passed between London and Cheltenham daily, and sometimes twice daily, and invariably by return of post. No one was more anxious to see the verses through to their final draft than Lord Holland, and Byron was beginning to grow impatient. Lord Holland, in spite of increasing pressures both at the House of Lords and at Drury Lane, continued with his conciliatory manner, gently persuasive, and like Ramsay's[*] 'Gentle Shepherd', strove to do his best and left the rest to Heaven.

> My dear Lord, I have but a moment as I am going to town where I shall find your prologue & be able to compare your corrections with the original. Perhaps it would be a good plan to get a few copies printed but what would be yet better would be for you to come up to Holland House the 9th October & hear the actor who is to deliver them recite it – I think your additional four lines very good – and victors even without the allusion to Virgil better than patriarchs – but where the question is between an allusion to the Prince of Poets & the unintelligible nonsense of that Hebrew nation can there be a doubt, – Worthies would be

---

[*] Allan Ramsay (1686-1758), Scottish poet. *The Gentle Shepherd*, a pastoral drama with rural scenes and rustic characters, set in the Scottish lowlands.

> flat but it is an old phrase worthies of a line. Intellectual is a heavy abstract Scotch Metaphysical word & as such most repugnant to the language of the Muses – who have I suspect a very female dislike to moral feelosife & eeliments of criticism &c &c &c – but yet per contra I do not very much admire genius gifted – nor is many-coloured an authority, for many is a sort of adverb adjective in most or I might say in many a language – multicolor – but I am really very imprudent in criticising your words – there is no doubt that Johnson would have said intellectual & after all it is more perspicuous than the others & perspicuity both of language & argument or train of thought a great & necessary beauty in all forms is eminently so in one that is to be spoken to an audience who may be called Athenians in an address but whom those who write & those who speak well know to be Milotians – you cannot flatter me more nor occupy me more agreeably than by discussing epithets & words in your verses —[20]

On 26 September, the same day that Lord Holland sent the above letter, Byron copied out and dispatched to Holland House a corrected version of the Address, complete with numbered lines for easy reference, and space below for comment. The idea was that Lord Holland's comments were to be initialled 'H' and an unnamed person in the character of Manager was to sign himself 'M'. It was quite fortuitous that the initial 'H', whilst intended to stand for the observations of a 'Hypercritic' or a supposedly rejected poetaster whose object was to find fault, only transparently veiled the identity of the writer. As to the secretive 'M', we discover from the manuscript that he was Samuel Whitbread, though this may not have been known to Byron. The rules of the game were simple and to the point, and Byron willingly accepted his role as he who is to be judged. The first two lines:

> In one dread night, our City saw & sighed
> Bowed to the dust the Drama's tower of Pride

were followed by the comments of the 'Hypercritic' thus:

> ….there is an incorrectness in this couplet – the City saw the Drama's tower bowed to the dust but it did not sigh the tower – in strict construction the words & sighed ought to come after the second line but as it stands it is intelligible & is an exercise of the reciter's talents. H.[21]

Chapter 7 – The Reluctant Poet: Execution or Persecution?

As to the second couplet,

> In one short hour beheld the blazing fane
> Apollo sink — & Shakespeare cease to reign —

'H' pronounced them 'faultless', and Byron never changed them from start to finish. He did find useful the comments of both 'H' and 'M' on the following lines:

> As flashed the volumed blaze, & ghastly shone
> The Skies with lightnings awful as their own,
> While crowds collected round the burning dome
> Shrank back appalled & trembled at their home.[22]

'H' found the first couplet 'very sonorous' & 'very good' but objected to the juxtaposition of 'As' and 'While'. 'M' found that the two clauses clogged the recitation: 'Few voices have variety of modulation enough to make them intelligible.'[23] He recommends omitting the couplet altogether, but in a footnote 'H' recommends that it be left in after all. Byron complied with their conflicting wishes by ingeniously altering the order of the lines, replacing 'flashed' with 'glared', and 'crowds collected' with 'thousands thronged' as suggested in his letter of the previous day. Thus the finished lines in the printed version became:

> While thousands, throng'd around the burning dome,
> Shrank back appall'd, and trembled for their home,
> As glared the volumed blaze, and ghastly shone
> The skies, with lightnings awful as their own,[24]

and everyone was satisfied, poet, manager, and critic. One problem that troubled 'H' and 'M' was: how many syllables has King 'Lear'?

> Though fled the Queen our Monarchs still remain
> Yes here old Lear shall be King again,

prompted the comments: 'This line must be left out for we have no one to act Lear' ('H') and 'Lear is only one syllable & this line must run: a king again' ('M'). Lord Holland's objection was well-founded.

The last great performance of Lear was Garrick's, at a time when there was a flare-up of the growing rivalry between the Theatre Royal, Drury Lane, and the Theatre Royal, Covent Garden. Spranger Barry had challenged Garrick to play Lear on the same night to see who could win the greatest audience. Thus only one play was being performed in both Patent theatres on that evening. Many of the audience, not to be outdone, commuted between Drury Lane and Covent Garden, passing on the news of the relative merits of the two performances to one another on the way. By the end of the evening, one or other of the actors would lose the floating part of his audience to his superior rival. Garrick won the contest for Drury Lane, as the Press reported:

> The town has found out different ways
> To praise the rival Lears
> To Barry they give loud Huzzas
> To Garrick they give tears.[25]

As Lord Holland affirmed, there was no longer an actor at Drury capable of giving even a tolerable portrayal of the role. Kemble had left for Covent Garden, and Kean, who would one day give Drury Lane its greatest Lear, had not yet stepped onto the London Stage.[26] 'M' rightly concerned himself with the problem of 'How many syllables are there in 'Lear'? 'H' took the heat out of the situation by amusing Byron with a story of a Frenchman who translated Shakespeare's plays 'very ill but made Le-ar two syllables – A critic asked a Lady why he did so & she answered: 'C'est apparamment parce qu'il n'avais jamais pu le faire Lire.'[27] Byron removed the couplet.

The rivalry of the two Patent theatres was of great topical interest, and it was a pity that Byron was persuaded to remove some lines [ll. 71-6] introduced into the earlier draft of the Address and which offended the Committee as a whole. In 1811, the management at Covent Garden had brought on stage a troop of horses in a performance of the pantomime *Bluebeard*. An elephant was encouraged onto the stage in a subsequent production, and Drury Lane ridiculed the practice in a burlesque entitled *Quadrupeds, or, The Manager's Last Kick*, which involved a group of tailors mounted on asses and mules. Byron's lines were characteristically to the point:

> Nay lower still — the Drama yet deplores
> That late she deigned to crawl upon 'all fours'
> When Richard roars on Bosworth for a horse
> If you command — the Steed must come in course,
> If you decree the Stage must condescend
> To sue the sickly taste we dare not mend.[28]

Chapter 7 – The Reluctant Poet: Execution or Persecution?

The view of the Committee was plainly expressed by 'M':

> However good the verses....we should recommend omitting these six for three reasons – first because the address is too long for a prologue, secondly because the general turn of it is serious, & fun will be more properly reserved for an epilogue – thirdly because we are still unwilling for various reasons generous & sordid to attack Covent Garden.[29]

He complains finally that, the usual number of lines in a prologue being from thirty to fifty, 'both Actors and Audience would be displeased with Shakespeare himself if he exceed 80 – Johnson's prologue on opening consisted of 62.....'.[30] He recommended that by cutting sixteen lines, Byron could get the length down to sixty-three, 'one line more than Dr. Johnson's.' Byron once more complied with his request, though he later added a further ten lines making the final version a total of seventy-three lines. The Holland House Papers in the British Library include a further draft of the Address with the numbered lines and footnotes and commentaries by 'M', but it would be a fruitless venture here to analyse any further than is necessary the working relationship that existed between Lord Holland and Lord Byron. It has been sufficient to show the nature of, and basis for, their personal and literary friendship, and the method of work adopted in the process of poetical refinement. The Holland House Papers provide a unique opportunity not only to see in detail the gradual path of a poem in progress, but to gain insight into the growth of the poet's mind at a particular stage in his development.

Byron was now in a state bordering on frenzy and scribbled a long but informative letter to Lord Holland:

> My dear Lord – You will think there is no end to my villainous emendations....as it now stands the conclusion of the paragraph "worthy his (Shakespeare) & <u>you</u>" [l. 18] appears to apply the "you" to those only who were out of bed & in Covent Garden market on the night of the Conflagration, instead of the Audience or the discerning public at large all of whom are intended to be comprised in that comprehensive & I hope comprehensible pronoun, – By the bye – one of my corrections in the fair copy sent yesterday has dived into the Bathos some sixty fathom.
>
> When Garrick died – & Brinsley ceased to write [l. 51][31] ceasing to live is a much more serious concern, & ought not be first therefore – I will let the old couplet stand –

with it's [sic] half-rhymes "<u>sought</u>" & "<u>wrote</u>" second thoughts in every thing are best, but in rhyme third & and fourth don't come amiss – I am very anxious in this business & I do hope that the sorry trouble I occasion you will plead it's [sic] own excuse, & that it will tend to show my endeavour to make the most of the time allocated. I wish I had known it months ago, for in that case I had not left one line standing on another. – I always scrawl in this way, and smoothe as much as I can but never sufficiently, & latterly I can weave a nine line stanza faster than a couplet. – for which measure I have not the cunning. – ....After all, my dear lord, if you can get a decent address elsewhere, don't hesitate to put this aside; why did you not trust your own Muse? I am very sure she would have been triumphant, & saved the Committee their trouble, "tis a joyful one" to me but I fear I shall not satisfy even myself. – After the second account you sent me tis no compliment to say, you would have beaten your candidates, but I mean that in that case there would have been no occasion for their being beaten at all. – There are but two decent prologues in our tongue

— Pope's to Cato — Johnson's to Drury Lane....[32]

My homage to Ly. H. – & best thanks for her kind remembrances.[33]

Behind the scenes, Lady Holland continued to hover attentively, offering comments when Lord Holland read her Byron's letters. She was thus able to follow as clearly as anyone the progress of events as the days came and went. Apart from their common interests, already alluded to, Byron seems to have been anxious to win her approval. When, earlier in the year, she had contracted an illness of some kind, Byron reproached himself for not having called on her sooner, and resolved to pay a visit to Holland House, on hearing from Lord Holland that she was only 'as well as could be expected.'[34]

At Cheltenham, Byron had been happy at the departure of the Lambs for Ireland, but following Lady Holland's return to London, he wrote that it was 'a sad event for me now reduced to a state of the most cynical solitude.'[35] He found her good-natured, even though she taunted Lady Caroline Lamb and told Lady Melbourne that Byron was getting fat.[36] Compared to his delicate constitution, Lady Holland was a hardy perennial, able to stand up to the freezing winters at Holland House. An entry in Byron's Journal records the effects of a cold November evening at Holland House when the Spartan Lady Holland's fire-screen added to

Chapter 7 – The Reluctant Poet: Execution or Persecution?

the discomfiture of the assembled guests:

> Why does Lady H. always have that damned screen between the whole room and the fire? I, who bear cold no better than an antelope....was absolutely petrified, and could not even shiver. All the rest, too, looked as if they were just unpacked, like salmon from a basket, and set down to table for that day only. When she retired, I watched their looks as I dismissed the screen, and every cheek thawed, and every nose reddened with the anticipated glow.[37]

Byron debated the acceptance or no of an invitation to Holland House. 'Shall I go? Um! Perhaps,' but having accepted in the end, found there a 'party numerous' which included Thomas Campbell in a blue suit and new wig ('He really looked as if Apollo had sent him a birth-day suit, or a wedding garment), the Marquis of Buckingham, George Lamb (a fellow-member of the Drury Lane Committee), the Marquis of Wellesley, and others of note, and presiding over all, 'milady in perfect good-humour, and consequently perfect.'[38]

After paying 'homage' to Lady Holland, Byron added to his letter to Lord Holland a postscript, for he had received the recently corrected draft with criticisms by 'H' and 'M' and now sent a new draft together with a proviso that Samuel Whitbread should not place the address in Elliston's hands until the alternative corrections had been settled. '....I have almost done. — E. will think it too long – much depends on the speaking, I fear it will not bear too much curtailing.'[39]

Byron was beginning to feel nervous. Whilst feeling some relief at nearing the end of his task, it was that very end that would be the judge of his work. He feared an outcry among the rejected poets, as Lord Holland had intimated in an earlier letter. But Byron's devotion to the Hollands spurred him on. 'All I have to do with it [the Address], he wrote, 'is with & and through you, & though I of course wish to satisfy the audience – I do assure you my first object is to comply with your request, & in so doing shew the sense I have of the many obligations you have conferred on me.'[40] To this Lord Holland replied in his coaxing and cajoling vein:

> I am delighted with your diligence – & anxious to rival it. Mine is an easier & less glorious task [,] that of finding fault but with so good humoured an author as yourself not an unpleasant one.
>
> We think that beautiful as is you[r] description of the fire you dwell too long on that subject not for composition but for policy, for the feelings of the audience...[41]

He voiced a further objection to the reference to Sheridan as 'Brinsley' [l.51]:

> Some say Brinsley is not known by that name, – the whole of that passage wants a little perspicuity....There is one observation made in [the] fourth line which I lament, as I like the line – can Shakespeare be said to have ceased to reign when he was acted constantly at Covent Garden?[42]

Byron was willing to accept Lord Holland's criticism of 'livid wave' and wrote on 28 September giving four alternatives:

> — Till slowly ebbed the Lava of the wave
> — Till slowly ebbed the spent volcanic wave
> — Till ebbed the Lava of the burning wave
> — Till ebbed the Lava of that molten wave.[43]

Nothing was decided. He was however reluctant to abandon some mention at least of the equestrian sensations at Covent Garden, and replied in a petulant tone: 'Is Whitbread determined to castrate all my cavalry lines? I don't see why t'other house should be spared. Besides it is the public who ought to know better, & you recollect Johnson's was against similar buffooneries of Rich[*] but certes I am not Johnson.'[44] As to Sheridan, Byron was not going to forsake the memory of his old friend. His feelings about him were strong enough to wish to record a conversation at Holland House on the dramatist's merits. It took place soon after Sheridan's death. Byron had spoken with feeling and admiration:

> Whatever Sheridan has done or chosen to do has been, par excellence, always the best of its kind. He has written the best comedy (School for Scandal) the best drama (in my mind, far before that St. Giles's lampoon, the Beggar's Opera), the best farce, and the best Address (Monologue on Garrick) and, to crown all, delivered the very best Oration (the famous Begum speech[†]) ever conceived or heard in this country.[45]

Sheridan was quite overcome on hearing of Byron's praise of his

---

[*] John Rich (1692-1761). Actor and theatre manager.
[†] Sheridan's famous 'Begum' speech (1787), lasting nearly six hours, concerned the imprisonment of the Begums of Oude and seizure of their moneys and lands.

Chapter 7 – The Reluctant Poet: Execution or Persecution?

speech.

> Poor Brinsley! If they were tears of pleasure, I would rather have said these few, but most sincere, words than have written the Iliad or made his own celebrated Philippic[*]. Nay, his own comedy never gratified me more than to hear that he had derived a moment's gratification from any praise of mine, humble as it must appear to "my elders and my betters".[46]

3. A Matter of Urgency

Now it was time for action. The fatal day was approaching. Lord Holland was staying at Bowood Calne, the Wiltshire home of his friend and fellow Whig, Lord Lansdowne, 'The whipper-in and huntsman of the pack' as Byron called him in *English Bards*. Because of the urgency of the situation, it was too risky to rely on the post. On 29 September, it was arranged that Byron should travel to Tetbury where Lord Holland would be waiting. Together, they would go over the Address in detail. Furthermore, precautions had to be made to foil the competitors in any protest that might ensue as a result of the announcement that in fact no one of their number had won the coveted laurels and that Lord Byron, as a member of the Committee, had been invited to compose the Address. Lord Holland wrote of this to Byron:

> It must be delivered to Elliston to 'conn by rote' next Monday at latest and if you cannot come up to give to him, I must. The Committee have determined to keep the whole matter a secret till the day, but their resolution was first 'that the Sub-Committee[47] having read the Competitors found notwithstanding some poetical merit in many of them that none would answer the purpose.' 2ndly. that Ld Holland then produced a rough copy of an address written by Ld Byron which with some few alterations seemed to the Committee well adapted to the purpose, & Ld Holld was required to ask Ld Byron's leave to have it spoken & at the same time to correspond & communicate with his Lordship on the subject.'
>
> Will that screen you sufficiently from the angry poetasters – I really think it must....[48]

---

[*] Philippic – a speech full of acrimonius invective.

The noble critic here seems to be adjusting the truth to suit the purpose. The numerous revisions and adjustments of the original draft – far more than there is space for in this chapter – can hardly be dismissed as 'some few alterations'. Had any of the slighted and rejected poets been fortunate enough to employ such a perspicacious mentor and adviser, they undoubtedly would have fared better. Their protests, consequent upon the forthcoming recitation of the Address, would appear to show them up as a bunch of conceited 'poetasters' (Lord Holland's word). One of them certainly, would, within a few days of the opening of the new theatre, cause a disturbance in the auditorium that was to give the readers of the London newspapers amusement for some days to come and form the subject of a spiteful parody by Byron. Meanwhile Lord Holland remained steadfastly loyal to his protégé:

> I can perceive a nobler flow in your verses that the shortness of a prologue will admit of or the nature of the couplet measure is adapted to – To bring yourself back to the standard, the best method is to read, repeat, and get by heart your favourite passages of Pope, whose fault God knows lies in the other way – His epistle to Harley, to Addison[*], or Medals,[49] & indeed all his versification would give you the jingle an audience like to hear in a prologue. I wonder you exclude Sheridan's beautiful epilogue to Semiramis or indeed his other prologues and epilogues, from your list of good models – perhaps if you acquiesce in the total murder of that topick (like Johnson) which we have so strangely mangled & emasculated, you might say a word on the Magic of that Name having carried the Committee through their labours. – a single word to the honour of the Committee would be well received by some of us, but among us there are others, & I am one, who would rather have nothing than a word too much – For a compliment to the Lane as it stands, there are other & stranger reasons into which a poet cannot enter but which must have their weight with the Managers, proprietors & actors – Half England will think the house what we call it – ....we can with the truth boast of its beauty.... The Stage is the only place where the same things are recited publickly to different ages & it becomes not only a receptacle to preserve the language but a sort of organ for conversing with past times past

---

[*] Joseph Addison (1672-1719)

Chapter 7 – The Reluctant Poet: Execution or Persecution?

> Characters & past Manners – .... As long as English lasts & an English stage is preserved uninterrupted, so long will the audience hear what Queen Elizabeth & the Wits of Charles the Second & Qn Anne's time heard – I don't know whether to explain myself in prose & therefore am not so unreasonable as to expect to be construed in verse....[50]

The reference to 'the Magic of that Name' was to Byron's suggestion that the phrase might replace the offending 'future flame' [l. 20] of which Whitbread did not approve. Lord Holland was happy neither with the original nor its substitute. Byron peevishly commented: 'There – the deuce is in it, if that is not an improvement to W[hitbread]'s content, adding a caustic reproach for his long-suffering adviser: 'But my dear Lord – your patience is not quite so immortal, therefore', though still conceding to signing himself 'yrs. Ever most affectionately BYRON.'[51] Nevertheless, the excision of the equestrian passage still rankled, thinking it 'unpardonable to pass over the horses & Miss Mudie &c[52].– as Betty is no longer a boy – how can this be applied to him? – he is now to be judged as a man – if he acts still like a boy.... I confess I wish that part of the address to stand – but if W. is inexorable een [even] let it – I have also new cast the lines & softened the hint of future combustion... – and sent them off this morning.'

In fact, Byron had dispatched yet another draft on 29 September, feverishly correcting as he copied it out, substituting Mrs. Siddons' 'varied art' for 'thrilling art' [l. 39] and in a covering letter, petulantly dismissing any criticism of Shakespeare ceasing to reign:

> My dear Lord – Shakespeare certainly ceased to reign in one of his Kingdoms, as George 3rd did in America, & George 4th may in Ireland....I have cut away you will see, & altered, but make it what you please – only I do implore you for my own gratification one lash on those accursed quadrupeds....I shall choak if we must overlook their d-----d menagerie. —[53]

The mental pressure of the approaching deadline was now making Byron ill. He was not only constantly revising and reshaping the Address, but was injecting much of his vital spark into the seemingly unending explanation and defence of his emendations against the criticisms, however well-meant, of Lord Holland and Samuel Whitbread. His apprehensions at the likelihood of charges of partiality being levelled against him in the newspapers further exacerbated his condition. Worried about Elliston's slow method of delivery, he feared further cuts would be necessary if the attention of the audience was to be held. Doubts assailed him as to the quality of his composition, thinking it tedious, and himself fortunate that whatever deficiencies remained would be overcome by its being read by a popular actor. 'I have cudgelled my brains with the greatest willingness – & only wish I had more time to have done better,' he wrote to Lord Holland on 30 September, sending his respects to Lady Holland, wistfully commented, 'How she must laugh at all this.'[54]

Two more letters followed on the same day, in which he expressed further fears as to the suspicious appearance of the rejection of all the competitors in favour of his 'rough copy never sent in'. Anxious to exonerate himself from any accusation of connivance, he asserted that 'my sole object is one I trust which my whole conduct has shown – viz – that I did nothing insidious – sent no address whatever – but when applied to did my best for them & myself – but above all that there was no undue partiality – which will be what the rejected will endeavour to make out – fortunately – most fortunately – I sent in no lines on the occasion – for I am sure that had they in that case been preferred – it would have been asserted that I was known & owed the preference to private friendship.

Byron feared what was largely true. He suffered feelings of guilt at the thought that he had enjoyed a unique privilege denied to the rejected poets, namely the valuable critical assistance of an erudite and urbane critic.

It was clear that Byron was now partially incapacitated by an attack of kidney stones and was under medication for the complaint. But the matter in hand had to proceed, and he made arrangements to meet Lord Holland at Tetbury on 3 October, taking with him the final draft of the Address. Lord Lansdowne asked him to Bowood Park, but Byron had already accepted an invitation from Lord and Lady Jersey. On 2 October, Lord Holland wrote again to congratulate Byron on the general improvement of the Address, which he had shown to Lord Lansdowne:

> Really the whole is admirable & will I think be far the finest address that has been spoken from the Stage since the Monody – you may sigh after the topicks of Johnson's prologue but there is not so much real poetry in it as in yours – not so much feeling in all his writing, save & except his description of old age in the 10th Satire, as in your verses on Siddons & Garrick.[55]

Byron copied out a second 'final' draft, still correcting as he went along. This time 'sulphurous' [l.7] was replaced by 'clouds of fire', one improvement among many that brought further refinement to a rough-hewn image.

It was now 9 October, the day before the opening. Byron scribbled a further frantic note with the last-minute corrections. Lord Holland reported that he had been to Elliston's to hear him read the address, found it satisfactory, enough anyway to please the ears of an author, and assured Byron there would be no likelihood of rioting by the disappointed poets on the scale of the Covent Garden O. P. [Old Price] riots. All now was as ready as it could possibly be. The poet and his critic could do no more. The work of the Competition Sub-Committee was done. Wyatt's splendid new theatre prepared to open its doors at last, but the winds of fate were blowing up a storm.

Phoenix of Drury Lane

CHAPTER EIGHT

Phoenix Triumphant

1. 'In one dread night...'

For the opening night of the Theatre Royal, Drury Lane, on Saturday 10th October the Management Committee chose to put on a performance of *Hamlet*, with Robert William Elliston in the part of Polonius.

As might be expected, the House was filled to overflowing with an excitable and enthusiastic audience. Lord Holland and Samuel Whitbread both received tremendous ovations. Garrick's widow was given three hearty cheers as she entered her box. When the curtain rose, the whole cast sang the National Anthem, after which the audience called for 'Rule Britannia',[1] and three thousand voices burst into triumphant song. Then Robert William Elliston stepped forward to recite the long-awaited Address. Byron had refused to be present, vehemently exclaiming to Lord Holland: 'I would not be within fifty miles of the place, on that night, for the universe.'[2] It was just as well he was not, for Elliston, incongruously attired as Polonius, recited the verses 'in a manner to drive an author mad.'[3] Not only was the delivery inadequate, but the audience could not hear. It became clear to everyone present that the stage was set too far back from the auditorium, the first of a number of defects in the new structure which would have to be rectified. The audience began to grow restive. Pockets of disturbance formed in various parts of the theatre. The murmuring of voices grew to such a pitch that cries of 'Silence!' rang throughout the House, causing Elliston to falter in his recitation. It is not known if any of the rejected poets were responsible for the *fracas*, but it seems likely that they were, in the light of subsequent events. Elliston continued with great difficulty, and it is doubtful if anyone heard the whole of the Address. If they had, it would have been as follows:

> In one dread night our city saw, and sigh'd,
> Bow'd to the dust, the Drama's tower of pride;
> In one short hour beheld the blazing fane,
> Apollo sink, and Shakespeare cease to reign.
>
> Ye who beheld, (oh! sight admired and mourn'd,   5
> Whose radiance mock'd the ruin it adorn'd!)
> Through clouds of fire the massy fragments riven,
> Like Israel's pillar, chase the night from heaven;
> Saw the long column of revolving flames
> Shake its red shadow o'er the startled Thames,   10
> While thousands, throng'd around the burning dome,

Chapter 8 – Phoenix Triumphant

Shrank back appall'd, and trembled for their home,
As glared the volumed blaze, and ghastly shone
The skies, with lightnings awful as their own,
Till blackening ashes and the lonely wall   15
Usurp'd the Muse's realm, and mark'd her fall;
Say — shall this new, nor less aspiring pile,
Rear'd where once rose the mightiest in our isle,
Know the same favour which the former knew,
A shrine for Shakespeare — worthy him and <u>you</u>?   20

Yes — it shall be — the magic of that name
Defies the scythe of time, the torch of flame;
On the same spot still consecrates the scene,
And bids the Drama <u>be</u> where she hath <u>been</u>:
This fabric's birth attests the potent spell —   25
Indulge our honest pride, and say, <u>How well</u>!

As soars this fane to emulate the last,
Oh! might we draw our omens from the past,
Some hour propitious to our prayers may boast
Names such as hallow still the dome we lost.   30
On Drury first your Siddons' thrilling art
O'erwhelm'd the gentlest, storm'd the sternest heart.
On Drury, Garrick's latest laurels grew;
Here your last tears retiring Roscius drew,
Sigh'd his last thanks, and wept his last adieu: 35
But still for living wit the wreaths may bloom,
That only waste their odours o'er the tomb.
Such Drury claim'd and claims — nor you refuse
One tribute to revive his slumbering muse;
With garlands deck your own Menander's head,   40
Nor hoard your honours idly for the dead.
Dear are the days which made our annals bright,
Ere Garrick fled, or Brinsley ceased to write.
Heirs to their labours, like all high-born heirs,
Vain of <u>our</u> ancestry as they of <u>theirs</u>;   45
While thus Remembrance borrows Banquo's glass

> To claim the sceptered shadows as they pass,
> And we the mirror hold, where imaged shine
> Immortal names, emblazon'd on our line,
> Pause — ere their feebler offspring you condemn,   50
> Reflect how hard the task to rival them!
>
> Friends of the stage! To whom both Players and Plays
> Must sue alike for pardon or for praise,
> Whose judging voice and eye alone direct
> The boundless power to cherish or reject;   55
> If e'er frivolity has led to fame,
> And made us blush that you forbore to blame;
> If e'er the sinking stage could condescend
> To soothe the sickly taste it dare not mend,
> All past reproach may present scenes refute,   60
> And censure, wisely loud, be justly mute!
> Oh! since your fiat stamps the Drama's laws,
> Forbear to mock us with misplaced applause;
> So pride shall doubly nerve the actor's powers,
> And reason's voice be echoed back by ours!   65
>
> This greeting o'er, the ancient rule obey'd,
> The Drama's homage by her herald paid,
> Receive <u>our</u> welcome too, whose every tone
> Springs from our hearts, and fain would win your own.
> The curtain rises — may our stage unfold   70
> Scenes not unworthy Drury's days of old!
> Britons our judges, Nature for our guide,
> Still may <u>we</u> please — long, long may <u>you</u> preside.[4]

No one in the whole of London was as familiar with the subtleties and nuances of Byron's Address as Lord Holland. He alone could gauge its success or failure. No doubt relieved that at last the fire of the occasion had burnt itself out, he scribbled a quick note to the anxious Byron, hoping for its speedy arrival before news of the performance could reach him, but the comforting words had a hollow ring:

> My dear Lord – I write from the box, to catch the post – It has succeeded admirably – Elliston repeated it well at

least that part of it which he was <u>perfect</u> in – His only fault was not having it by heart & the cry of silence put him out – ....but it succeeded admirably & will more & more every night. I wish you had been here. I shall be too late. Good bye

Yrs. Vll [*Vassall*]. Holland

The more perfect Elliston get[s] in it – the more it will be approved of.[5]

Lord Holland's apprehensiveness over the reactions of the Press was justified. Lewis Goldsmith reported in *The Antigallican Monitor* that the Address was indeed the production of Lord Byron, and 'if it be really (as has been stated) the pick and choice of all the poetical talent in the country, we cannot but lament that dearth of genius and excellence which it too woefully proves.'[6] The critic of *The Times* could not bring himself to believe the lines could have been written by Byron. The Address, he wrote, was throughout 'of the lowest order of taste, conception, and knowledge of poetic language.' James Perry's *Morning Chronicle* expressed the view that 'We cannot suppose that it was selected as the most poetical composition....But, perhaps by its tenor, by its allusions to the fire, to Garrick, to Siddons, and to Sheridan, it was thought most applicable to the occasion, notwithstanding its being in parts unmusical, and in general tame.'[7]

Certainly, among the hundred or so rejected Addresses there were to be found verses of equal merit, and the public, excited by the sensational rumours that heralded the event, had been expecting rather more from the belaurelled poet than the disappointingly conventional couplets they heard (and in many cases failed to hear) on the occasion of the grand opening of their glorious new 'Temple of the Muses'. The Phoenix, exhausted by its three score flights and ten in the cause of poesy had no longer any strength to spread its wings. To Lady Holland, Byron scribbled a note saying: 'I have had sad work to keep out the Phenix [*sic*] – I mean the *fire office* of that name – it has *insured* the theatre & why not the address!' On 14 October, Byron wrote to Lord Holland:

> My dear Lord, – I perceive that the papers yea even Perry's [*Morning Chronicle*] are somewhat ruffled at the injudicious preference of the committee; my friend Perry has indeed "*et tu Brute*"'d me rather scurvily for which I will send him for ye. M[*orning*] C[*hronicle*] the next epigram I scribble as a token of my full forgiveness. Do the Committee mean to enter into no explanation of their proceedings? You must see there is a charge of partiality.

> – You will at least acquit me of any great anxiety to push myself before so many elder & better anonymous to whom the 20 gs. [*guineas*] – (which I take to be about two thousand pds. bank currency) & the Honour would have been equally welcome. – ....I wish to know how it went off at the second reading, & whether anyone has had the grace to give it a glance of approbation. – I have seen no paper but Perry's & two Sunday ones, Perry is severe & the others silent. – If however you and your Committee are not now dissatisfied with your own judgment, I shall not much embarrass myself about the brilliant remarks of the journals. – My own opinion upon it is what it always was, perhaps, pretty near that of the public. – Believe me my dear Ld.
>
> ever yrs most obliged & sincerely
>
> P.S. – My best respects to Ly. H. whose smiles will be very consolatory even at this distance. — .[8]

Byron, content with his Address and, regarding 'the nonsense in the papers', had not thought it proper to answer 'because they did not wish to give the publication of their proceedings in a controversial form.'[9] As to Elliston's performance: 'I hear he has continued to murder rather than recite it. He read it well to me but he evidently did not <u>then</u> understand it – & he repeats it imperfectly & ill'[10] – Byron wrote in similar vein to Lady Melbourne two days later:

> Talking of addresses put me in mind of my <u>address</u> which has been murdered (I <u>hear</u>) in the delivery & mauled I <u>see</u> in the newspapers, & you don't tell me whether you heard it recited, I almost wish you may not, if this be the case.[11]

The murder of Lord Byron's Address rankled in the minds of both its author and his critic almost to the point of being an obsession, Byron seeking constant reassurance for what he knew to be an inferior piece, and Lord Holland earnestly wishing Byron to think it quite otherwise. In his last words on the subject, Lord Holland reiterates the thoughts of earlier letters to Byron:

> There is not fault to find with you but the choice of the man to deliver it who really murdered it worse than he did Polonius in the play. – I quite find a chasm since I have no criticisms to bother you with. I have derived so much pleasure from our correspondence that I could wish you no worse than to write a poem every fortnight for me to

try to pull to pieces. I have however been employed ever since the opening of Dry. Lane with your verses for I have read over & over again.[12]

To the question 'How good was Lord Holland for Lord Byron?' one is constrained to reply with reservations – judging at least from the impressions of those who were present on the occasion of the first public performance of his Address. Comparing the first and final drafts we discern a number of praiseworthy refinements, but we also regret the inclusion of certain later emendations. There are lines of real poetical effect interspersed with lines of utter bathos, and here and there a tendency to fill out thoughts unnecessarily. Unhappily, Byron, as with all the rejected poets, was hampered by the straightjacket of tradition. Like them, he could not bring himself to exorcise the shades of Dryden, Pope and Johnson. The spirit of Old Drury was too powerful to resist. If only he could have been allowed to exercise his original genius, with an open mind, free of the trammels of the past, the brilliant young author of the first Cantos of *Childe Harold's Pilgrimage* might have produced an Address worthy of his name. But the pressures of time and tradition were too great. Whatever wish he may have had to compose a dramatic prologue of an original kind, his profound respect for the critical acumen of Lord Holland would have dissuaded him. There were, as we have seen, other more profound personal reasons for Byron's friendship with Lord and Lady Holland which absolutely forbade any expression of reluctance or unwillingness on Byron's part to accommodate the wishes of the Committee. He had no choice but to follow the thorny path of composition laid down for him by conditions common to all the competitors. He graciously accepted the word of Lord Holland and, like the knight in Browning's *Childe Roland to the Dark Tower Came*:

> .....acquiescingly
> I did turn as he pointed: neither pride
> Nor hope rekindling at the end descried,
> So much as gladness that some end might be.[13]

For the hopeful band of competitors, the bright 'Temple of the Muses' had become a place not only of rejection but of *de*jection, the 'Dark Tower' at the 'end descried' of a futile quest for honours and glory. 'Childe Harold' had tried a different path to 'Childe Roland', in some ways over smoother ground, but nevertheless with its own dangers along the way, and Byron's feelings of doubt in his appointed task foreshadowed, admittedly less ominously, the apprehensions of *Childe Roland*:

> Thus, I had so long suffered in this quest,
>> Heard failure prophesied so oft, been writ
>> So many times among 'The Band' — to wit,
> The knights who to the Dark Tower's search addressed
> Their steps — that just to fail as they, seemed best,
>> And all the doubt was now — should I be fit?[14]

Byron's reminder to his first-night audience that they should not expect to find talents on the new stage of Drury Lane equal to the great dramatists and actors of the past, paralleled the relationships between the authors of the Drury Lane Addresses and the authors of the Drury Lane Prologues:

> While thus Remembrance borrows Banquo's glass,
> To claim the sceptered shadows as they pass,
> As we the mirror hold, where imaged shine
> Immortal names, emblazoned on our line,
> Pause – ere their feebler offspring you condemn,
> Reflect how hard the task to rival them. [15]

As we have seen, the critic of *The Times* had charged Byron's Address with being of the lowest order of taste, conception and knowledge of poetic language, an unfair judgment for what was, after all, a more than adequate attempt at a form which Byron was almost wholly unused to as a poet. But it was criticisms of this kind which aroused the resentment of the rejected authors. When it was known that the offending lines were by Lord Byron, and that in fact no competitor had been chosen as winner of the hoped-for prize, there was an uproar. 'At this outrage, the poetic wrath boiled over, and one furious competitor determined to give public expression to the rage that filled his soul.'[16]

2. Lord Byron's Real Sir Fretful

On Wednesday 14 October 1812, after an evening performance of Bickerstaffe's* *The Hypocrite*, 'a Gentleman'[17] stood up in the Pit of the

---

* Isaac Bickerstaffe, died c.1812. Irish playwright, popular comedies and comic operas include *Love in a Village* (1762), *The Hypocrite* (1769), adapted

Theatre Royal, Drury Lane, and attempted to address the audience.[18] He was prevented from being heard by the ensuing clamour and the repeated calls for calm from the theatre management. It was ironically suggested by a few waggish spectators in the gallery that he should mount the stage to proclaim his oration, which, to everyone's surprise, he proceeded to do. Once in position, and some semblance of meaning could be attached to the mumbled sounds that came from his mouth, silently opening and closing as it was, like a fish out of water, it became clear to those that could hear, that he was 'one of the aggrieved sons of Apollo'[19] whose Address had been among those rejected by the Committee.

The farce, *The Beehive*,[20] was about to be performed as an afterpiece, and George Raymond, the prompter and stage-manager, came forward in the hope of announcing it, taking up a position close to the agitated intruder. He bowed to the audience, then to the stranger beside him, who returned the compliment. They continued bowing to the audience, then to each other, back and forth for some time, then, ridiculous as it was, began at one and the same time to address the restless spectators, who were by now much given over to hooting and hissing. The tumult grew, and the ludicrous piece of miming the two luckless speakers appeared to be acting out on the stage, became more of a farce than that which was about to be performed. At length, Raymond announced that 'if it was the wish of the house to hear that gentleman, he would give place to him.'[21] Left to his own devices, and in full possession of the stage, the stranger struggled to make himself heard, 'but the simmering excitement of the house could not be reduced to silence.'[22] His 'impassioned gestures' made it apparent that he had something of importance to say, but not a syllable could be heard. It became clear that the audience wished the scheduled farce of *The Beehive* to replace, with the greatest possible speed, the one which was at that moment holding the stage. The two-man farce turned into a dramatic quartet when two policemen were called on, and not without a scuffle, the embarrassing intruder was briskly removed. The matter did not, however, end there.

On the following evening, another troublesome spectator appeared in the Theatre and, at the end of the play, rose to his feet to address the audience, this time from the third tier of the boxes. It appeared that the intruder of the previous evening had been George Frederick Busby, one of the authors of the Drury Lane Addresses, who, out of a touching filial devotion, had chosen to recite, not his own rejected Address, but that of his father, Dr. Thomas Busby. The good Doctor, in Jerrold's view 'a fussy, self-advertising busy-body',[23] had already addressed a circular

---

from Molière's *Tartuffe* and Cibber's *The Non-Juror* containing the popular hypocrite, Mawworm.

letter to his friends announcing his intention of making a demonstration that evening and requesting their support by being present, having decided to make his own personal appearance to defend the name and reputation of the rejected poets, among whom he also numbered.

George Frederick's aim had been to offer to the reluctant audience the opportunity of hearing (though, as it turned out, not hearing through lack of any performing voice) a rendering of his father's rejected composition. His sense of hurt over the wrong that had been done his father by the unconscionable attitude of the Committee had compelled him to brave the storm of public ridicule and thus to redeem the honour of his eccentric and seemingly over-bearing parent.

The House was crowded and filled with an air of expectancy. After the play was ended (ironically a performance of Sheridan's *The Rivals*), Dr. Busby rose to his feet and, in spite of the uproar, began his speech:

> I am Dr. Busby, a lover, a member of the drama, and a friend to the theatre [*cheers and hisses*]. Ladies and gentlemen, it is well known that for several weeks the Committee appointed to manage the public concerns of this theatre have, by public advertisement, courted the exertions of the literary world – to prepare an Address to be spoken at the opening of this truly magnificent structure. This was on their part noble and praiseworthy; but it must be allowed on all hands that, however right they have been in intention, they have most lamentably erred in judgement.

For some minutes, he was forced to remain silent for the volume of noise and tumult to subside. Shouting, to make himself heard, he began again:

> Ladies and Gentlemen, you are doubtless aware that the Committee for conducting the affairs of this Theatre, very laudably and patriotically advertised for Addresses to be spoken at its opening. A great number, to the extent of more than 100, I am told, were sent. Of that composition which was adopted, I need not say more than it does not diminish my respect for the talents of the Noble author, which I before expressed. [*Cries of 'To the point, to the point!'*] If you entertain the same opinion that I indulge regarding the literary abilities of the nation, you cannot help coming to the conclusion that many pieces of the highest excellence were sent for approbation in consequence of this general challenge. I know of at least three or four, and I did not let slip this favourable

opportunity of exerting my own poor talents.[24]

At this point, he was interrupted by shouts and yells from the impatient audience, a number of whom walked out in protest, but the Doctor was undeterred. As a desperate measure, the orchestra started up in competition in an attempt to drown his voice, and after some minutes the farce of *The Beehive* was allowed to proceed. After it was over, the Doctor rose to his feet again, and with a powerful voice delivered his parting peroration:

> I have a strong, a powerful motive for requesting your attention. I am a friend of this theatre. I wish to open the way for super-excellence, to bring forward strong and powerful talent, instead of letting it sink into oblivion. Gentlemen, I am a friend to merit, and more especially to modest merit – my son is now in the house with an Address which I had prepared for the opening of this theatre, and nothing would be a greater pride and satisfaction to me than that he should be allowed by the managers to rehearse it on the stage, if you will give him leave.[25]

The sensational behaviour of Dr. Busby was made more dramatic at this moment, for, just as he was bowing to the audience, who by now had become resigned to hearing the Address, two Bow Street officers burst into the box, grappled with the offending protester, and dragged him, struggling, out into the corridor. Many of the audience protested, making it clear that they were now on the Doctor's side in the matter, and would not tolerate brute force being applied to one of their number. 'On the stairs, however, the Doctor squatted himself with a vigorous adhesiveness, and defied the efforts of the officers to remove him. Some of the audience interfered in his favour, and he was borne back in triumph to his box, from which he once more harangued the house,' greeted, as *The Antigallican Monitor* reported, by the 'plaudits and huzzas' of the rest of the House, who now were wildly enthusiastic to hear the rest of the Address.[26] Raymond, the stage-manager, meekly agreed, if only to see a speedy conclusion to these embarrassing proceedings. The young Mr. Busby was now encouraged to return to the stage, where he set off on his perilous path through the opening lines of his father's Address, with frequent interruptions from the audience. Little or nothing could be understood, so weak was his voice; the fledgling failed to crow louder than the parent bird, barely able to utter more than a twitter. He had to stop again when a voice stronger than his shouted from one of the boxes:

> Mr. Busby, - I would advise you to go home, if you

cannot make use of a stronger voice. You ought not to presume to get on that stage to detain the company if you cannot speak so that we may distinctly hear; and I must tell you, that not a word of what you say can be understood here from the smallness of your voice, however elegant and large your ideas may be.'[27]

Thus the Address was begun again:

> When energising objects men pursue,
> What are the prodigies they cannot do, —

but more interruptions eliminated any effect the rapidly weakening voice from the stage could make, and the remainder of the Address was inaudible. Raymond came forward to ask the audience if they had heard enough. With one voice they answered in the affirmative, the young Mr. Busby was led from the stage at last, and the witnesses to this extraordinary spectacle went home none the wiser.

It had been Sir Fretful Plagiary's view that newspapers were villainous, and like him, Dr. Thomas Busby would have been wise to follow his example never to read them, for the next day after the Drury Lane fiasco, he became the subject of ridicule in almost every journal. It was generally agreed that such an event should never be allowed to happen again, otherwise any disappointed poet or dramatist could step onto the stage uninvited, whenever his work was rejected, and insist on its being played in the pit. In the opinion of one newspaper, the Committee had done well to reject all the Addresses:

> ....for, however deficient Lord BYRON's successful Address may be as a picked and chosen production.... It is sufficiently superior to the effusions of all those who have hitherto dared to publish the competitory essays....It is not known, nor we believe surmised, that any poets of consequence condescended to engage in the contest. Even Lord BYRON (young and unsettled as is his reputation as a poet) thought, it appears, the occasion unworthy of his pen, and did not enter the lists, but sent his production to his friend Lord HOLLAND, openly avowing himself as the author; and by Lord HOLLAND, Mr. WHITFIELD*, and the rest, it was at once decreed to be better than all the *anonymous* pieces which had been submitted.[28]

---

* Printer's error for Whitbread.

The paper agreed however that certainly one or two pieces were 'superior to Lord Byron's', and in consequence, 'the Committee have unwarrantably swerved from that impartial line of conduct which they pledge themselves to in their public advertisement.'[29]

3. A Man of Many Parts: Busby the Polymath

Who was Dr. Thomas Busby? The facts of his life are few. He was born in 1755 and educated at Cambridge, where he read music and the Humanities and obtained his doctorate. It is probable that his interest in Lucretius began about that time, for his philosophy of life seems to have developed side by side with his gradual discovery of *De Rerum Natura* (*On the Nature of Things*), by the Roman poet Lucretius, which he began to translate about 1794 and with which he had a personal sympathy. He was also an 'active minor composer' and author of a number of musicological works which included, in 1801, *A Complete Dictionary of Music*, so successful was it that an American edition was brought out in 1827, *A Grammar of Music* (1826), and his most successful and much-quoted work, *Concert Room and Orchestra Anecdotes of Music and Musicians*, published by Clementi & Co. in 1825. Judging him by his behaviour at the Theatre Royal, Drury Lane, on the night of his protest, we may consider him to have been a man of deep emotions, and a devoted *littérateur* with a pride in his achievements as poet and translator. His *Monologue* was not a work of the highest quality – something it had in common with all the other Addresses, including Byron's – but neither was it the worst of those submitted, and words which he had written in 1786 about another poem of his seemed equally applicable in 1812:

> If the Poem possesses merit, that merit will be its own index with real judges, and survive all the attacks of false criticism: if, on the contrary, it should be found destitute, instead of transmitting its author's name to posterity, it will as certainly sink into oblivion; a circumstance which every unsuccessful writer, not as void of understanding as of literary talents, will deem the more tolerable fate.[30]

It is perhaps in *The Age of Genius: A Satire on the Times, in a Poetical Epistle to a Friend* that we may surmise something of the nature of the man. His protest over the much-criticised behaviour of the Drury Lane Committee had shown him to be a man of principle, prepared to stand up with courage and tenacity when those principles were put to the test. He was also prepared to stand up for justice and truth, for pride of country, and the values that derived from proper educational theory and the true Augustan concept of Learning as an essential prerequisite for the civilised man. There was a time:

> When all were <u>chastely</u> honest, greatly good;
> Untempted, or temptation still withstood;
> When patriotism in <u>patriots</u> found support
> And Virtue at St. James's kept her <u>court</u>;....[31]
> A time:
> When ev'ry heart beat *Amor Patriae*
> And Britain's strength was Britain's liberty;[32]

The fruits of Genius, however, could not belong to everyone. We could not all be Sheridans and Colmans*, Kembles and Holmans[33]:

> Did Genius fall the lot of ev'ry one,
> How wou'd the bus'ness of the world be done?
> If all were wits, who'd wreath the poet's bays?
> Originals, who furbish up old plays? [34]

In an extended metaphor of Lucretian fire, he sees the body and the soul of Learning enveloped by 'the bright flame of Genius', but warns of the dangers of our inability to control the processes of the mind:

> When we a spark wou'd rouze [*rouse*] the active flame,
> We only need to fan and feed the same:
> Once rais'd the more we heap the kindling pyre,
> Sparks thicker rise, and fiercer flames aspire;
> Catch at each part, their growing vigour raise,
> And spread, and burst into an universal blaze!
> Not so the mind! — A spark found only there,
> We less must heap, and with a nicer care;
> The mental spark but such a pile will light,
> Bear but much chafing, and but burn so bright.
> The fuel duly measur'd to its pow'r,

---

* George Colman (1762-1836). Dramatist, author of *The Heir-At-Law* (1797), which included a depiction of the Voltaire's greedy, pompous, pedantic Dr. Pangloss. He came to recognise that ultimately, in spite of the cruelties and misfortunes of the world, we must continue to work and metaphorically 'cultivate our gardens'.

Chapter 8 – Phoenix Triumphant

> If faintly glimm'ring, may exist its hour;
> Illumine all its little pyre around,
> And, by its own, the kindred sparks their bound.
> But if, ambitious, it wou'd spread, (Behold!
> Behold! the fate of little sparks too bold!)
> Stifled by what it vainly strives to light
> Its rashness brings its own eternal night.[35]....
>
> As flames unfed, must transiently expire,
> So without learning must the mental fire;
> Nay, as more bright, more genral [sic] the flame,
> E'en so the mind the wider it expands,
> More knowledge for its maintenance demands.[36]

In terms now familiar from Pope, Johnson, and the authors of the Drury Lane Addresses, he tells us that Learning can thrive, given the vital spark of Genius, and thus combat Folly and Pride. The 'sons of Literature' can pursue the stream of inspiration to the 'fountain-head' and thus Taste, Sense and Wit. But how many fail in this endeavour:

> How many with their learning, error drink,
> And make the brink of knowledge, folly's brink;[37]

He is aware of the great dangers of the effects of the Enlightenment on the untrained and unsophisticated mentality. Though knowledge is power, it also has the power to corrupt:

> Some are to barbarism so strong inclin'd
> By nature, they can never be refin'd;
> Or arts, or letters, teach them what you will,
> You only give to vice new pow'rs and skill:
> Bound or to frailty's, or to folly's side,
> Or vice, or folly, still their conduct guide;[38]

These ideas were very much in the minds of educationists at the turn of the century. Hester Chapone[*], Dr. Gregory[†] and Hannah More[*] were

---

[*] Hester Chapone (1727-1801), largely known for her *Letters on the Improvement of the Mind*.

[†] John Gregory (1724-1773), educationist and author of *A Father's Legacy*

just as concerned in their way with the nurturing and flowering of the young mind, whether boy's or girl's, as Henry Brougham, Dr. Birkbeck and the professors of the 'March of Mind' movement were in their way for the education of the adult. Thomas Hood shows this in his etching, *The Progress of Cant*, though in the case of children corporal punishment remained one of the principal means of control:

> There I was birch'd! There I was bred!
> There like a little Adam fed
>   From Learning's woeful tree!
> The weary tasks I used to con! —
> The hopeless leaves I wept upon! —
>   Most fruitless leaves to me! —[39]

Thirty-eight years before Hood wrote those lines, Thomas Busby was advocating education for life and not for its own sake:

> Some boys, at most, seem only sent to school,
> To complement the universal rule;
> Just thro' a certain course of study run,
> Just to return to where they first begun:
> Acquire a little with a deal of pain,
> For bus'ness to resign it all again:
> Just as their sisters, in their maiden lives,
> Learn music — to forget it when they're wives.
>
> Behold them, tolerable scholars made,
> Throw by their books to make a way for trade
> At certain age, see them of course begin
> To let out learning, to let commerce in;
> Till from all lit'rature's attractions wean'd,
> And losing e'en the little they had glean'd,
> In spite of all their Greek, and all the praise
> Acquir'd by misconstruing Latin plays,
> They turn out just as wise, and just as bright

---

to his Daughters (1761).

   [*] Hannah More (1745-1833), a religious writer and author of a pastoral drama for children, *The Search after Happiness*. Established several schools in the Mendip area. Issued a series of *Cheap Repository Tracts*.

As they who've only learn'd to read and write.[40]

This caring, sensible attitude to the growth and education of the mind of the child is far from the image we have gained of the arrogant, fretful, and faintly absurd author of the Drury Lane *Monologue*. Indeed, we sense in the following lines the semblance of a fond father for whom little George Frederick was the centre of his affections:

> What parent but admires his children's babble,
> And sense and humour hears in all they gabble?
> Between papa and company hemm'd in,
> How dicky's wit provokes the circling grin!
> And if 'mongst all the rattle of the day,
> One random repartee shou'd break its way,
> Which the child neither means nor understands,
> What laughing plaudits! And what clap of hands!
> How oft the table bids the joke resound!
> The standing bye-word of a whole year round![41]

There is nothing here of Busby's namesake, the rigid disciplinarian, Richard Busby, the celebrated, and to some boys notorious, headmaster of Westminster School in Dryden's day, who birched Dr. Burney's father mercilessly for playing truant. No! Not at all! The impression we have from reading between the lines is of a proud and loving father, who provided a carefully prescribed, largely classical, education for his sons which he administered with a firm yet gentle hand, thus earning the touching devotion which manifested itself in such extraordinary circumstances, to the astonishment of both the public and the press, on the stage of the Theatre Royal, Drury Lane. The proof of this mutual affection is to be found in the Preface to Thomas Busby's translation of *De Rerum Natura*. After offering his thanks to the many subscribers, he pays the following tribute:

> Impressed, not only with the sensations of a father, but with those of one individual benefited by the exertions of another, I cannot conclude my catalogue of obligations without mentioning the extensive aid this version of Lucretius has derived from the readings by Mr. G. F. Busby; whose style of conveying the sense of the author afforded every advantage to the language of the translator. If any farther credit be wanting to him with my friends, on account of the service he has rendered me, it will not be

withheld when I acquaint them, that, to promote my great object, he has, from time to time, voluntarily withdrawn his attention from a work on which he himself is sedulously engaged: – An Entire Translation of the *Thebaid* of Statius.[42]

4. 'Inspiring Apollo' and 'Lucretian Fire'

Having now established two of the conflicting faces of Dr. Thomas Busby – the passionate but seemingly ridiculous campaigner for poetic justice, and the firm but affectionate parent, we may now proceed to a third – the highly respected but now forgotten translator of Lucretius. *The Nature of Things: A Didascalic Poem, translated from the Latin of Titus Lucretius Carus: accompanied with Commentaries, Comparative, Illustrative, and Scientific, and the Life of Epicurus* is a monumental work of scholarship by a translator skilled in the craft of poetry.[43] It is only proper to say that two editions of Lucretius had already been published in the years immediately preceding Busby's work.[44]

The controversial Greek scholar, Gilbert Wakefield,[*] to whom Busby pays tribute by including George Dyer's[†] poem in praise of Wakefield, brought out his edition in 1796-99. Another edition, translated by John Mason Good[‡] appeared in 1805-7. As Thomas Busby claims to have begun his translation about 1794, neither of these works could have influenced him until he began Books 3, 4, 5 and 6, which he completed between the summer of 1810 and the following February. Even then, it is impossible to discover on the known evidence, whether he gave as much as a cursory glance at these works, though he was almost certainly familiar with the 1682 verse translation of Thomas Creech,[§] and may have

---

[*] Gilbert Wakefield (1756-1801). Greek scholar of Unitarian persuasion. Translator of Lucretius (1796-9). Despised Pitt. Imprisoned for seditious pamphlet.

[†] George Dyer ((1755-1841). Converted to Unitarian sect. Charles Lamb thought him gentle, kind and eccentric. His doctrine of benevolence to the poor, influenced Coleridge and Wordsworth. Being short-sighted (caused by editorial exertions), he nearly drowned by accidentally walking into the New River (Islington). Author of *Complaints of the Poor People of England* (1793) and *Poems and Critical Essays* (1801). A translation of his Latin tribute to Gilbert Wakefield was included in Busby's *Lucretius* pp xx-xxi.

[‡] John Mason Good (1764-1827). Physician, member of Guys Hospital. Translator of *The Song of Songs* (1803) and *Lucretius* (1805-07). Spoke several languages, including Russian.

[§] Thomas Creech (1659-1700). Translator of Lucretius (1682). Also *Odes*.

known of Dryden's fragments and those of Alexander Pope. It is not within the scope of this work to determine the incidence of imitation and borrowing, plagiaristic or otherwise that Thomas Busby may or may not have done in composing his own translation. It is sufficient to say that his version of *De Rerum Natura* is a testimony to the dedication and sense of purpose, the imagination and insight, the craftsmanship and poetic sensibility of this unusual man. One dares to say, in the face of his critics, that there are even many moments of sublime poetry. 'Lucretius,' he wrote, 'has been my inspiring Apollo.'[45] The statement confirms inferences already made in *The Age of Genius*. In that poem too, Busby had tried his hand at the rhyming couplet – a conventional enough pursuit in 1786 – and managed it with some success. Now, with the *Lucretius*, he would do the same, fearing the dangers of the freedom of blank verse:

> The delicacy, as well as the energetic compression, inherent in the couplet; the advantage of occasionally departing from its uniformity; the powerful climax natural to the triplet, and the majestic pomp of the Alexandrine; these appeared not only to embrace every accommodation of which a translator can be solicitous, in regard to authentic expression, but to afford peculiar opportunities for melody, force, magnificence. And all the great qualities of superior versification.[46]

Thomas Busby first became publicly known for his translations of Lucretius through the series of recitations which he organised at his home in Queen Anne Street, Cavendish Square, the circumstances of which he explains in the *Preface*:

> I offered to characters high in rank, literary repute, and poetical taste, opportunities of forming their judgment of the style in which I had executed the whole of my arduous task. Numerous and distinguished parties honoured my invitations to three annual series of recitations, in Queen-Anne-Street; and the very favourable manner in which the efforts of the reciter of the "Nature of Things" were received, procured the work a name highly flattering to my feelings, and the most promising of its future

---

Satires and Epistles of Horace (1684) and other Greek and Latin writers. Committed suicide from disappointed love and pecuniary difficulties. Busby's criticism of Creech's translation lay in its inaccuracy and lack of harmony. His version 'frequently omits whole paragraphs, and as often renders the sense obscurely, with so little of the spirit and beauty of his author.' Thomas Busby *Lucretius* Vol. I Preface p vii.

success.⁴⁷

Busby's 'glorious hope of praise' was echoed in the lines of Lucretius:

> Warms my bold heart, and animates my lays;
> Exalts my soul to energy divine,
> And fires with all the raptures of the Nine.
> Daring I follow where the Muses lead;
> Through paths untrod with new delight proceed.⁴⁸

Book the Fourth begins:

> Fired by my theme, transported I proceed,
> Through paths untrod my steps the Muses lead.⁴⁹

And Book the Fifth:

> What bard sublime, with sacred fury fired,
> By Phoebus rapt, and every Muse inspired,
> Can lift his number to that height supreme,
> To match the Majesty of NATURE'S THEME? ⁵⁰

Lucretius derived his inspiration from three principal sources, all of which Busby found to be entirely in keeping with his own philosophy of life: Epicurus's belief that happiness derives from the enjoyments of the mind, an idea that appears in a disguised form in his Drury Lane Address when he tells the audience:

> A double blessing your rewards impart,
> Each good provide, and elevate the heart,
> Our twofold feeling owns its twofold cause:
> Your bounty's comfort — rapture, your applause.⁵¹

Anaximander, whose theory that the sun was a circle of fire, which gave light to the moon and brought life to man and nature by its beams, and Democritus, whose theory that the world was composed of a concourse of atoms, were both fundamental influences on Lucretius, who also speculates on the first use of fire and the importance of dreams and waking visions:

> Though oft upon the lofty mountain's brows,
> Where trees shoot thick, and interweave their boughs,
> Branch presses branch, as driving blasts arise,
> Chafes into flame and blazes to the skies;
> Yet in the wood exists no actual fire,
> But, roused by friction, ardent seeds conspire,
> And burst to flame. But were their fire within,
> Quick would that fire to rage and blaze begin;
> Quick, without wind or friction, kindle round,
> And groves and woods with ashes strew the ground.[52]

Again, in his Drury Lane Address, Dr. Busby does not attempt to hide his literary indebtedness in the opening lines:

> When energising objects men pursue,
> What are the prodigies they cannot do?
> A magic Edifice you here survey,
> Shot from the ruins of the other day,
> As Harlequin had smote the slumberous heap,
> And bade the rubbish to a fabric leap.
> Yet at the speed you'd never be amazed,
> Knew you the zeal with which the pile was rais'd:
> Nor ever here your smiles would be represt,
> Knew you the rival flame that fires your breast.
> Flame! Fire and flame! Sad, heart-appalling sounds,
> Dread metaphors, that ope our healing wounds —
> A sleeping pang awake — and — But away
> With all reflections that would cloud the day
> That this triumphant, brilliant prospect brings;
> Where Hope reviving, re-expands her wings;
> Where generous joy, exults — where duteous ardour springs.[53]

These lines do not match the quality of the Lucretius translation, nor even of *The Age of Genius*, and we must assume that, like all the other Drury Lane competitors, including Byron, he was not temperamentally suited to the writing of occasional verse. One contemporary comment took the view that Dr. Busby had united the solemn with the familiar and that he was mistaken in mixing the two styles:

A metaphor should always have a double purpose, that of giving a resemblance, and that of embellishing and improving the effect of a lesser object, by investing it with the characteristics of a greater; but Drury-Lane is here sunk into a Harlequinade, instead of being elevated into a poetical image. The epithet <u>slumberous heap</u> is nonsense, and the word <u>bade,</u> according to the frequent practice of some of our worst poetasters, is the application of a word of personal quality to a thing totally incapable of all personal action; that is to say, which can never be so personified, to render it reasonable to believe than it can receive or obey a command. Would not a man, for example, in common discourse, be justly deemed mad, if he were to command a millstone to move out of his way, or a turnpike gate to fly off its hinges before his horse. And is it not equally nonsensical to address a command to brick and mortar. We have dwelt upon this because it is a frequent and abominable fault of our present versifiers. The 7th line – '<u>Yet at the speed you'd be amaz'd</u>,' contains an ungraceful syllabic contraction. The next line, <u>You knew</u> (for did you know) '<u>the zeal with which the pile was raised</u>,' is a true example of the bathos, and it is a problem whether the poet meant to praise the bricklayers or the committee. The two following lines are worse and worse; the <u>rival flames</u> in the 10th verse, in allusion to the actual burning of the theatre, is a vile conceit, which it almost freezes one to think of. The beginning of the 11th verse, which the author seems to have intended as a thunder clap, reminds us only of the tremendous titles which are usually put upon our Lottery-bills to catch attention – MOSCOW BURNT. BONAPARTE IN FULL RETREAT; KING OF NAPLES PRISONER. [54]

Phrases like 'exalting sanction', 'fond remembrance', and 'straining nerves' were, according to another critic 'all in the true namby-pamby of the day; the merest ordinary prose versified,' and as for exploring 'rich novelty', prizing 'all merit', and revering 'Th'illustrious dead', all might be passed over, 'if they were not brought forward as examples of true poetry.' In the lines:

> This spirit drives Britannia's conquering car,
> Burns in her ranks — and kindles every Tar.[55]

the critic understandably objects on the ground that the word 'tar' is 'a familiar jollification' for 'sailor' and stylistically inappropriate. Such judgments of the *Monologue* are irrefutable and only substantiate, even more, Dr. Busby's opinion that the verses were the product of his own 'poor talents', things of 'modest spirit'. If this was so, why did he speak out with such vehemence in full view and hearing of the assembled audience at the Theatre Royal, Drury Lane on 15 October? Was it personal vanity? An excess of poetic zeal? The damaged pride of the rejected author? In Lucretius's phrase, was he a man obsessed by 'the blind longing for honours' (*honorum coeca cupido*)?[56] A contemporary versified version of his Drury Lane speech confirms these impressions:

> Hear, Ladies and Gentlemen, I, who address you,
>   Dr. BUSBY, by name,
>   A man of great fame,
> Would with all the deep wrongs I have suffered, impress you.
>
> You must know I'm a Poet, right clever and easy;
>   Lucretius of old,
>   His sterling fine gold
> I've exchang'd into brass, just such as you see me.
>
> Notwithstanding all this, that the Drury Committee,
>   Overlooking my merit,
>   Pretensions, and spirit,
> Have preferr'd a poor snivelling Lord! Lack; the pity!

These paltry verses end:

> And now lest you doubt, that my poetry's pretty,
>   The son shall recite,
>   What his parent did write,
> BOBBY* BUSBY, stand up, boy, and give 'em a ditty.[57]

---

* Bobby – a soubriquet for a person who bobs up and down in his seat.

5. Battle of Wits: Byron versus Busby

All this time, Lord Byron remained silent, unlike the intrepid Dr. Busby, for, as we have seen, the Doctor was ever a fighter. On 23 October 1812, Busby wrote a letter to the newspapers, defending his 'strange conduct' at Drury Lane Theatre the week before. That he felt the need to do so suggests that he was in some way aware of having gone too far, with the resulting loss of his natural dignity as a classical scholar and musicologist:

> I had learnt what has since been publicly stated, that the Address brought forward was not the composition of one of the Candidates; and I considered that the Committee, by accepting any other than one of those submitted to them, had lapsed into a breach of good faith. The obligation between this Committee and the Authors of the presented verses was reciprocally binding: the poetical tribunal was to have the privilege of deciding upon their comparative merits without appeal, and the Candidates to enjoy the certainty that some one of those they offered should be chosen. It will, Sir, avail nothing, the Committee saying that the best of these was indifferent: that assersion [sic] would not dissolve the bond into which they had voluntarily entered. But how, Sir, do the Committee act? Totally forgetting the obligation they have contracted, they cast aside those who have an exclusive claim upon their choice, and resort to abilities not comprehended within the pale of their engagement. This, Sir, was a violation of justice that called for an open and oral demonstration of the indignant feeling universally excited among the Candidates. The dignity and rights of British literature were deeply involved in this act of injustice, and demanded the determined interference of some zealous member of the republic of letters. This interference, Sir, I undertook.[58]

Compared to the rest of Busby's works, which bear the mark of a consistent and finished craftsmanship, the Drury Lane *Monologue* is hardly more than a temporary aberration of little merit. Yet it is this one work which has sent Thomas Busby's name and reputation into the darkest regions of oblivion. The reason for this was the publication of some verses in the *St. James's Chronicle* on 24 October 1812, the day following Dr. Busby's letter of self-justification. If the Doctor had seemed to the rejected authors of the Drury Lane Addresses like some

Gawain striking off the head of the Green Knight, his image was miraculously transformed on the instant into that of a Don Quixote tilting at windmills. These verses established for ever in the minds of a fickle public that Thomas Busby was a hollow man, full of 'vain and self-conceit',[59] a man who signified nothing but a poetasting buffoon, who strutted and fretted his hour upon the stage and then was heard no more.

The devastating verse came from the pen of Lord Byron, who now could contain his anger no longer. No one knew better than he how to destroy a reputation with such deadly accuracy. The elaborate title is difficult to understand today if the exact circumstances are not known of Dr. Busby's protest and the abortive recitation of his devoted but feeble-voiced son. In an instant, Sir Fretful Plagiary had stepped into the den of the literary lions and was torn to pieces.

A Parenthetical Address, by Dr. Plagiary, half-stolen, with acknowledgements, to be spoken in an inarticulate voice by Master — , at the opening of the next new theatre is a parody,[60] and to see into its workings, the following selected passages may be compared with the relevant lines from Busby's *Monologue* which precede them. Byron lifted the phrases underlined direct from Busby's text[*]:

Busby: When energising objects men pursue,
What are the prodigies they cannot do?
A magic Edifice you here survey.
Shot from the ruins of the other day!
As Harlequin had smote the slumbrous heap,
And bade the rubbish to a fabric leap.[†]
Yet at the speed you'd never be amazed,
Knew you the zeal with which the pile was rais'd.

Byron: 'When energising objects men pursue,'
Then Lord knows what is writ by Lord knows who.
'A modest monologue you here survey,'
Hiss'd from the theatre the 'other day',
As if Sir Fretful wrote 'the slumbrous verse',
And gave his son 'the rubbish' to rehearse.
'Yet at the thing you'd never be amazed',
Knew you the rumpus that the author raised.

---

[*] See Appendix A for the complete version of Busby's *Monologue*.
[†] Harlequin leapt out of a box or through a window in stage representations of him.

Busby: Nor ever here your smiles would be represt,
Knew you the rival flame that fires our breast.
Flame! fire and flame! sad, heart-appalling sounds,
Dread metaphors, that ope our healing wounds —
A sleeping pang awake — and — But away
With all reflections that would cloud the day....

Byron: 'Nor even here your smiles would be represt',
Knew you these lines — the badness of the best,
'Flame! fire! and flame!' (words borrowed from Lucretius),
'Dread metaphors which open wounds' like issues!
'And sleeping pangs awake — and — but away'
(Confound me if I know what next to say);

Busby: For British Poesy — whose powers inspire
The British pencil and the British lyre.
Her we invoke! — her sister Arts implore;
Their smiles beseech whose charms yourselves adore.
These, if we win, the Graces too we gain, —
Their dear belov'd, inseparable train;
Three who their witching airs from Cupid stole,
And Three acknowledged sovereigns of the soul;

Byron: 'Oh British poesy, whose powers inspire'
My verse — or I'm a fool — and Fame's a liar,
'Thee we invoke, your sister arts implore'
With 'smiles', and 'lyres', and 'pencils', and much more.
These, if we win the Graces, too, we gain
Disgraces, too! 'Inseparable train!'
'Three who have stolen their witching airs from Cupid'
(You all know what I mean, unless you're stupid):

Busby: Thus lifted, gloriously we'll sweep along,
Shine in our music, scenery, and song;
Shine in our farce, mask, opera, and play,
And prove Old Drury has not had her day.

Nay more — to stretch the wing, the world shall cry,
<u>Old Drury never, never soared so high</u>!

Byron: '<u>Thus lifted gloriously</u>, you'll soar <u>along</u>',
Borne in the vast balloon of Busby's <u>song</u>;
'<u>Shine in</u> your <u>farce, mask</u>, scenery, <u>and play</u>'
(For this last line George had a holiday):
'<u>Old Drury never, never soared so high</u>',
So says the manager, and so say I.[61]

    Though it is difficult to forgive his pun on Graces and *Dis*graces, the techniques he employed – in retaining the largely identical rhymes (used here to good effect), and keeping close to the sound of the original – are the traditional techniques of parody:[*] Busby's 'smote' and 'bade' with Byron's 'wrote' and 'gave'; and even more so Busby's 'lyre' and Byron's 'liar'. The more successful of Busby's lines Byron wisely chose to ignore. By careful selection of the less successful lines, he was able effectively to annihilate any serious intention in the original and, to paraphrase Addison, the Colossus (of Lucretius) was reduced to the Pygmy (of Drury Lane).
    In spite of this setback, Dr. Busby, in quieter vein, succeeded in keeping his name before the public with his recitations of *The Nature of Things,* as well as keeping up his musical activities for which he was best known and liked. It would be churlish not to digress a little at this point by including a brief account of the Doctor's professional life as a talented musicologist, impresario and composer. Assuming that the world of music could not immediately provide him with an adequate income, we find him in his earlier years settling into a career in journalism and parliamentary reporting in the 1760s.
    A performance was announced for 31 May 1814, at the Covent Garden Opera House, showing him to be a man of a certain originality as a talented musician and concert promoter:

> To accommodate the magnitude and novel plan of Dr. Busby's grand triple Orchestra, and to open to the audiences a full view of its height and depth, the painted drapery over the curtain of the Opera stage, is, we hear it stated, to be entirely cleared away; the whole scenic result of the contrivance will present to the eye, band behind band, each stationed in the rear of lofty arches, supported

---

[*] For discussion on parody see Chapter Four.

by magnificent pilasters, and forming a display of orchestral preparation equally superb and unprecedented.[62]

Dr. Busby's Musical Journal, the first number of which appeared in January 1801, containing printings of his own songs, news on new British and foreign music and a 'variety of excellence and combination of distinguished talents', continued its successful run, one announcement referring to it as 'a rich treat' for masters and amateurs alike, a proof of its author's 'acknowledged science and refined taste.'[63]

Busby's connection with Drury Lane and Covent Garden did not begin with his notorious appearance on the opening night of the new Theatre Royal. He had written twice to Sheridan in 1799 with the purpose of persuading him to let out the theatre to him for the performance of oratorios during Lent (since there were no theatrical performances allowed), but as far as is known Sheridan never replied. Busby was forced to address himself to Peake, the treasurer, asking him to intercede:

> Mr Busby presents his comp[ts] to Mr Peake – Has written twice to Mr. Sheridan on the subject of engaging the theatre for a performance of Oratorios [for] Lent, but has not yet received any answer. Learning that he is expected in Town to-morrow, will therefore be obliged to Mr. Peake if he will press the business. Mr. B. spent last evening with Dr. Arnold, who promises to the enterprise every assistance in his power and if B. should prefer it, will be a joint manager and proprietor. Mr. Peake will be so obliging as to mention that particular to Mr. S. and to represent to him that Mr. Busby is anxious to immediately treat with him and the other gentlemen concerned in the property of the Theatre.[64]

In letters to Robert Elliston (1819-20), there are references to dramatic pieces, such as *The Gypsy Girl*, a comedy in five acts, *Copper Dick*, a farce, *Nightmare Abbey*, and another entitled *Man and Wife* (possibly the play by George Colman, the Elder). It seems that Busby entered into some sort of agreement with Elliston to become a reader of plays. The arrangement does not appear to have been very successful, however, if we are to believe an announcement in the press to the effect that 'the friends of Dr. BUSBY assert that although he enjoys the appointment of reader to Mr. ELLISTON, not one of the various pieces which have hitherto been produced were submitted to his inspection.'[65] Any further connection with the Theatre seems to have been doomed to failure in the literary field, but he continued to provide music for after-

Chapter 8 – Phoenix Triumphant

pieces and the like, and wisely settled to writing his more successful musicological works. Apart from his *General History of Music* and his *Grammar of Music*, his most popular work was the *Concert Room and Orchestra Anecdotes*, published in 1825:

> Dr. BUSBY has assembled, in three elegant volumes, every anecdote and fact connected with the Art and its Professions; and the work is at once so rich in curiosities, amusement, and instruction, that it ought to be attached to every pianoforte, and found in every drawing-room and boudoir in the three kingdoms. [66]

In conclusion, we must return to some surprising facts about the translator of Lucretius. Two introductions took place which were to assist the success of *The Nature of Things*. A Dr. Fryer[*], possibly a musical man, but at all events with valuable connections in high society, introduced Thomas Busby and his son to the Prince Regent's brother, the Duke of Sussex, a 'strange, shambling giant, half sage, half buffoon, with his multitude of piping bullfinches, his library of fifty thousand volumes and fifteen pairs of spectacles to read them by.'[67] The Duke kindly honoured the two enthusiastic Lucretians by allowing the younger of the two to recite a portion of the work in his presence, for which the father publicly acknowledged his gratitude.[†] More important, Earl Moira, Governor-General of India, interceded and secured the patronage of the Prince Regent himself. The rest of the royal Dukes, Kent, Cumberland, Cambridge, and Sussex all followed in giving their support. When the work was published, Dr. Busby wrote a letter to the last of these, from his home in Queen Anne Street, on 7 June 1813:

> Dr. Busby presents his profound respects to his Royal Highness, the Duke of Sussex – has the honour to transmit to his Earliest Royal Patron, a copy of the new English Lucretius. Dr. Busby requests the Duke of Sussex to believe that he shall be greatly anxious to learn His Royal Highness's opinion of his labours; and that should they be approved by a Prince of the distinguished talents which the Duke of Sussex had repeatedly displayed, his highest ambition will be gratified. [68]

---

[*] Dr. Edward Fryer (1761-1826). Licentiate of the Royal college of Physicians. Physician to the Duke of Sussex. Attended the painter, James Barry, in his last illness. Wrote account of his life.

[†] Augustus Frederick, Duke of Sussex (1773-1843). 6th son of George III and Queen Charlotte. Supported progressive political policy. President of Society of Arts (1816) and The Royal Society (1830-39).

Prince Augustus-Frederick, Duke of Sussex
(from a painting by Thomas Phillips)

The Dedication to the Prince Regent was even more grandiloquently phrased:

> To him, who, Combining with a Munificent Regard for Literature and the Arts, a Spirit purely British, has magnanimously declared that 'A prince holds his Power but as a trust for the good of his People,' the present Translator of Lucretius is proud to present these Volumes, the Offering of his devoutest Homage; and to express his indelible sense of the Honor [*sic*] conferred on his work by the Sovereign Authority of his Country.[69]

Whilst these honours were of vital importance in gaining a wider support for his work, Dr. Busby needed, above all, the public approval of a distinguished scholar. He had sent 'Book the First' to Baron Grenville, whose admiration of the translation he had no difficulty in securing, and now, as Chancellor of the University of Oxford, Grenville was pleased to accept the dedication. Thus among the impressive pages of such dedications as those already quoted, we find the following letter to the Right Honourable William, Lord Baron Grenville, Chancellor of the University of Oxford, D.C L., F.S.A.:

> My Lord
>
> With the respect due to a great Statesman, a profound Scholar, and the Supreme Head of a Learned

University, I inscribe to your Lordship this Translation of Lucretius.

    Feelings, my Lord, the most gratifying, accompany my reflection, but when the Party Politics and Transient Events of the present day shall be forgotten, it will continue to be known that my labours in rendering the most abstruse and most sublime of the Roman Classics were sanctioned by the Commendation of Yr. Lordship, and protected by the Name of Grenville.

    I have the honour,
    My Lord,
        To subscribe myself,
        Your Lordship's much obliged
        and most devoted humble servant,
        THOMAS BUSBY

Mus.Doc.Cantab. [70]

The first and second Books had been completed about 1794-95 and following Grenville's approval and encouragement, Busby set to work on the remaining four books, including the greater part of the Preface, his Dissertation on the life of Lucretius, and the Commentaries, all this between midsummer 1810 and the following February. He was a man of passion and no obstacle was so great as to blench his determination in promoting the philosophy of Lucretius.

6. The Flickering Flame of Fame

Sadly, it was a vain hope of Thomas Busby's that his inspired translation of *De Rerum Natura* should survive the 'Transient Events' of his day, for we know more about the Franco-Prussian War, Napoleon, Scott's *Rokeby*, Jane Austen's *Pride and Prejudice*, Southey's *Life of Nelson*, and Schubert's First Symphony – all of them 'news' in 1813 – than we know of the long-forgotten translator of Lucretius. Yet his star shone more brightly in 1813 than he could ever have hoped. He had achieved his greatest ambition. The public support he received was a phenomenon in itself.

    The List of Subscribers to the translation covers nineteen quarto pages. Apart from the Prince Regent and the Royal Dukes of York, Kent, Cumberland, Cambridge and Sussex, and not forgetting their royal sister, the Princess Charlotte Augusta, other Dukes included those of Grafton, Leeds, Bedford, and Devonshire. Among the Marquises were those of

Bath, Hertford, Queensberry and Blandford, and among the Earls, those of Plymouth, Coventry, Dartmouth, Bristol, Radnor, Romney, and Earl Grey. There were Viscounts Hood, Curzon, Falmouth, Palmerston, and Perceval, and among Privy Councllors were Spencer Perceval (assassinated while the book was going to press) and Richard Ryder.

Baronets and knights included Sir Andrew Agnew (the Sabbatarian campaigner, pilloried by Thomas Hood in his *Ode to Sir Andrew Agnew*),[*] Sir Francis Burdett, Sir William Curtis (Sheriff of London), Sir Rowland Hill (hero of the Spanish Wars), Henry Brougham (later to defend Queen Caroline at her trial in 1820), and it is unexpected to find the name of Samuel Whitbread included here. The Headmaster of Harrow School, Dr. George Butler is listed, together with the King's physicians, Dr. Robert Willis and Dr. Bailie, James Alan Park (the judge), Capel Lofft (discoverer of Robert Bloomfield[†] author of *The Farmer's Boy*), Samuel James Arnold (first manager of Wyatt's new Theatre Royal), C.A. Busby (architect and engineer, and brother to George Frederick), Rudolph Ackermann (publisher of prints and illustrated books), James Asperne (proprietor of *The European Magazine*), John Braham (the celebrated singer), Thomas Campbell (the author of *The Pleasures of Hope*), Samuel Taylor Coleridge the poet), Muzio Clementi (the pianist and composer), Paul Colnaghi (Italian print-seller), Josiah Conder (bookseller and editor of *The Eclectic Review*), Henry Cary (translator of Dante's *Divine Comedy)*, Henry Colburn (the publisher of Thomas Hood's works), Messrs Cradock and Joy (publishers of Thomas Hood and John Hamilton Reynolds' *Odes and Addresses*),[71] William Gifford (translator of *Juvenal* and author of *The Baviad*), Robert William Elliston (lessee of Drury Lane), John Philip Kemble (actor), Charles Knight (publisher of popular literature), Thomas Moore (poet and translator of Anacreon), Thomas Lawrence (portrait painter), James Rivington (publisher), Henry James Pye (former Poet Laureate), John Soane (professor of Architecture to the Royal Academy), Martin Tupper (author of *Proverbial Philosophy*), a number of Royal Academicians, including Michael Shee, Richard Westall, Richard Westmacott, and their President, Benjamin West, Jeffry Wyatt (the architect, and later restorer of Windsor Castle), Messrs Taylor and Hessey (publishers of Keats and Hood's employers), and, worthy of mention here, Messrs. Vernor, Hood and Sharpe, publishers.

Though only a fraction of the formidable list of nineteen pages of

---

[*] Sir Andrew Agnew (1793-1849). Committed Sabbatarian. Hood protested at the Parliamentary campaign to protect and respect 'the Lord's Day' and wrote his powerful 'Ode to Sir Andrew Agnew'.

[†] Robert Bloomfield (17766-1823). Worked as a shoemaker. Lived in dire poverty for most of his life. As well as the successful *The Farmer's Boy* (1800) he wrote *The Banks of the Wye* (1811).

Chapter 8 – Phoenix Triumphant

subscribers can be mentioned here, it will be seen that they represented every walk of life: Politics, the Law, the Church, the Professions, the Arts, Music, Painting, Literature and Publishing, Science, the Theatre, and Architecture, being only a few of the more obvious sections of society who believed enough in Thomas Busby's translation of Lucretius to allow their names to be inscribed in it. Lord Byron, after his angry accusations against Busby of arrant plagiarism, might be supposed to have expressed some contempt at such a prodigious success as Thomas Busby had achieved with his translation. It is all the more surprising, therefore, to find Byron's name among the distinguished subscribers! A special tribute is paid to him in the *Preface*,[72] which suggests that all was forgiven and forgotten between the author of the newly-published *Childe Harold's Pilgrimage* and the champion of the authors of the Drury Lane Addresses:

> The name of Lord Byron, among my subscribers, demonstrates the candid expectations entertained respecting this translation, by one of the most distinguished poets of the age.[73]

We no longer remember the brilliant, multi-talented, eccentric, ebullient, versatile Thomas Busby, and, in spite of accusations of plagiary, we can admire and appreciate his life-long devotion to classical literature and music. His flame flickered brightly for a moment and was gone. It only remains for some future scholar of the work of Lucretius to restore the balance. Whatever our judgment of Thomas Busby's *The Nature of Things* may be as a translation, it is, like Fitzgerald's *Rubayat of Omar Khayyam*, a poem of some stature in its own right, a 'golden lay', as Tennyson wrote of it:

> Than which I know no version done
> In English more divinely well.[74]

In the year following the appearance of *The Nature of Things*, a surprising development occurred. Thomas Busby sent to Byron's publisher, John Murray, the manuscript of a long satire in prose and verse entitled *Anti-Byron*. Murray sent the manuscript to Byron for his opinion. Byron replied that he could not, in the circumstances, consider himself a fair judge on the subject, 'nor can I perceive what Dr. B. has to do with the matter except as a translator of Lucretius – for whose doctrines he is surely not responsible.'[75] The matter would be tantalisingly obscure if it were not for an informative letter Byron wrote to Annabella Milbanke on 15 March 1814:

> .....the author's object is to prove that I am the <u>systematic</u>

reviver of the dogmata of Epicurus* – & that I have formed a promising plan to overthrow these realms their laws and religion by dint of certain rhymes....of such marvellous effect that he says they have already had the "most pernicious influence on civil society". – Howbeit – with all this persuasion of mine evil intents – what I saw was....a great deal about Gassendi Locke &c.† ....and a learned refutation of my supposed doctrines.[76] The preface is all about the 8 lines (ye. tears) – which have U believe given birth to as many volumes of remarks answers epigrams &c. &c.....In addition to these, I do not think that there be 50 lines of mine in all touching upon religion – but I have an ill memory – & there may be more – however I had no notion of my being so formidable an Encyclopaedist – or a Conspirator of such consequence.‡ Now – can anything be more ludicrous than all this? – yet it is very true – I mean the Anti-person of whom I am speaking – he assumes at first setting out my <u>Atheism</u> as an incontrovertible basis & reasons very wisely upon it – the real fact is I am none – but it would be cruel to deprive one who has taken so much pains of so agreeable a supposition – at least unless he believed that he had convinced me of that which I never doubted. – – I will send it to you ye. moment it is out to shew you what an escape you have had – for there is a long prose passage against <u>my marrying</u> – or rather anyone's marrying me – on account of ye. presumed philosophy wherewithal I am to lecture ye. future Ly. B. And the young Spinozas tutored in the comfortable creed§ dualism with which I

---

* Epicurus. Greek philosopher, for whom the highest good (*summum bonum*) could be best achieved and expressed through happiness, that is, peace of mind. Byron is referring to the later interpretation which came to emphasise a decline towards a belief in more sensual enjoyment.

† Gassendi Locke. Pierre Gassendi's philosophy of empiricism and experimentalism lead him to promote in France the ideas of Bacon's *New Organum*. He argued against the eclecticism and dogmatism of Descartes, anticipating John Locke's more tolerant English empiricism and pragmatism.

‡ French 18th century Encyclopédistes numbered over 100 'philosophes', the principal among whom were Jean-Jacques Rousseau, Denis Diderot, and Voltaire. Promoted rational science, preached tolerance, and encouraged learning.

§ Spinoza (1632-1677). Dutch rationalist philosopher. Important influence on the Enlightenment. Brought new approach to Bible criticism and the concepts of the self in relation to the universe. Opposed Descartes's mind-body in his

have already inoculated "civil society" & which they are to take instead of the Vaccine. — .....[77]

Byron was surprised at Busby's attack on his supposedly atheistic views, and though he was inclined towards the belief that both his 'pious' *Anti-Byron* Busby and the future Lady Byron were bent upon his conversion, he was able to feel impartial enough to advise Murray to print the work, thinking some parts of the verse very good, the whole very grave, lacking in humour and personality, but with very decent invective. To Murray, he wrote:

> I tell you openly & really most sincerely – that if published at all there is no earthly reason why you should not – on the contrary I should receive it as the fairest compliment you could pay to your good opinion of my candour – to print & circulate that or any other work attacking me in a manly manner – & without any malicious intention from which as far as I have seen I must exonerate this writer. – He is wrong in one thing – I am no Atheist – but if he thinks I have published principles tending to such opinions he has a perfect right to controvert them. – Pray publish it – I shall never forgive myself – if I think that I have prevented you. — — — Make my compts. to the Author – & tell him I wish him success – his verse is very deserving of it – & I shall be the last person to suspect his motives.[78]

It seems that Murray was of two minds. Perhaps he feared the onset of another sensational crisis. Thomas Busby had proved himself to be capable of vociferous public expression and in that alone had acquired a certain notoriety. Byron, in serious financial straits by this time, having been forced to sell Newstead Abbey, the family seat, was wooing a wealthy heiress, Annabella Milbanke, and could not afford to risk public exposure of his moral and ethical position. Already, Annabella had heard stories that he was 'dreadfully perverted' and 'an infidel'. In short, she found Byron too 'Byronic'. Nevertheless, on 2 January 1815, he married his clever young amateur mathematician, Annabella, his 'Princess of Parallelograms'[79]

It appears that Byron was foolhardy in advising Murray to publish a work which exposed too much his unconventional religious attitudes at a time when he was bent on what had all the characteristics of a *mariage de convenance*. Murray was perhaps right to decide against the publication of Busby's *Anti-Byron*, and, as far as is known, no other publishers

---

principal work, Ethics. His books prohibited reading on the Papal Index.

considered doing so, if in fact they were ever propositioned by the author at all. 'If you do not publish it,' wrote Byron to Murray, 'some one [*sic*] else will – you cannot suppose me so <u>narrow</u>-minded – as to shrink from discussion – I repeat once and for all – that I think it a good poem...'[80]

Busby's name appears a number of times in Byron's letters up to 1814, at first with a growing irritation over the matter of the Drury Lane protest, but later with a deepening respect for Thomas Busby, the translator and poet, a respect reciprocated by Byron's consent to become a subscriber to *The Nature of Things*. Mutual respect was at last restored. There it would seem the matter had ended. Their attempt at rivalry had burnt itself out.

John Murray, Byron's publisher   Dr. Thomas Busby

7. 'Mad, bad and dangerous to know'

These famous words have now become a cliché, much abused in recent times, yet they ring true enough when we consider the last year of Byron's life in England. Dr. Thomas Busby had made, in his poem, *Anti-Byron*, a powerful attack on Byron's arid atheism. Since he could deny the love of God, he could embrace Free Love, which could go hand-in-hand with freedom from personal responsibility for his actions. His impulsive separation from natural tenderness and affection was, in practice, a form of self-denial, which in turn brought only feelings of emptiness and despair.

Byron had not been blessed with the best of parents. His father,

Chapter 8 – Phoenix Triumphant

Captain John Byron, known as 'Mad Jack', was a dissolute drunkard and womaniser, who married two wealthy heiresses and gambled away their fortunes. His mother, Catherine Gordon of Gight, surrounded by a family of suicidal relatives, was an hysterical, overbearing, coarse, vulgar woman, given to violent tempers. Such an ancestral trio would hardly augur well for the infant George Gordon Byron. His great uncle, William, 4th Lord Byron, called 'The Wicked Lord Byron', from whom the ten-year old Byron would one day inherit the title of 5th Baron Byron, was a brutish fellow, who had killed a neighbour and was a harsh master to his servants.[81]

The Hours of Idleness, composed during Byron's days at Oxford, had shown Byron to be an outspoken critic of order and authority, having little respect for the controlling hand of his guardian, Lord Carlisle. In *English Bards and Scotch Reviewers*, he had committed the youthful solecism of attacking Lord and Lady Holland in return for their generous hospitality. In spite of that, they had judiciously treated him with respect, introducing him to fellow Whigs in the elegant surroundings of Holland House, where they could hone and temper his views to the needs of the party. Above all, for one so sensitive to criticism, they had given him the one thing he needed most – affection.

Unlike the devoted Lady Holland, Byron's support for Napoleon waned when the defeated Emperor failed to commit suicide after losing the Battle of Waterloo. Later, Byron bought up reams of the Emperor's Malmaison writing paper, made an offer for his Coronation Robes and spent £500 on a crude copy of Napoleon's carriage, complete with its bed, library and dining suite.

Annabella sought to retrieve their ill-fated marriage, for she had an urge not only to help Byron but to save him. She set out on a crusade to purge him of his more extreme predilections and bring him to understand the natural order of normal relationships. She failed however to realise the extent of the turmoil in his mind that could secretly send him running to prostitutes and the gambling houses. Desperate to avoid bankruptcy, he was forced to put up for sale his estate at Newstead Abbey, the scene of his notorious orgiastic parties.

Through his aristocratic dislike of 'business', Byron failed to meet his debts and was reduced to giving away his manuscripts rather than demeaning himself by selling them. All this filled him with uncontrollable anger. His neurosis let loose a spate of violent hostility, interspersed with long periods of ennui, frustration and emotional imbalance. He was thought by some to be losing his mind. The family feared he would take his own life so as to release himself from the torment in his soul.

Any signs of a rapprochement between Byron and Annabella were finally dashed when her parents learned the truth about their daughter's unusual marital intimacies. They consulted Lady Caroline Lamb, whose powerful sexual obsession with the young Byron had by now turned to a seething hatred of him. She laid her bitterness at the feet of the mortified parents and to their horror all was revealed.

Lady Anne Isabella (Annabella) Milbanke, wife of Lord Byron

Caroline had fallen for the handsome young Byron in 1812, soon after the publication of the first cantos of *Childe Harold,* and it did not take her very long to decide that he was "mad, bad, and dangerous to know." Yet once entrapped in a frantic affair with her, he was at first reluctant to subject himself to her exotic, byzantine sexual fantasies. He had once upon a time laid himself open to her spell. Now, in Greece, especially following sensational revelations about his open relationships with young boys, his dignity and self-respect as a poet was irrevocably damaged. The situation was grave, especially since sodomy was punishable by long prison sentences, or even, in extreme cases, death by hanging.

Byron was to leave England in disgrace in 1816 – a place, he considered, of cant and hypocrisy. Bishop Heber[*], in 1822, attacked

---

[*] Bishop Reginald Heber (1783-1826) Bishop of Calcutta, poet and hymn-writer, Preacher at Lincoln's Inn in 1822.

Byron by writing of him as "a systematic poet of seduction, adultery, and incest, the contemner of patriotism, the insulter of piety, the raker of every sink of vice and wretchedness." Thomas Busby did not go so far as that in his criticism of Byron's atheistic views. Nevertheless, Heber's out-and-out rejection on such strict moral grounds was to reverberate throughout Victorian society for decades to come and continues today, even in our more permissive digital age.

Four principal female protagonists played their parts in this drama of passions, despair and humiliation: Lady Holland through her admiration and support for Byron the poet; Augusta Leigh, for the constancy of her incestuous love for Byron, and his for her; Lady Byron in her earnest wish to restore his soul and self-respect; and Lady Caroline Lamb who demonised him. By an unexpected twist of fate, the latter had now become the principle protagonist in the drama, who, ironically, was herself to become 'mad, bad and dangerous to know' and become his merciless chastiser.

None of this would necessarily concern us here, however, if there were not a final episode in which literature would play its part, this time in the manifestation of a more popular kind. Three years after Byron's departure from England, a scurrilous pamphlet made its sensational appearance in Grub Street. It was entitled *The Men in the Moon: or, The Devil to Pay.* Surprisingly, it was not listed in Albert M. Cohn's *George Cruikshank: A Catalogue Raisonné of the Work during the years 1806-1877.* It was possibly a rogue publication, considered too libelous to publish openly. A better known, equally scathing pamphlet, *The Man in the Moon* in 1820 - a vicious lampoon of the Prince Regent, was printed by the radical publisher, William Hone. It was dedicated to 'The Rt. Hon. The Lord of the Faithless', criticising Byron for his atheistical beliefs, accusing him of 'deriding Religion, debasing Society, creating Discord, indicting Abuse', and 'levelling Distinction in a Christian country.' The woodcuts were by George Cruikshank, a sharp observer of the social and political scene.

The first woodcut is a grim reminder: a deserted gallows, the knotted noose having previously completed its grim 'business', awaits the arrival of the next 'recipient' (Byron). On the post nearby is a dunce's cap with ass's ears, below which are two flails that have been used for whipping the prisoner in the nearby stocks. Atop the crossbar squats the Devil, gloating and squirming triumphantly. A quotation from *Don Juan* makes its point:

> The Devil's in the Moon for mischief,
> And yet she looks so modest all the while.

A further woodcut has the mark of genius about it. Byron is in the grip of the Devil, who takes possession of him, body and soul, grips him by the shoulder with a clawed hand, and points with a withered finger towards the gallows on the white cliffs (England). The ravening birds hover overhead, ready to feed on his corpse. Byron raises his hand at the horrific prospect of being hanged for his sins. He makes a reluctant farewell to his native land forever. In this Faustian vision, his native country had set the 'Lord of the Faithless' adrift in foreign lands:

> Me, miserable, which way shall I fly—
> Infinite wrath, and infinite despair?
> Which way I fly is Hell, myself am Hell;
> And in the lowest depth, a lower deep,
> Still threat'ning to devour me, opens wide,
> To which the Hell I suffer seems a Heaven.[82]

Chapter 8 – Phoenix Triumphant

In *Satan's Address to his Friend* that follows, the Devil accuses Byron of his misdemeanours and warns him of the punishment to come:

> Start not, My Lord!
>   'Tis only I,
> Your *primogenial* Deity:
>   Who stop'd to say,
> That if you wish
>   Your *end* to know;
> I'd point the way.
> 'Tis pity to perplex your brains,
> Musing on *future groans* and *pains*,
>   Just now—
>   For know,
> Your *crew* below,
>   Have fram'd,
>   A *Resolution*,
> Swearing to *overthrow*
> The CONSTITUTION;
>   REFORM's their *word*,
> "*Meaning, of course, Rebellion, Blood, and Riot,*"

> And hope to raise
> A direful blaze
> When men are hush'd and quiet.

to which His Lordship replies:

> Go! Get thee hence, thou hellish fiend,
> I *ne'er believ'd*, not *fear*, and *end*.
> No thoughts of future life have I;
> But wait the *stream* of destiny.
> Scorning the high control of youth;
> I learn'd to hate: THE WORD OF TRUTH.
> So thus I spurn THE BOOK OF GOD,
> And only heed thy MASTER's nod.

Caricaturists in Byron's day were quick to include any quirks in the physical appearance of their human targets and, in Byron's case, made much of his deformed foot, from which he had suffered humiliation from childhood. Cruikshank cruelly, yet ingeniously, arranged his design to merge Byron's left foot with the Devil's cloven hoof. Hone takes no prisoners in the vehemence of his vicious wit and the political perspicacity of his observations and opinions.

In 1823, the Greek Committee in London asked Byron to look into the plight of Greece under the Turkish yoke. Byron, by espousing the Greek Cause, was to become a national hero to all the Greek revolutionaries. At last he would find fame and honour of the kind he could never have achieved in England.

Byron died at Missolonghi on 19 April 1824. His body was refused a place with other great poets laid to rest in Westminster Abbey on moral grounds and was taken to the small country village of Hucknall Torkard near Newstead Abbey - the final rejection of his fellow countrymen. In 1997, when England failed to celebrate his bi-centenary, it was up to Russia, where he is universally admired, to strike a Byron anniversary medal. Today, he is admired throughout Europe and across the world.

We have already noticed that the Theatre Royal, Drury Lane, can be seen in a disguised form in the centre of Thomas Hood's etching of 1825, *The Progress of Cant*.[*] Hood adapts Hone's idea by depicting Byron in the guise of the Devil with a tail from under his tail-coat and feet shown as cloven hooves. A dissolute female, a prostitute with painted eyebrows and beauty spot, an inmate of Newgate Prison, tries to entrap the Devil by treading on his tail. She carries a banner marked *Fry for Ever*, which,

---

[*] See Preface p xiv

typical of Hood's astonishing propensity for multiple interpretations in his puns, encourages the eye to search for more in the surrounding images. A banner on the far side announces THE CAUSE OF GREECE, which connects the 'reader' to the now familiar image of the building of St. Pancras New Church in Greek style – see frontispiece.

A secondary, subliminal interpretation of the image as Benjamin Wyatt's new Theatre Royal, Drury Lane, is indicated by the prominent banner boldly protesting: NO THEATRE, held aloft by Edward Irving, the charismatic preacher, condemning the London playhouses for their immorality. He was justified, for since the opening of the theatres on the return of Charles II to the throne in 1660, playwrights responded with enthusiasm to the new-found freedoms that allowed them to present sexually implicit scenes on stage, a situation the authors of the *Genuine Addresses* were keen to remedy.

The range of imagery adopted by the poets of the *Genuine Addresses* provides a window through which we can understand the principles and ideas that collectively filled their thoughts as they feverishly scribbled down their first drafts. For them, Shakespeare, in his completeness, provided the perfect interpretation of the human condition, a benchmark by which they could judge their own creations. Addison, Johnson, and Garrick had provided the means and the method. Spanish aggression and Napoleon were no longer a threat. Freedom and liberty had returned and the Phoenix had found peace from its labours at last. The Muses had reclaimed their right to reign over the New Drury and Apollo was once more in the ascendant.

Phoenix of Drury Lane

23. Lord Byron in Albanian dress, painted by Thomas Phillips (1813)

24. Portrait of Lady Caroline Lamb by Thomas Lawrence, c.1805

25. The Honorable Augusta Leigh, half-sister of Lord Byron.
Portrait by James Holmes.

26. Catherine Gordon, mother of Lord Byron.
Portrait by Thomas Stewardson.

27. Extract from Hood's cartoon *Progress of Cant* depicting Byron in the guise of the Devil with a tail coming out from under his tail-coat and feet shown as cloven hooves. (*by kind permission of Aberdeen University*)

28. Frederick Howard, 5th Earl of Carlisle, guardian of the young Lord Byron, viciously lampooned in *English Bards and Scotch Reviewers*. Painted by Thomas Lawrence, 1794

29. Charles Maurice de Talleyrand. Bishop, versatile politician and influential diplomat, supporting the Bourbon legitimacy.

30. Bonaparte crossing the Alps on a white stallion. A magnificent propaganda painting by Jacques-Louis David, 1802.

31. Bonaparte crossing the Alps on a mule. A more accurate record of the expedition. Here a peasant is leading him over the Great St Bernard Pass on his way to his victory at Marengo, Italy, in 1800. Painting by Paul Delaroche, 1850.

32. *The King of Brobdingnag and Gulliver.* Caricature of George III and minuscule Napoleon in the role of 'Gulliver' (from Jonathan Swift's *Gulliver's Travels*). The dwarf Grildrig was the Queen's Court Jester.
Artist: James Gillray. Published by Mrs H Humphrey, print-seller, in 1803.

33. Nottingham market place, the site of the frame-breakers' riots. Painted by William Goodacre, c.1827

34. Ned Ludd, the leader of the Luddites. Engraving, 1812.

35. Frame breakers. The drawing depicts two men superimposed on an 1844 engraving from the Penny magazine of a post-1820s Jacquard loom.

36. The Grande Théâtre de Bordeaux.
Considered the finest opera house in Europe when it was built in 1780, and was the inspiration for Wyatt's design for Drury Lane.

37. The fourth and present Theatre Royal, Drury Lane, designed by Benjamin Wyatt and constructed at a cost of almost £152,000. It opened in 10th October 1812 with a production of 'Hamlet Prince of Denmark'

38. Portrait of Henry Richard Vassall-Fox, 3rd Baron Holland, by Sir George Hayter (1820)

39. Portrait of the Revd. Gilbert Wakefield by James Green, c.1800

40. Sketch for a Prime Minister, or how to purchase a Peace
Published in *The Satirist* February 1st 1811

Lady Holland, ever ambitious for her husband's promotion in Government, attempts to enter the Treasury in the hope of seeking a meeting with the Chancellor of the Exchequer, Spencer Perceval, who was in charge of trade with neutral countries to combat Napoleon's embargo on British trade. He raised money for the wars against Napoleon. He threatens Lord and Lady Holland with a blunderbuss and shouts: "Away rogues - you can't come in here." A banner falls from the window announcing: "I shall be Prime Minister". A voluptuous Lady Holland holds a paper in her hand marked: 'Lord Wellington'' and comments: "Then I shall be Bang Up to everything." Napoleon mutters: "Et moi aussi." He hides under her cloak for fear of discovery and offers a sack full of gold as a peace offering. But he holds a dagger in his right hand to show he is still ready to defend himself in an emergency. The comical door-knocker depicts an alarmed First Lord of the Treasury, Spencer Perceval, having his chin pulled. Elected Prime Minister in 1809, he was assassinated as he entered the Lobby of the Houses of Parliament on 1 May 1812. The point of the caricature is that Her Ladyship wears the trousers and His Lordship wears the skirt.

41. Edmund Kean as Richard III (published by M. & M. Skelt, London, between c1837 and 1840)

42. William Charles Macready as Macbeth

43. Sir Henry Irving, from photo by Samuel A Walker, 1883, published in *The Pictorial World*

44. Cartoon in *The Examiner* by George Cruikshank. *The Four Mr. Prices* is a dig at Stephen Price's scheme of four different ticket prices to suit the pockets of a wide range of clients. It shows a small group of comical figures walking arm-in-arm along a country road, presumably on their way to the theatre: a very tall dandy in a ridiculously small 'Petersham' hat and pinch-waisted, high-collared tail-coat (High Price), is followed by an absurdly minuscule manikin in hunting habit, top hat and riding-boots (Low Price), who in turn is firmly attached to a large rotund figure wearing capacious, balloon-like pantaloons, a broad-brimmed hat, and tight-buttoned jacket, bursting at the seams (Full Price), arm-in-arm with a pathetically thin top-hatted, half-starved figure with spindly legs (Half Price).

A secondary interpretation may have something to do with tradespeople. For example, manufacturing candles began in 1830, when a 'Mr. Price' advertised his candles as a 'new portable, adaptable, even edible' commodity, still to be found world-wide.

CHAPTER NINE

The Rejected Addresses

- *A Sensational Sequel*

1. Horace and James Smith: Parody Personified

In 1812 a small book of brilliant parodies entitled *Rejected Addresses*, by two learned and witty brothers, Horace and James Smith, made its appearance. It professed to be a collection of Addresses by famous authors – Byron and Busby among them. Its astonishing popularity took it to 25 editions in as many years.

The Smith brothers, James (1775-1839) and Horace (1779-1849), were irrepressible humourists who regularly produced reams of comic copy for Thomas Hood's father's *Monthly Magazine*. Horace also wrote novels and articles for the *London Magazine*. The editor was John Taylor, a friend and partner of the publisher, Thomas Hood the Elder.

Horace Smith

James Smith

Horace was an assiduous writer, publishing five books in three years, including *Gaieties and Gravities* (1825), a collection of essays, comic tales and fugitive pieces. His best novel was *Brambletye House* (1826), a tale of cavaliers and roundheads in the style of Walter Scott's *Woodstock*.[1] Horace was a friend of many authors, Thackeray among them. Shelley said of him: 'Is it not odd that the only truly generous person I ever knew who had money enough to be generous with, should be a stockbroker.'[2] In his avuncular role, Horace befriended the young Thomas Hood, who gave a charming account of their first meeting. He wrote to his Scottish friend, Robert Balmanno:

> I called on Horace Smith yesterday but he was out. Today I have had better luck though he was out still – for we met at his door, & I gave him your letter on the steps. I was

Chapter 9 - The Rejected Addresses

delighted with him…he was all that is kind and gentlemanly. …I hope that he & I are to be quite thick ere I leave. If such a stick as I may be thick with anyone.'[3]

Looking through the poetical works of Horace Smith and his brother today, we would find few of the poems to satisfy our modern sensibilities. They are all very much of their own time, where an abundance of whimsical themes and a plethora of wry archaisms form the major part of the *oeuvre*. Nevertheless, at a time when the reading public was rapidly increasing, the verses were popular among the more informed of their readers. We can find some daunting titles, including all thirteen verses of an 'Address to a Mummy', with lines such as:

> And thou hast walked about (how strange the story!)
> In Thebe's street three thousand years ago,
> When the Memnonium was in all its glory,
> And time had not begun to overthrow
> Those temples, palaces and piles stupendous,
> Of which the very ruins are tremendous.
>
> Speak! For thou long enough hast acted Dummy.
> Thou hast a tongue – come – let us hear its tune;
> Thou'rt standing on thy legs, above-ground Mummy!
> Revisiting the glimpses of the moon…[4]

In December 1817, Horace Smith did battle with his friend Percy Bysshe Shelley, over which of them could compose the best sonnet on a mutually chosen theme, the River Nile. They both chose the Egyptian Pharaoh, Rameses II, of whose tomb in the desert only a few fragments remained. Shelley called his poem 'Ozymandias':

> I met a traveller from an antique land,
> Who said – "Two vast and trunkless legs of stone
> Stand in the desert….Near them, on the sand,
> Half sunk a shattered visage lies, whose frown,
> And wrinkled lip, and sneer of cold command,
> Tell that its sculptor well those passions read
> Which yet survive, stamped on these lifeless things,
> The hand that mocked them, and the heart that fed;
> And on the pedestal, these words appear:
> My name is Ozymandias, King of Kings;

> Look on my Works, ye Mighty, and despair!
> Nothong beside remains. Round the decay
> Of that colossal Wreck, boundless and bare
> The lone and level sands stretch far away."

Shelley won the contest; his sonnet was included in countless anthologies.[5] The poem is remarkable for its rhyming pattern of the fourteen lines, which has the rhymes petering out (abab-cdcd-efef-ef), showing that everything achieved by man throughout history slowly decays and falls into oblivion. Thus Shelley's obscure pen-name, 'Glaristes' (approximately 'preaching dormouse') reflects the process. Time has proved 'Ozymandias' to be by far the more successful of the two poems.

Horace's poem was published under the impressive title: *A Stupendous Leg of Granite, Discovered Standing by itself in the Deserts of Egypt.*[6] Horace's first line is an indication of how the poem proceeds: 'In Egypt's sandy silence, all alone, stands a stupendous Leg...'. Another of Horace's sonnets, *To the Setting Sun,* begins: 'Thou central Eye of God, whose lidless ball/Is vision all around....', lines which fail to inspire, except as parodies of themselves.

For all that, both Horace and James were much admired for their quirky verse, with its multitude of classical references, Latin quotations, and a variety of unrewarding themes, many relating to celebrities and events of the day, now long since forgotten. However, as fêted as they were for their society verses, their fame was to be fixed forever in the remarkable little volume *Rejected Addresses: or, The Theatrum Poetarum*, published in 1812 to great acclaim.[7]

Horace's brother, James, was Solicitor to the Board of Ordnance. Unlike his more taciturn brother, he was a brilliant conversationalist and held sway at many a sparkling social gathering of the London *literati*. He made a great success with his skittish volumes *A Trip to Paris* and *A Trip to America,* titles inspired by Sheridan's comedy, *A Trip to Scarborough.* His publisher, Charles Matthews, commented that James was 'the only man who can write clever nonsense.' His speech was always kindly and devoid of sarcasm. The irreverent *Fraser's Magazine* included him in a gallery of portraits as 'a gouty and elderly painstaking joker'.[8]

The idea for the *Rejected Addresses* was thought up almost overnight, encouraged by a close friend of the brothers, Charles Ward, the inveterate imbiber of good port - a fact that explained the size of his large crimson nose, inflamed no doubt by the hellish heat of the crumbling Theatre Royal. He gave the brothers a fiery theme on which to exercise their talents. It was during the plans to set up the competition for the opening Address that Charles Ward alerted the brothers to the challenge. Horace immediately began to compose an Address himself, which was duly entered and registered according to the elaborate rules. In spite of such alacrity, his poem eventually joined the rest of the rejects.

However, all was not lost. It seemed that on 21 August 1812 James Smith dined with Charles Ward at the Piazza Coffee House in Covent Garden, the very place where Sheridan had sat drinking a glass of wine, watching his theatre go up in flames and waiting for his insurance money. Ward claimed that the bulk of the genuine Addresses were of unacceptable quality, whereupon James improvised an Address that set Ward off into peals of laughter, for by this time he had consumed the greater part of a magnum of old port. James told Horace the story and Horace suggested they should share the parodies of their chosen authors to speed the work forward. They feared that they had little time to beat the clock, for they had only six weeks to go before the opening of the theatre; the poems would have to be rapidly composed, the book printed and published ready for the opening night.[9]

The brothers had to think hard about which poets of the day might well have contributed to the Competition. Another difficulty was shortage of time in which to allow the idea to mature in their minds and the variety of styles they were to parody. Faced with the principal names of the day from Sir Walter Scott, William Wordsworth, Lord Byron, Thomas Moore, #George Crabbe, Samuel Johnson, and harking back to earlier Drury days, dramatists William Davenant and Sheridan, the brothers had a hard and wearisome task. They had to allow their familiarity with these literary models to fill up the blank pages in front of them with uncommon speed. It is to their credit that, ironically, they succeeded in producing a work touched with the mark of genius.

The concept of composing a number of parodies based on the style of well-known poets, as if they themselves had entered the competition for the opening Address at the new Theatre Royal, turned out to be a sensation, one that would seal the reputation of the Smith brothers and fix their names firmly in the hall of fame. There were rumours that some of their more revered contemporaries had ventured to enter the fray and sent in their own offerings with the assurance of anonymity under the prescribed secrecy arrangements. Out of the 112 Addresses, only 21 were selected for the short list, wryly described as a 'fair example of the present state of poetry in Great Britain.'[10] It was regretted that the brothers were put in the same embarrassing position as the Selection Committee, who had 'culled what had the appearance of flowers from what possessed the reality of weeds.'[11]

Established authors as they were, the task of finding a publisher prepared to print *Rejected Addresses* in time proved to be a considerable stumbling block. Moreover, they were not prepared to pay the costs themselves. As Horace remarked: 'We had no objection to raise a laugh at the expense of others, but to do that at our own expense, uncertain as we were to what extent we might be involved, had never entered our contemplation'.[12] They first approached John Murray, offering him the copyright for £20. However, he refused them and suggested one, Thomas Cadell, a relative of the Smiths. This would have been a risk as his business was in a questionable state, and more to the point, he was known to be 'close' in business deals. Eventually, they approached the publisher of plays, John Miller, who accepted a 50 per cent deal.

Within a week of the opening of the new theatre, London was awash with reviews. Everyone was curious as to the true identity of the authors. When finally they were exposed, the brothers were welcomed into the literary salons. *The Edinburgh Review* for 12 November 1812 devoted eighteen pages, and in America, the *Analectic Magazine* of Philadelphia gave ten pages. Thus:

> In the prime of life – thirty-seven and thirty-three respectively – of eminently gentlemanly manners and bearing, and of remarkably handsome personal appearance, highly educated, and possessed of an inexhaustible fund of literary knowledge, James and Horace Smith were exactly fitted to shine in the presence of the highest and most learned.[13]

Not all contemporary critiques of the parodies of the *Genuine Addresses* were entirely complimentary. Francis Jeffrey, editor of T*he Edinburgh Review*, noted for its scathing criticism, did not consider them to be of the highest form, possessing 'a certain ludicrous and light air, not quite suitable to the gravity of some of the originals,' imparting to some of them 'a sort of mongrel character in which we may discern the feature both of burlesque and imitation.'[14]

Francis Jeffrey

Chapter 9 - The Rejected Addresses

For the most part, the verse was recognisable. Parodies of Scott, Southey, Crabbe, Coleridge, Colman, Byron, and 'Monk' Lewis figured among the better examples. Jeffrey did however appreciate that a certain value in the *Rejected Addresses* lay in their lack of malice. It appeared also that none of the poets caricatured seemed to have taken offence. Byron and Scott are recorded as saying they 'could hardly believe that they had not written the Addresses themselves.'[15]

After all the excitement was over, James settled back into his life as a solicitor. Horace had had retired from the stockbroker business in 1812, at the peak of his fame as one of the poets of the *Rejected Addresses* and by 1826 had settled at No 10 Hanover Crescent, an elegant Regency terraced house in Brighton. After some years of success, the brothers sold John Miller their half share for £1000, with which they were well pleased.[16]

Horace became a successful stockbroker and made a considerable fortune sufficient to retire very comfortably to his fine house in Brighton, where, as we have seen, he continued to write poetry and historical novels. He brought out an edition of James's writings under the title *Memoirs, Letters, and Comic Miscellanies in Prose and Verse*. Horace had a proverbial wit. Commenting on the social life of Brighton, he remarked: "If I mount my little white nag and ride from Kemp Town to Brunswick Terrace I am sure of half-a-dozen invitations to dinner. That I call enjoying life." Horace died ten years after his brother, in 1849.

The following sections are commentaries on the first eight out of the 21 *Rejected Addresses* and the authors parodied therein:

>*Loyal Effusion* by W.T.F.
>*The Baby's Début* by W.W.
>*An Address Without a Phoenix* by S.T.P.
>*Cui Bono?* By Lord B.
>*Hampshire Farmer's Address* by W.C.
>*The Living Lustres* by T.M.
>*The Rebuilding* by R.S.
>*Drury's Dirge* by L.M.

2. *Loyal Effusion* by W.T.F. (William Fitzgerald)

The Phoenix Rises Again!

The first of the published *Rejected Addresses*, *Loyal Effusion* by W.T.F. was a parody of the now-forgotten William Thomas Fitzgerald (1759-1829), described as a 'versifier' by his critics, who composed in an inflated patriotic style and was thus a gift to the parodist. Son of a military officer in the Dutch service, he was educated at the University of Paris and the Inner Temple. Until about 1805, he was employed at the Navy Pay Office, a safe sinecure, in contrast to his radical support of human rights. For much of his life he was a loyal Laureate and Founder of the Literary Fund.

In 1799, he published *Nelson's Triumph, or, The Battle of the Nile,* and in 1815, *Wellington, or The Battle of Waterloo,* a patriotic panegyric to feed the passions of the pit and the gallery. He took care to print the salient rabblerousing words in capital letters as a guide to the actor chosen to read his *Address:*

> Thus long defensive BRITONS stood,
> And brav'd the overwhelming flood,
> With constancy divine!
> 'Till the brave PRUSSIAN'S distant gun
> Induced the GLORIOUS WELLINGTON
> To form the BRITISH line;
>
> His eagle eye discerns from far
> That moment which decides the war,
> "FORWARD! he cries, "FOR ENGLAND'S GLORY!"
> The veteran bands of GALLIA yield,
> And WATERLOO'S triumphant field
> Shall shine the BRITISH story.

Genuine as his love of country was, fate brought him untimely ill-heatlth the consequence of which he was forced to retire early from his Navy Office post. For the last thirty years of his life he suffered from dropsy and a debilitating asthmatic condition. His lack of strength did not prevent him from continuing to compose powerful patriotic prologues. Some critics have praised him as being one of the foremost 'loyalist' versifiers of his day, vehemently denouncing Napoleon. It seems however

Chapter 9 - The Rejected Addresses

that his contemporaries considered him mediocre, William Cobbett calling him the 'Small Beer Poet'. Thomas Hood referred to him in his *Address to Mr. Cross* as lying on 'his small bier'.[17] The Smith brothers remembered him at the Pic-Nic Theatre in Tottenham Street, 'wearing a wig too small for his head,'[18] and Byron petulantly scorned him for his recitations at the Literary Fund Annual Dinner:

> Still must I hear? – shall hoarse Fitzgerald bawl
> His creaking couplets in a tavern hall. [19]

The discovery of Fitzgerald's Address, printed by Boyle in his notes,[20] allows us to judge for ourselves how effective his poem was, since it reveals some degree of competence:

> When wrapped in flames, terrific to the sight,
> Old Drury perish'd in one fatal night,
> The troubled shade of GARRICK, hovering near,
> Dropt on the burning pile a pitying tear!

These lines are followed by a fanciful assertion that 'Departed spirits watch the place they love.' Then follows an attack on the depravity of Charles II's reign, 'Encouraged by Vice, it gave fair Virtue pain':

> Licentious Plays debauch'd – the Actors too,
> They copied manners which their Authors drew,

No! this was not the stuff the Committee was looking for. With regard to the tear, James Smith noted: 'What a pity that, like Sterne's recording angel, it did not succeed in blotting the fire out for ever! That failing, why not adopt Gulliver's remedy?' – a reference to an incident in which the ever pragmatic Gulliver, alarmed at the burning down of the Princess of Lilliput's palace, saved the situation by urinating over it, causing a considerable stench.

The Smiths cruelly deflate Fitzgerald as a puffed-up patriot in their parody and adroitly convert the serious into the comic by perpetuating the over-used 'phoenix' image in their parody:

> A phoenix late was caught: The Arab host
> Long ponder'd - part would boil it, part would roast;
> But while they ponder, up the pot lid flies,
> Fledged, beak'd, and claw'd, alive they see him rise

> To heaven and caw defiant in the skies.
> So Drury, first in roasting flames consumed,
> Then by old renters to hot water doom'd,
> By Wyatt's trowel patted, plump and sleek,
> Saws without wings, and caws without a beak. [21]

Predictably, Napoleon does not escape their wit:

> Gallia's stern despot shall in vane advance
> From Paris, the metropolis of France;
> By this day month the monster shall not gain
> A foot of land in Portugal or Spain.
> See Wellington in Salamanca's field
> Forces his favourite general to yield,
> Breaks through his lines and leaves his boasted Marmont,
> Expiring on the plain without his arm on;
> Madrid he enters at the cannon's mouth
> And then the villages still further south.
> Base Bonaparte, fill'd with deadly ire,
> Sets, one by one our playhouses on fire. [22]

Here, in these lines, the parody of Fitzgerald's style is mere imitation, but the sentiments are exactly what the Drury Lane pit-dwellers wanted to hear, lines nevertheless, that were doomed to die a natural death on the Committee's pile of rejections.

We can imagine Fitzgerald's powerful delivery of the lines as he recites his poignant couplet:

> The sweetest tribute to the fallen brave
> Are Soldier's sorrows on a Soldier's grave! [23]

However, much the imitation of Fitzgerald's style attempts to become a parody, it fails to impress because of its closeness to the original, which tells us perhaps that the original was already a parody of itself.

In the concluding lines Fitzgerald descends into bathos:

> Bless every man possess'd of aught to give;
> Long may Long Tylney Wellesley Long Pole live,
> God bless the Army, bless their coats of scarlet,
> God bless the Navy, bless the Princess Charlotte. [24]

Jeffrey comments that the lines 'render with effect the vulgarity, servility, and gross absurdity of the newspaper scribblers.'[25]

As for the worthless William Wellesley Pole, we remember little of him now. He carried off the attractively wealthy Miss Long, daughter and heiress of Sir James Tylney Long, on whose death Pole took the names for his own. His squandering of the vast fortune, his outrageous demolition of the great palace of Wanstead House in Essex led him into insolvency. As a consequence of his debts (only a part of which were paid off by the sale of its fabulous contents), his cruel arrogance in his marital relations, his moral and physical decline and fall into poverty inevitably led to his death in a miserable garret on 1st July 1857. The *Morning Chronicle* came to the conclusion that he was 'a profligate, and a gambler in his youth, he became debauched in his manhood, redeemed by no single virtue, adorned by no single grace, his life gone out even without a flicker of repentance.' We can only wonder what effect Fitzgerald's implied plea for forgiveness made on the reading public. The parodist, presented with such an object of derision, had no compunction about making fun of such an outrageous profligate. In the words of another famous Fitzgerald:

> The Moving Finger writes, and having writ,
> Moves on. Not all your Piety and Wit
> Shall lure it back to cancel half a line,
> Nor all your Tears wash out a word of it.'[26]

3. *The Baby's Début* by W. W. (William Wordsworth)

Images of Innocence

The second poem in *Rejected Addresses* was *The Baby's Debut* by W.W., immediately recognized as an attack on Wordsworth's poetry about childhood. The poem was intended to pillory the 'Alice Fell' style devised by Wordsworth to create an effect of untutored simplicity in evoking the mind of the child, seen through the more mature sensibilities of an adult. Such artificial devices irritated Byron, who wrote of 'the simple Wordsworth':

> Who both by precept and example, shows
> That prose is verse, and verse is merely prose... [27]

The tone of the parody was foreshadowed by a particularly vicious epigraph lifted from one of Cumberland's plays (much admired by Horace Smith):

> Thy lisping prattle and thy mincing gait,
> All thy false mimic fooleries I hate;
> For thou art Folly's counterfeit, and she
> Who is right foolish hath the better plea:
> Nature's true idiot I prefer to thee. [28]

Parodists are like journalists. They look for the newsworthy, a choice angle on a story that will catch the attention of the sensation-loving public. James Smith hit upon a theme that would promote *Rejected Addresses* to an even wider readership and put the book straight into the pit of public controversy. As one critic has pointed out, Wordsworth's 'excursions into the mawkish' were singled out for imitation. The criticism was patently levelled at the simple style employed in his poem, *We are Seven*, in which the poet meets a child visiting the graves of her siblings. The ballad style is spare and simple and immediately claims the sympathy of the reader:

> I met a little cottage Girl:
> She was eight years old, she said;
> Her hair was thick with many a curl
> That clustered round her head.
>
> "Sisters and brothers, little maid,
> How many may you be?"
> "How many? Seven in all," she said,
> And wondering looked at me.

The Baby's Debut is crafted in identical style lends itself well to the Smith brothers purpose, namely to society's widespread sentimental view of childhood. Wordsworth was subsequently taken to task in the pages of the *Ediburgh Review* for 'his mawkish affectations of childish simplicity and 'nursery stammering'.[29] Charles Lamb, shocked at the cruelty of the parody, wrote to Wordsworth in sympathetic tones, saying: 'I should guess, one of the sneering brothers, the vile Smiths. are responsible.'[30] Francis Jeffrey complained that the author did not attempt to copy 'any of the higher attributes of Mr. Wordsworth's poetry; but has succeeded perfectly in the imitation of nursery stammering. It will make him ashamed of his *Alice Fell*....of which it is by no means a parody, but a very fair, and indeed we think a flattering imitation.' This view reflects the damning remark that Wordsworth was none other than 'a purveyor of puerilities'.[31]

The poet is on a journey by post-chaise to Durham and hears a faint moan. The driver is going at a fair pace, the racket of the chaise and the clattering hooves of the horses obscuring the low moaning. Once or twice, the poet calls to the groom to stop, and when they do, there is only silence. 'What can it be, this piteous moan?' Eventually, the poet finds a small girl had hidden herself away and was weeping inconsolably. She has lost her cloak. He finds it trapped in the wheel.

> 'Twas twisted betwixt nave and spoke;
> Her help she lent, and with good heed
> Together we released the Cloak;
> A wretched, wretched rag indeed.

He invites the child to come with him into the chaise:

> She sate [*sic*] like one past all relief;
> Sob after sob she forth did send
> In wretchedness, as if her grief
> Could never, never have an end,
>
> 'My Child, in Durham do you dwell:'
> She check'd herself in her distress,
> And said, 'My name is Alice Fell;
> I'm fatherless and motherless.'

On arrival at the Tavern door, he gives money to the host, with instructions to buy her a new cloak. So ends the story:

> 'And let it be a duffel grey,
> As warm a cloak as man can sell!'
> Proud creature was she the next day,
> The little Orphan, Alice Fell.

The outcome is all very unsatisfactory. What happened to Alice as she went off into nowhere, anywhere? Was she grateful to her kindly benefactor? Did she write a thank you note? Ask him to come and see her? Did he never wonder what happened to her? Did she arrive safely at her mysterious destination? Did her new cloak get caught in another wheel? Better still – was she a ghost? Was there an endless series of kind gentlemen travelling the lonely road in the ghostly post-chaise and a string of little Alices to save from starvation?

A whole new area of expertise awaits the eager parodist. Flights of fancy spring into action. The quill is poised and ready dipped. Inspiration flows and Horace feverishly puts pen to paper, for time is pressing. He imagines himself attending a performance at the newly built Theatre Royal, Drury Lane. Everyone is waiting for the Prologue but which of the great actors available may walk on? Which of the great themes of Drury has been chosen for the occasion? Naturally it will be a celebratory ode on the splendours of Benjamin Wyatt's new theatre. Of course we know what really happened, but here, after all the fuss has died down, here we are in the fantasy world of the parodist with no holds barred.

Parody of Innocence

In *The Baby's Début*, Alice Fell is replaced by Nancy Lake, a child of eight, who is wheeled on to the stage of Drury Lane. Instead of the customary Address, she relates in verse, an incident which, though lamentably laughable to the audience, feigns something of the poignancy of the original.

Papa has bought Nancy a wax doll, and a spinning top for her brother Jack, who is jealous that his might be the cheaper of the two presents.

> Jack's in the pouts, and this is it, —
> He thinks mine came to more than his,
>   So to my drawer he goes,
> Takes out the doll, and, O my stars!
> He pokes her head between the bars
>   And melts off half her nose!
>
> Quite cross, a bit of string I beg,
> And tie it to his peg-top's peg,
>   And bang, with might and main,
> Its head against the parlour door:
> Off flies the head, and hits the floor,
>   And breaks a window-pane.
>
> This made him cry with rage and spite;

Chapter 9 - The Rejected Addresses

> Well, let him cry, it serves him right,
>   A pretty thing, forsooth!
> If he's to melt, all scalding hot,
> Half of my doll's nose, I'm not
>   To draw his peg-top's tooth!
>
> Aunt Hannah heard the window break,
> And cried: "O naughty Nancy Lake,
>   This to distress your aunt;
> No Drury-Lane for you to-day!"
> And while Papa said, "Pooh, she may!"
>   Mamma said:" No, she sha'n't! [*sic*]"

In spite of reprimands, the 'chaise' was prepared, the porter came to collect her and deliver her to the Theatre post-haste. On arrival, she marvels at Wyatt's fine new building:

> My father's walls are made of brick,
> But not so tall and not so thick
>   As these; and, goodness me!
> My father's beams are made of wood,
> But, never, never half so good
>   As those that now I see.
>
> What a large floor! 'tis like a town!
> The carpet when they lay it down,
>   Won't hide it, I'll be bound;
> And there's a row of lamps! –my eye!
> How do they blaze! I wonder why
>   They keep them on the ground.

Nervous at going on stage, she keeps hold of the side-wing, only to be pushed forward, urged on by the prompter, making an encouraging reference to the child actor, William Betty, known as 'the Young Roscius (the 'Older' being Garrick), describing his style of acting:

> "You've only got to curtsy, whisp-
> er, hold your chin up, laugh, and lisp,
>   Then you're sure to take:

> I've known the day when brats, not quite
> Thirteen, got fifty pounds a night;
> > Then why not Nancy Lake?"
>
> And now, good gentlefolks, I go
> To join mamma, and see the show;
> > So, bidding you adieu,
> I curtsy, like a pretty miss,
> And if you'll blow to me a kiss,
> > I'll blow a kiss to you.   [*She blows a kiss and exits*]

The difference in the simplicity of both the original poem and its parody is worthy of comment. Both poems tell a story, the style of one necessarily determines the style of the other. In *Alice Fell*, the story is darkened by grief and bereavement, the lost orphan in a hostile environment, vulnerable to the dangers around her, dependent on the sudden appearance of a guardian angel, who helps her to safety. There is a touching expression of a love for humanity that overrides the threatening world around her. The damaged cloak is a symbol of hopelessness, the new cloak, of security. The light tone of the poem belies its seriousness which, paradoxically, is not apparent to us at first reading.

The Baby's Début is composed in the style of a monologue to be delivered before an audience and contains some secret ingredients necessary for performance. Not least of these is a verse form common to comic readings, with a shortened third and sixth line to play against each other, just as an amusing after-thought or aside can cause laughter. The subject appears to be more trivial – sibling jealousy and rivalry. It is all about the age-old story of favouritism and ambition, of striving to keep ahead of a rival, wanting to be valued equally by each parent. There is, however, one very important difference between the two poems, which will become clearer by reminding ourselves of the Romantic view of childhood.

Foundations of Adulthood

The 17th and 18th century treatment of children as miniature adults, both in life and in art, was overturned by the new Romantic sensibility, and is evident throughout the 19th century. The cultural sea-change that engendered a new idea of Nature and its direct relationship with God the Father meant that children came to be more closely observed. This school of thought was a more free-thinking interpretation of Nature, encouraged

Chapter 9 - The Rejected Addresses

by the French Encyclopédistes, especially in the works of Jean-Jacques Rousseau's *Émile*. In Wordsworth's case, he had the advantage of countless conversations with his sister Dorothy, the delightful subject-matter of which is recorded in her copious diaries.

Dorothy had a particular affinity for, and cared for, many children in her lifetime. Wordsworth learnt from her at first hand a deeper understanding of a child's 'centre of being' and of the maturing of the child's mind and personality into adulthood. This theory of the loss of innocence is comparable to child psychology today. Wordsworth expresses his thoughts on this theme succinctly in the now famous lines:

> My heart leaps up when I behold
> A rainbow in the sky;
> So was it when my life began,
> So is it now I am a man,
> So be it when I shall grow old,
> Or let me die!
> The Child is Father of the Man,
> I could wish my days to be
> Bound each to each in natural piety.

The innocence of childhood was paramount throughout the romantic period. In the previous century it had become clear that parental and educational disciplines were required if children were to have a good and useful life. Such an attitude began to take on an important role in attempts by certain educationists to control unwanted tendencies and emotions in a child's path towards maturity. The instructive poems of Isaac Watts were a real advance in paving the way for an improving kind of literature for children.

Since the soul was seen as good, the problem was how to deal with a mind prone to evil thoughts. The method was to encourage suitable alternatives through the work ethic and organised playtime - a case of adults attempting to protect the child from evils and cruelties of a world created by adults. In *Intimations of Immortality from Recollections of Early Childhood,* Wordsworth looks back wistfully to innocent halcyon days of his childhood:

> There was a time when meadows, grove and stream,
> The earth, and every common sight,
> To me did seem
> Apparelled in celestial light,

> The glory and the freshness of a dream.
> It is not now as it hath been of yore ;—
> Turn wheresoe're I may,
> The things which I have seen I see no more.[32]

Wordsworth thought of 'natural piety' as being, in Coleridge's words, 'the continuity of self-consciousness' between childhood and adulthood. William Blake believed there was no such thing because 'the Natural Man is at enmity with God'.[33]

The sophisticated reading public of the day would have been able to discern subtleties of parody much more than the reading public today because they were familiar with the originals. This had ever been the case since the days of the 18th century Enlightenment, but with significant improvements in education throughout Victorian times, the tropes and puns of light verse were an expected pleasure demanded by the reading public. The wit of Alexander Pope, Jonathan Swift, and the raucous ribaldry of Restoration comedies were a fitting expression of the cynicism of their times.

The humour of Horace and James Smith, Praed, Thomas Hood and all that Regency and Victorian band of comic writers entertained their insatiable public in a more gentle fashion. With the publication of *Lyrical Ballads* in 1800, which included all but one of the 'Lucy Poems', *The Prelude* (1805), and *Poems in Two Volumes,* including his ode, *Intimations of Immortality* (1807), Wordsworth was at the height of his powers. James Smith, for his parody of Wordsworth, chose to ignore the greater Nature poetry and settled for a parody of *Alice Fell*, a story of jealousy and violence between two spiteful siblings, keeping to the form of a traditional comic prologue.

4. *An Address Without a Phoenix* by S.T.P.

An Attempt at Mystification

The third of the *Rejected Addresses* was entitled *An Address without a Phoenix,* purporting to be by the mysterious 'S.T.P.', with no clue as to the identity of the author. This poem has a gentle, dignified lilt, an unexceptional tone and style, and, fortunately for the phoenix-battered committee, there was not a single mention of the bird:

> Slow crept the silent flame, ensnared its prize,

> Then burst resistless to the astonished skies.
> The glowing walls, disrobed of scenic pride,
> In trembling conflict stemmed the burning tide,
> Till crackling, blazing, rocking to its fall,
> Down rushed the thundering roof, and buried all!

Such lines might be considered to be some of the best in the whole book, or at the very least a thoroughly competent imitation. But imitator of whom? Alexander Pope, perhaps? Certainly not Byron, who at that time shunned rhyming couplets, though, as we have seen, relented under pressure from Lord Holland. Parody these lines were not, yet strangely familiar to a *côterie* of readers. The *Edinburgh Review* made nothing of it, professing 'our ignorance of the author' designated by his mystery initials. The reviewer, judged the poem 'decent and mellifluous', but failed to see how it could justify its place in a volume of parodies, a view we can concur with today: [34]

> O! may we still, to sense and nature true,
> Delight the many, nor offend the few,
> Though varying tastes our changeful Drama claim,
> Still be its moral tendency the same,
> To win by precept, by example warn,
> To brand the front of Vice with pointed scorn,
> And Virtue's smiling brows with votive wreaths adorn.

Who, then, was S.T.P.? Readers might have been tempted to solve the mystery of the identity of the author by assuming that 'Samuel Taylor, Poet' had to wait another twenty-one years for the true identity to be revealed. In the Preface to the 1833 edition, Horace Smith finally admitted that he, not Coleridge, was the mystery author. He had written the poem as his genuine contribution to the competition for the opening Address, and not being fortunate enough to have it among the chosen entries, decided to include it as 'Rejected' to provide bulk. Thus it was that the perspicacious reviewer saw 'no very prominent trait of absurdity' in it and did not fall into the trap that had been deftly laid for him. Horace had nevertheless pulled off the trick by hiding behind the screen of a spurious academic, a Professor of Theology (Holy Scriptures) – SANCTAE THEOLOGIAE PROFESSOR![35] In a sense, the poem is an oddity in the collection, a bogus intruder that masquerades as a parody when it is in fact a close imitation of the genuine article in its own right. No wonder it caused confusion among the critics.

5. *Cui bono?* By Lord B. (Byron)

The Tormented Hero

After ridiculing Wordsworth, the Brothers chose Byron as their next victim, even though he had not numbered among the rejected poets. He was, nevertheless, the most controversial poet of his day and was a sitting target. Their chosen poem was *Childe Harold's Pilgrimage*, a long, self-absorbed narrative written between 1812 and 1818. The world-weary Byron is morbidly reflective about the universe and his place in it, and has found no answer in the pleasures of this life as represented by what he considered to be the hypocritical English society of his day. He seeks solace in foreign lands, as if he were a young medieval knight (Childe) searching for the Holy Grail of ultimate happiness and fulfilment, and finding only disillusionment and the end of things:

> Oh! that the desert were my dwelling-place,
> With one fair Spirit for my minister,
> That I might all forget the human race,
> And, hating no one, love but only her!
> Ye Elements! – in whose ennobling stir
> I feel myself exalted – Can ye not
> Accord me such a being? – do I err
> In deeming such inhabit many a spot?
> Though with them to converse can rarely be my lot …
>
> Roll on! thou deep dark ocean – roll!
> Ten thousand fleets sweep over thee in vain;
> Man marks the earth with ruin – his control
> Stops with the shore; upon the watery plain
> The wrecks are all thy deed, nor doth remain
> A shadow of man's ravage, save his own,
> When, for a moment, like a drop of rain,
> He sinks unto thy depths with bubbling groan
> Without a grave, unknelled, uncoffined, and unknown.

The poem, in deftly-chosen Spenserian stanzas, was bound to be the perfect butt of the parodist. Its brilliance lay not only in the texture of the language and the sorrowful symmetry of the poet's thoughts, but also the overriding power of life's futility. As with the companion verses, James

Smith, leaving Horace to complete the poem, draws on images of a new Drury, invoking the Nine Muses along the way:

> Sated with home, of wife, of children tired,
> The restless soul is driven abroad to roam;
> Sated abroad, all seen, yet nought admired,
> The restless soul is driven to ramble home;
> Sated with both, beneath new Drury's dome,
> The fiend Ennui awhile consents to pine,
> There growls, and curses, like a deadly Gnome,
> Scorning to view fantastic Columbine,
> Viewing with scorn and hate the nonsense of the Nine.

Horace continues:

> Ye reckless dupes, who hither wend your way,
> To gaze on puppets in a painted dome,
> Pursuing pastimes glittering to betray,
> Like falling stars, in life's eternal gloom,
> What seek ye here? Joy's evanescent bloom?
> Woe's me! The brightest wreaths she ever gave
> Are but as flowers that decorate a tomb.
> Man's heart, the mournful urn o'er which they wave,
> Is sacred to despair, its pedestal the grave.

Unfortunately, the parodist in the first verse, in this case, James Smith, was too adept at his craft, for his verse proved to be convincing enough to have been composed by Byron himself, who, though smarting from the criticism of *Childe Harold,* admired the *Rejected Addresses* from the very first. On 19 October 1812, he wrote to his publisher, John Murray: 'I think the Rejected Addresses by far the best thing of the kind since the Rolliad and wish *you* had published them. Tell the author I forgive him, were he twenty times over a satirist....He must be a man of very lively wit, and less scurrilous than wits often are.' [36]

Parodies give, as a rule, a bad impression of the originals, but in the *Rejected Addresses* the reverse is the fact.' Smith wisely chose not to use any of Byron's earlier attempts at the rhyming couplet. As we have seen, Byron vehemently resisted the scheme until Lord Holland encouraged him to – or more accurately, emotionally blackmailed him into – applying himself to the task.

The author has succeeded better in copying the moody misanthropic diction in which his noble biographer has embodied then. The attempt, however, indicates very considerable power; and the flow of the verse and the construction of the poetical period are imitated with no ordinary skill.[37]

This parody is considered to have outshone the rest of the *Rejected Addresses*. Robert Southey, the Poet Laureate, wrote: ' I liked Lord Byron the best. There were others equally good but here the mode of thought as well as the manner is happily caught.'[38] Byron wrote similar thoughts to Francis Hodgson in the same month: 'I am a great admirer of R. A. [*Rejected Addresses*], though I have had so great a share in their publication, and I like the C. H. [*Childe Harold*] imitation one of the best.'[39] However, looked at in the light of more contemporary criticism, it might join the multitude of other parodies of Byron that flourished both during his lifetime and afterwards.

Undoubtedly, Byron wondered how the whole alarming episode could possibly benefit in any way the reputations of the original victims. A complete absence of any critical acclaim consigns an author's work to virtual oblivion, whereas a negative response at least keeps a work in the pubic memory. Byron himself need not have cared a jot, for, dubbed the leader of the 'Satanic School of Poetry', he was regularly pilloried in the caricatures of the day.

There was, too, a political aspect to Byron's *ennui* following the ending of the Napoleonic Wars, in which an estimate of some 5 million men died, considerably affecting the balance of male to female in the population. In spite of successfully defeating Napoleon's *Grande Armée* at Waterloo, and Bonaparte's subsequent exile to the island of St. Helena, an invasive melancholy settled upon a generation weary of war and post-revolutionary social deprivation. It all helps to explain the Smith brothers' use of the Latin tag, quoted by Cicero from the orations of Milo and Roscius, in the title, 'Cui bono?', often misapplied as 'What's the good of it?' but more correctly, 'Who gains by it?' or 'To whose advantage is it?'[40]

Childe Harold gives the image of Byron as romantic hero – intelligent, perceptive, cultured, sensitive, courageous, sophisticated, brave, adventurous, but above all radical, visionary, and determined to break through social and political boundaries. The hero also has a negative side: arrogance, cynicism, self-indulgence, self-pity, often with a powerful sexual drive, all to the point of self-destruction. All these qualities make up the exceptional man: the leaders, the tyrants, the passionate lovers – in short, the heroes and heroines of sagas, tragedies, novels, and narrative poetry – in a word: the generic hero and heroine. These attributes in Byron were propagated and encouraged to some extent through his Whiggish *liaisons dangereux* formed in his Holland House days.

Like Byron, the despised exile from polite English society, Napoleon, the ruthless conqueror and subjugator of nations, was transformed into a hero. The impressive painting of Napoleon by Jacques-Louis David depicts the Emperor astride a white horse. In real life, he rode on a tired-looking mule, if the earlier painting of him is a true picture. David, his devoted admirer, chose to change all that. But pride must have a fall, and, for both Byron and Napoleon, exile was their inevitable fate. Horace Smith's closing lines reflect that dilemma:

> And Wisdom weeps, and Folly plays her pranks
> And moody Madness laughs and hugs the chain he clanks.

The lines are a nice parallel with those of Thomas Love Peacock's parody of Byron as 'Mr Cypress', who sings of the destructive fever of the spirit that

> Burns, blasts, consumes its cell, the heart,
> Till, one by one, hope, joy, desire,
> Like dreams of shadowy smoke depart.[41]

6. *Hampshire Farmer's Address* by W.C. (William Cobbett)

The Headstrong Heckler

The Hampshire Farmer's Address is a hidden commentary on Samuel Whitbread, chairman of the Selection Committee, whom it was discovered had contributed an Address himself. Its principal feature was a florid account of the phoenix, which led Sheridan to retort that Whitbread had 'entered into particulars, and described its wings, beak, tail, &c. in short, it was a poulterer's description of a Phoenix.' The poem had mysteriously disappeared, and we can assume that Whitbread had surreptitiously slipped into the Committee's office and withdrawn it. Or it may be that he made a request to Charles Ward for his Address to be returned to him. Whatever the case, it remains a bland, conventional piece of little merit. The failure of Whitbread's abortive entry was immortalised with a paean of praise in the robust style of William Cobbett. *The Hampshire Farmer's Address* by W. C., was a surprising choice for one of the *Rejected*

Addresses, especially since poetry, not prose, was specified as a requirement by the Selection Committee.

William Cobbett

If we are to believe William Hazlitt's description of Cobbett in *The Spirit of the Age*, then not only was he an unpredictable supporter of both sides of a political argument, and a forthright, headstrong, capricious critic of human behaviour and waywardness, he also had a complete lack of interest in the world of theatre. He was a political chameleon, changing sides as it suited and a terror to those who abused the rule of law and offended against social proprieties. Yet, he was a true patriot, and a staunch advocate of propriety in all things, even the social niceties of relationships between young men and women. His belief, for example, in the necessity for proper household management is expressed in a diatribe on the deleterious effects of drinking tea:

> The drink which has come to supply the place of ale has, in general, been tea. It is notorious, that tea has no useful strength in it; that it contains nothing nutricious [*sic*]; that it, besides being good for nothing, has badness in it, because it is known to produce want of sleep in many cases, and in all cases to shake and weaken the nerves. It is, in fact, a weaker kind of laudanum, which enlivens for the moment and deadens afterwards. ... Then comes the great article of all, the time employed in this tea-making affair. It is impossible to make a fire, boil water, make the tea, drink it, wash up the things, sweep up the fire-place and put all to rights again in a less space of time upon average, than two hours. However, let us allow *one*

hour; and here we have a woman occupied no less than three hundred and sixty-five hours in the year, or, thirty whole days, at twelve hours in the day; that is to say, one month in the year, besides the waste of the man's time in hanging about waiting for the tea! Needs there anything more to make us cease to wonder at seeing labourers' children with dirty linen and holes in the heels of their stockings.

Cobbett relished in being controversial and often landed himself in trouble for being outspoken on politically divisive subjects. Like his contemporary, Thomas Hood, he was independent of party and was not afraid to be on the attack and stick to his principles. Observing the degree of moral degradation among the poor, he became a passionate campaigner against the evils of gin-drinking. His *Political Register*, *Rural Rides* and *The English Gardener* make good travelling companions. They are written in a refreshingly clear, forthright style, employing few Latinate expressions, and exploiting the natural power of Anglo-Saxon vocabulary. His collections of accounts of parliamentary debates eventually formed the basis for parliamentary proceedings now known as Hansard. In the light of this briefest of accounts of his virtues and peccadilloes, we can understand why the Smith brothers should choose him as one of their authors. He was a true 'Hampshire man' but not by any means a man from Hampshire. Nor was he, by any measure, as we have said, a man of the theatre:

Thus 'Cobbett' addresses his playgoers with some typical down-to-earth advice:

MOST THINKING PEOPLE,

When persons address an audience from the stage, it is usual, either in words or gesture, to say: "Ladies and Gentlemen, your servant." If I were base enough, mean enough, paltry enough, and *brute beast* enough, to follow that fashion, I should tell two lies in a breath. In the first place, you are *not* Ladies and Gentlemen, but I hope something better, that is to say, honest men and women; and in the next place, if you were ever so much ladies, and ever so much gentlemen, I am not, *nor ever will be,* your humble servant. You see me here, most thinking people, by mere chance. I have not been within the doors of a playhouse before for these ten years; nor, till that abominable custom of taking money at the doors is discontinued, will I ever sanction a theatre with my

> presence.... You are now, (thanks to *Mr. Whitbread*), got into a large, comfortable house... Who routed you from a rat-hole, five inches by four, to perch you in a palace? Again and again I answer, *Mr. Whitbread*.[42]

The style here has more in common with Byron's frame-breakers' speech in the House of Lords than with a theatrical prologue, yet there is, in the oratory of the speech, a certain theatricality. Cobbett's writings are peppered with pithy sayings. In such generally ill-mannered times, his *Advice to Young Men* was a useful guide to relationships, but on feminine grace he wrote:

> It is not enough that a young woman abstain from everything approaching indecorum in her behaviour towards men; it is, with me, not enough that she cast down her eyes, or turn aside her head, with a smile when she hears an indelicate allusion; she ought to appear not to understand it, and to receive from it no more impression than if she were a post.[43]

and in his essay on 'Temperance' he ends with a sharp rebuke for those with a tendency to gluttony and over-indulgence:

> Security of all is to eat little, and to drink nothing that intoxicates: He that eats till he is full is little better than a beast; and he that drinks till he is drunk is quite a beast.

Cobbett was a politician who really cared about the political health of the nation and, in particular, living conditions of the poorer classes.

Whitbread, too, was an accomplished, plain speaker in the House of Commons; his powerful voice, with its broad, rolling country tones, reverberated across the Chamber, giving an impression of genuine emotional commitment. He was much praised for his humanitarianism, strengthened by his liberalism and his tireless sense of duty. He devoted himself to countless charitable works, and as an ardent social reformer and plain speaker he was able to achieve much in the fields of religious and civil rights. He supported the proposal for a national education system and was, with Wilberforce, a leading light in the movement for the abolition of slavery. With his controversial radical tendencies, he made an effective leader of the Whigs. Such was his fervour for liberty, equality and fraternity, that he became one of the foremost supporters of Bonaparte and hoped for the self-styled Emperor's eclectic reforms to be introduced into the more empirical structure of the British Constitution.

Samuel Whitbread was a rough-cut brewer and, like Cobbett, a plain man's politician, and just the right man to bring the Theatre Royal Drury Lane back to life by stabilising the finances and restoring something of the old vitality, but on a much safer foundation. Above all, he had learnt the value of money the hard way and quickly learned how to manipulate the dissolute Sheridan and his wayward band of actors. Though the Smith brothers' parody is a fair attempt at a political rant of the Cobbett kind, it is more an appeal to the new patrons, 'the thinking people', whom he has 'routed from their rat-hole' to 'perch them in a palace'.[44]

7. *The Living Lustres* by T.M. (Thomas Moore)

A Passable Parody

Thomas Moore (first published under the whimsical pseudonym of 'Tom Little') was of an unusually small stature, so much so that, on a visit to America, President Thomas Jefferson mistook him for a child, which accounts for Moore's title of his second volume of poems, *Poetical Works of the Late Thomas Little* in 1801. His years at Trinity College, Dublin, coincided with the oncoming turmoil of the French Revolution and a number of his friends like Robert Emmett were members of the 'United Irishmen' movement, which supported the Jacobins, an influential political club, meeting in secret at the Dominican Convent in the Rue St. Jacques in Paris. Their leader was Maximilien de Robespierre. Their members were hunted down during the Reign of Terror in 1793 and executed. Ironically, their English counterpart, the subversive London Revolution Society, founded in 1788, far from being an off-shoot of the faction, was their original inspiration. When things got too dangerous for him in England, Moore fled to America, but in Norfolk, Virginia, he fell foul of officialdom by criticising the slave trade and, thinking better of it, soon returned to England.

Moore, in spite of his convivial nature, could easily be ruffled by adverse criticism. A critical article in the *Edinburgh Review* led to his challenging its distinguished editor, Francis Jeffrey, to a duel. They agreed to meet at Chalk Farm, North London and, who knows, he or his opponent might have been killed. As it happened, the authorities were apprised of the event and both contestants were arrested. It did not end there. A short time afterwards, Moore, in one of his fiery moods, sent a threatening letter to Byron, following his critical review of Moore's verses. Fortunately, Byron had gone abroad and did not receive the letter. By the time he returned, all was forgotten and friendship was restored.

Moore's lyrical poetry remains his greatest achievement and it was this part of his *opus* that Horace Smith chose to parody in *The Living Lustres*. In some ways the parody falls short of our expectations. With such carefully measured lines and control of imagery, we would find it hard, in spite of the simple sentimentality of the song, to criticise a particular genius so satisfying and complete:

> Believe me, if all those endearing young charms,
> Which I gaze on so fondly today,
> Were to change by tomorrow, and flee to my arms,
> Live-fairy gifts fading away.
> Thou wouldst still be adored, as this moment thou art,
> Let thy loveliness fade as it will,
> And around the dear ruin each wish of my heart
> Would entwine itself verdantly still.

In reading the simple words of many of Thomas Moore's *Irish Melodies* - if we have any memory for tunes - then we will more than likely be singing the music of Moore's musical collaborator, Sir John Stevenson. His melodies have been sung by Irishmen throughout the world, particularly in the United States, and by immigrants in former British Empire dependencies. The nostalgia brought about by distance was largely responsible for the survival of these enduring tunes, and their meaningful message to the dispossessed turned them into a special category of composition:

> There is not in the wide world a valley so sweet
> As that vale on whose bosom the bright waters meet.
> Oh! the last rays of feeling and life must depart
> Ere the bloom of that valley shall fade from my heart.

This tranquil, romantic haven in the heart of the Vale of Avoca is alive in the hearts of all Irish men and women who, by circumstance, dwell in far-off parts of the world. It was not only a haven, it is a heaven, a spiritual home and a place literally to die for. These gently emotive first lines of the *The Meeting of the Waters*, bring with them not only a strong personal response but possess a subliminal political appeal, whether for patriot and ex-patriot. There can be no better target for parody than these simple lines, which, to many devoted admirers would seem almost blasphemous, choosing to play on Moore's more amorous inclinations rather than concentrating on the required topic of the 'Theatre Royal Drury Lane':

> O why should our dull retrospective addresses

Chapter 9 - The Rejected Addresses

> Fall damp as wet blankets on Drury Lane fire?
> Away with blue devils, away with distresses,
>   And give the gay spirit to sparkling desire.
>
> Let artists decide on the beauties of Drury,
>   The richest to me is when woman is there;
> The question of houses I leave to the jury;
>   The fairest to me is the house of the fair.
>
> When woman's soft smile all our senses bewilders,
>   And gilds, while it carves, her dear form on the heart,
> What need has New Drury of carvers and gilders?
>   With Nature so bounteous, why call upon Art?
>
> How well would our actors attend to their duties,
>   Our house save in oil, and our authors in wit,
> In lieu of yon lamps, if arrow of young beauties
>   Glanced light from their eyes between us and the pit!

But in his mood of nostalgia, he is helplessly drawn back to 'the roseate blushes' and 'the love-breathing-smile' of the nymphs of his desires, though not without the intrusion of some political point-scoring:

> For dear is the Emerald Isle of the ocean,
>   Whose daughters are fair as the foam of the wave,
> Whose sons, unaccustomed to rebel commotion,
>   Though joyous, are sober – though peaceful are brave.
>
> The shamrock their olive, sworn foe to a quarrel,
>   Protects from the thunder and lightning of rows;
> Their sprig of shillelagh is nothing but laurel,
>   Which flourishes rapidly over their brows.
>
> O! soon shall they burst the tyrannical shackles
>   Which each panting bosom indignantly names,
> Until not one goose at the capital cackles
>   Against the grand question of Catholic claims.

After 1806, Moore devoted himself to writing lyrics for Irish tunes, deserted his old radical ways, gave his turncoat allegiance to the Tories, and supported Catholic emancipation, though he had an uneasy relationship with its adherent, Daniel O'Connell. Most of all, Moore will be remembered for one act of literary vandalism: in collusion with publisher John Murray, he burnt Byron's memoirs at the request of the poet's family. He has never been entirely forgiven for being party to such a conspiracy.

As for the success of Horace Smith's parody, it is difficult to agree entirely with his verdict: '*The Living Lustres* appears to us to be a very fair imitation of the fantastic verses which that ingenious person, Mr. Moore, indites when he is merely gallant, and, resisting the lures of voluptuousness, is not enough in earnest to be tender.'[45] In other words, a passable parody. After reading Moore's *Lalla Rookh: the Fire Worshippers*, H. S. Field could not resist a poke of musical fun:

> From my cot that lies buried a short way from Lerida
>   Love and a diligence lent me their wings.
> Swift as a falcon I flew to thy balcony.
>   (Is it bronchitis? I can't sing a bar.)
> Greet not with merriment Love's first experiment;
>   Listen, Pepita! I've brought my *catarrh*![46]

8. *The Rebuilding* by R.S. (Robert Southey)

Polymath and Wordsmith

History abounds with political turncoats and Southey was no exception. His conversion may well be one of the reasons why he was largely forgotten by the educated reader until, more recently, modern scholars began to take up the challenge. Party politics rarely forgives outright apostasy, though it still has ardent admirers today among the reading public, especially American literary scholars. Southey had a phenomenal skill in managing words, the complexity of their sound and sense within the forms and rhythms of the poetic idiom. He was not afraid to tackle major themes and consequently was remarkably ingenious and dextrous in the management of his elaborate subject matter and its relationship with the expression of it in every line of his verse. His principal downfall was that he appealed to a highly sophisticated literate élite, educated to relish his work at private recitals in the luxury of the drawing-room. Nevertheless he was a man of great scholarship and consummate artistry.

Chapter 9 - The Rejected Addresses

Southey began as a romantic poet, inextricably associated with the 'Lake Poets', William Wordsworth and Samuel Taylor Coleridge, through whose reputations he retains a devoted number of admirers. *The Cataract of Lodore*, written to amuse Southey's children, is a masterpiece of invention which would keep any of today's children busy with their dictionaries for hours on end.

One by one, the children beg their father to put into words the wonderment they experienced on their many visits to the Falls:

>They had seen it before,
>So I told them in rhyme,
>For of rhymes I had store;
>And 'twas in my creation
>That so I should sing;
>Because I was Laureate
>To them and the King.

From its source in the tarn on the fell, the stream creeps gently through meadow and glade, increasing in pace until it emerges through caverns and rocks:

>Rising and leaping,
>Sinking and creeping,
>Swelling and sweeping,
>Showering and springing,
>Flying and flinging,
>Writhing and ringing,
>Eddying and whisking,
>Turning and twisting.

The length of the line increases as the elemental power of the tumbling water increases. Now there is no time for end-rhymes: the children would be standing in awe of the great falls plunging eternally onto the rocks below:

>Dividing and gliding and sliding,
>And falling and brawling and sprawling,...
>And grumbling and rumbling and tumbling,
>And clattering and battering and shattering;

until, through the sensations and impressions of the children, we, the readers, are caught up in the maelstrom:

> Recoiling, turmoiling and toiling and boiling,...
> And rushing and flushing and brushing and gushing,....
> And thumping and plumping and bumping and jumping,
> And dashing and flashing and splashing and clashing,
> And so never ending, but always descending,
> Sounds and motions for ever and ever are blending,
> All at once and all o'er, with a mighty uproar, -
> And this way the water comes down at Lodore.

The tranquillity of the Lake District allowed Southey to live the simple life in a rural setting. He indulged himself in the midst of his children and thus, like every doting parent, played an important role as guide and mentor. It is an irony that, in among the complexity of his writings, we find the work he is best known for – his children's tale, *The Story of the Three Bears* who live a contented life in their woodland cottage.[47] One day, while they were are out walking in woods waiting for their porridge to cool, their peaceful life is threatened by an ugly old woman who creeps into their home and samples their porridge, sits in their chairs, and, most offensive of all, tries out their beds. It is all about the invasion and protection of innocence in a world of unknown dangers. (Later versions of the story changed the ugly old woman into a pretty young girl, Goldilocks.)

Evil has its subtle and frequently brutal ways of attempting to stifle and destroy the good of the world. In Southey's metrical tales, he shows the terrors of cruelty and revenge through more sophisticated means. In a similar way Thomas Hood reveals in his poem the thoughts and emotions of Eugene Aram, the murderer, his harrowing feelings of guilt compelling him to confess his crime to his innocent young pupil. Employing that same simple, innocent tone in *The Battle of Blenheim*, the father explains the horrors of war:

> "Now tell us what 'twas all about,"
> Young Peterkin, he cries,
> And little Whilhelmine looks up
> With wonder-waiting eyes,
> "Now tell us all about the war,
> And what they fought each other for.
>
> "It was the English," Kaspar cried,

"Who put the French to rout;
But what they fought each other for
I could not well make out;
But everybody said," quoth he,
"That 'twas a famous victory."...

"They said it was a shocking sight
After the field was won;
For many thousand bodies here
Lay rotting in the sun;
But things like that, you know, must be
After a famous victory."

And every body praised the Duke
Who this great fight did win."
"But what good came of it at last?"
Quoth little Peterkin.
"Why, that I cannot tell," said he,
"But 'twas a famous victory."

A prolific letter-writer, Southey was also extraordinarily versatile as historian and biographer, writing significant works on the lives of Horatio Nelson (1813), John Wesley (1820), John Bunyan (1844) and Oliver Cromwell (1844), all of whom satisfied his personal view that greatness and radicalism were opposite sides of the same coin. He wrote eclogues, lyrics, metrical ballads, melodramas, fiction and autobiography. His minor poems, published in 1815, are contained in three volumes; his substantial literary output in total was published in ten volumes (1837-8). He was, in Coleridge's words, 'the complete man of letters'.

It is Southey's biographical works that reveal a profound admiration and preference for certain kinds of historical figures who from small beginnings grew to be powerful masters of their own destinies, and perpetrators of irreversible religious and political change. His father had been something of a renegade, cherishing the memory of his ancestor who fought in the Monmouth Rebellion.

The young Southey began school at Bristol, where he was mercilessly bullied, and from there proceeded to a Welsh school, where he was on one occasion beaten about the head with a fiddle stick. He learnt his lesson early in life - that there is no advancement without pain. But it was there that he developed a preference for the medieval rather than his own times. He discovered Malory's *Le Morte d'Arthur*, Spenser's *The Faerie Queene*, and Milton's *Paradise Lost*. Many of his works reveal a deep-seated obsession with the inevitability of punishment with little chance of redemption.

Of all the poets chosen by the Smith Brothers for *Rejected Addresses*, Robert Southey is the most obscure and tantalisingly arcane. There are elements of distress, suffering, sadism, violent death and grim forebodings. Perverse, irreligious, and expressly sexual themes lurk beneath the surface of his poetic narratives, giving a macabre expression to the passionate feelings of his doomed heroes. His creativity arose out the dark regions of his soul, obfuscating, primitively prurient – tantalisingly attractive to the more sophisticated minds of his classically educated readers.

At twenty years of age, he was developing radical political views in long poems of protest like *Wat Tyler* (1794). This radical poem, challenging the established order, was originally published anonymously, re-emerging again in 1817, when Southey had already been appointed Poet Laureate, causing considerable discomfort to the establishment. A review by Hazlitt forced Southey to own up to its authorship. *The Edinburgh Review* judged the poem 'un-Laureate-like'. In 1796, *Joan of Arc* was published, again in twelve books, with more assurances of a radical repeat of violent themes, and in particular, intellectual violence.

Southey possessed a prodigious creative energy allowing him to carry in his brain at any one time a multitude of ideas, philosophies and historical facts to challenge any of his contemporaries. His curiosity was insatiable and that, coupled with a phenomenally retentive memory, allowed him to draw on his vast knowledge at will. He could mastermind a host of concepts at any one time and arrange them in a complex framework with great artistry.

In 1801, Southey published the first of his long mythological poems, *Thalaba the Destroyer*. The story takes place in the Zorastrian period long before the coming of Islam and pursues a violent path through episodes containing child cruelty, mass murder, vengeance, abject love and self-sacrifice. It is written in the stars that Thalaba shall give up his life for his faith so that he can join his beloved Oneiza in Paradise.

All this was far from the pantisocratic society envisaged by Coleridge in the early days of their friendship. What utopian ideals there existed then! with all members ruling equally, spending their time working for the common good, with a minimum of laws and regulations. But it had all been done before in theory at least, with Plato's *Republic*, Thomas More's *Utopia*, and Francis Bacon's *New Atlantis*. The idea of settling the community in a remote part of Wales failed to excite luminaries of the movement and initial enthusiasm for the venture quickly waned.

The key to Southey's development lay in his classical education at Westminster School, where he soon became an enthusiastic reader of Homer, Ossian, and the Bible as literature. He had an obsession for the Gothic, with its macabre themes, subliminal sexual cravings, and terrifying racial bloodlust. George Augustus Sala was terrified at the thought of corporal punishment as a child but had a fascination for the sexual role of flagellation.[48]

In 1799, Southey began to work on the legend of *Madoc*, a prose version that arose from his private reading, concerning the legendary Welsh prince, who was reputed to have discovered America long before Columbus and whose siblings had been murdered by King David. As we may anticipate, the poem proceeds through a series of violent adventures, including child sacrifice, racial blood-lust and the final brutal conquering of the Aztec hoards.

Central to Southey's own character was his radicalisation, through the harsh treatment at Westminster School, at a time when boys were frequently beaten, caned even for minor, one might say, 'breeches' of the regulations. The punishment incensed him sufficiently to contribute an article to the school magazine, *The Flagellant*, an abrasive piece '+on the evils of flogging (29 March 1792). William Vincent, Southey's headmaster at the time, was enraged at Southey's suggestion that Vincent himself actually enjoyed a sadistic (therefore sexual) pleasure from the 'exercise'. The young Southey was bemused at the dramatic effect his article had on the boys and masters alike. For his explosive article he was promptly expelled.[49]

Southey's powerful heroes had at the centre of their being the seeds of their own destruction. In the three major works, *Thalaba*, *Madoc* and *Kehama* we see the ultimate dissolution of their beliefs and the disintegration of their personal hopes and aims..

For the setting of *The Curse of Kehama* (1810), we must go back to the pre-Christian, pre-Islamic times, to the one of the oldest of world religions, Zoroastrianism, a monotheistic religion with dualistic overtones Founded about 1000BC by Zoroaster, or Zarathrustra, a Persian of the 6th century, who changed the polytheistic Arya folk-religion he founded, Its world is one of universal opposites: Zoroastrians have an either/or choice between good and evil, in a world governed by 'The Lord of Truth', who, in words familiar to Christians, 'created the Heavens and the Earth, night and day, darkness and light'. The individual, of his own free will, can choose the eternal gift of the Heavens or be condemned to live out his afterlife in Hell. This is a far cry from Southey the idealist, who had once attempted to dabble with the idea of a pantisocratic egalitarian society. Kehama's world is a world of lust, cruelty and the struggle for power.

Southey was approaching middle-age when he finally published *The Curse of Kehama*, but the idea for the poem stems from his school days, a time when he suffered from insomnia and spent the long hours of the night recalling the episodes of the legend and assembling in his mind images that were to form the basis of this remarkable poem.

Lurking in the deep recesses of his memory were troubling visions of a mysterious, evil-looking fellow-pupil and the nightmarish terror he planted in the young poet's mind. At one point Southey gave up the project, perhaps disturbed by a recall of those frightening experiences, but Walter Savage Landor persuaded him to take up his pen again and complete the Kehama poem.

The Curse of Kehama (1810) is an epic poem with at its centre the evil Brahmin priest, Kehama, who, in his quest to become a god, gains a destructive, demonic power that will in the end serve to bring about his own destruction. His efforts are frustrated by the sudden death of his son, Arvalan, who has attempted to seduce a peasant girl, Kailyal, and is brutally killed by Yamen, the God of Death. Enraged by this, Kehama wages war on Yamen and puts a curse on the killer, Ladurlad, who, bravely resisting torture, becomes a hero and, joining forces with the Hindu gods, sets out to destroy Kehama. After a number of adventures, Kailyal is restored to safety and freed from Kehama's curse. The rest of the story involves a complexity of incidents including Vishnu assuming human form to save humanity, Kailyal falling in love with the entrancing Ereenia, Kehama determined to seduce her, Shiva coming down to earth to restore Yamen to power, and Ladurlad, absolved from the curse at last, enters Paradise.[50] The Smith brothers chose the passage describing the funeral of Arvalan:

> MIDNIGHT, and yet no eye
> Through all the Imperial City closed in sleep!
> Behold her streets ablaze
> With light that seems to kindle the red sky,
> Her myriads swarming through the crowded ways!
> Master and slave, old age and infancy,
> All, all abroad to gaze;
> House-top and balcony
> Clustered with women, who throw back their veils
> With unimpeded and insatiate sight
> To view the funeral pomp which passes by,
> As if the mournful rite
> Were but to them a scene of joyance and delight.

Vainly, ye blessed twinklers of the night,
Your feeble beams ye shed,
Quenched in the unnatural light which might outstare
Even the broad eye of day;
And thou from thy celestial way
Pourest, O moon, an ineffectual ray!
For lo! ten thousand torches flame and flare
Upon the midnight air,
Blotting the lights of heaven
With one portentous glare.
Behold the fragrant smoke in many a fold
Ascending, floats along the fiery sky,
And hangeth visible on high,
A dark and waving canopy.

Hark! 't is the funeral trumpet's breath!
'T is the dirge of death!
At once ten thousand drums begin,
With one long thunder-peal the ear assailing;
Ten thousand voices then join in,
And with one deep and general din
Pour their wild wailing.
The song of praise is drowned
Amid the deafening sound;
You hear no more the trumpet's tone,
You hear no more the mourner's moan,
Though the trumpet's breath and the dirge of death
Swell with commingled force the funeral yell.
But rising over all in one acclaim
Is heard the echoed and re-echoed name,
From all that countless rout;
Arvalan! Arvalan!
Arvalan! Arvalan!
Ten times ten thousand voices in one shout
Call Arvalan! The overpowering sound
From house to house repeated rings about,

From tower to tower rolls round.

The death-procession moves along;
Their bald heads shining to the torches' ray,
The Brahmins lead the way,
Chanting the funeral song.
And now at once they shout,
Arvalan! Arvalan!
With quick rebound of sound,
All in accordant cry,
Arvalan! Arvalan!
The universal multitude reply.
In vain ye thunder on his ear the name;
Would ye awake the dead?
Borne upright in his palankeen,
There Arvalan is seen!
A glow is on his face,—a lively red;
It is the crimson canopy
He moves,—he nods his head,—
But the motion comes from the bearers' tread,
As the body, borne aloft in state,
Sways with the impulse of its own dead weight.

Close following his dead son, Kehama came,
Nor joining in the ritual song,
Nor calling the dear name;
With head deprest and funeral vest,
And arms enfolded on his breast,
Silent, and lost in thought he moves along.
King of the world, his slaves unenvying now
Behold their wretched Lord; rejoiced they see
The mighty Rajah's misery;
That Nature in his pride hath dealt the blow,
And taught the Master of Mankind to know
Even he himself is man, and not exempt from woe.

By 1825, the year of publication of *Rejected Addresses,* Southey had left behind his old principles and prejudices and would in the following year be rewarded with the position of Poet Laureate. The Queen was far more concerned with the political leaning and reputation of a poet-laureate than his literary merit and high reputation as a poet. ' ...he would have declined the offer had the Queen not relieved his worries by telling him that no one would ask him to write anything on demand but only commemorate royal events,' and as things turned out, he cleverly avoided putting pen to paper for any occasion whatsoever.[51]

James Smith had chosen his subject wisely and confined himself to a less controversial minor masterpiece, choosing imitation rather than parody, thus avoiding any trivialisation of the original concept. Like traditional prologues, it is intended to be spoken, and such a plan requires appropriate diction and measure. Jeffrey considered the Address 'almost perfect', the descriptions being 'quite as good as the original.'[52]

> Midnight, yet not a nose
> From Tower-hill to Piccadilly snored!
> Midnight, yet not a nose
> From Indra drew the essence of repose!
> See with what crimson fury,
> By Indra fann'd, the god of fire ascends the walls of Drury!
>
> Tops of houses, blue with lead,
> Bend beneath the landlord's tread,
> Master and 'prentice, serving-man and lord,
> Nailor and tailor,
> Grazier and brazier,
> Through streets and alleys pour'd –
> All, all abroad to gaze,
> And wonder at the blaze.
> Now come the men of fire to quench the fires;
> To Russell Street see Globe and Atlas run,
> Hope gallops first, and second Sun;
>   On flying heel,
> See Hand-in-Hand
> O'ertake the band!
> View with what glowing wheel
>   He nicks
>   Phoenix!

> While Albion scampers from Bridge Street, Blackfriars—
>> Drury Lane! Drury Lane!
>> Drury Lane! Drury Lane!
> They shout and they bellow again and again.
>> All, all in vain!
>> Water turns steam;
>> Each blazing beam
> Hisses defiance to the eddying spout;
> It seems but too plain that nothing can put it out!
>> Drury Lane! Drury Lane!
>> See, Drury Lane expires!...

Suddenly, the Hindu god, Vishnu, the Preserver, appears, (appropriately in the form of Samuel Whitbread, the saviour of the New Drury):

> There lay the buried god, and Time
> Seemed to decree eternity of lime;
> But pity, like a dew-drop, gently prest
> Almighty Veeshnoo's adamantine breast [note]:
>> He, the preserver, ardent still
>> To do whate'er he says he will,
>> From South-hill wing'd his way,
>> To raise the drooping lord of day....

The preliminaries over, the lawyers produce the documents to sign, but the evil Yamen intervenes:

> Yamen beheld, and wither'd at the sight ;
> Long had he aim'd the sunbeam to control
> For light was hateful to his soul:....
> "Thy toils of the morning, like Ithaca's queen,
> I'll toil to undo every night"....
> This had shall tear your paper bonds to pieces;
> Ingross your deeds, assignments, leases,
> My breath shall every line erase
> Soon as I blow the blaze."

Yamen's threat of destroying the plans to restore the theatre is ignored by Veeshnoo [Whitbread], who invokes the Nine Muses:

> Ye sons of song, rejoice!
> Veeshnoo has still'd the jarring elements,
> The so heres hymn music;
> Again the god of day
> Peeps forth with trembling ray,
> Wakes from their humid caves, the sleeping Nine,
> And pours at intervals a strain divine.

And at last the spirit of New Drury appears in the form of Harlequin:

> Now Veeshnoo turn'd round to a capering varlet,
> Arrayed in blue and white and scarlet,
> And cried: "Oh! brown of slipper as of hat!"
> Lend me, Harlequin, thy bat!"
> He seized the wooden sword, and smote the earth;
> When lo! Upstarting into birth
> A fabric gorgeous to behold,
> Outshone in elegance the old,
> And Veeshnoo saw, and cried: "Hail, playhouse, mine!"….
> More bright, more glorious than before!"

As might be expected, the plot and choice of subject matter received very mixed critical acclaim, though no-one could deny the quality and subtlety of the language. However, since British India was in the making, an increasing interest in the multiplicity of religions was of paramount importance in the wider understanding of exotic cultures to which the new British arrivals were exposed.

There was much controversy over Southey's exotic verse tales. 'It seems,' reported the *Monthly Mirror,* 'Mr. Southey labours under a great disadvantage, through the choice of his machinery…Being what it is, however, we pronounce it a splendid specimen of a daring poetical imagination, fed and supported by vast sources of knowledge and observation.'[53] John Forster, whilst he praised the 'admirable' diction, 'strong, various, and free', said Southey had 'grown out of that affected simplicity of expression', the versification was in 'complete defiance of all rule and all example', with a 'wild wantonness of amplification'.[54]

We can understand Byron's irritation with Southey's poetry, 'so quaint and mouthey', distanced from today's less patient and discerning readers, with little time to fathom the meanings and complexities of abstruse and unfamiliar references:

> O! Southey! Southey! Cease thy varied song!
> A bard may chant too often and too long;
> As thou art strong in verse, in mercy spare!
> A fourth, alas, were more than we could bare,
> But if, in spite of all the world can say,
> Thou still wilt verseward plod thy weary way,
>
> The babe unborn, thy dread intent may rue,
> 'God help thee, Southey, and thy readers too!'[55]

Southey's narrative poems can make unpalatable reading to the uninitiated. Thomas Moore made a neat assessment in a short epitaph, the first and last verses of which run:

> Beneath the poppies buried deep,
> The bones of Bob the bard lie hid;
> Peace to his manes;[*] and may he sleep
> As soundly as his readers did!
>
> Death, weary of so dull a writer,
> Put to his books a *finis* thus:
> Oh! May the earth on him lie lighter
> Than did his quartos upon us![56]

Wordsworth, in his epitaph on Southey, has a kinder and less partisan view:

> Whether he traced historic truth with zeal
> For the state's guidance, or the church's weal;
> Or Fancy, disciplined by studious Art,
> Informed his pen, or Wisdom of the heart,
> Or Judgments sanctioned in the patriot's mind
> By reverence for the rights of all mankind.
> Large were his aims, yet in no human breast
> Could private feelings find a holier nest.

Southey was a man of great spirit and prodigious intellectual energy

---

[*] manes: deified souls of departed ancestors: Revered shade of departed person.

all the same. Once, in more radical times, he had been the ardent supporter of Napoleon, proposed the transportation of offenders guilty of libel and sedition, spoke out against Catholic emancipation, and blamed the Peterloo Massacre on the revolutionary rabble killed and injured by government militia. He went out of his way to antagonise manufacturers, and was a passionate critic of new factory systems that thrived on misery. He was dismayed to see overcrowded living conditions of factory workers in Manchester and was horrified by the sight of children working close to dangerous machinery.

Politically, Southey had shown himself to be no mean thorn in the flesh of the establishment. With honours and sinecures appearing on the horizon, his fellow rebels saw him as betraying the socialist ideals set out by reformers like Robert Owen, abhorring the embracing of Tory doctrine, just as Thomas Moore had done, to suit his own advancement. Byron's contempt for this outrageous *volte-face* was viciously expressed in *Don Juan*, and brilliantly elaborated in his scathing parody of Southey's elegy in praise of George III, *A Vision of Judgment*. Furthermore, Byron had never forgiven him for his sneering attack on himself and the Shelleys as being part of a 'League of Incest' and labelling them 'the Satanic School of Poetry', an extraordinary accusation since the satanic element plays such a significant role in their own exotic tales.

Horace Smith recalls a revealing visit to Southey in retirement at Keswick:

> Not without emotion did I push back the swing-gate, giving access to the large rambling garden....not without a reverent curiosity did I gaze upon the books of which his collection was so large that they overflowed their appropriate receptacles, and thickly lined the sides of the stairs up which we ascended. Nothing could be more cordial than the reception I experienced. His quick eye and sharp intelligent features might have enabled him to pass for a younger man than he really was, had not his partially grizzled hair betrayed the touches of age. His limbs, too, seemed to share the activity of his mind, for in the course of our conversation, requiring reference to some particular book, he ran with agility up the rail-steps which he had rapidly pushed before before him for the purpose, and instantly pounced upon it.[57]

Horace remarked on the 'multifarious reading' displayed on the shelves, but especially noted:

> I remember to have brought way with me an impression – perhaps an erroneous, perhaps a presumptious one – that

> he betrayed occasionally more party spirit that was becoming....Old age has taught me to abjure all dogmatism; to distrust my own sentiments, to respect those of others....That so good, so kind-hearted a man as Southey should write with so much acrimony, not to say bitterness, whenever he became subject to a political or religious bias, has excited surprise in many persons who did not reflect that his residence in a remote country town, surrounded by a little coterie of admirers, whose ready assent confirmed him in all his prejudices and bigoted notions, must have had a perpetual tendency to arrest his mind and to prevent its moving forward with the general march of intellect and liberality.[58]

If we remember Southey as living the life of a 'Lake Poet', the simple country life, enjoying the company of friends, the happy father writing poems and stories for his children, regularly attending Sunday services in his parish church at Keswick, we will find his last days a tragic end to a brilliant career. Horace astutely observed Southey's dilemma:

> '...he maintained and acted upon the theory, that change of mental labour is equivalent to rest, and if he alternated between history, poetry, and criticism he would not require any relaxation or repose. For any man this would be a perilous error, but for one whose sequestered life, however charming might have been his domestic circle, admitted little other social enjoyment and allowed hardly any varieties of amusement, a long course of monotonous labour could not fail to grow doubly hazardous.'[59]

Southey became increasingly forgetful, not recognising those who had known and loved him, gradually losing his memory altogether, his teeming brain slowly atrophying, all that phenomenally prodigious knowledge obliterated forever by a ruthless dementia.

He remains, to anyone who comes to appreciate his work, one of the most learned and mystifying of Poet-Laureates. In the present century, his writings remain largely out of print and thus largely unread, though with the coming of the internet, more have become available through a number of useful website publishers. All that remains is for Thelaba and Kehama to be rediscovered by the television reseachers to provide plots and action for some bloodcurdling late-night drama.

9. *Drury's Dirge* by L.M. (Laura Matilda)

A War of Words

The identity of the poet parodied in this Address was hidden by the Smiths from all but the literary *cognoscenti*. The Smiths were 'anxious to disavow any revelation' of her identity and, 'as in gallantry bound, wish this lady to continue anonymous.'[60]

The lady in question was discovered to be Hannah Cowley (1743-1809), the daughter of a Devon bookseller.[*] From her very earliest years Hannah had to hand every type of reading in her father's library. After some years, the family moved to London, where the father became an official of the Stamp Office. He took her to see her first play and thereafter her enthusiasm for the life of the theatre began to grow, encouraging her to try her hand at play-writing. For a woman of her day, her achievement was remarkable: the fast-flowing action of her comedies and sparkling dialogue, would captivate her audiences for decades to come. Among the most delicately articulate of playwrights, she was admired by Garrick and Sheridan, with roles acted by such distinguished personages as John Phillip Kemble and Mrs. Jordan.

Her plots were ornate fabrications bordering on the farcical, involving a host of lovelorn suitors, scheming mothers, handsome soldiers, marriageable widows, jealous rivals, wicked schemers, rich uncles, embroiled in secret passions, broken vows, confused identities, ruined reputations, deathbed confessions, all manner of subterfuge, forged or missing documents, and an abundance of confessions, repentance, lies and deceits, ending in disgrace for some and honour or justice for others.

By 1775, she completed her first play, *The Runaway*, and in the following year it was staged at Drury Lane by Garrick. With a record 17 performances, her success was assured. A farce, *Who's the Dupe?* (1779), followed with equal success, but her next attempt, a tragedy, *Albina*, failed to impress.

Garrick was an unusual tutor in the craft of play-writing and, a rare attitude for the times, encouraged and nurtured the talents of a number of women playwrights, who were generally dismissed as having copied from their male rivals. Neither could the anti-feminine views of the press be considered in any way encouraging, judging by the comment in *The Gazetteer* of 18 May 1779: 'We are tired of indulging Authours [*sic*] because they are Female.' The theatre was a man's world and women

---

[*] Hannah Cowley's collected works were brought together in 1813 (Anon. *The Works of Mrs. Cowley, Drama and Poems.* London: Wilkie and Robinson. 1813) but rarely heard of again.

writers had no place in it. Garrick had great faith in Cowley's talent and was able to guide her through the complexities of script-writing, dialogue, scene-structure and plot.

Elements of the plot of *Albina* are typical of countless plays and operas of the period: a young widow, Albina, is courted by Edward, a handsome young soldier. Reluctant to break her mourning vows, she finally agrees to the union. On the eve of the wedding, her brother-in-law, Lord Gondibert, is persuaded by the jealous Editha to intervene, and tells Edward that Albina has been unfaithful. A duel is arranged, so the king banishes Gondibert, who has by this time vowed to murder Albina and commit suicide. He bursts into her bedroom, unwittingly stabbing Editha, who has unwisely hidden there, at which point Albina rushes in and begs the expiring Gondibert's forgiveness – and the lovers live happily ever after.

Hannah Cowley   Hannah More (by H.W.Pickersgill)

Sheridan declined to put the play on at Drury Lane, so the determined Mrs. Cowley took it to the rival Theatre Royal, Covent Garden. Unfortunately she was out of luck as Hannah More's *Fatal Falsehood* (1779) was already in production. Mrs. Cowley was convinced that More had outrageously plagiarised *Albina* and in her preface to the printed edition of *Albina*, claimed that the two plays did in fact possess 'wonderful resemblances'. According to one report, she stood up in the theatre and shouted: 'That's mine! That's mine!'[61]

The accusation was exacerbated by an article in the *St. James's Chronicle* with Mrs. More protesting: 'I am under the solemn necessity of declaring, that I never saw, heard, or read, a single line of Mrs. Cowley's Tragedy.'[62] The affronted Mrs Cowley replied with equal defiance: 'I wish Miss More had been still more sensible of the indelicacy of a newspaper altercation between women, and the ideas of ridicule which the world are apt to attach to such unsexual hardiness...'[63] The contentious dialogue grew to fever pitch in what Ellen Donkin calls 'The Paper War',[64] for it took place between two rival newspapers and became more interesting than the plays themselves. During that time the two ladies never met face to face.

Thomas Cowley, cautiously admitted that, given the loose system of the day, 'Amidst the croud [*sic*] of Plots, and Stage Contrivances, in which a Manager is involv'd, *recollection* is too frequently mistaken for the suggestions of *imagination*" His proposed a public enquiry into the feud, probably encouraged by Captain Cowley, who was connected with the newspaper – a clever ploy to avoid criminal proceedings. *Albina* ended its days at the Theatre Royal, Haymarket, where it filled the 'tragic' gap in the Summer Season of comedies.[65]

Following the plagiary *débâcle*, the two Hannahs pulled their punches and settled down to a quiet life, More to retirement to the country and Cowley to the gentle pursuit of versifying (her complete works were published in 1813). Clearly, fashions changed and Hannah Cowley's dramatic skills were soon outdated with the rapidly changing tastes. Thomas, having previously travelled to to America in search of a fortune, and returned penniless, set out on another course of action, accepting a position in India with the British East India Company. He never returned home to England and died there in 1797.

Why did Thomas take the decision to cut himself off from his roots in mid-life, abandoning wife and children, to bury himself in a far-off land? Hannah's last play may hold a clue. The plot concerns Don Carlos, who has deserted his wife, Victoria, for the alluring courtesan, Laura and makes her a gift of his estate. In spite of the situation, Laura invents a ruse to dress Victoria as a man, Florio, pretends to be in love with him, and breaks off her affair with Don Carlos now she has ownership of his property. The plot thickens, ending with Don Carlos repenting and promising himself to Victoria. Significantly, the title of the play was *A Bold Stroke for a Husband*, performed in the very year Thomas left for India. Perhaps Hannah, who from the start clearly had a mind of her own, and possibly a supply of left-over passion, was tempted to stray from the accepted path and found solace in the arms of another. William Gifford, in his satirical attack on the Della Cruscan group of poets, the *Baviad*, hints strongly at the reason her husband left:

> See Cowley frisk it to one ding-dong chime,

And weakly cuckold her poor spouse in rhyme....
[*Baviad* ll. 23-24]

Vers de Société

Hannah Cowley's poetry was published under the *nom de plume* of 'Anna Matilda'.[66] However, her work first appeared under her own name in the pages of a journal called *The World*, in the form of a poetic correspondence between herself and another anonymous poet. They chose to sign their effusions under the secretive sobriquet: 'Della Crusca'.

The story really begins further back in time with an English dilettante, Robert Merry (1755-1794) who, after selling his commission in the Horse Guards, spent three years or so indulging himself on the Grand Tour through Germany, the Low Countries, France, and Switzerland, and ending by savouring the artistic and social delights of Florence during the time of the Habsburg-Toskana dynasty. Italy lay under the yoke of the Austro-Hungarian Empire. Whilst this was painful and humiliating to the Italians, to the English emigrés, life was full of enjoyable daily indulgences.

Merry began to scribble for two local journals, the *Arno Miscellany* (1784) and the *Florence Miscellany* (1785), collections of verse contributed by Italian and ex-patriot English writers including Hester Thrale Piozzi:

> See Thrale's grey widow with a satchel roam,
> And bring, in pomp, her labour'd nothings home.
> [*Baviad* ll. 7-8]
> The summons her blue-stocking friends obey,
> Lured by the love of Poetry – and Tea.
> [*Baviad* ll. 37-38]

Flamboyant by nature, Merry rapidly became a much-noticed figure about town, and very soon the subject of scandal through publicly entering into a *liaison dangereuse* with the footloose Countess Cowper, wife of the third Earl Cowper.* She was, in her turn, being courted by Leopold, the Grand Duke of Tuscany, who lived with his family at the sumptuous ducal residence, the Villa Palmieri. It soon became impossible for Merry to remain part of this sensational threesome and he was forced to make a

---

* George Nassau Clavering-Cowper, 3rd Earl Cowper (1738-1789), had travelled on the Grand Tour of Europe and later emigrated to Italy, where he added the title of Prince of the Holy Roman Empire to empower his status in Florentine society.

hasty retreat in 1787 and return to England. His arrival was greeted with some curiosity, for he was recognised as a member of a much–ridiculed band of Della Cruscan poetasters.

Robert Merry, in his self-appointed role of editor of the *Miscellanies*, had adopted the ideas and manners of the 16th century linguist, Alessandro Della Crusca, after whom the Florentine Accademia Della Crusca was founded.[67] The principal ideas centred round the insistence of classical simplicity and in the first of the poems, by Bertie Greathead, 'The Dream', he bemoaned the paucity of talent at the time, and recommended a return to the Miltonic style. Translations of Dante and Petrarch provided the way forward, a soft bread of medieval etiquette buttered with solicitude and 'kindness'.*

Byron, whose emotional attachment to Italy had been well-established in his undergraduate days at Cambridge, was a willing recipient to the Della Cruscan school of thought, in particular with the liberalising effect on *The Hours of Idleness* poems. The mood and treatment was personal and in some ways political. He began to experiment with *terza rima* and *ottava rima*, bringing a kind of personal dialogue between himself and the object of his thoughts and feelings, coated in a thin veil of erotic sentimentality. His youthful *ennui* was one of the characteristics that gave the Smith brothers the idea for the style of their parody *Cui Bono?* Politically, Byron was able to sympathise with the Grand Duke Leopold's unwelcome dominance and control over the lives of the subjugated Florentines. Erudite classical and other references could hide subversive attitudes under a cloak of comparative safety.[68]

Merry's first appearance in print, 'The Adieu and Recall to Love', was signed under the pen name 'Della Crusca' and accurately followed the 'kindness' recipe by addressing a characteristically epicene Cupid, now brought struggling back to life thus:

> Go, idle Boy! I quit thy pow'r,
> Thy couch of many a thorn, and flow'r,
> Thy twanging bow, thy arrow keen,
> Deceitful Beauty'd timid mien;
> The feign'd surprise, the roguish leer,
> The tender smile, the thrilling tear,
> Have now no pangs, no joys for me,
> So fare thee well, for I am free! [69]

---

* Hester Thrale Piozzi wrote that the group only wished 'to say kind things to each other' and 'had no reason to be ashamed of our mutual partiality.'

Clearly missing his former Florentine amatory adventures, he makes a desperate attempt to call up the petulant muse:

> O hasten back, then, heav'nly Boy,
> And with thine anguish bring me joy!
> Return with all thy torments here,
> And let me hope, and doubt, and fear.
> O read my heart with ev'ry pain!
> But let me, let me love again.[70]

A consoling reply came almost by return of post from a devoted admirer:

> "To Della Crusca: The Pen"
>
> O! seize thee again the olden quill,
> And with its point my bosom thrill;
> With magic touch explore my heart,
> And bid the tear of passion start....
>
> It fell from Cupid's burnished wing
> And forcefully he drew his string;
> Which sent his keenest, surest dart
> Thro' a rebellious frozen heart....
>
> APOLLO, CUPID, shall inspire,
> And aid thee with their blended fire.
> The one, poetic language give,
> The other bid thy passion live;
> With soft ideas fill thy lays,
> And crown with LOVE thy wintry days.
>
> Signed ANNA MATILDA [71]

But Hannah was not to be allowed to have the last word:

> "To Anna Matilda"
>
> I know thee well, enchanting Maid,

Chapter 9 - The Rejected Addresses

> I've mark'd thee in the silent glade....
> O well thy form divine I know—
> When youthful errors brought me woe....
> With glowing ardours rouse my soul,
> And bid the tides of Passion roll.
> But think no longer in disguise,
> To screen thy beauty from mine eyes,
> Nor deign a borrow'd name to use,
> For well I know—thou art *the* Muse!
>
> DELLA CRUSCA [72]

There are orgasmic overtones in such pleading lines as:

> Shake from thy lock ambrosial dew
> And thrill each pulse of joy a-new;
> With glowing ardours rouse my soul,
> And bid the tides of Passion roll.

And still comes, the very same morning, another erotic declaration of undying love, as the blush of youth fades:

> My tresses sprinkle with the snow,
> Which boasted once the *auburn glow*;
> Warp the slim form that was ador'd
> By him, so lov'd, my bosom's LORD –
> But leave me, when all these you steal,
> The *mind* to taste, the *nerve* to feel!
>
> ANNA MATILDA [73]

The mood and tone of these 'epistolary' pieces have all the mannerism of Marlowe's 'Come live with me and be my love', echoed with the sharp, ironic parody in Raleigh's clever reply. The tradition of the medieval lover protesting his worthlessness when brought face to face with the virginal perfection of his love seemed to be dying a very slow death. The self-denial of courtly love had lost its charm. Not only had Anna Matilda's youth faded, but her style of poetry was out of fashion.

Byron sneered a little:

> Though Crusca's bards no more our journals fill,
> Some stragglers skirmish round the columns still –

calling them 'the howling host' - 'Matilda snivels yet…'[74]

It would be difficult not to agree with the standard academic view of the Della Cruscans as 'the nadir of the art which 'united pretentiousness with imbecility after a fashion not easy to parallel elsewhere', who 'drank themselves drunk at the heady tap of German *Sturm-und-Drang* romanticism, blending French sentimentality with Italian trifling,' and 'producing almost inconceivable balderdash.'[75]

Such outright condemnation of this small coterie of amateurs (in the sense of devotees) enjoying their 'Poetry with Tea' and their wine with *canapés* at poetical *soirées* in the romantic environment of Florence seems a hard judgement, especially when we come to a consideration of the poet who called herself 'Laura'. Whilst their motives for the play they were acting out were sincere, their 'dramatis personae' appeared to the London *cognoscenti* to have an element of the ridiculous about them. Here indeed was the perfect target for the Smith brothers, a prime opportunity to make a frontal attack on the Cruscan cult of sensibility.

Having satisfied ourselves as to the real identity of Anna Matilda, who, then, was *Laura Matilda*, the supposedly pseudonymous author of the 'Rejected Address' entitled *Drury's Dirge*?

Poetry with Passion

Leaving aside the 'Anna Matilda' half, the most likely candidate for the other half would be another Della Cruscan, the actress Mary Robinson, who wrote poetry under the *nom de plume* 'Laura Maria'. Hannah Cowley had graciously retired from the stage, turning herself into her fictional character Laura. Now, in the mind of Horace and James Smith, Anna Matilda and Laura Maria became one in 'Laura Matilda'.

From small beginnings, Mary Robinson. rose to become one of the most brilliant poets of her day, admired by Coleridge and Godwin, though unjustifiably neglected by posterity.

Chapter 9 - The Rejected Addresses

Mrs Mary Robinson, the celebrated 'Perdita'

Mary's story did not begin with poetry.[76] It began with a life-changing scandal that shocked the nation and all but ruined her. She was born in Bristol in 1757. Her father, Nicholas Darby, a sea captain, soon deserted her mother, took a mistress, indulged in many affairs and squandered the family monies. Her mother, Hester, fearing penury ahead, achieved her wish to marry Mary off to an articled clerk, Thomas Robinson, who, though professing to have a fortune, proved to be penniless and as much a profligate as the father. Hester decided to move the family to London to avoid local gossip and disgrace, but it was not long before Thomas was imprisoned for debt in the Fleet Prison, voluntarily joined as was the custom of the day by the family, including Mary. During this time she began to compose poetry, producing a small volume entitled *Captivity*, which providentially came to the notice of Georgiana, Duchess of Devonshire, who became her patron. Mary showed her gratitude to her with a sonnet:

> 'Tis not thy flowing hair of orient gold,
> Nor those bright eyes, like sapphire gems that glow,
> Nor cheek of blushing rose, nor breast of snow,
> The varying passions of the heart could hold.
>
> Those locks, too soon, shall own a silv'ry ray.
> Those radiant orbs their magic fires forego,
> Insatiate TIME shall steal those fires away,

> Warp thy fine form, and bend thy beauties low.
>
> But the rare wonders of thy polish'd MIND
> Shall mock the empty menace of decay;
> The GEM that in thy SPOTLESS BREAST enshrin'd,
> Glows with the light of intellectual ray,
> Shall, like the Brilliant, scorn each borrow'd aid,
> And deck'd with native lustre NEVER FADE!
> [*Sonnet inscribed to Her Grace The Duchess of Devonshire.*]

By this time Mary had become a very beautiful young woman and would one day be painted by Gainsborough and Reynolds. She began to make her mark as an actress. She was soon noticed by David Garrick and began acting at the Theatre Royal, Drury Lane, playing Juliet, and had great success with 'breeches' parts, particularly Viola in *Twelfth Night*. Her performance as Perdita created a sensation in *Florizel and Perdita*, an adaptation of *A Winter's Tale,* a performance sufficient to bewitch the young Prince of Wales, then only 17 years of age, with her exceptional beauty. He feverishly penned a note to her signed 'Florizel'. At first she resisted his advances, but with a combination of patience and persistence, he persuaded her to accept an emolument of £20,000 to become his mistress.[*]

With a wastrel husband in the wings, Mary's financial circumstances were such that she was forced to make a virtue of necessity by accepting the offer. Though the Prince had given her a promissory note, four years went by and the bond was still not paid, by which time the Prince was enjoying other amorous adventures, leaving Mary destitute. It was a national scandal, an embarrassment to the Court and spread a degree of consternation in government circles.

All this time, many love letters and *billets doux* had passed between the lovelorn couple. Mary realised that she would have to take drastic action if she were to save herself from destitution.

> ....passion mocks the empty boast of fame,
> Tell him no joys are sweet, but joys of love,
> Meeting the soul, and thrilling all the frame!
> Oh! May th'ecstatic thought in bosom move,
> And sighs of rapture, fan the blush of shame.
>   [Sonnet VIII]

---

[*] An extravagant sum, a measure of his blind infatuation for her – a sum in today's terms of approximately £750,000.

Chapter 9 - The Rejected Addresses

She threatened to make the affair public if the Prince did not pay her the sum agreed. The Crown finally promised to settle with her and the letters were handed over, though in the .end payments to her continued to be few and far between.

A reading of Mary Robinson's exceptional poetry can only lead us to believe that there remained a strong affection between her and the errant young Prince, and even though no direct reference may or not be intended, there is a vibrant tenderness, a reflective passion that suffuses even the white of the page in the first and last verses of 'Absence':

> When from the craggy mountain's pathless steep,
> Whose flinty brow hangs o'er the raging sea,
> My wand'ring eye beholds the foamy deep,
> I mark the restless surge and think of THEE.
> The curling waves, the passing breezes move,
> Changing and trech'rous as the breath of LOVE,
> The 'sad similitude' awakes my smart,
> And thy dear image twines about my heart.
>
> When at the still and solemn hour of night,
> I press my lonely couch to find repose,
> Joyless I watch the pale moon's chilling light,
> Where thro' the mould'ring tow'r the north-wind blows;
> My fev'rish lids no balmy slumbers own,
> Still my sad bosom beats for thee alone,
> Nor shall its aching fibres cease to smart,
> 'Till DEATH's cold SPELL is twin'd about my HEART.

Throughout the vicissitudes of her troubled life, Mary Robinson succeeded in writing three plays, five volumes of poetry, eight novels, and a memoir. Her last 15 years of life were spent in a secret off-and-on liaison with Colonel Banastre Tarleton, a hero from the American war, whom she had come to know possibly at Thomas Gainsboroug's studio whilst having her portrait painted.

Fate has a way of bringing an end to 'the primrose path of dalliance'.[77] Her relationship with Tarleton continued sporadically until 1784 when it seems the couple had a serious falling out over the nature of her illness.

At the age of only 26, the beautiful creature that was Mary Robinson, was ravaged by a mysterious disease which left her partly paralysed. She had to be carried to and from her house and lifted in and out of her carriage. 'See Robinson forget her state, and move/On crutches towards the grave....'[78] Mary's mother, Hester, harboured fears that her daughter, in her wish to go on the stage, would fall prey to the unwelcome attentions of her fellow actors, and the more notorious upper class part of the Drury Lane audiences. In this she was right. A vicious dilettante, Lord Lyttleton, furious at Mary's refusal of his lustful advances, set out to ruin her husband Thomas by 'taking him to gaming houses and brothels.'[79] One speculative opinion suggests Mary was suffering from some form of sexually transmitted disease.[80] In spite of her disability she struggled on and in the main succeeded in turning this near tragedy round, through her passion for poetry. She strove to gain greater access to the contemporary scene, enjoying the admiration and subsequently the friendship of established figures like William Godwin and Samuel Taylor Coleridge, the latter of whom greatly admired her work and sometime in 1796, showed her his poem, *Kubla Khan*, long before it was published (1816).[81]

It would be tempting here to enter into a more detailed discussion about the influence of Mary's meeting with Coleridge and the deep impression that *Kubla Khan* must have had on her imagination; following on his *Lyrical Ballads*, came her own *Lyrical Tales*. The most effective, though addictive, palliative for sickness was opium, an inspiration for Mary's poem '*The Maniac*' (1791), based on a local madman who begs someone to tell him the reason for and cause of his sickness, and written some five years *before* Coleridge's *Kubla Khan*. Only a modest sample of quotations from both poets can give an indication of their communion of spirit.

Coleridge (*Kubla Khan*)	Robinson
1.'And there were gardens bright with sinuous rills	1.'When with the Sylvan train I seek the grove
2. Where blossomed many an Incense-bearing tree.'	2. Where MAY's soft breath diffuses incense round' (*Absence*)
3.'A damsel with a dulcimer In a vision once I saw.'	3.'tuneful maids' (*Sonnet VII*) 'The dulcet numbers vibrate in my heart.' (*Sonnet VIII*)
4. Could I revive within me Her symphony and song'	4.'I think I hear thy fascinating song Join the melodious minstrel's tuneful song' (*Absence*)

Chapter 9 - The Rejected Addresses

Through Mary's Florentine connections, she would have been encouraged to read the poetry of the 14th century Italian poet, Petrarca (anglicised to 'Petrarch'), and in particular his form of the sonnet, encouraging her to compose a longer sequence. Until the coming of the Shakespearean sonnet, Petrarch's treatment seemed gently appropriate to the demands of the poets of sensibility and therefore of the Della Cruscans in general.[82]

A well-known story was told of Petrarca going to mass in Avignon where he was captivated by the beauty of a young maiden in the cathedral, whose name was Laura. She would become, for the rest of his life, the primary inspiration for his poetry. Throughout his many diplomatic missions across Europe, in the service of Cardinal Colonna, the cherished image of Laura was etched in his memory. His unrequited passion for her, or perhaps it should be said, adoration, was to be the driving force of his sonnet sequence in praise of her. It was the perfect vehicle for Mary Robinson to assuage her own deeply emotional sense of loss. Her intense emotional and physical distress were transmogrified into a kind of spiritual adulation. Locked into the prison of her own paralysis, Mary too could become Laura. As Laura Maria, she could conceal her identity.

The English Sappho

Mary gave up her frail friendship with the Della Cruscans, and as we have seen, her poetry stands far above the aspirations and capabilities of the poets of *The Florentine Miscellany*. In the later part of her life she remembered the Petrarchan ideals drawn from Ovid (after Pope's translation) and the Greeks, and settled upon the life and work of Sappho, the poet from the island of Lesbos, to whom she dedicated her *Sonnet XVIII*, with poignant memories possibly of her young royal lover:

> Why hast thou chang'd? dear source of all my woes?
> Though dark my bosom's tint, through ev'ry vein
> A ruby tide of purest lustre flows,
> Warm'd by thy love, and chill'd by thy disdain;
> And yet no bliss this sensate Being knows;
> Ah! why is rapture so allied to pain?

Whatever the amount of posturising the Della Cruscans may have indulged in, there was invariably the urge to titillate the reader with a dose of eroticism. Their rediscovery of the 7th century Greek poet, Sappho,[83] gave the female part of their society the opportunity to express the inexpressible with daring and without shame:

> Why through each aching vein with lazy pace
> Thus steals the languid fountain of my heart,
> While, from its source, each wild convulsive start
> Tears the scorch'd roses from my burning face?
> In vain, O Lesbian Isles! Your charms I trace,
> Vain is the poet's theme, the sculptor's art,
> No more the Lyre its magic can impart,
> Though wak'd to sound, with more than mortal grace!
> Go, troubled maids, go bid my Phaon prove
> That passion mocks the empty boast of fame.
>
> Mary Robinson *Sonnet VIII*

Women were not as yet wholly acceptable to the male-dominated world of authorship. However, Hannah Cowley and Mary Robinson, hiding as they did behind their pseudonyms of Anna Matilda and Laura Maria, were eventually able to break the bonds of 18th century male domination in the theatre as well as in the literary salon. Anti-feminism had dominated the stage from the days of Nell Gwynn and Sarah Siddons. New views of the role of women in society were making their mark in works like Mary Wolstonecroft's *A Vindication of the Rights of Woman* (1794), Hannah More's *The Story of Sinful Sally. Told by Herself)*, published in the *Cheap Repository* (1796), and Mary Robinson's outspoken *A Letter to the Women of England, on the Injustice of Mental Subordination* (1799).[84]

Not every woman measures her independence in the same way and it was no exception that More and Robinson approached the problem from opposite viewpoints. More proposes the idea of educating women out of the drudgery of domesticity and raising them to a position of intellectual freedom in society. Her primarily evangelical approach rested on 'Christian duty and self-improvement.' Her path of 'goodness' was paved with good intentions. Robinson, on the other hand, promoted respect for sexual dignity rather than purity, equal to that appropriated by men from Biblical times, and ultimately to find an independent social and even political voice. Robinson returned to some of her old Florentine *vers de société* ways to make her point in these lines selected from *Female Fashions 1799*:

> Cravats like towels, thick and broad,
> Long tippets made of bear-skin,
> Muffs that a RUSSIAN might applaud,

Chapter 9 - The Rejected Addresses

> And rouge to spoil a fair skin....
>
> A bush of hair, the brow to shade,
> Sometimes the eyes to cover;
> A necklace that might be display',
> By OTAHEITAN lover!....
>
> Such is CAPRICE! But, lovely kind!
> Oh! Let each mental feature
> Proclaim the labour of the mind,
> And leave your charms to NATURE.

Another of Mary's poems, *All Alone,* is almost a companion to Wordsworth's *Alice Fell,* which belied his dislike of the Della Cruscan style. A child is discovered abandoned in a churchyard. The technique is identical:

> Ah! Wherefore by the Church-yard side,
> Poor little LORN ONE, dost thou hide?
> Thy wavy looks do thinly hide
> The tears that dim thy blue-eyes ray;
> And wherefore dost thou sigh, and moan,
> And weep, that thou art left alone?
>
> Thou art not left alone, poor boy.
> The Traveller stops to hear thy tale;
> No heart, so hard, would thee annoy!
> For tho' thy mother's cheek is pale
> And withers under yon grave stone,
> Thou art not, Urchin, left alone.

The grim story of how the waif came to be left alone in the cold is almost identical in style and concept to *Alice Fell,* but the story-telling is far more skilled. It strongly suggests that Wordsworth had known of this poem before writing *Alice Fell.*

Drury's Dirge Unveiled

The parody here is based on a fusion of Mrs. Cowley and Mrs Robinson's Della Cruscan styles. The Smiths took for their model Jonathan Swift's *Song by a Person of Quality*, with its absurd alliterations, *non sequiturs* and oxymorons, and adoption of the identical measure:

> Fluttering spread thy purple pinions,
> Gentle Cupid, o'er my heart,
> I a slave in thy dominion,
> Nature must give way to art.
>
> Mild Arcadians, ever blooming,
> Nightly nodding o'er your flocks,
> See my weary days consuming,
> All beneath your flowery rocks.
>
> Thus the Cyprian goddess weeping
> Mourned Adonis, darling youth,
> Him the bear, in silence creeping,
> Gored with unrelenting tooth.
>
> Cynthia, tune harmonius numbers,
> Fair Discretion, string the lyre,
> Soothe my ever-waking slumbers,
> Bright Apollo, lend thy choir.

The poem was an example of what was called in 18th century France an 'amphigouri' or 'amphigory',[*] a form of intentional nonsense, 'a rhyme without reason', 'a meaningless rigmarole', an absurd piece of trivia.[85] Gilbert Wakefield, editor of Pope's works, thought Swift's poem was 'disjointed and obscure.'

Laura Matilda's poem of 15 verses parodies the nonsensical use of classical references, but what are we to make of Verse 10 for example? :

---

[*] *Amphigouri*. Its descent can be traced from the verbal trickery of *A Midsummer Night's Dream* to the Anti-Jacobins, Henry Carey's *Chrononhotonthologos,* Sheridan's *The Critic,* and onwards to Lewis Carroll and Edward Lear.

Chapter 9 - The Rejected Addresses

> Pan beheld the Patroclus dying,
> Nox to Niobe was turned;
> From Busiris Bacchus flying,
> Saw his Semele inurn'd.

Certainly on a first reading the poem appears to wander through a wonderland of nonsense into which are thrown a crowd of Greek gods and goddesses who today may well bring the modern reader to a state of confusion and consequent indifference. Certainly it is evidence of the classical education received by Horace and James in their school days. Would there be any point in making a closer study of these references? Would it be worth solving the mystery, if there is one, of what had been described as 'inconceivable balderdash'? Yet if taken seriously, it might just be considered one of Horace Smith's most ingenious contributions to the volume of *Addresses*.

Taking the positive view, perhaps a study of the classical references might bring to light some obscure secrets encrypted within the text. In fact, a little research uncovered some surprising references, links and parallels to hidden images of fire and water (highlighted in italics), as may be discovered in the following tentative commentaries:

> Balmy Zephyrs, lightly flitting,
> Shade me with your azure wing;
> On Parnassus' summit sitting,
> Aid me, Clio, while I sing.

The soft west wind, Zephyrus, clouds over the blue sky of day. The poet invokes the Muse of History, Clio, to come down from the heavens, (Mount Parnassus, the seat of Apollo, the god of poetry and song so much beloved of Drury's audiences), to aid Laura Matilda in the task of describing the momentous event about to happen.

> Softly slept the dome of Drury
> O'er the empyreal crest,
> When Alecto's sister fury
> Softly slumb'ring sunk to rest.

It is night-time. Everything is peaceful, everyone asleep. The high dome of Drury, soon to be a place of fire, falls victim to Alecto, one of the avenging Furies (Eumenides), who comes to wreak vengeance and, by tradition, bearing flaming torches.

> Lo! Lemnos limping lamely,
> Lags the lowly Lord of Fire,
> Cytherea yielding tamely
> To the Cyclops dark and dire.

Amidst an outrageous Vulcan, Lord of Fire, who, in falling from the heavens, landed on the island of Lemnos, breaking his leg, now arrives, limping, to stoke Drury's fire, accompanied by the gigantic, human-devouring Cyclops. Even Cytherea (Venus), goddess of love and beauty, has conceded defeat. All that is good about Drury is shrouded in darkness and despair.

> Clouds of amber, dreams of gladness,
> Dulcet joys and sports of youth,
> Soon must yield to haughty sadness;
> Mercy holds the veil of truth.

An orange glow spreads across the London sky as the fire begins to rage. The fun and high spirits of Drury are rapidly being reduced to a heap of burning embers. All that remains is universal grief and condolence. And, still, a veil hangs over the truth about the cause of the fire.

> See Erostratus the second
> Fires again Diana's fane;
> By the Fates from Orcus beckon'd,
> Clouds envelop Drury Lane.

Just as Erostratus (reduced by a syllable from 'Eratostratus' for scansion) had once burned down the fane (temple) of Diana, now a second burning down of Drury Lane, the 'Temple of the Muses', was taking place (it was first destroyed by fire in 1672.) Vulcan is triumphant. Clouds of smoke billow through the beleaguered theatre, attracting the unwelcome attention of Orcus (Pluto), the god of Hell, who orders the cruel Fates, daughters of Nox and Erebus, to lay a thick wreath of smoke, cutting fateful Drury's last threads of life. Atropos, a sister Fate, comes, wielding her deathly scissors.

> Lurid smoke and frank suspicion
> Hand in hand reluctance dance;

Chapter 9 - The Rejected Addresses

> While the God fulfils his mission,
> Chivalry resign thy lance.

As the smoke thickens, suspicion grows as to the cause of the fire, and the Hand-in-Hand Insurance Company are reluctant to pay up (i.e. join the dance, co-operate). Vulcan, god of fire, does his worst, as the life of Drury is suffocated and delivered up to the flames. Nobility and integrity are no weapons against total immolation.

> Hark! The engines blandly thunder,
> Fleecy clouds dishevell'd lie,
> And the firemen, mute with wonder,
> On the son of Saturn cry.

The noise of the fire-engines adds to the pandemonium. Wisps of smoke hang over the débris, as the firemen stare, stunned at the spectacle, and call on Neptune, son of Saturn, God of the ocean, to bring more water.

> See the bird of Ammon sailing,
> Perches on the *engine's peak*,
> And, the Eagle firemen hailing,
> Soothes them with its bickering beak.

The phoenix, bird of Ammon, (probably originating from Phoenicia), sails in on the wind and perches on the top of the Eagle fire-engine, offering itself up to be sacrificed to the flames of Drury. The firemen hail it as their saviour, strangely comforted by its irritating screech (its 'bickering')

> Juno saw, and mad with malice
> Lost the prize that Paris gave;
> Jealousies ensanguined chalice.
> Mantling pours the orient wave.

Jealous Juno, daughter of Saturn, looked down from the heavens, full of malice and mischief. She had not forgotten that Paris had given Venus (Cetherea) the golden apple instead of to her. Through his infidelity she had handed him the poisoned chalice of infidelity and Troy was destroyed in a blood-soaked ('ensanguined') battle. From her eastern throne, in consequence, out of jealousy, she would drown Drury in a mantle of water.

> Pan beheld Patroclus dying,
> Nox to Niobe was turned;
> From Busiris Bacchus flying,
> Saw his Semele inurn'd.

Drury lies in almost ruins as the fire takes its toll. Now Pan has come from his home in Arcadia, looking fearsome, like a hairy goat with his horns, and cloven hooves. He had witnessed the dying throes of the Trojan hero, Petroclus, he who had once burned down the Temple of Diana, and has come to gloat. Ever the cause of numerous pranks, Pan lived up to his name in Drury's case and caused widespread panic.

Nox, daughter of Chaos, and mother of the Furies, joins Niobe, mother of Discord, to add to the confusion. The tyrant, Busiris, son of Neptune, forces Bacchus, the god of wine, and his fellow imbibers to flee from Drury. Just as Jupiter had once brought water to the army of Bacchus, dyimg of thirst in the deserts of Libya, so now water came to slake the raging fire of Drury. Nox, in her principle role as goddess of Night brought her offspring, the Day and the Night to hurry things on. Dawn was approaching. Bacchus is reminded of his mother Semele's first sight of Jupiter. So overawed was she by the majesic presence of the Father of the Gods, combined with the intensity of her physical desire, that she was consumed by fire.

> Thus tell Drury's lofty glory,
> Levell'd with the shuddering stones;
> Mars, with tresses black and gory,
> Drinks the dew of pearly groans.

The beautiful lofty interiors of the theatre are burnt to cinders and the walls of stones, like Troy itself, have tumbled to the ground. Mars, the god of war, has done his worst. Resentful of Apollo's intervention in his passionate extramarital affair with Venus, he determined to persecute the children of Apollo.

> Hark! what soft Aeolian numbers
> Gem the blushes of the morn!
> Break, Amphion, break your slumbers,
> Nature's ringlets deck the thorn.

So the dread night is over. Calm is restored to the stricken Drury.

Chapter 9 - The Rejected Addresses

The gods have been busy but not kind. The early morning sun brings, as in Aeolia far away in Asia Minor, a soft winter glow, and poetry, not water, begins to flow. It is the Lesbian home of Sappho. Amphion, son of Jupiter, the spirit of poetry, is alive and well. Mercury had taught him music and gave him his lyre, and it is said that he moved the fallen stones of Thebes and raised the walls to the tune of his lyre. Through his sublime eloquence he persuaded a wild and uncivilised people to to read and write and build a new town. Thus at Drury Lane, a new Theatre Royal was built, and the poetry and songs of Apollo returned at last.

> Ha! I hear the strain erratic
> Dimly glance from pole to pole;
> Raptures sweet and dreams ecstatic
> Fire my everlasting soul.

The sounds of Drury gradually return, haphazardly at first, memories of the old raptures and dreams come crowding back and fire the poet's 'everlasting soul'.

> Where is Cupid's crimson motion?
>   Billowy ecstasy of woe,
> Bear me straight, meandering ocean,
>   Where the stagnant torrents flow.

Will Cupid come to play his old tricks? Whatever troubles may lie in store, the poet asks for a straight path ahead on his voyage through the 'meandering ocean' of life. Cupid, god of love, whose dominion extends over the sea, the earth, and the heavens, has departed, his work done, taking with him the troubles of old Drury and replacing them once more with love and beauty. The 'crimson ecstasy', the spirit of Drury, has overcome the 'meandering sea' of uncertainty, and a new Drury is about to be reborn from the ashes, like a phoenix.

> Blood in every vein is gushing,
>   Vixen vengeance lulls my heart;
> See the Gorgon gang is rushing!
>   Never, never let us part!

The spiteful vengeance of the three Gorgon sisters, their hair crawling with serpents, their bodies cloaked in impenetrable scales, and their single swivelling eye with its power to turn human beings to stone, has wreaked their spiteful vixen vengeance. Heroic Perseus has saved the day, the blood of their sisters' severed heads dripping out over the sands of Libya.

Jeffrey, in the *Edinburgh Review*, was not impressed. The parody, he wrote, 'was not of the first quality', and 'very non-sensical'.[86]

The plethora of largely unfamiliar gods and goddesses in *Drury's Dirge* is clearly a deterrent to read on for more than three or four verses into the poem. Yet the erudite, classically brilliant Horace Smith chose to write 15 virtually unintelligible stanzas purporting to have been written by two largely forgotten ladies, presumably with the wish that his readers would read the poem to the bitter end, though it is not known whether anyone ever did.[87] What is far more important than the poem itself is that it brought about the resurrection of two neglected women playrights and poets, both of whose reputations had suffered from the indifference of the male–dominated ethos and prejudices of actor-managers. It would be a century before any sign of organised protest would come about and violence erupt sufficient to bring a real change in women's rights.

CHAPTER TEN

The Shape of Things to Come

1. Edmund Kean: A Tempestuous Spirit

Just when it seemed that the Theatre Royal, Drury Lane, was at one of its lowest points, the long-suffering Phoenix flapped its tireless wings once more and summoned help. At a small theatre in Dorchester, sometime in 1787, a little-known actress named Anne Carey, gave birth to an illegitimate child and called him Edmund. The father was an architect's clerk, an impoverished descendant of the ancient line of O'Catháin (anglicised to O'Kane/Kean) of Donegal. It is likely that little Edmund Kean inherited something of his maternal grandfather, the composer and playwright, Henry Carey. In time, his mother, unable to cope with his arrant wilfulness and uncontrollable temper, deserted him and followed her own undistinguished path as an actress on the Dublin stage

Little attention was given to Kean's upbringing. He enjoyed the dubious, wayward pleasures and adventures of life behind the scenes, his vagabond experience conjoined with a wilful and passionate nature. His uncle, a ventriloquist, gave the boy some useful lessons in elementary stagecraft and soon little Edmund began to make appearances in small parts, not always without causing pandemonium on stage and embarrassment to his fellow actors.

We next hear of the young tearaway at Drury Lane, being sacked for bad behaviour – he accidentally fell against a row of children next to him, causing a domino effect which turned tragedy into farce and brought peals of laughter from the audience. After this mishap, he was condemned to appear only in pantomimes. Skilled at mimicry, Kean seriously upset actor John Phillip Kemble, a man not to be trifled with, who angrily pushed the child away, causing him to fall through a trapdoor, rendering him lame for a time. Luck was not on little Edmund's side when he ran away to Bartholomew Fair, a place of immorality and all manner of dangers for a young child. Eventually he joined Saunder's Circus where, during an accident as a tumbler, he broke both legs, which may have led to his temporary retirement. Spending some years wandering from town to town looking for work, he found himself a wife, Mary Chambers, and eked out a life that left the young couple hardly able to feed themselves and their small son.

By 1806, he was playing small parts at the Haymarket Theatre. Not wishing to try his hand on the London stage, he relied on finding enough work in the provinces. Eventually, while acting at Dorchester, he was noticed by the Drury Lane stage-manager, and took up the offer of work at Drury Lane for three years as an apprentice, where he had an ideal opportunity to learn the disciplines and secret ways of a great theatre.

Kean comes on to the scene at Drury on 26 January 1814, when he made a triumphant appearance as Shylock, followed equally by Hamlet, Othello and Iago. He was praised by Hazlitt, Kemble and Byron. Further triumphs eventually came with a variety of performances as Macbeth, Sir Giles Overreach, young Norval, King John, and Rolla in the Kotzebue/Dryden production of *Pizarro* with a sensational performance as Lear in 1820. After a tour in America, he returned to Drury to repeat his success as Richard III.

The Lessee of the Theatre Royal at this time was Robert William Elliston, the actor who had recited Byron's *Address* at the riotous opening of the Theatre Royal in 1812.

Passion and frustration do not make good companions in real life, but once on stage again, Kean's feelings were released with such emotional force that audiences flocked to see him. His Shylock was one of the greatest first appearances in the history of the Theatre Royal. By now his passion had become an obsession of prodigious proportions – a massive outpouring of pent-up emotion, expressed through the language and images of Shakespeare and the turbulent characters of his imagination, particularly Richard III. His performances of the great Shakespearean roles had such visceral power, such flagellation of the soul, that no other great tragedian in history could match them.

Kean's sexual energy exhausted itself in countless affairs with upper-class women. He became reckless and irresponsible, spending much of his time drinking and carousing in low taverns, causing him to be late for performances, forgetting his lines and indulging in wild extravagances that left him penniless.

His progress towards self-destruction was hastened by sickness and alcohol. Disaster came when he was involved in a criminal conviction, which adversely affected his run of popularity even in his established roles. By 1827, it appears that his popularity had returned with his performance as Shylock, though his Henry V was a failure. On 12 March 1833, he played for the last time in the play he had made his own, Richard III. During his last years, his energies were dissipated by drunkenness and prodigality. He collapsed on stage in his son's arms during a performance of *Othello*, and died at Richmond, Surrey, in May 1833 at the age of 46.0

2. Stephen Price: An American Means Business

Stephen Price (1783-1840) was an American entrepreneur who had little or no interest in becoming an actor, but he had drive enough to put on 450 performances at the Theatre Royal in 220 days. He leased Drury Lane for a term of fourteen years at a rental of £10,000 per annum, paid the rent to the shareholders and finally got on with the job of running the Theatre as a real business.[1] There is little evidence to tell us how popular he was, though we can comfortably assume that there were tensions with his actors where expenses were concerned. One of a new breed of impresarios, he had the idea of introducing an inventive scheme of ticket prices ranging from high price, full price, half price to low price to suit the pockets of a wide range of devotees. A George Cruikshank caricature, *The Four Mr. Prices*, shows a small group of comical figures walking along a country road, presumably on their way to the theatre, personifying these different prices (see illustration no. 44 in the colour plates).

Stephen Price (engraving based on a portrait by Samuel Reynolds)

Stephen Price was the brash product of his own particular cultural inheritance which, as far as the English classical theatre was concerned, was in its comparative infancy. The American professional theatre of his time was strongly based on profits rather than expensive quality entertainment. This change had begun with more high-minded managers aware of the growing need for more polished performances as the theatre-going middle classes began to assert themselves. It had not yet, however, reached that point by the time Kean arrived in 1820 to play at the Park Theatre, New York.

Previously, the original 'American Company', who had come to England in 1752, had little in common with the virtuosic wit of Farquhar and Sheridan, nor of the sophisticated staging of Garrick's Shakespeare productions. Price, ever a man of ideas where money was concerned, had the brilliant notion of presenting to his New York audiences, great English actors and actresses as visiting 'stars' of the English stage, representing the very highest level of performance. That the working-class audiences of the Bowery, a street notorious for dance halls and gambling houses, were ready for such innovation proved to be grossly out of key with their taste for melodramas, comic songs and monologues, echoing the already established tradition of London's East End entertainments. Gradually, the middle classes began to frequent the more salubrious Park Theatre and to appreciate the English style of acting.

As with the English theatres, immorality was rife in the upper parts of the theatre, especially with the infiltration of prostitutes, pimps, pickpockets and other undesirables. Rowdiness and occasional uproar from the pit and galleries were a great annoyance to those in the more elegant parts of the theatre. Even there, social graces were more in favour of the audience than actors on stage, who frequently could not hear themselves speak.[2]

Even though Price tended to be tight-fisted with actors' salaries, he was honest and honourable when it came to finance generally, a rare quality in the pull and thrust of the world of theatre, but even he could not maintain his position in the face of a decline in 'legitimate theatre', so he chose to buck the trend at Drury Lane by putting on more popular operas and light musical entertainments. This policy appears to have been a mistake and he failed in his attempts to save Drury. He is said to have been a man of 'coarse manners, repulsive conduct, and vulgar conversation,' a condition which cannot have helped his relationship with his actors and back-stage staff. That, and his serious lack of knowledge and judgment of, and even interest in, the thespian arts, led him to lose over £9000 in two seasons alone.[3] The Committee attempted to eject him, forgetting that he had once been a lawyer. He refused to surrender his lease without negotiating a sizeable compensation and they were forced to pay him an appreciable allowance over several weeks. He was, all the same, declared bankrupt and quit Drury in 1830, after only four years of his hoped-for 14. In March of that year he took his leave of Drury Lane and returned to America.[4]

Good came out of ill in the end. Price's short stay in England gave him the chance to appreciate that English talent could fill the Price coffers back home at the Park Theatre, New York, if marketed in the right way. However, it was hard-going for his actors introducing their untutored audiences to Shakespeare and other English classics for the first time, and to convince them that the pure genius of Kean and Macready was an experience not to be missed.

3. Pride shall have a fall: Alfred Bunn and William Macready

Our image of Elliston is of an actor berated by the First Night audience at the opening of the new theatre, on which occasion, as we have seen, he could not be heard over the voices of the poetasting protesters. His performance of Byron's Prologue could hardly be said to have been 'eloquent'. Much given in his younger days to gambling, drinking and fornication, he did, in spite of his personal failings, flourish and became a substantial if ruthless Lessee of the Theatre Royal, succeeding in acquiring other smaller theatres.

> Oh! Great Lessee! Great Manager! Great Man!
> Oh, Lord High Elliston! Immortal Pan....
> Do anything! — Thy fame, thy fortune, nourish!
> Laugh and grow fat! be eloquent, and flourish![5]

Elliston's principal headache had been in managing Kean's erratic life-style, but all too soon he was to have trouble with an arrogant, self-opinionated Macready, and had to cope with the unpredictable tempers of Madame Vestris. By 1826, he was bankrupt to the tune of £5,500. He had spent £22,000 of his own money on redecorating the interior of the theatre and was, in spite of his misplaced generosity, poorly treated by the proprietors.

Alfred Bunn was appointed stage manager, Drury Lane, in 1823, then after ten years was promoted to manager, in which role he remained until 1848. Dumpy in appearance and bouncy by nature, he put on very successful performances of Balfe's *The Bohemian Girl* during the 1843 Christmas season. As the next Lessee of Drury Lane, he was all for novelty, over and above serious drama and much preferred reptiles and elephants on stage to any morose Hamlet or guilt-ridden Macbeth. He would never have tolerated Kean, but he realised that the moralising William Macready was tragedian enough to fit the bill if the audiences clamoured for him.

Bunn was considered a vulgar little man with a coarse tongue and flashy appearance and was the model for Thackeray's luckless *Pendennis*:

> ...a portly gentleman with a hooked nose and a profusion of curling brown hair and whiskers: his coat was covered with the richest frogs [an ornamental fastening for coats], braiding and velvet. He had under waistcoats, many

Chapter 10 - The Shape of Things to Come

splendid rings, jewelled pins [tie or cravat pins], and neckchains. When he took out his white pocket handkerchief with the hand that was cased in kids [pigskin leather gloves], a delightful odour of bergamot and musk was shaken through the house. [6]

Alfred Bunn, drawn on stone by R.J.Lane A.R.A

Like Sheridan, Bunn was sharp on actors' wages, keeping them to a bare minimum, but he managed to sign up William Charles Macready for the 1835-36 season. Bunn had taken over the old Royalty Theatre, putting on pantomimes and burlettas, but after a few years of failure, the theatre burnt down.

Macready was in complete contrast to Bunn in everything – moral, upright, a good family man, moody, and often overbearing. Disapproving of Kean, he had no regard for Bunn either, saying he was devoid of honour and 'double-tongued'. [7] He spoke of Charles Kemble at Covent Garden as one with whom he could not even bring himself to shake hands; it would have been 'tantamount to making alliance with fraud, treachery, falsehood, the meanest and most malignant species of intrigue'. [8]

In return Bunn found Macready less of a draw than he had originally thought and started to give him after-pieces and half-price shows. In due course, a violent struggle took place in Bunn's office. Though it was a potentially dangerous situation, it was equally laughable as Macready was still in his hunchback costume. 'I struck him, as he rose, a backhanded slap across the face. I did not hear what what he said, but I dug my fist into him as effectively as I could; he caught hold of me, and got at one time the little finger of my left hand in his mouth, and bit it.'[9] Bunn sued

Macready for assault and that was the end of the matter. Macready stormed off to join Covent Garden. Bunn, in desperation, brought in performing animals (Ducrow's horses were a popular entertainment), but it turned out to be a *déjà-vu* experiment which did not appeal, just as it had not in the days of Grimaldi. In 1839, Bunn was declared bankrupt.

Bunn's legacy to the English stage was, in spite of his personal vagaries, remarkably invigorating for the continuance of the Theatre Royal as the principal venue for major performances. His support for operas by the Irish composer, Michael Balfe, in particular *The Bohemian Girl,* for which Bunn wrote the libretto (including the song 'I dreamt I dwelt in marble halls'), was one of the more positive contributions during his reign as joint manager of both the Theatre Royal and Covent Garden.[10]

A comedian named W. H. Hammond came out of the blue to take on the lease and immediately lured Macready back from Covent Garden to play Macbeth and a version of *Mary Stuart* by James Haynes, both of which lasted only 20 nights. Hammond, with an eye to the main chance, absconded with the takings and was declared bankrupt in his absence.

Who should come to the rescue as Drury's next actor-manager but William Charles Macready himself, who began by reviving Shakespeare for, as it happened, an indifferent audience. During one performance, as Macready lay prone after a death scene, one of the actors accidentally stood on his hand. He, the corpse, sat bolt upright and shouted to his assailant: 'Beast of hell!' causing the audience, prepared for tragedy and grief, to collapse into uncontrolled laughter.[11]

Despite these upsets Macready put on the phenomenal number of 96 Shakespeare performances, against all likelihood that they would capture public interest, and 148 operas and pantomimes, before he decided to leave the Theatre Royal for good. He gave one farewell performance as Macbeth in February 1851, and set off for America.

4. Dion Boucicault Saves the Day

Bunn's desperate struggle to keep Drury alive by balancing the books with circuses and pantomimes could not in the end avoid his own bankruptcy. In spite of his successor, Frederick Gye, one of many long-since forgotten managers, attempting to bring into being the inflated notion of Drury Lane as 'The Grand National Opera House', no such grandiose future was forthcoming. A sequence of ineffectual managers failed to revive the fortunes of the ailing Theatre Royal. Next came Edward Tyrrell Smith, a newspaper owner and land agent, who kept the theatre ticking over with a variety of circus and vaudeville turns, mixed in with the occasional opera, and a touch or two of Shakespeare. At this

Chapter 10 - The Shape of Things to Come

point, a forty-year-old Irish scientist and writer, Dionysius Lardner, arrived on the London scene, having been elected professor of natural philosophy and astronomy at University College. He brought with him Anne Boursiquot, with whom he had lodged in Dublin, and her children. One of the children was Dion, almost without doubt Lardner's son, for he was given full financial support by Lardner until he could make his own way as an actor. In London, Dion began by studying at University College School and thence on to university, but the lure of the stage was much in his mind. After a period of study at London University, he left to join William Charles Macready in Cheltenham, and soon after began to write plays, his first being *The Legend of Devil's Dyke*, performed in Brighton in 1838.

Dion Boucicault

Dion Boucicault 1820-1890, as he came to be known, proved to be the saviour of Drury, having great success with his extravaganza, *London Assurance,* produced at Covent Garden in 1841, with a cast including the prestigious Charles Mathews and Madame Vestris. The play included characters redolent of Sheridan' creations – the fop, Sir Harcourt Courtly, Lady Gay Spanker, the horse-riding temptress, and Mark Meddle, the lawyer – in a crowded cast.

Another of Boucicault's successes was *The Corisican Brothers; or, The Fatal Duel*, a tragedy adapted from the original by Alexandre Dumas, author of *The Count of Monte Cristo* and *The Three Musketeers.* The plot simplifies down into a 'rivalry in love' theme that ends in a double tragedy. The play ends with a scene of horror when Fabiano and Madame De Laparre are transfixed as they watch the ghost of Louis drift across the stage. After Sir Henry Irving's famous performance of the play, Oscar Wilde composed a note of praise in a sonnet, entitled 'Fabiano Dei Franchi,' and addressed it to 'my friend Henry Irving':

> The silent room, the heavy creeping shade,
> > The dead that ravel fast, the opening door,
> > The murdered brother rising through the floor,
> The ghost's white fingers on thy shoulders laid
> And then the lonely duel in the glade,
> > The broken swords, the stifled scream, the gore,
> > The grand revengeful eyes when all is o'er.[12]

As a brilliant actor-manager and playwright to boot, Boucicault had a great talent for understanding what his audiences needed. Above all, in this more trivial age, they demanded light entertainment; they wanted extravagant productions with plenty of spectacle, mixed in with music hall, comic characters and plenty of banter, and as a supreme showman he could give it to them in full measure. He was popular for his originality in the construction of elaborate plays, and his grasp of social *minutiae*. His major contribution to any London theatre he performed in was to vastly increase money, and bundles of it.

Boucicault moved to America, where he settled for the rest of his life. He was appointed manager of Burton's New Theatre on Broadway and renamed it the Winter Garden Theatre, where, in 1859, he produced his sensational play about anti-slavery, entitled *The Octoroon*. On a visit to London in 1875, he made a re-appearance at Drury Lane to rapturous applause, but soon afterwards returned to the United States, where he died in New York City in 1890.

5. The Great 'Gussie': Pantomime versus Opera

From 1879 onwards, the tradition of putting on pantomimes at Christmastime came to pass, through the enthusiasm and foresight of a remarkable actor-manager, Sir Augustus Harris, popularly known as 'Gus' or 'Gussie', and that Christmas tradition survives to this very day. His first two productions were *Bluebeard* and *The Forty Thieves*, followed by a whole string of what were to become perennial favourites: *Babes in the Wood*, *Jack and the Beanstalk*, *Beauty and the Beast*, *Humpty Dumpty*, *Dick Whittington*, and *Cinderella*, spectacular productions involving hundreds of participants and all of them starring a remarkable new comic talent, Dan Leno. Harris's brilliance did not stop there. He put on an impressive historical extravaganza entitled *The Spanish Armada*, reviving some of the old political fervour of Dryden's days. Above all, he restored Shakespeare to respectability.

Sir Augustus Harris, by Spy

Harris had grown up in a theatrical household, his father being something of an actor-manager and dramatist himself, and his mother a theatre costumier. The Theatre Royal had fallen on hard times and here was a talented, energetic young man with ideas of his own who would come along and transform the old ailing *ancient regime* into a successful business.

Undaunted, Harris went down to the East End pubs, traditional homes of working-class Music Hall, to root out artists for his pantomimes. Dan Leno, Marie Lloyd and Vesta Tilley, who was brave enough to enter the male arena with her 'Burlington Bertie' costume, were all enticed into the bright lights of the West End stage. From the Music Hall came the fashion for pantomime dames, when male performers could dress as women with great comic effect and get away with any amount of sexual innuendo, reducing their audiences to fits of laughter. Many subsequent acts were to join the list: Old Mother Riley, and many more since, but none of these cross-gender acts could surpass the sublime Dan Leno. Whatever great things Harris gave to Drury Lane, his greatest innovation was to make working class entertainment respectable for his middle class

West End admirers.

However, he was not content in supplying the more frivolous part of his audiences with light entertainment; he wanted to reach out further to the more sophisticated theatregoers and with them in mind he began to introduce operas in their original languages, particularly the operas of Wagner, inviting great singers from abroad like Dame Nellie Melba and Jean de Reszkes to sing to eager late 19th century audiences.

Harris's death in 1896 made little difference to the precarious path the Theatre Royal was taking towards broad, elaborate performances with sensational happenings on stage. The scenery was magnificent, exquisitely painted – a wonder world of enchanted castles and magical forests. At the turn of the century, Cecil Raleigh's *The Great Millionaire*, which included elaborate, realistic scenes on the cliffs at Paignton and in the luxurious Carlton Hotel, portrayed a realistic car crash, fifty-six speaking parts and a variety of seventeen scene settings. In another extravaganza, a chariot race is described in *The Era*:

> Four great cradles, 20 feet in length and 14 feet wide, movable back and front on railways supported by a bridge structure capable of supporting twenty tons... Each cradle bears four horses and a chariot. Horses are secured by invisible steel cable traces. As the horse gallops the treadmill revolves [backwards] under its feet. The wheels of the chariot are worked on rubber rollers, operated by electrical motors. An impression of great speed is created by the presence of a panoramic background, thirty-five feet high, representing the walls of the arena. This is made to revolve rapidly in the opposite direction to the chariots. [13]

However much these extravagant theatrical exploits succeeded in titillating the audiences of the last decades of the century, the costs could never continue to be viable given the changing economic trend of the times. Vast government funding was going towards the political upheavals in South Africa. Theatre managers had to return to common sense book-keeping and the only way to achieve that was to find a new 'star' in the theatrical firmament.

At this point in its long and turbulent history, the Theatre Royal Drury Lane, was to retrieve its dignity in the form of an outstanding performance of *The Merchant of Venice* with a cast brought together for the Actors' Association Benefit, and starring one of the greatest actors to appear on any London stage: Henry Irving.

6. Arthur Collins: From Seedsman to Saviour

It is a rare event in life when one great man is found to follow on from another. When Harris died, a dark and sinister rumour spread through the streets and alleyways around Drury Lane that the doughty old Theatre Royal was once more to face demolition. The phoenix was exhausted - reluctant to be called upon to suffer once more its fiery fate yet again, to flap its tired old wings to save the ancient lady from her inevitable fate. Talk was going about that the Duke of Bedford intended to refuse to renew the lease, that the beloved playhouse was no longer fit for purpose and would have to be demolished. After clearance, the site was to be merged with Covent Garden Market. It was very clear, with no Gussie Harris to help, that a saviour was desperately needed.

A seedsman who had joined the well-known firm of Carters, Arthur Collins, a young man with a passion for things theatrical, got wind of the situation. He had a skill in drawing and painting and, in 1881, had joined the scene-painting room. From Paint Frame at Drury, he was rapidly promoted by Harris to stage manager, but, as fate would have it, Harris was taken ill and died. His grieving widow could go on no longer, so Collins was constrained to seek desperate measures to find the necessary £1000 to pay for the transfer of the remainder of the lease. Collins decided to visit Harris's executor, who refused to negotiate the deal. Not having the funds himself, the situation seemed hopeless, until a chance meeting with an Australian theatre enthusiast, who generously paid the Duke's agent, enabling Collins to set up a Limited Liability Company with himself as Managing Director. He had idolised Harris and remained true to his principles and ideals, which, in many ways, Collins transcended. He knew in his bones that he had to choose the right seeds to make Drury Lane flower again with spectacular shows. Once more he employed the talents of the duo, Cecil Raleigh and Herbert Campbell, 'the Gilbert and Sullivan of melodrama'.[14] Raleigh was vivacious and quick-witted and had a fine opinion of himself, in contrast to the urbane, cultured and equally talented Campbell, who excelled in more dramatic writing. Just as Beaumont and Fletcher had discovered the key to their success two centuries before, Raleigh and Campbell wrote better together than apart.

Arthur Collins as 'The Guv'nor' (from Vanity Fair, 28 Dec 1910)

Towards the end of the century, Arthur Collins staged one of his many extravaganzas, *Hearts are Trumps*, which included elaborate scenes from the Botanical Gardens in Regent's Park and in particular a Private View at the Royal Academy, with a sensational 'curtain scene' that scandalised the more respectable spectators. The villain of the piece had a portrait painted of a female nude, which became the notorious centre-piece of the exhibition. A solitary woman moves forward as if to get a closer view, takes out a knife and "slashes the picture to ribbons" before the attendants can stop her. In true melodramatic style they cry: "By what right have you done this deed?" She violently shakes them off. Defiantly facing the audience, she speaks the shocking reply: "By the greatest right that God or man ever gave a woman. I am — her Mother!" A dismayed audience gasped and burst into enthusiastic applause.[15]

It was an archetypal moment in the history of Victorian melodrama. The actress playing the part was one of the most celebrated leading ladies of her time – Violet Vanbrugh, whose manager was Dion Boucicault's son.[16] Her career spanned over 50 years of theatre, in performances of plays by Arthur Pinero (Rose in *Trelawny of the Wells*), Oscar Wilde (Lady Markby in *An Ideal Husband*) George Bernard Shaw, J. M. Barrie, Somerset Maugham, A. A. Milne, and Noel Coward.

7. Nights out for the Working Classes

Of over 130 theatres in London that survived into modern times, only a handful remain. The new improvements of the Strand obliterated the old Olympic, Globe and Opera Comique. The Lyceum, once famed for sensational performances by Madame Vestris and Sir Henry Irving, also disappeared under the powerful path of redevelopment.

Philip Astley's elegant circus-style Royalty Amphitheatre, once a circus, was burned down in 1794, only to be replaced by another itself destined to be accidentally incinerated. Undeterred, Astley built a new hippodrome in which he could stage spectacular displays of horsemanship under the management of Andrew Ducrow, including an exciting equestrian adaptation of Byron's *Mazeppa*. Boucicault later renamed the building 'The Theatre Royal, Westminster', but it in turn was abandoned as the taste for more sophisticated drama developed. Astley however was a man of determination. With timbers from a French warship, the "Ville de Paris", he built a theatre in Wych Street, and named it 'Little Drury Lane'. Even then, though it received its first audience on 1st December 1818, financial losses soon forced him to sell to actor-manager, Robert William Elliston, who had played a major role in the opening of Benjamin Wyatt's new Theatre Royal, Drury Lane in 1812.

Grimaldi's Sadler's Wells, subsequently kept alive in a later technological age for many years as a picture house, had once more returned to the dignity of a working theatre. As for the Prince of Wales's, it sank under a plethora of past names such as the Queen's, the Regency, the Fitzroy, and 'The Dust-hole', whilst Boucicault's 'The Princess's' became 'a dusty, mouldering vault with who knows how many ghosts from the past!'[17]

Outside the City of London walls it was a different picture altogether. A myriad of taverns, public houses, night-clubs and similar drinking venues had sprung up in every part of the East End. The Grecian Theatre in the City Road, once known as the Grecian Saloon, and later the more grandiose Olympic Saloon, was situated opposite the rowdy Eagle Tavern in the City Road, and hence was frequently referred to by the local working-class, music-hall-loving clientèle as the Eagle Saloon which occupied the site of the old 18th century 'Shepherd and Shepherdess Tea Gardens', with its arbours for refreshments and dancing platform. In 1825, The Eagle was rebuilt as a music hall. The entrepreneur-proprietor Thomas 'Brayvo' Rouse had the novel idea of bringing light opera to the masses there, and selected popular masterpieces from the Paris Opera repertoire. His Hoxton playhouse opened in 1832 as a venue for light opera, the legitimate theatre remaining the proprietary right of the patented theatres: the King's Theatre (later called the Haymarket Theatre), Royal Drury Lane and Covent Garden. For the first time Londoners could hear Auber's *Fra Diavolo*, Rossini's *La Gazza Ladra* (*The Thieving Magpie*), Donizetti's *L'Elisir d'Amore*, and Weber's *Der Freischütz*.

The famous manufacturer, John Brock, brightened up the night skies from 1825 onwards with his firework displays to entertain the jostling crowds roaming the streets in search of pleasure. On any night, thousands of pleasure-seekers gathered in the narrow alleys, where they could spend their hard-earned money on all kinds of nefarious pleasures in tavern, inn, and places of ill-repute. In its dog-days, it was as a hot house, a black hole, for the number of human beings packed in every night.

The principal entertainment was melodrama (plays bound by law to include some music). The Grecian audiences were vociferous in their noisy appreciation of these blood-curdling 'screamers', especially if they had partaken of the regular brandy and water, and strong beer available, though tea was a calming alternative among the less adventurous part of the crowd. If cash was short, then the working man could, in extremity, pawn his 'weasel' for a few more drinks:

> Half a pound of tuppenny rice,
> Half a pound of treacle,
> That's the way the money goes,
> Pop goes the weasel!
>
> Up and down the City Road,
> In and out the Eagle,
> That's the way the money goes,
> Pop goes the weasel!
>
> Every night when I go out
> The monkey's on the table.
> Take a stick and knock it off,
> Pop goes the weasel!
>
> A penny for a ball of thread,
> Another for a needle,
> That's the way the money goes,
> Pop goes the weasel!
>
> All around the cobbler's bench

Chapter 10 - The Shape of Things to Come

> The monkey chased the people;
> The donkey thought 'twas all in fun,
> Pop goes the weasel!

Alternative interpretations of this jingle are at variance in the detail. One suggests the origin lies in Cockney rhyming slang: If 'weasel' is a variant of 'whistle', then 'whistle and flute' = suit. Equally, 'weasel and stoat' = coat. Another suggestion is that 'weasel' was the name for a tailor's flat iron, or a hatter's tool. A more plausible explanation is derived from spinning and weaving, in which a 'spinner's weasel' was part of the wheel used to measure the silk thread to create a skein. Here we are entering the world of the 13,000 impoverished Huguenots, forced to flee persecution following the Edict of Nantes in 1685. They settled in Spitalfields in the East End of London. Economic depression came when imports of French silk ruined their trade so much that serious riots occurred in 1769, leading to further violence.

By 1832, *The Poor Man's Guardian* for 18 February was reporting a grim picture of deprivation:

> The low houses are all huddled together in close and dark lanes and alleys, presenting at first sight an appearance of non-habitation, so dilapidated are the doors and windows – in every room of the houses, whole families, parents, children and aged grandfathers swarm together.

Henry Heatherington's *The Poor Man's Guardian*, with its slogan 'Knowledge is Power', was first published on 1st October 1830, highlighting the plight of 'the poor, the suffering, the industrious, the productive classes', with the message: 'We will teach this rabble their power – we will teach them that they are your master, instead of being your slaves.' He supported the recently-formed National Union of the Working Classes to campaign for universal suffrage and trade union rights, and achieving an astonishing circulation of 22,000. He was brave and abrasive, making bold and revolutionary statements: 'The poverty of the poor man is essential to the riches of the rich man. The desire of one man to live on the fruits of another's labour is the original sin of the world.'

Looms were fast becoming redundant, owing to imports of contraband silk from abroad, causing abject deprivation. Pawning the weasel was one way to satiate body and soul in the hundreds of taverns and clubs that sprung up in the East End of London. The Eagle was eventually acquired by General William Booth in 1882 for the Salvation Army.

8. The Monologue: The Comic Genius of Dan Leno

Countless actors and actresses down the centuries had come from poor backgrounds, though a small number began life in the middle classes, several even from the aristocracy, like Barton Booth in the late 1680s, who was descended from the Booths of Cheshire, the family name of the Earls of Warrington at Dunham Massey. Booth rebelled against family tradition by abandoning undergraduate life at Trinity College Cambridge and running away to Dublin to join a theatrical company there. Mention of his name takes us back to the old days at Drury Lane when Booth managed the theatre jointly with Thomas Doggett and Colley Cibber. He made famous the role of Cato in Addison's play of the same name. It was typical of his nature that he had taken the rebellious role and made the part his very own. No other actor could match his performance.[18]

At this point in the history of the Theatre Royal, Drury Lane, two iconic figures emerged from deprived backgrounds and made their remarkable rise to the very top of the tree: Dan Leno (1860-1904) and Henry Irving (1838-1905). Melpomene and Thalia, the muses of Drama and Comedy so beloved of the writers of the *Rejected Addresses*, had at last returned to save their 'Temple'. The benighted phoenix could heave a sigh of relief and sink into its nest, in the hope that it would never be disturbed again.

Leno was a man of prodigious energy, performing almost every day of his working life for 36 years, 24 of which he appeared regularly at the Theatre Royal, Drury Lane. At the age of four, his parents paraded him on the music-hall stage as 'The Infant Wonder'. By the age of nine, he began to do solo performances, one of his great skills being improvisation. In his early years, he played low comedy roles and filled in with busking and developing a clog-dancing routine for which he became well-known, playing mostly to working-class audiences. He had a quick perception of the quirks of habit and mannerisms of speech displayed on the streets of the East End of London. His ability to enter into the true character of a beefeater, a huntsman, a fireman, or a henpecked husband, had the mark of genius about it.

Most of all, it is to Leno that we owe the tradition of cross-dressing, enabling him to create truly traditional comic roles as pantomime dame. His garrulous old women had a touch of pathos about them, which created a mixture of amused sympathy in his devoted audiences. In 1884, he began to beguile the more sophisticated audiences of Drury and he remained the most popular of pantomime dames for the next 15 years.

Thanks to the acuity and encouragement of Augustus Harris, the diminutive Dan Leno formed a brilliant comic partnership with the burly

Chapter 10 - The Shape of Things to Come

Herbert Campbell and together they regularly appeared in numerous productions: *Jack and the Beanstalk* (1889), *Beauty and the Beast* (1890), *Humpty-Dumpty* (1891), *Little Bo-Peep* ((1892), *Robinson Crusoe* (1893), *Dick Whittington* (1894), *Cinderella* (1895), *Aladdin* (1896), *Bluebeard* (1901), *Mother Goose* (1902), and many others.

Dan Leno as Shopwalker (from *Hys Booke*, by Dan Leno, 1901)

It is, however, Leno's monologues that distinguish him from other performers at this time. A direct descendant of the 18th century prologue, the monologue represents the continuing tradition of the kind of entertaining recitation that speaks directly to each member of the audience, just as it did in the days of Addison and Garrick. Nell Gwynn in her breeches and broad-brimmed hat was not so dissimilar to Leno with his broad Cockney accent, comical flounces and frills in his roles as Widow Twankey and Mother Goose. Even from the titles of his recitations, 'My Wife's Relations', 'The Grass Widower' and 'I'm waiting for him tonight', it is easy to tell why his devoted audiences repeatedly called for their favourites, with their hilarious situations and bold, suggestive content. There was a touch about them of the wife's nightly greeting with 'a hit on the head with a rolling pin'. Harlequin's slapstick of the old 'commedia dell'arte' days had become a recognisable style of its own. With Leno, among the several qualities that made him so popular was this engaging, endearing nature of his performances that set him above most of his contemporaries.

Leno's generosity was legendary. Given the intensity of his commitment to his craft, Leno gave time to charitable works, especially the Terriers Association, to help retired artists. He became the first President of the Music Hall Benevolent Fund and was an early member of the theatrical charity, the Grand Order of Water Rats. In the late 1890s, he formed a cricket team called 'The Dainties', for which he recruited many leading comedians and music hall stars. 'Dan Leno's Cricketers' were given full billing in the *Sheffield Evening Telegraph* on 20 June 1899.[19] He fitted them out in comical costumes and there was little observance of the rules of the game. There was more comedy on the pitch than off, which the crowds of his supporters came to expect and enjoy in the atmosphere of pantomime that prevailed throughout the game. He was ever the kindly neighbour, making gifts of his home-grown vegetables, and eggs from his own chickens. Yet he always found time for his fellow actors and their troubles, a remarkable contrast to the harsh and precarious times of Charles Macklin and Christopher Rich.

To seal his fame, on 26 November 1901, he was invited to Sandringham to perform before King Edward VII and Queen Alexandra, who presented him with a jewelled royal tie-pin – and he made the Princess Royal laugh. Such success does not always come without a price to pay. In the end Leno followed in the path of his father and grandfather and gave in to alcoholism, 'the demon drink' much feared by Victorian reformers like Father Mathew and General Booth. His physical condition gradually deteriorated, and mentally he began to show signs of angry, even violent behaviour towards the very people he loved, his fellow actors. After such outbursts he grew remorseful and apologetic.[20] What followed was the final act of his personal tragedy. An obsession led him to believe that he had the makings of a serious actor and he began to harbour thoughts of leaving Mother Goose behind and taking on the part of *Richard II* and Shakespeare rôles, currently being played by the great Henry Irving. The story goes that he attempted to persuade the actress, Constance Collier, to play opposite him in a Shakespeare season. She gently declined on the grounds of his mental state.

Two days later, Dan Leno was admitted to Camberwell House asylum for the insane.[21] He died, aged only 43, after a short life crammed with incident, a little man with a big heart, a true genius of comedy, whose influence on a whole new generation of 20th century music-hall comedians was without equal.[22]

9. Henry Irving: All Bells and No Vampires

Henry Irving was born into a working-class family in the West Country. Christened John Henry Brodribb, he was a cousin of the poet, W. H. Davies, author of *The Autobiography of a Super-Tramp*, but Davies's rough endurance of poverty was not for young John. From school he went on to join a law firm, but a chance visit to the theatre to see a performance of *Hamlet* opened a new world of opportunity.

In 1876, a remarkable meeting took place in Dublin. Irving was playing at the Theatre Royal, and arranged to meet a young man at the Shelbourne Hotel who had published reviews of Irving's performances for the *Dublin Evening Mail* and the *London Daily Telegraph*. His name was Bram Stoker. Over dinner, Irving entertained his young guest with a recitation of Thomas Hood's *Dream of Eugene Aram* after which Stoker burst into hysteric excitement at the description of Aram's tormented confession to an innocent young child that he had murdered a man out of greed. The meeting turned out to be a life-changing moment for Stoker, who became a loyal and devoted business manager to Irving for the next 27 years. However, Irving's devotion was not sufficient to agree to acting in the stage adaptation of Stoker's novel, *Dracula*, but it may have been the underlying sexual content of the play that may have influenced his decision.[23] At all events, the idea of an outwardly happy man tormented by inner guilt would become the subject of one of Irving's greatest performances as Dr. Frankenstein.

Real success, however, did not come easily. It would be some 15 years before he was able to land a key role that would make his name a household word with the partisan audiences of Drury Lane. In 1869 he married Florence O'Callaghan, an unfortunate liaison since she despised the theatre and was no support to him in his ambitions. Nevertheless, two years later, in 1871, Irving began a long association with the Lyceum Theatre in London which until 1809 had been the home of Philip Astley's circus. The Theatre Royal, Drury Lane company moved in for the duration until the Wyatt's new theatre opened in 1812. From 1816, the Lyceum, after surviving on a variety of motley musical entertainments, miraculously transformed itself into the English Opera House.

The Lyceum, almost opposite the Theatre Royal, had stolen Drury's reputation for brilliant productions of Shakespeare, with a new emphasis on technical innovation and historical accuracy. Irving achieved his long-wished-for chance to play Hamlet to Ellen Terry's Ophelia (1878); this was followed by *The Merchant of Venice* (1879), *Much Ado About Nothing* (1882), and *Twelfth Night* (1884). Oscar Wilde admired the high style and subtle psychological realism of Irving's performances.[24] George

Bernard Shaw was jealous of Irving's friendship with his leading lady, who some suspected of being a more than romantic attachment, and he did everything he could to steal her away for performances of his own plays. His continuous practice of demeaning Irving was little short of contemptible.

Irving's crowning achievement was a version of *Le Juif polonais: The Polish Jew* (translated by Leopold Lewis as *The Bells*), a play by the French playwrights, Émile Erckmann (1822-1899) and Alexandre Chatrian (1826-1890), life-long friends who wrote numerous plays and stories together, as well as individual essays, political tracts and a number of highly controversial works in a macabre vein (*The Man-Wolf* and *The Crab Spider*). Their writings frequently supported anti-monarchist and anti-German themes, both of which were prevalent in the France of the revolutionary 1880s and much praised at the time by Victor Hugo and Émile Zola. The ghost stories of Erckmann-Chatrian (as the two were known) suited perfectly the spirit of the times, following in the wake of the horrific tales by 'Monk' Lewis and Bram Stoker.

The pair's popular trend for the *macabre* exactly matched Irving's talent for the melodramatic style of acting – full of sound and fury, with long-drawn-out vowels, moans and groans, and melodramatic gestures.[25] This image of his acting style belies defamatory reports that he was 'a most peculiar actor, prone to peculiar gestures and with a peculiar voice.' His voice is said to have been thin and his body of lean appearance.[26] This description does not tally with another report of his performance of the death scene in *The Bells*:

> The gradual stupefaction, the fixed eye, the head bent down on the chest and the crouching humility before a stronger will…the very ugly picture of a dead man's face…the low terrified wail as the awful sentence is being pronounced and Mathias sinks kneeling on the floor of the court…

First performed at the Lyceum, *The Bells*, a play about a man haunted by a murder he has committed, turned round the ebbing fortunes of the Lyceum and brought it back into the world of serious theatre, with an enhanced reputation for more polished productions of drama. The play's earlier performances at the Royal Alfred Theatre had not attracted audiences sufficiently, but Irving managed to persuade the Drury Lane management that he could transform it into a popular thriller. Even so, the first night was ill-attended and, instead of the triumphant final curtain he had expected, the audience sat in an uncomfortable silence. An anxious pause for Irving, standing alone on stage, was suddenly transformed into rapturous applause followed by a standing ovation.

Chapter 10 - The Shape of Things to Come

In fact, *The Bells* was an important turning-point in the history of dramatic productions at Drury Lane. The reason for this was the new psychological content of the play. Mathias, the central character in the play, is depicted as a highly-respected burgomaster, beloved of everyone in the community, a jovial, genial, happy soul without a care in the world. The weather is bitterly cold. Mathias comes in out of the driving snow, kisses his wife affectionately, and warms his hands by a blazing log fire. There is much merriment. Such is the public face of Mathias, but the face of the inner man is more sinister for he is tormented within by the horrifying memory of the murder of a Polish Jew he had committed fifteen years before. Suddenly his temporary peace of mind is disturbed by the sound of jingling bells as a sledge approaches and a man dressed in Polish costume enters, asking for hospitality. His arrival has all the innocence of any welcome proffered to a traveller in such conditions. Is it just coincidence that he is attired in the identical costume of the murdered man? Mathias falls down in a fit and in his delirium he imagines, with all the dreadful reality of dreams, that he is being hanged for his crime. The amiable old doctor pronounces that the tortured death of Mathias is the result of too much wine-drinking. Such was the terror of mortal suffering compellingly portrayed by Irving that, George R. Sims reported, a woman in the audience fainted:

> The play left the first-nighters a little dazed. Old fashioned playgoers did not know what to make of it as a form of entertainment. But when the curtain fell the audience, after a gasp or two, realised they had witnessed the most masterly form of tragic acting that the British stage had seen for many a long day, and there was a storm of cheers.[27]

The evening ended on a strange and disturbing note for, as Irving was leaving the theatre with Florence, still pregnant with their second child, she asked: "Are you going on making a fool of yourself like this all your life?" He alighted from their carriage at Hyde Park Corner and never saw her again. Their two sons, H. B. Irving and Laurence Irving, grew up under the influence of their embittered mother and inherited her jaundiced views of their father, whom they called 'The Antique'. Both became actors of talent. In later life there came about a gradual *rapprochement* between father and sons.

In 1895, Irving received a knighthood from Queen Victoria, after which Florence, in spite of being irreparably separated from her husband, insisted on calling herself 'Lady Irving'.

Henry Irving brought to the English stage a fresh vision, one of technical innovation, visual splendour and real historical accuracy. He revived and restored to favour the great tragedies of Shakespeare, succeeding in filling the theatre with more affluent and sophisticated audiences from the newly-built suburbs.[28] In the United States, he had played opposite Sarah Bernhardt and Eleonora Duse. He had enjoyed an affectionate friendship and professional partnership with Ellen Terry. He had become the most eminent tragedian of his age. For his farewell performance, he chose Victorien Sardou's *Dante* (1903), a free interpretation of the great Italian poet's life. Cheering rose up throughout the vast theatre. It would be his last performance in London before a final tour of the provinces. In Bradford, after playing Tennyson's *Becket*, he returned to the Midland Hotel, collapsed in the foyer and died. He was buried in Westminster Abbey near to David Garrick. Inexplicably, he left Stoker nothing in his will, after 27 years of service as his manager, 27 years of loyalty and unflagging devotion. The fashion for Irving's declamatory histrionics still persisted in part, though spectators occasionally complained of his 'thinnish voice, strange diction, and odd mannerisms.'[29] Nevertheless, Irving was part of the process of change that was to transform the theatre experience from pure entertainment into the drama of ideas - in other words, the demise of old-style Victorian theatre and the advent of realistic drama. From this moment on, English drama was to change inexorably, leading the way for the harrowing domestic dramas of Ibsen: *Hedda Gabler* (London 1890), *The Doll's House* (1889), *Ghosts* (1891)], so admired by George Bernard Shaw and promoted by his friend, the influential critic and translator of Ibsen's plays, William Archer.

About this time, the New Royalty Theatre was putting on challenging performances of Ibsen's *Ghosts* (1875) and *The Wild Duck*, Shaw's *Widowers' Houses,* with Brandon Thomas's *Charley's Aunt* brought hilarity into the mix. There was much to choose from, for London by now had 57 licensed theatres and 415 music halls, a situation which led to reduced prices, increased profits, and higher wages for actors.[30] By contrast with past practice, there came realistic settings, contemporary themes to suit the tastes of increasingly literate audiences, and a greater interest in motive and hidden passions. William Archer was of the opinion that drama should be an intellectual enjoyment, should stimulate thought and consider questions of justice and injustice,[31] which lends credence to Shaw's view that 'good plays illuminate truth by forcing the spectator to face facts.'[32]

Chapter 10 - The Shape of Things to Come

10. Curtain Up on a New Era

Although pantomimes continued to flourish with successful performances of *Dick Whittington, Aladdin, Jack-and-the-Beanstalk* and *Humpty-Dumpty*, with a plethora of revivals to keep the audiences interested, new names came to keep tradition in place. Sir Johnstone Forbes-Robertson brought in adaptations of serious drama, and gave outstanding performances in Kipling's *The Light that Failed,* Jerome K. Jerome's *The Passing of the Third Floor Back*, Steinbeck's *Of Mice and Men*, as well as Shakespeare revivals, *Othello,* and *Julius Caesar*. After his emotional farewell performance in *Hamlet*, the members of the audience wept, as did he, when he came forward to thank them personally, shaking their hands in an unusual display of emotion in a mood reminiscent of Garrick's own departure from the stage.

By 1915, the Theatre Royal, Drury Lane, became almost a theatre of war, for a German Zeppelin set out for London with bombs aboard. In 1916, the Shakespeare Tercentenary celebrated with a matinée performance of *Julius Caesar*, with the veteran actor, Frank Benson. King George V unexpectedly attended and had the idea of conferring a knighthood on Benson, but no suitable sword was available, not even a cardboard one in the property department. Eventually a more authentic one was found in a nearby shop and the deed was done.

A refurbishment was planned in 1921. The old boxes were dismantled and re-sited in the circle with a full view of the stage, and new entrances improved access to the stalls. The stage was divided into a series of lifts, which could be raised, lowered or tilted to give greater effects, ingeniously employed in the production of Noel Coward's *Cavalcade*. It enabled a troopship to be seen departing, a realistic scene at a railway station, men marching to war, and a scene at Queen Victoria's funeral: during which the audience could hear:

> ...the clatter of the horses' hooves and the jingle of chains and accoutrements as the cortège went by out of sight. That this effect, which moved many to tears, was produced by two property men, one just manipulating two halves of a coconut and the other shaking a chain, did not matter at all. Nobody saw that, but they visualised one of the most solemn moments in history....a picture of the serried mass of players on the lifts with a background of the national flag stirred the deepest emotions.

Stephen Price's experience at the Park Theatre, New York, had proved to be invaluable. His American spirit came through to haunt the old theatre again. With the magnificent refurbished interior in place, Sir Alfred Butt, in Price's same spirit, introduced a new series of large-scale musicals from America, the first of which, *Rose-Marie*, ran for over 800 performances from 20th March 1925 to 26th March 1927, during which the King came on three occasions. *The Desert Song* followed with 422 performances between 7th April 1927 and 14th April 1928. With such wild successes, it was inevitable that 'stars' would be born, singers of great quality like Paul Robeson (*Show Boat* –'Ole man river') and Richard Tauber (*The Land of Smiles* – 'You are my heart's delight'), each of whose fame rests on performances of one particular song.

The Second World War brought in a new trend in patriotic 'musicals' by a new young composer, Ivor Novello, with a skill in creating memorable tunes. He succeeded in marrying sentiment with song in shows like *The Dancing Years* and *King's Rhapsody*.that reflected the triumph over the terrors of war-time in musical dramas perpetuated in countless amateur performances all over the United Kingdom. From then on, sensational American successes like *Oklahoma!* (1947-53), *My Fair Lady* (1958-63), *42nd Street* (1984-89), and *Miss Saigon* (1989-1999), filled the theatre with capacity audiences.

In 2000 the Theatre was purchased, lock, stock and barrel, by Andrew Lloyd Webber, the composer of some of world's best-known musicals – a prodigious gesture of incalculable generosity. Since 2014 it has been managed by LW Theatres, Lloyd Webber's management company. Then in 2019 the theatre closed its doors for a 20-month, £60m restoration, re-opening in 2021 to great acclaim.

Andrew Lloyd Webber

No English theatre has had such a rich and chequered history as the Theatre Royal, Drury Lane. From its beginnings under Davenant and Killigrew, it never ceased to be a place of tears and laughter, of triumphs

Chapter 10 - The Shape of Things to Come

and disasters, of riot and celebration, of speculation and intrigue, of great tragic acting and sublime comedy.

This book has been about two of the most momentous occasions in its turbulent history: the burning down of Henry Holland's theatre in 1809 and the rebuilding of Benjamin Wyatt's new theatre in 1812. As we have seen, the burning down and demolition of the Theatre Royal, Drury Lane, in 1809 was one of the most disastrous events of Regency times. It was not the first London theatre to end its life in ashes, but like the mythical phoenix to which it was frequently compared, it arose again and again, amidst ridicule and controversy. Charles II's preoccupation with the raucous, cross-dressing Nell Gwynne may well have had more to do with the frequency of his visits to the Royal Box, but it is always to the great actors and actresses who trod its boards over the centuries, and provided their audiences with unrivalled perfomances.

The happenings and personalities of these times were reflected in the countless prologues with which it was customary to introduce a play. We remember that they were not necessarily composed by the playwrights themselves, but that some were written by established authors like Samuel Johnson and David Garrick, and were to be the prototypes which the authors of the 112 Addresses emulated for the opening of the new Theatre Royal in 1812.

The unusual friendship between radical Lord Byron and the Whiggish Lord and Lady Holland, bound by their hero-worship of Napoleon, explains why the reluctant Byron was persuaded to concede to Lord Holland's pressing demands to compose the perfect Address – traditional prologue, epilogue, and monody providing Byron and his fellow authors of the Drury Lane Addresses with the vital substance of their verses. The subsequent riotous response to Elliston's reciting of the Address at its first performance is one of the most astonishing events in the history of British drama. It brought about the phenomenal success of two brothers, Horace and James Smith, with their composing of *Rejected Addresses, or, The Theatrum Poetarum,* which continued throughout the rest of the century, with over 25 editions - one of the most extraordinary moments in 19th century publishing history.

The range of imagery adopted by the poets of the *Genuine Addresses* provides a window through which we can understand the principles and ideas that collectively filled their thoughts as they feverishly scribbled down their first drafts. For them, Shakespeare, in his completeness, provided the perfect interpretation of the human condition, a benchmark by which they could judge their own creations. Addison, Johnson, and Garrick had provided the means and the method. Spanish aggression and the threat of Napoleon were no longer a threat. Freedom and liberty had returned and the Phoenix had found peace from its labours at last. The

Muses had reclaimed their right to reign over the New Drury and Apollo was once more in the ascendant.

Across the nation there was beginning to be a mood for change. Thomas Busby's protest was endemic of a general desire for improvement in the moral tone in theatrical productions and a deeper treatment of character and theme.

Samuel Whitbread had been the guiding force in unravelling the tangled web of Sheridan's financial affairs. We owe to him the survival of a great theatre. Now owned by another great benefactor, Andrew Lloyd Webber, the Theatre Royal Drury Lane that we know today has been restored to its former 1812 glory, to be enjoyed by theatre-goers for many years to come.

APPENDIX A

ANTHOLOGY

1. John Dryden Prologue to *The Rival Ladies*

2. Dryden A Second Prologue

3. Alexander Pope: Prologue to Addison's *Cato*

4. Samuel Johnson: Prologue for the opening of the Theatre Royal 1747

5. Richard Brinsley Sheridan: Monody on death of Garrick

6. Byron: Monody of the death of Sheridan

7. Thomas Busby: Monologue for the opening of Drury Lane Theatre

8. Byron: A Parenthetical Address [to Dr. Busby]

John Dryden

PROLOGUE
to *The Rival Ladies*

'Tis much Desir'd, you Judges of the Town,
Would pass a Vote to put all *Prologues* down;
For who can snow me, since they first were Writ,
They e'r Converted one hard-hearted Wit?
Yet the World's mended well; in former Days   5
Good *Prologues* were as scarce, as now good *Plays*
For the reforming Poets of our Age,
In this first Charge, spend their Poetique rage;
Expect no more when once the *Prologue*'s done;
The Wit is ended e'r the *Play*'s begun.   10
You now have Habits, Dances, Scenes, and Rhymes;
High Language often; I [aye?], and Sense, sometimes:

As for a clear Contrivance doubt it not;
They blow out Candles to give Light to th' Plot.
And for Surprize, two Bloody-minded Men   15
Fight till they Dye, then rise and Dance agen:
Such deep Intrigues wou'd welcome to this Day:
But blame your Selves, not him who Writ the Play;
Though his Plot's Dull, as can be well desir'd,
Wit stiff as any you have e'r admir'd;   20
He's bound to please, not to Write well; and knows
there is a mode in Plays as well as Cloaths:
Therefore kind Judges —

A SECOND PROLOGUE

Enters.

   — Hold; would you admit
For Judges all you see within the Pit?
Whom would he then Except, or on what Score?   25
   All, who (like him) have Writ ill Plays before:
For they, like Thieves condemn'd, are Hang-men made,
To execute the Members of their Trade.
All that are Writing now he would disown;
But then he must Except, ev'n all the Town.   30
All Chol'rique, losing Gamesters, who in spight
Will Damn to Day, because they last last Night.
All Servants whom their Mistress's scorn upbraids;
All Maudlin Lovers, and all Slighted Maids:
All who are out of Humour, or Severe;   35
All, that want Wit, or hope to find it here.

Alexander Pope

PROLOGUE
to Addison's *Cato*

To wake the soul by tender strokes of art,
To raise the genius, and to mend the heart;
To make mankind in conscious virtue bold,
Live o'er each scene, and be what they behold: 5
For this the Tragic Muse first trod the stage,
Commanding tears to stream thro' ev'ry age;
Tyrants no more their savage nature kept,
And foes to virtue wonder'd how they wept.
Our author shuns by vulgar springs to move
The hero's glory, or the virgin's love;   10
In pitying Love, we but our weakness show,
And wild Ambition well deserves its woe.
Here tears shall flow from a more gen'rous cause,
Such Tears as Patriots shed for dying Laws:
He bids your breasts with ancient ardour rise,   15
And calls forth Roman drops from British eyes.
Virtue confess'd in human shape he draws,
What Plato thought, and godlike Cato was:
No common object to your sight displays,
But what with pleasure Heav'n itself surveys,   20
A brave man struggling in the storms of fate,
And greatly falling, with a falling state.
While Cato gives his little Senate laws,
What bosom beats no in his Country's cause?
Who sees him act, but envies ev'ry deed?   25
Who hears him groan, but does not wish to bleed
Ev'n when proud Caesar 'midst triumphal cars,
The spoils of nations, and the pomp of wars,
Ignobly vain and impotently great,
Show'd Rome her Cato's figure drawn in state;   30
As her dead Father's rev'rend image past,
The pomp was darken'd, and the day o'ercast;
The Triumph ceas'd, tears gush'ed from ev'ry eye;

The World's great Victor pass'd unheeded by;
Her last good man dejected Rome ador'd, 35
And honour'd Caesar less than Cato's sword.
　　Britons, attend; be worth like this approv'd,
And show, you have the virtue to be mov'd.
With honest scorn the first fam'd Cato view'd
Rome learning arts frin Greece, whom she subdu'd; 40
You scene precariously subsists too long,
On French translation, and Italian song,
Dare to have sense yourselves; assert the stage,
Be justly warm'd with your own native rage:
Such Plays alone should win a British ear, 45
As Cato's self had not disdain'd to hear.

Samuel Johnson

PROLOGUE
spoken by David Garrick
at the opening of the new Theatre Royal Drury Lane 1747

When Learning's Triumph o'er her barb'rous Foes
First rear'd the Stage, immortal SHAKESPEARE rise;
Each change of many-colour'd Life he drew,
Exhausted Worlds, and then imagin'd new;
Existence saw him spurn her bounded Reign, 5
And panting Time toil'd after him in vain:
His pow'rful Strokes presiding Truth impress;d,
And unresisted Passion storm'd the Breast.
　　Then JOHNSON came, instructed from the School,
To please in Method, and invent by Rule; 10
His studious Patience, and laborious Art,
By regular Approach essay'd theHeart;
Cold Approbation gave the ling'ring Bays,
For those who durst not censure, scarce cou'd praise,
A Mortal born he met a general Doom, 15
But left, like *Egypt*'s Kings, a lasting Tomb,

The Wits of *Charles* found easier Ways to Fame,
Nor wish'd for JOHNSON's Art, or SHAKESPEARE's Flame;
Themselves they studied. As they felt they writ,　20
Intrigue was Plot, Obscenity was Wit.
Vice always found a sympathetick Friend;
they pleas'd their Age, and did not aim to mend.
Yet Bards like these aspir'd to lasting Praise,
And proudly hop'd to pimp in future Days.
Their Cause was gen'ral, their Supports were strong,　25
Their Slaves were willing, and their Reign was long;
Till shame regain'd the Post that Sense betray'd,
And Virtue call'd Oblivion to her Aid.

　　Then crush'd by Rules, and weaken'd as refin'd,
For Years the Pow'r of dignity declin'd;　30
From Bard, to Bard, the frigid Caution crept,
Till Declamation roar'd, while Passion slept.
Yet still did Virtue deign the Stage to tread,
Philosophy remain'd, though Nature fled.
But forc'd at length her antient Reign to quit,　35
She saw great *Faustus* lay the Ghost of Wit:
Exulting Folly hail'd the joyful Day,
And Pantomime, and Song, confirm'd her Sway.

　　But who the coming Changes can presage,
And mark the future Periods of the Stage? —　40
Perhaps if Skill could distant Times explore,
New *Behns*, new *Durfeys*, yet remain in Store.
Perhaps where *Lear* has rav'd and *Hamlet* dy'd,
On flying Cars new sorcerers may ride.
Perhaps, for who can guess th' Effects of Chance?　45
Here *Hunt* may box, or *Mahomet* may dance.

　　Hard is his lot, that here by Fortune plac'd,
Must watch the wild Vicissitudes of Taste;
With ev'ry Meteor of Caprice must play,
And chase the new-blown Bubbles of the Day.　50
Ah! let not Censure term our Fate our Choice,
The Stage but echoes back the publick Voice.

> The Drama's Laws the Drama's Patrons give,
> For we that live to please, must please to live.
>   Then prompt no more the Follies you decry,   55
> As Tyrants doom their Tools of Guilt to die;
> 'Tis yours this Night to bid the Reign commence
> Of rescu'd Nature, and reviving Sense;
> To chase the Charms of sound, the Pomp of Show,
> For useful Mirth, and salutary Woe;   60
> Bid scenic Virtue form the rising Age,
> And Truth diffuse her Radiance from the Stage.

Richard Brinsley Sheridan

VERSES
To the Memory of
GARRICK
spoken as
A MONODY
at the Theatre Royal in Drury Lane

> If dying EXCELLENCE deserves a Tear,
> If fond Remembrance still is cherished here,
> Can we persist to bid your Sorrows flow
> For fabled suff'rers and delusive Woe?
> Or with quaint Smiles dismiss the plaintive Strain,   5
> Point the quick Jest — indulge the Comic Vein —
> Ere yet to be buried ROSCIUS we assign —
> One kind Regret — one tributary Line!

> His Fame requires we act a tenderer Part:
> His MEMORY claims the Tear you gave his ART!   10

> The general Voice, the Meed of mourning Verse,
> The splendid Sorrows that adorned his Hearse,
> The Throng that mourn'd as their dead Favourite pass'd,
> The grac'd Respect that claim'd him to the last,

While SHAKESPEARE's Image from its hallow'd Base, 15
Seem'd to prescribe the Grave, and point the Place, —
Nor these, — nor all the sad Regrets that flow
From fond Fidelity's domestic Woe, —
So much are GARRICK's Praise — so much his DUE —
As on this Spot — One Tear bestow'd by YOU.   20

Amid the Arts which seek ingenuous Fame,
OUR toil attempts the most precarious Claim!
To HIM, whose mimic Pencil wins the Prize,
Obedient Fame immortal Wreaths supplies:
Whate'er of Wonder REYNOLDS now may raise,   25
RAPHAEL still boasts contemporary Praise,
Each dazling [sic] Light and gaudier Bloom subdu'd,
With undiminish'd Awe HIS Works are view'd:
E'en Beauty's Portrait wears a softer Prime,
Touch'd by the tender Hand of mellowing Time.   30

The patient SCULPTOR owns a humbler Part,
A ruder Toil, and more mechanic Art;
Content with slow and timorous Stroke to trace
The lingering Line. And mould the tardy Grace:
But once achieved — tho' barbarous Wreck o'erthrow   35
The sacred Fane, and lay its Glories low,
Yet shall the sculptur'd Ruin rise to Day,
Grac'd by Defect and worship'd in Decay;
Demands his Honors, and asserts his Fame.   40

Superior Hopes the POET's Bosom fire, —
O proud Distinction of the sacred Lyre! —
Wide as the inspiring PHOEBUS darts his Ray,
Diffusive Splendor gilds his VOTARY's Lay.
Whether the Song Heroic Woes rehearse,   45
With Epic Grandeur, and the Pomp of Verse;
Or, fondly gay, with unambitious Guile
Attempt no Prize bit favouring Beauty's Smile;
Or bear dejected to the lonely Grove

The soft despair of unprevailing Love, — 50
Whate'er the Theme — thro' every Age and Clime
Congenial Passions meet the according Rhyme;
The Pride of Glory — Pity's Sigh sincere —
Youth's earliest Blush — and Beauty's Virgin Tear.

Such is THEIR Meed — THEIR Honors thus secure, 55
Whose Arts yield Objects, and whose Works endure.
The ACTOR only, shrinks from Time's Award;
Feeble Tradition is HIS Memory's Guard;
By whose faint Breath his Merits must abide,
Unvouch'd by Proof — to Substance unallied! 60
Ev'n matchless GARRICK's Art to Heav'n resign'd,
No fix'd Effect, no Model leaves behind!

The GRACE and ACTION — the adapted MIEN
Faithful as Nature to the varied Scene;
Th' EXPRESSIVE GLANCE — whose subtle Comment draws
Entranc'd Attention, and a mute Applause;
GESTURE that marks, with Force and Feeling fraught,
A Sense in Silence, and a Will in Thought;
HARMONIOUS SPEECH, whose pure and liquid Tone
Gives Verse a Music, scarce confess'd its own; 70
As Light from Gems, assumes a brighter Ray
And cloathed with Orient Hues, transcends the Day! —
PASSION's wild Break — and FROWN that awes the Sense
And every CHARM of gentler ELOQUENCE —
All perishable! — like the Electric Fire 75
But strike the Frame — and as they strike expire;
Incense too choice a bodied Flame to bear,
Its Fragrance charms the Sense, and blends with Air.
WHERE then — while sunk in cold Decay he lies,
And pale Eclipse forever close those Eyes! 80
Where is the blest Memorial that ensures
Our GARRICK's Fame? — whose is the Trust? — 'tis YOURS![17]

And O! by every Charm his Art essay'd

To soothe your Cares! — by every Grief allay'd!
By the hush'd Wonder which his Accents drew!   85
By his lasting parting Tear repaid by you!
By all those Thoughts, which many a distant Night,
Shall mark his Memory with a sad Delight! —
Still your Hearts' dear Record bear his Name;
Cherish the keen Regret that lifts his Fame;   90
To YOU it is bequeath'd, assert the Trust;
And to his WORTH — 'tis all you can — be Just.

What more is due from sanctifying Time,
To chearful [sic] WIT, and many a favour'd RHYME,
O'er his graced Urn shall bloom, a deathless Wreath,   95
Whose blossom'd Sweets shall deck the Mask beneath.
For these, — when SCULPTURE's votive Toil shall rear
The due Memorial of a Loss so dear! —
O loveliest Mourner, Gentle MUSE! be thine
The pleasing Woe to guard the laurell'd Shrine.   100
As FANCY, oft by Superstition led
To roam the Mansions of the sainted Dead,
Has view'd, by shadowy Eve's unfaithful Gloom,
A weeping Cherub on a Martyr's Tomb —
Do thou, sweet MUSE, hang o'er HIS sculptur'd Bier,   105
With patient Woe, that loves the ling'ring Tear;
With Thoughts that mourn — nor yet desire Relief,
With meek Regret, and fond enduring Grief;
With Looks that speak — He never shall return!
— Chilling thy tender Bosom clasp his Urn!   110
And with soft Sighs disperse the irreverend Dust,
Which TIME may strew upon his sacred Bust.

Lord Byron

MONODY
on the Death of
THE RIGHT HON. R. B. SHERIDAN
spoken at Drury Lane Theatre

When the last sunshine of expiring day
In summer's twilight weeps itself away,
Who hath not felt the softness of the hour
Sink on the heart, as dew along the flower?
With pure feeling which absorbs and awes   5
While Nature makes that melancholy pause,
Her breathing moment on the bridge where Time
Of light and darkness forms an arch sublime,
Who hath not shared that calm, so still and deep,
The voiceless thought which would not speak but weep, 10
A holy concord, and a bright regret,
A glorious sympathy with suns that set?
'Tis not harsh sorrow, but a tenderer woe,
Nameless, but dear to gentle hearts below,
Felt without bitterness, but full and clear,   15
A sweet dejection, a transparent tear,
Unmix'd with worldly grief or selfish stain,
Shed without shame, and secret without pain.

   Even as the tenderness that hour instils
When Summer's day declines along the hills.   20
Si feels the fulness of our heart and eyes
When all of Genius which can perish dies.
A mighty Spirit is eclipsed — a Power
Hath pass'd from day to darkness — to whose hour
Of light no likeness is bequeath'd — no name,   25
Focus at once of all the rays of fame!
The flash of Wit, the bright Intelligence,
The beam of song, the blaze of Eloquence,
Set with their Sun, but still have left behind
The enduring produce of immortal Mind;   30

Fruits of a genial morn, and glorious noon,
A deathless part of him who died too soon,
But small that portion of the wondrous whole,
these sparkling segments of that circling soul,
Which all embraced, and lighten'd over all, 35
To cheer, to pierce, to please, or to appal.
From the charm'd council to the festive board,
Of human feelings the unbounded lord;
In whose acclaim the loftiest voices vied,
The praised, the proud, who made his praise their pride. 40
When the loud cry of trampled Hindostan
Arose to Heaven in her appeal from man,
His was the thunder, his the avenging rod,
The wrath — the delegated voice of God!
Which shook the nations through his lips, and blazed 45
Till vanquish'd senates trembled as they praised,

    And here, oh! here, where yet all young and warm,
The gay creations of his spirit charm,
The matchless dialogue, the deathless wit,
Which knew not what it was to intermit; 50
The glowing portraits, fresh from life, that bring
Home to our hearts the truth from which they spring;
These wondrous beings of his fancy wrought
To fulness by the fiat of his thought,
Here is their first abode you still may meet, 55
Bright with the hues of his Promethean;
A halo of the light of other days,
Which still the splendour of its orb betrays,

    But should there be to whom the fatal blight
Of failing Wisdom yields a base delight, 60
Men who exult when minds of heavenly tone
Jar in the music which was born their own,
Still let them pause — ah! little do they know
That what seem'd Vice might be but Woe.
Hard as his fate on whom the public gaze 65
Is fix'd for ever to detract or praise;

Repose denies her requiem to his name,
And Folly loves the martyrdom of Fame,
The secret enemy whose sleepless eye
Stands sentinel, accuser, judge, and spy,   70
The foe, the fool, the jealous, and the vain,
The envious who but breathe in others' pain,
Behold the host! delighting to deprave,
Who track the steps of Glory to the grave,
Watch every fault that daring Genius owes   75
Half to the ardour which its birth bestows,
Distort the truth, accumulate the lie,
And pile the pyramid of Calumny!
These are his portion — but if join'd to these
Gaunt Poverty should league with deep Disease,   80
If the high Spirit must forget to soar,
And stoop to strive with Misery at the door,
To soothe Indignity — and face to face
Meet sordid Rage, and wrestle with Disgrace,
To find in Hope but the renew'd caress,   85
The serpent-fold of further Faithlessness:–
if such may be the ills which men assail,
What marvel of at last the mightiest fail?
Breast to whom all the strength of feeling given
Bear hearts electric — charge with fire from Heaven, 90
Black with rude collision, inly torn,
by clouds surrounded, and on whirlwinds borne,
Driven o'er the lowering atmosphere that nurst
Thoughts which have turn'd to thunder — scorch and burst.

   But far from us and from our mimic scene   95
Such things should be — if such have ever been;
Ours be the gentler wish, the kinder task,
To give the tribute Glory need not ask,
To mourn the vanish'd beam, and add our mite
Of praise in payment of a long delight.   100
Ye Orators! whom yet our councils yield,
Mourn for the veteran Hero of your field!

The worthy rival of the wondrous *Three!*
Whose words were sparks of Immortality!
Ye Bards! to whom the Drama's muse is dear,　　105
He was your Master — emulate him *here*!
Ye men of wit and social eloquence!
He was your brother — bear his ashes hence!
While Powers of mind almost of boundless range,
Complete in kind, as various in their change,　　110
While Eloquence, Wit, Poesy, and Mirth,
That humbler Harmonist of care on Earth,
Survive within our souls — while lives our sense
Of pride in Merit's proud pre-eminence,
Long shall we seek his likeness, long in vain,　　115
And turn to all of him which may remain,
Sighing that nature form'd but one such man,
And broke the die — in moulding Sheridan!

Thomas Busby

MONOLOGUE

for the opening of the Drury Lane Theatre

　　When energising objects men pursue,
What are the prodigies they cannot do?
A magic Edifice you here survey,
Shot from the ruins of the other day!
As Harlequin had smote the slumbrous heap,　　5
And bade the rubbish to a fabric leap.
Yet at the speed you'd never be amazed,
Knew you the seal with which the pile was rais'd:
Nor ever here your smiles would be represt,
Knew you the rival flame that fires our breast.　　10
Flame! fire and flame! sad, heart-appalling sounds,
Dread metaphors, that ope our healing wounds —
A sleeping pang awake — and — But away
With all reflections that would cloud the day

That this triumphant, brilliant prospect brings; 15
Where Hope reviving, re-expands her wings;
Where generous joy exults — where duteous ardour springs.
    Oft on the boards we've proved — no, not these boards —
Th'excelling sanction your applause affords;
Warm'd with the fond remembrance, every nerve 20
We'll strain, the future honour to deserve:
Give the great work our earnest, strenuous hand,
And (since new tenements new brooms demand)
Rich novelty explore; all merit prize,
And court the living talents as they rise: 25
Th'illustrious dead revere — yet hope to show,
That modern bards with ancient genius glow.
Sense we'll consult e'en in our farce and fun,
And without *steeds* our *patent stage* shall run;
Self-actuated whirl — not you deny, 30
While you're transported, that you gaily fly;
Like Milton's chariot, that it lives — it feels —
And races from the spirit in the wheels.
    If mighty things with small we may compare,
This spirit drives Britannia's conquering car, 35
Burns in her ranks — and kindles every Tar.
NELSON displayed its power upon the main,
And WELLINGTON exhibits it in Spain;
Another MARLBOROUGH points to Blenheim's story,
And with its lustre blends his kindred glory, 40
    In Arms and Science long our Isle hath shone,
And SHAKSPEARE — wond'rous SHAKSPEARE — rear'd a throne
For British Poesy — whose powers inspire
The British pencil and the British lyre.
Her we invoke! — her sister Arts implore; 45
Their smiles beseech whose charms yourselves adore.
These, if we win, the Graces too we gain, —
Their dear belov'd, inseparable train;
Three who their witching airs from Cupid stole,
And Three acknowledged sovereigns of the soul; 50
Harmonious throng! With nature blending art;
Divine Sestetto! warbling to the heart:
For Poesy shall here sustain the upper part.
    Thus lifted, gloriously we'll sweep along,
Shine in our music, scenery, and song, 55
Shine in our farce, masque, opera, and play,

And prove Old Drury has not had her day.
Nay more — to stretch the wing, the world shall cry,
Old Drury never, never soared so high!
"But hold," you'll say, "this self-complacent boast; 60
Easy to reckon thus without your host."
True, true — that lowers at once our mounting pride;
'Tis your's alone our merit to decide;
'Tis our's to look to you — you hold the prize
That bids our great, our best ambition rise. 65
A double blessing your rewards impart,
Each good provide, and elevate the heart,
Our twofold feeling owns its twofold cause:
Your bounty's comfort — rapture, your applause;
When in your fostering beam you bid us live, 70
You give the means of life, and gild the means you give.

Lord Byron

PARENTHETICAL ADDRESS

by Dr. Plagiary

Half stolen, with acknowledgements, to be spoken in an inarticulate voice by Master P. at the opening of the next new theatre. Stolen parts marked with the inverted commas of quotation — thus ' — '

'When energising objects men pursue,'
The Lord knows what is writ by Lord knows who,
'A modest monologue you here survey,'
Hiss'd from the theatre the 'other day,'
As if Sur Fretful wrote 'the slumbrous' verse, 5
And gave his son 'the rubbish' to rehearse.
'Yet at the thing you'd never be amazed,'
Knew you the rumpus which the author raised,
'Nor even here your smiles would be represt,'
Knew you these lines — the badness of the best, 10
'Flame! fire! and flame!' (Words borrowed from Lucretius,)
'Dread metaphors which open wounds' like issues!

'And sleeping pangs awake — and — but away'
(Confound me if I know what next to say).
'Lo Hope reviving re-expands her wings,'   15
And Master G— recites what Dr. Busby sings! —
'If mighty things with small we may compare,'
(Translated from the grammar for the fair!)
Dramatic 'spirit drives a conquering car,'
And burn'd poor Moscow like a tub of 'tar,'   20
'This spirit Wellington has shone in Spain,'
To furnish melodramas for Drury Lane.
'Another Marlborough points to Blenheim's story,'
And George and I will dramatise it for ye.

   In arts and sciences our isle hath shone'   25
(This deep discovery is mine alone),
'Oh British poesy, whose powers inspire'
my verse — or I'm a fool — and Fame's a liar,
'Thee we invoke, your sister arts inspire'
With 'smiles,' and 'lyres,' and 'pencils,' and much more.   30
These, if we win the Graces, too, we gain
Disgraces, too! 'inseparable train,'
'three who have stolen their witching airs from Cupid'

(You all know what I mean, unless you're stupid);
'Harmonious throng' that I have kept *in petto*   35
Now to produce in a 'divine sestetto'!!
'While Poesy,' with these delightful doxies,
'Sustains her part' in all the 'upper' boxes!
'Thus lifted gloriously, you'll soar along,'
Borne in the vast balloon of Busby's song;   40
'Shine in your farce, masque, scenery, and play'
(For this last line George had a holiday).
'Old Drury never, never soar'd so high,'
So says the manager, and so say I.
'But hold, you say, this self-complacent beast;'   45
Is this the poem which the public lost?
'True — true — that lowers at once our mounting pride;'

But lo:– the papers print what you deride.
'Tis ours to look on you — you hold the prize,'
'Tis *twenty guineas*,as they advertise! 50
'A double blessing your rewards impart' —
I wish I had them, then, with all my heart.'
Our *twofold* feeling *owns* its twofold cause,'
Why son and I both beg for your applause.
'When in your fostering beams you bid us live,' 55
My next subscription list shall say how much you give!

APPENDIX B

Poems, Plays and Prologues mentioned in the text

Apology (Cibber)
A Trip to Scarborough (Sheridan, after Vanbrugh)
A Winter's Tale (Shakespeare)
Cato (Addison)
Endymion, the Man in the Moone (Lyly)
Everyman (Prologue)
Douglas (Home)
Gorboduc (Norton and Sackville)
Guy Mannering (Sir Walter Scott).
Hamlet (Shakespeare) (see Garrick)
Harlequin Fortunatus, or, The Wishing Cap
King Lear (Shakespeare)
King Lear (Tate's adaptation)
La Dernière Chemise de l'Amour (see *Love's Last Shift*)
Les Fêtes Chinoises (Jean Noverre)
Love for Love (Dryden)
Love in a Bottle (Farquhar)
Love in a Village(Isaac Bickerstaffe)
Lovers' Vows (Kotzebue. Trans. Elizabeth Inchbald))
Love's Last Shift, or, The Fool in Fashion (Cibber)
Macbeth (Shakespeare)
Monody (Sheridan on Garrick's retirement)
Pasquin (Fielding)
Pizarro (Sheridan)
Prologue to Addison's *Cato* (Alexander Pope)
Prologue to *Macbeth* (Colman the Younger) (see New Drury opening)
Prologue to *Wit Without Money* (Beaumont and Fletcher)
Richard III (Cibber's adaptation)
Romeo and Juliet (Shakespeare)
Tartuffe (Molière) (translated by Cibber)
The Beaux' Stratagem (Farquhar)
The Beggar's Bush (Beaumont and Fletcher)
The Beggar's Opera (John Gay)
The Bohemian Girl (Balfe)
The Careless Husband (Cibber)
The Clandestine Marriage (Colman)
The Conquest of Granada (Dryden)
The Constant Couple Farquhar)

Appendices

The Critic (Sheridan)
The Cruelty of the Spanish in Peru (Davenant)
The Election (parody in Sheridan's *The Critic*)
The Emperor of the Moon (Ahpra Behn)
The Fair Penitent (Rowe)
The Fatal Dowry (Massinger and Field)
The Fatal Marriage (Southerne)
The History of Sir Francis Drake (Davenant)
The Honeymoon (Tobin)
The Hypocrite (Isaac Bickerstaffe)
The Indian Emperour (Dryden)
The Indian Queen (Dryden)
The Life and Death of Common Sense (parody in Sheridan's *The Critic*)
The Life and Death of Tom Thumb (Fielding) (see *Pasquin*)
The Merchant of Venice (Shakespeare) (see Garrick)
The Mourning Bride (Congreve)
The Non-Juror (Cibber) (see *Le Tartuffe*)
The Padlock (Isaac Bickerstaffe)
The Princess of Cleves (La Fayette)
The Rehearsal (Buckingham)
The Relapse, or, Virtue in Danger (Vanbrugh) (see *A Trip to Scarborough)*
The Rival Ladies (Dryden)
The Royal Hunt of the Sun (Peter Shaffer)
The Secret Love of the Maiden Queen (Dryden)
The School for Scandal (Sheridan)
The Stranger, or Misanthropy and Repentance (Kotzebue)
The Victory and Death of Lord Nelson (Cumberland)
The Way of the World (Congreve)
The Wild Gallant (Dryden)
The Winter's Tale (Shakespeare)(see *Florizel and Perdita*)
The Wonder (Mrs. Centlivre)
Threnody (Dryden) on Charles II
Twelfth Night (Shakespeare)
Two Gentlemen of Verona (Shakespeare)
Tyrannic Love, or, The Royal Martyr (Dryden)
Venice Preserv'd (Otway)
Wit Without Money (Beaumont and Fletcher)(see Prologue)
Whistle for it! (George Lamb).

APPENDIX C

1. Published authors of the *Genuine Addresses*

2. Index of first lines in *Rejected Addresses*

3. Authors parodied in *Rejected Addresses*

PUBLISHED AUTHORS OF THE GENUINE ADDRESSES

A Checklist

The Genuine (Rejected) Addresses, presented to the Committee of Management for Drury-Lane Theatre: preceded by that written by Lord Byron, and adopted by the Committee. Printed and sold by B. McMillan, 6, Bow Street, Covent Garden. Sold also by Hatchard, Piccadilly; Sherwood and Co., Paternoster-Row; Turner, 87 Strand; Cawthorn, Cockspur Street; Underwood, 32, Fleet-Street; Martin, Holles-Street, Cavendish Square; and Nunn, Great Queen-Street. 1812. Price Six Shillings.

Numbers in brackets indicate the order of placing in the folios in the British Library Dept. of MSS. Cat. Add. MSS. 27899 and 27900. q. v. Appendix A. 1

Page	
iii - ix	Introduction
1-3	Address, written by Lord Byron. Spoken by Mr. Elliston.
5-7	Address, transmitted on the 6th September, 1812, to the Secretary of the Committee. By Horace Twiss, esq.
8-11	Address, sent to the Committee. (33)
12-14	Address, sent to the Committee on the 9th Sept. 1812. By Anna, a Young Lady in the Fifteenth Year of her Age. (19)
15-16	Address, sent to the Committee, August 31, 1812, by William Thomas Fitzgerald, Esq. (9)
17-18	Address, presented to the Committee. By John Taylor, Esq. (40)

Appendices

19-20	Address. By Alicia Lefanu. (5)
21-23	Address. By C. T. (115)
23-24	Address. By C. T. (74)
25-27	Address. By T. J. Z. Z. (49)
28-30	Monologue. By Dr. Busby.
31-32	Unalogue. By G. F. Busby, Esq. (27)
33-35	Address.
36-38	By Josephus. (68)
39-41	By Walter Henry Watts. (17)
42-45	Address, presented to the Committee. By Edmund l. Swift, Esq, (90)
46-48	Address, left with the Secretary of the Drury-Lane Committee, 9th September, 1812, By Levet Desdaile. (22)
49-51	Address. By J. S. (43)
52-55	Address. By E. N. Bellchambers. (15)
56-57	By J. H. B.
58-61	Address. No. I
61-64	Address. No. II (7)
65-66	Address. (28)
67-70	Address, presented to the Committee.
71-73	Address. By Eugene Roach. (51)
74-75	Address. By Edward Simpson.
76-79	Address. By George Taylor. (37)
80-81	Address. By John Pytches, esq., of Groton House, Suffolk.
82-86	Essay for the Address, on the Re-Opening of Drury-Lane Theatre. By

                    Hugo Arnot, Esq.   (98)

67-88   Address.   By Icarius.   (66)

89-91   Address.   By J. H. C.   (55)

92-94   Address, sent to the Drury-Lane Committee by William Wastell, Esq.
   (31)

95-96   Monologue.   By John Gorton.   (50)

97-98   Address, sent to the Committee, sept. 16, 1812. By J. N. R. (83)

99-101   Address by J. G.   (78)

102-104   Address, submitted, Sept. 1812, to the Drury-Lane Committee by David Huston. (4)

105-108   Address. By H. G. Moir.(71)

109-110   Address.   (91)

111-112   Address.   By George Terry.(86)

113-117   Address.   By Samuel Lock Francis.   (52)

118-120   Address.   By F. T. (67)

121-122   Address.   By T. J. (101)

123-125   Address.   By Bavius.   (75)

126-130   Address.   Sent to the Committee.

Appendices

INDEX OF FIRST LINES IN THE GENUINE REJECTED ADDRESSES

Asterisks indicate those Addresses published in 1812. Numbers in brackets indicate the order of placing in the two folios in the British Library Dept. of MSS. Cat. Add. MSS. 27899, 27900.

1.	A certain Gentleman of worth and Fame	(11)
2.	*All hail the day that yields such brilliant sights	(55)
3.	A new Theatre is the modern style	(56)
4.	As from the ashes of her pristine form	(103)
5.	As he whom fate condemns awhile to roam	(58)
6.	As round the World night's shadowy volumes roll	(3)
7.	As springs the Phoenix from her glowing Bed	(45)
8.	As when an antient kingdom falls a prey	(36)
9.	As when the Phoenix in Parnassian lore	(60)
10.	*As when the Sun, through veil of darkening clouds	
11.	As when the Water [couched?] by heavenly Sway	(34)
12.	*Bards ask but honest fame to Stimulate	(52)
13.	*Before a British audience I appear	(19)
14.	Behold from ruins a new fabric springs	(114)
15.	*Britons, all hail! behold you have again	(91)
16.	Britons once more from midst the wreck of flames	(69)
17.	*Ere Antient Carthage saw her greatness wane	(75)
18.	Exiled by adverse Fate, by wayward fortune driven	(88)
19.	Friends of the Arts, of Science & the Stage	(38)
20.	Friends of the Drama, ye whose raptured eyes	(26)
21.	Friends, Patrons, Lovers of Dramatic lore	(70)
22.	Friends, Patrons, Britons, this our grateful theme	(24)
23.	From early Greece to these our modern Times	(62)
24.	From Times creation to its dread decease	(79)
25.	From whence the pile, that meets my wondering eyes	(29)
26.	Good folks, pray list one minute while I speak	(100)
27.	Hail splendid pile — thou newly risen sun	(42)
28.	*Has not the Sun withdrawn his wintry beam	(51)
29.	Here on this hallow'd ground the magic earth	(72)
30.	How oft have we, this night assembled here	(16)
31.	*Impartial Judges of the Thespian Band	
32.	Imperfect, Rude, Misshapen, Unrefined	(32)
33.	*In antient times when Greece & Rome bore Sway	(5)
34.	*In earliest ages ere Mankind began	(115)
35.	*In early times when first the Muse's tongue	(49)
36.	*In every clime to art & learning known	(33)
37.	*In Orient clime, when years decreed have run	(28)
38.	Ladies and Gentlemen, the Proprietors of this Theatre	(53)
39.	Lo in Majestic pride behold sublimely rise	(102)

351

40.	Long had the Muse o'er fallen Drury wept	(97)
41.	*Long o'er the spots where Drury glory slept	(7)
42.	Long tho our Pile in mould'ring ruins lay	(110)
43.	*Methinks some Voice in wond'ring accents cries	(66)
44.	Nature herself [exalts?] the Dramas cause	(46)
45.	New Drury, — compilation. Let me see.	(57)
46.	No more do thorns at Drurys grave appear	(23)
47.	Now Phoenix like New Drury rears her head	(2)
48.	Now Phoenix like New Drury rears her head	(14)
49.	*Now Phoenix like New Drury rears her head	(86)
50.	Of genius wild and savage nature sprung	(21)
51.	*Oh ever welcome to this spacious dome	(4)
52.	Oh for a muse of water, if our State	(109)
53.	Oh Sacred Muses, ye who deign t'inspire	(63)
54.	Once more to Drury to our hopes restored	(63)
55.	*Once more the scenic Muse beholds a dome	(40)
56.	*On our prompt labour cast a lively look	
57.	Revived by a distinguished Patriots aid	(35)
58.	Rais'd from her ashes to the promised pile	(48)
59.	Say shall the hand of antient time in vain	(84)
60.	*See like the Phoenix on aspiring wing	(37)
61.	Shakespeare exclaims Oh for a muse of Fire	(18)
62.	*Shrouded in gloom, when frozen whirlwinds sweep	
63.	Since ruin wrapt that prouder Mansions height	(94)
64.	Sweets to the sweet, & be this Classic shrine	(30)
65.	The exulting throb demands a transient pause	(25)
66.	The moral uses of the Mimic stage	(82)
67.	The Muse kind friends after a long adieu	(106)
68.	The Stage at first by wisdom was design'd	(59)
69.	*Tho' when the Grecian sages reared the Stage	(67)
70.	'Tis done, the War of opposition's o'er	(65)
71.	*To catch the manners living as they rise	(78)
72.	To conquer prejudice & hearts refine	(6)
73.	*To grace the mystic rites to Bacchus paid	(15)
74.	To rouse the energies new nerve the heart	(13)
75.	Welcome thrice welcome to this antient bound	(95)
76.	*Welcome thrice welcome generous friends once more	(83)
77.	Were we hardhearted we could lay before ye	(85)
78.	*What pride what pleasure fill the flowing breast	(43)
79.	What sounds, what joys, now greet my pensive ears	(112)
80.	*What strange reverses mock his baffled skill	(22)
81.	What throng of feelings agitate the breast	(39)
82.	*What throng of feelings agitate the breast	(98)
83.	What time the fierce barbarian sallied forth	(68)
84.	When barbarous Man from Savage fierceness broke	(92)
85.	When divine order saw together hurl'd	(41)
86.	*When energising objects men pursue	

87.	When first in early Britain's gothic days	(64)
88.	When first on Earth the arts their radiance threw	(54)
89.	When first the comic Muse stepped forth to view	(8)
90.	When first Vesuvius with tremendous ire	(73)
91.	*When Grecian fury doomed proud Troy to blaze	(71)
92.	When her Triumphant Chariot ploughs the Wave	(1)
93.	*When Ilion's Sons, o'erwhelm'd by Grecia's ire	
94.	*When lowering clouds proclaim along the shore	(31)
95.	When o'er our Isle dark superstition reign'd	(108)
96.	When one long exiled from his native land	(10)
97.	When Rome's proud Chieftain to the winds unfurl'd	(61)
98.	When Shakespeare reigned on this our native shore	(104)
99.	*When that appalling Element whose rage	(17)
100.	*When the fierce Saracen relentless poured	(90)
101.	When the great Architect divine display'd	(47)
102.	When the great Architect divine displays	(113)
103.	*When wrapt in flame terrific to the sight	(9)
104.	*While conquering Greece in generous triumph saw	(101)
105.	While on your call our grateful zeal attends	(99)
106.	*While wasting Time still spares th' Ephesian's fame	
107.	*While years revolving sweep the human race	(74)
108.	While yet uncurbed the passions held their sway	(81)
109.	*Whilst yet sad mem'ry paints the mournful sight	
110.	*Whoe'er the world's vast theatre surveys	
111.	With verdant laurels of immortal bloom	(12)
112.	Ye Britons of Glory, read here a plain story	(105)
113.	*Ye social energies that link mankind	(27)
114.	Yes it is past, the gloomy day is o'er	(44)
115.	Yet once again tho numbered with the Dead	(20)
116.	*You see old Time his Scythe & Hour glass too	(50)

AUTHORS PARODIED IN *REJECTED ADDRESSES*
A Checklist

Horace and James Smith, *Rejected Addresses, or, The New Theatrum Poetarum.* London. Printed for John Miller, 25, Bow-street, Covent Garden; and John Ballantyne and Co., Edinburgh. 1812. Printed by W. Pople, 67, Chancery Lane.[1]

Page	Title and Authors	Code Initials	Parody of
v-xii	*Preface*		
1-4	*The Loyal Effusion.*	By W. T. F.	(William Fitzgerald)
5-1	*The Baby's Debut*	By W. W.	(William Wordsworth)
11-13	*An Address Without a Phoenix*	By S. T. P.	(Horace Smith)
14-20	*Cui Bono?*	By Lord B.	(Byron)
21-27	*The Hampshire Farmer's Address*	By W. C.	(William Cobbett)
28-31	*The Living Lustres*	By T. M.	(Thomas Moore)
32-41	*The Rebuilding*	By R. S.	(Robert Southey)
42-46	*Drury's Dirge*	By Laura Matilda	(Hannah Cowley)
47-58	*A Tale of Drury*	By W. S.	(Walter Scott)
57-63	*Johnson's Ghost*		(Samuel Johnson)
64-70	*The Beautiful Incendiary*	By the Hon. W. S.	(William Spencer)
71-74	*Fire and Ale*	By M. G. L.	(Matthew Gregory Lewis)
76-80	*Playhouse Musings*	By S. T. C.	(Samuel Taylor Coleridge)
81-84	*Drury Lane Hustings: A New Halfpenny Ballad.*	By a Pic-Nic Poet	(Harry Greville)
85-94	*Ancestral Atoms*	By Dr. B.	(Dr. Thomas Busby)
95-10	*Theatrical Alarm Bell*	By the Editor of the M.P.	(Daniel Stuart)
101-109	*The Theatre*	By the Rev. G. C.	(George Crabbe)
110-121	1. *Macbeth Travestie (Case No. 1)* By Momus Medlar		(William Shakespeare)
	2. *The Stranger Travestie (Case No. 2)* By Momus Medlar		(August von Kotzebue)
	3. *George Barnwell Travestie (Case no. 3)* By Momus Medlar		(George Lillo)
122-127	*Punch's Apotheosis*	By T. H.	(Theodore Hook)

The Theatre Royal, Drury Lane: A Timeline

1662	Killigrew's patent. 25 April.
1663	Opened 8 April.
1666	Nell Gwynne performed. Theatre burnt down with 60 houses.
1672	Theatre burned down together with 60 houses.
1674	Rebuilt by Sir Christopher wren. Opened 26 March.
1712	Cibber, Wilkes, Booth.
1742	Garrick's first appearance at Drury.
1747	Garrick and Lacy tenure. Revival of Shakespeare.
1766	Theatre fund founded by Garrick.
1775	Interior rebuilt by Adam brothers.
1776	Garrick's farewell.
1776	Sheridan takes over management.
1782	10 October. Mrs. Siddons first appearance as a 'star'.
1783	John Philip Kemble's *début* as Hamlet.
1794	Theatre rebuilt by Henry Holland on large scale and re-opened.
1794	Charles Kemble's first appearance
1800	11 May. Attempted assassination of the King by Hatfield.
1809	24 February. Theatre burnt down.
1812	10 October. Theatre rebuilt by Benjamin Wyatt. Re-opened, with Prologue by Byron.- spoken by Robert Elliston.
1814	Edmund Kean as Shylock.
1819	New lessee, Robert William Elliston.
1820	Madame Vestris's first appearance.
1803	27 October. Real water used in *Cataract of the Ganges*.
1826	New lessee. Stephen Price.
1827	Ellen Tree appears as Violante.
1827	Charles Kean appearance as Norval.
1830	New management of Alexander Lee and Captain Polhill.
1831	New lessee, Alfred Bunn.
1839	New management by Hammond.
1841	William Macready's management. Season of German operas.
1843	Bunn returns as lessee.
1844	16 December. Clara Webster burnt on stage and died.
1849	Management under Anderson.
1851	26 February. Macready's 'Farewell'.
1852	Bunn back again as lessee-manager.
1858	English opera introduced.

1859	Italian opera introduced (until 1878).
1874	Balfe's statue unveiled.
1875	Wagner's *Lohengrin*.
1879	4 February. Theatre closed. Actors' strike.
1879	Augustus Harris, new lessee and manager, to 1892.
1883	Carl Rosa opera company, through to 1885. Re-opens the House 1886.
1889	Pantomime, *Jack and the Beanstalk*. Many performances.
1890	Carl Rosa's *Romeo and Juliet*.
1891	Pantomime, *Beauty and the Beast*. House closed. Troubled times. Occasional performances.
1892	Pantomime, *Humpty Dumpty*.
1892	Pantomimes, *Little Bo-Peep*, *Red Riding Hood*, *Hop o' My Thumb*, to 1893.
1893	April. Comédie Française, plays by Racine and Molière (also at Windsor Castle).
1893	Balfe's *The Bohemian Girl*. Wagner's opera, *Die Walküre*, etc.
1893	Duke of Bedford renews lease for 7 years. Pantomime, *Robinson Crusoe*.
1895	Pantomime, *Dick Whittington*.
1895	Eight performances by Eleonora Duse.
1896	Pantomime, *Cinderella*, *Aladdin*.
1896	Cheap summer season.
1896	Autumn season. English Opera.
1897	Arthur Collins, managing director.
1898	Pantomime, *The Babes in the Wood*.
1916	Shakespeare Tercentenary – performance of *Julius Caesar*
1921	Refurbishment of theatre. Noel Coward's *Cavalcade*.
1925	Musical, *Rose-Marie*
1927	Operetta, *The Desert Song*
1939	Ivor Novello's *The Dancing Years*
1947	Rodgers and Hammerstein's, *Oklahoma*
1958	Lerner and Loewe's, *My Fair Lady*
1984	Musical, *42nd Street*
1989	Musical, *Miss Saigon*
2000	Andrew Lloyd Webber purchases theatre
2021	Theatre reopens after £60m refurbishment

SOURCES AND FURTHER READING

HOLLAND HOUSE PAPERS - 0312.51639 [Selected references]
British Museum (Prints and Drawing Dept.)

Volume One

Volume Two

Correspondence between Lord Byron and Lord Holland.
pp204-14 passim. pp219-227 passim: Ref: Napoleon Bonaparte.

Volume Three

p239 and note. Ref: John Allen
p239. Ref: Congreve
Henry Fox, son of Lord Holland.
Lord and Lady Holland.
p265. Ref: 'Monk' Lewis. See poems
p249. Ref: Congreve
p256. Ref: Napoleon Bonaparte
Alexander Pope
Sheridan's conversation, sentimentality.
Byron, Drury Lane Addresses
Lord Holland
Lady Holland

Volume Four

Napoleon Bonaparte: See Lord Holland's *Memoirs*.
pp 61, 73, 320 and note: Lord Holland. Portrait of Lord Holland: see *Memoirs*
John Hamilton Reynolds
Johnson

Add. MSS. 51641

Letter from Sheridan to Ld Holland. 17 July 1811.
Entry 43: Exhibition of the two models [of Wyatt's new theatre] unavoidably delayed to Friday at 3 pm. The first at Benjamin Wyatt's (Foley? Place) – then Philips at Carlton House.
Entry 44: Letter Samuel Whitbread to Sheridan re. site for the new building.

HOL 1312.51645

Correspondence of Sidney Smith, Blanco White.

HOL 0312.51639

pp5-6: Autograph copy of Byron's Address. Cf. for this Address. ref. to Johnson's line 'And Passion stormed the heart'.

pp13-14: Letter from Byron to Lord Holland. 10 Sept. 1812. 'The lines which I hatched off....' [See Byron LJ2 p191]

pp15-1: Lord Holland to Byron 'I am really concerned to find...'

pp18-20: Byron to Lord Holland. 'If the sound of your excellent verses run in my ears...'

p22: 23 Sept. Byron to Lord Holland. 'Keep my name a secret – or I shall be beset by all the rejected....'

pp23-24: Byron to Lord Holland. [See Byron LJ2 p204] 'Ecco! I have marked some passages with dual readings....' Refs. To phoenix.

pp25-27: First draft of Byron's Address sent to Lord Holland 23 Sept. 1812. See pencil notes re differences with final printed version. Instructions for him as to how to proceed.

pp29-30: Drury address [probably the one read by Lord Holland] with different beginning: 'While wasting Time, still spares the Ephesian's fame'.

pp31-34: Another Address. (Possibly the one read by Ld Holland). Beginning: While expectation [sits?] on thousand eyes,
  Eager to see the Virgin curtain rise'
  I scarcely dare entreat a short delay,
  But we must have a Prologue for our play.
And continues with refs. to Sheridan's ode to Garrick.

p35. Byron to Lord Holland. 24 Sept. 1812. Requesting revisions - with apologies. [LJ2 p205].

pp36-37: On same day, sent more revisions. ' I must bore you still further with alterations ....' [LJ206]

pp38-39: 24 Sept. Sent yet more revisions: I believe this is the third scrawl...' **pp38-39**]

pp40-43: Lord Holland to Byron. 25 Sept 'Your verses are better and better every time...' (See p 7 of pencil script for whole letter).

p44: Lord Holland to Byron. 'As I perceive you are inclined to be diligent from correction....'.

pp45-46: Another from Byron with further corrections. 'Still more matter for a May morning having hatched the middle & the end....'

pp47-9: Corrected copy of Address with some omissions. And one addition: 'but I fear still too long.'

pp50-51: 25 Sept. Lord Holland replies the by the next post.

pp52-57: Address written out with numbered lines. With space below for notes. By Lord Holland.
The identity of the readers was to remain secret. Initialed 'H' for

Sources and further reading

'Hypercritical'. Drury Lane Manager [Whitbread] to intitial 'M'. There follows in the pencil notes a list of comments by 'H' and 'M'.

pp58-59: Another copy of the Address with numbered lines, with 'M's' footnotes and commentaries.

pp60-63: Frenetic, scribbled letter from Byron to Lord Holland. with further emendations. 'I always scrawl in this way...' Letter is followed by a long postscript.

pp64-67: Lord Holland to Byron. 'I am delighted with your diligence...'
Reference to objection about Sheridan's being referred to as Brinsley.

pp68-69: Byron to Lord Holland. 'Is Whitbread determined to castigate all my cavalry...'

pp70-78: Lord Holland to Byron. Lord H. (staying at Lord Lansdowne's seat, Bowood, Calne), to meet at Tetbury to go over the address with Byron (at Cheltenham). 'It must be givent Elliston to conn by rote...' Followed with comment by 'M' on the length. Later Lord Holland writes: 'I can perceive a nobler flow in your verses....' There follows a long addendum.

p84: 30th Sept. 'you will find a sort of clap-trap lauditory...'

p86: Byron's Copy Penultimate. Still correcting as he copies the Address out.

p96: Lord Holland to Byron. 2nd October. Receipt of corrected copy at Drury Lane. 'I must congratulate you on the general improvement...' Lord Holland asks for an urgent viva-voce conference with Byron. 'I see you long for satire & I hope you will still vent your indignation...' One competitor seems to have found favour with Lord Holland regarding 'horses'.

p102: Final draft on large paper for clarity to help Elliston. Still last minute corrections go on. 'sulphurous corrected to 'clouds of fire'.

p106: 9th October. Corrections even the day before.

p107: Lord Holland to Byron. 'I write from Mr. Elliston's & have had the satisfaction of hearing him read your Address...'

p109: Lord Holland to Byron: I write from the box, to catch the post—It has succeeded admirably...'

Byron writes to Lord Holland two days later on 14th October. 'I perceive that the papers yea even Perry are somewhat ruffled...'

p113: Lord Holland to Byron. 15th October. 'the committee are content & have not thought it proper to answer the nonsense in the papers...'

p118: 20 October. From Holland House. Lord Holland. 'Busby who is your [Melbourne?] is excellent & and I think must give you an itching for a Satire or an epigram...'

BIBLIOGRAPHY

Addison, Joseph. *The Spectator*. London 1827
Anthony, Katherine. *The Lambs: A Study of Pre-Victorian England*. Hammond. nd.
Ashbee, C. R. *Caricature*. Chapman & Hall. 1928.
Baddeley, Clinton *Burlesque Tradition in the English Theatre after 1660* London 1952
Beavan, Arthur. *James and Horace Smith: A Family Narrative* Hurst and Blackett, London 1899.
Blackstone, Bernard *Byron: A Survey* Longman 1975
Blakeney,E.H. Ed. *A Smaller Classical Dictionary*. J.M. Dent. London. 1910.
Blunden, Edmund 'The Rejected Addresses' (in *Votive Tablets*) London 1931
Brandreth, Gyles. *The Funniest Man on Earth: The Story of Dan Leno*. Hamish Hamilton London ISBN 978-0-89810-9]
Bratton, Jacky. The Making of the West End Stage. CUP, 2011.
Brewer. *Dictionary of Phrase and Fable*. Cassell London.1971.
British Drama: A Collection of the most approved Tragedies, Comedies, Operas, and Farces. Two volumes. Jones & Co. 1824. pp554-566.
British Library Catalogue No 91. P.177 re Drury Lane.
Browning, Robert. *Selected Poems*.
Buckingham, Richard. *Memoirs of the Court of the Regency.* pp169-70.
Burlesque Plays of the Eighteenth Century. OUP 1969. Includes Buckingham's *The Rehearsa*l and Fielding's *Tom Thumb the Great*
Busby, Thomas. *The Nature of Things: A Diascalic Poem, translated from the Latin of Titus Lucretius Carus: accompanied with commentaries.*
Busby, Thomas. *Comparative, Illustrative, and Scientific of the Life of Epicurus.* J. Rodwell, New Bond Street, London. 1813
Busby, Thomas. *The Age of Genius: A Satire on the Times in a Poetical Epistle to a Friend.* Printed for Harrison & Co. No.18 Paternoster Row.
Byron, Lord *Don Juan* ed. Elizabeth F. Boyd. Humanities Press 1958
Byron. Lord. *English Bards and Scotch Reviewers*
Byron, Lord. *Poetical Works*. OUP 1904. Reprinted 1906 and 1945.
Byron, Lord, *The Poetical Works of Lord Byron.* 'Monody on the Death of the Right Hon. R. B. Sheridan, spoken at Drury Lane Theatre'. Suttaby 1888. pp63-4.
Byron, Lord http://en.wikipedia.org/wiki/Childe_Harold's_Pilgrimage
Byron, Lord. *Byron's Letters and Journals*. Vol. 2. 1810-1812 'Famous in My Time.'Ed. Leslie A. Marchand. John Murray 1973.
Byron, Lord. *Byron's Letters and Journals*. Vol.3. 1813-1814 'Alas! The Love of Women!' Ed. Leslie A. Marchand. John Murray 1974.
Byron, Lord. *Byron's Letters and Journals*. Vol.4 1814-1815 'Wedlock's The Devil' Ed. Leslie A. Marchand. John Murray 1976.
Chesterton, G. K. *The Victorian Age in Literature* 1913
Chilcott, Tim. *A Publisher and His Circle*. Routledge & Kegan & Paul. London 1972
Cibber, Colley. *Apology for the Life of Colley Cibber.* Ed. Robert W. Lowe.

Sources and further reading

Clubbe, John. Byron paper.
Clubbe, John. *Thomas Hood: Selected Poems* Harvard UP 1970
Cochran, Peter. Ed. *Byron and the Theatre.* Cambridge Scholars Publishing. 2008.
Courthope, W. J. *Addison* 1884
Clayton Tim and Sheila O'Connell. *Bonaparte and the British.* British Museum 2015.
Croot, Patricia. 'Before and after Drury House: Development of a Suburban Town House 1250-1800'. Article drawn from *A History of the County of Middlesex, Vol. XIII Part 1: Landownership and Religious History.*
Cumberland, Richard. *The British Theatre.* 1823-31. Edited George Lamb.
Cumberland, Richard. *The Dramatic Works of Richard Cumberland, written by himself.* (1806-7). For a comprehensive list of his works, see Myers *Dictionary.*
Davis, Paul. E. H. *From Castle Rackrent to Castle Dracula.* University of Buckingham Press 2011. Ch. 8 'Bram Stoker – The Eternal Vampire'
Dobbs, Brian. *Drury Lane: Three Centuries of the Theatre Royal 1663-1971.* Cassell 1972
Donkin, Ellen, 'The Paper War of Hannah Cowley and Hannah More'. *Curtain Calls: British and American Women and the Theater, 1660-1820.* Mary Anne Schofield and Cecilia Macheski, eds. Ohio UP. 1991, 153.
Donkin, Ellen, *Women Playwrights in London 1776-1829* (1995).
Dryden, John. *The Poetical Works of John Dryden.*
Elwyn Malcolm. *Lord Byron's Wife.* Macdonald. 1962.
Everitt, Graham. *English Caricaturists and Graphic Humourists of the Nineteenth Century.* Swan & Sonnenschein. 1873.
Finberg, Melinda C. *Eighteenth-Century Women Dramatists.* Oxford.World's Classics. 2001.
Fleming, Anne. *The Myth of the Bad Lord Byron.*
Fleming. Anne. *Byron the Maker.* Vol. I of *Byron in England.* Book Guild Publishing. 2006.
Fox, Henry Richard Vassall. *The Diary of....,* See Holland,Lord.
Fraser, George. *Alexander Pope.* Routledge 1978
Freud, Sigmund. *Der Witz.*
Gentleman's Magazine 1747
Gifford.*Genuine Rejected Addresses.* Printed and sold by B. McMillan. London 1812.
George, Dorothy. *English Political Caricature. 1792-1832.* OUP. 1959.
Goldsmith, Lewis. Ed. *The Antigallican Monitor and Anti-Corsican Chronicle.*
Goldsmith, Lewis. Ed. *The Argus, or London Reviewed in Paris.* (1802)
Greville. *Memoirs 1837-52.* Vol. I pp 245-6
Groot, Patricia. *'Before and After Drury House: Development of a Suburban Town House 1250-1800.* Victoria County History: Middlesex.
Gross, Jonathan David. *Byron: The Exotic Liberal.* Rowman & Littlefield Publishers Inc. New York 2001.
Harwood, Ronald. *All the World's a Stage.* Secker and Warburg,/British Broadcasting Corporation. 1984

Haydn. *Dictionary of Dates*. Ward, Lock 1889.
Holland House Papers. Department of Manuscripts, British Museum. Add. MSS HOL 51318-52254.
Holland House Papers. Department of Manuscript, British Museum. Ref: Add. MSS HOL 0312.51639. *Correspondence between Lord Byron and Lord Holland.*
Holland, Lady Elizabeth. *Elizabeth, Lady Holland to Her Son. 1821-1845*. Ed. Earl of Ilchester. John Murray 1948.
Holland, Lord *The Rejected Addresses*. 'The Original Manuscripts forwarded to the Committee of Drury Lane *Theatre in Sept 1812 in accordance with the Advertisement of August 8th*, comprising upwards of 100 Poems, Letters, and Interesting documents, arranged and bound in 2 vols. British Museum. Department of Prints and Drawings.
Holland, Lord. *Memoirs of the Whig Party*. 2 vols. John Murray 1905
Holland, Lord. *The Diary of Henry Richard Vassall Fox, third Lord Holland*, with extracts from the diary of Dr. John Allen. Edited with an introductory essay and notes by Abraham D. Kriegel. Routledge and Kegan Paul. 1977 The diary was kept by Lord Holland from 1831 to his death in 1840.
Hollis, Leo. *The Phoenix*. Weidenfeld & Nicolson 2008.
Hood, Thomas. *The Letters of Thomas Hood*. Ed. Peter Morgan. Oliver and Boyd.
Hood, Thomas. *The Poetical Works of Thomas Hood.* Ed. Walter Jerrold, Henry Frowde. OUP. 1911.
Hudson, Derek *Holland House in Kensington* Peter Davies 1967
Hyland, Paul. Editor. *Ned Ward's Classic Account of Underworld Life In Eighteenth Century London.* 1993. See Edward Ward.
Ilchester, The Earl of. *The Home of the Hollands*. John Murray 1917.
Jerdan, William. *Autobiography*.
Jerrold, Walter. 'The Centenary of Parody'. *Fortnightly Review* No. DXLVI New Series. Vol. II. August I, 1912.
Jerrold, Walter (ed). *A Century of Parody.* London 1913.
Johnson, Samuel. *The Idler*. 1734-1789.
Johnson, Samuel. *The Poems of Samuel Johnson*. Ed. David Nichol Smith and Edward L. McAdam. Oxford. Clarendon Press.
Jump, John D. *The Ode*. Methuen. 1974.
Kensington Public Library. Miscellaneous collection of MSS, books, engravings, and photographs.
Lemprière, ,J.. *A Classical Dictionary*. Second Edition. Routledge.. London.
Liechstenstein, Princess Marie. *Holland House*. Vols. 1 & 2. Macmillan. London 1874
London County Council. *Survey of London*: 'The Theatre Royal, Drury Lane, and the Royal Opera House, Covent Garden.' Ed. F. H. W. Sheppard. Vol. 35 pp9-29.1970.
Lowe, Robert W. '*The Real Rejected Addresses: A Chapter in Theatrical Literature'. Blackwood's Magazine* No DCCCCXXXI Vol CLIII May 1893.
MacQueen-Pope, W. *Theatre Royal Drury Lane* W. H. Allen 1945
Marchand, Leslie A. *Byron; A Biography*. 3 vols. Alfred A. Knopf. New York.

Sources and further reading

1957. London 1958.
Marchand, Leslie A. *Byron's Letters and Journals.* John Murray. 1973.
Marchand, Leslie Alexis http://www.nytimes.com/1999/07/16
Martin, Philip E, *Byron: A Poet before his Public* CUP1982
Maurois, André *Byron. Trans. Hamish Miles. Bodley Head 1930*
Mitford, Mary Russell. *Our Village.* 1819.
Moore, Doris Langley. *Lord Byron: Accounts Rendered.* John Murray. 1974.
Moore, Thomas. *The Life and Letters of Lord Byron: with Notices of His Life.* 2 vols. London, 1830.
Moore, Thomas. *Life of Sheridan.*
Myers, Robin. *Development of the English Book Trade 1700-1899.* Ref. Peter Thorogood: 'Thomas Hood: A Nineteenth-Century Author and his Relations with the Book Trade to 1835.' 1981.
Myers, Robin. *Dictionary of Literature in the English Language.* 2 vols. Pergamon Press Ltd. 1970. Oxford.
Oxford Dictionary of National Biography.
Pierson, Joan. *The Real Lady Byron.* Robert Hale. 1992.
Pope, Alexander, *Complete Works.*
Price, Cecil *The Dramatic Works of Richard Brinsley Sheridan* OUP 1973
Price, Cecil. *Lady Caroline Lamb: A Biography.*
Price, Cecil. *The Theatre of David Garrick.* 1975.
Price, Cecil. *Monk Lewis: a Critical Biography.*
Redding, Cyrus. *Fifty Years' Recollections*, iii pp176-8
Rejected Addresses.. 'The Original Manuscripts forwarded to the committee of Drury Lane *Theatre in Sept 1812 in accordance with the Advertisement of August 8th*, comprising upwards of 100 Poems, Letters, and interesting Documents, arranged and bound in 2 vols. British Museum. Department of Prints and Drawings.
Roberts Michael. *The Faber Book of Comic Verse.* Faber&Faber. 12th Impression 960.
Rogers, Pat. *An Introduction to Pope* Methuen 1975
Rogers, Pat *Henry Fielding* Paul Elek 1979
Rosebery, Lord. *The Last Phase* 1901
Russell, Dr. Terry. *The Drury Lane Chronicles* (1826-30). Download from http:/drurylanechronicles.neocities.org/trcontents.htm
Segar, Mary Gertrude. Editor. *Namby Pamby: The Poems of Ambrose Philips.* p248. Berg Reprints xiv 1938. Also 'Ambrose Philips. TLS 7 Dec. 1933 p875
Shelley. Ref. 'Ozymandias': http.//genius.com/Percy-bysshe-shelley-annotated
Sheridan, Elizabeth. *Betsy Sheridan's Journal: Letters from Sheridan's Sister.* Ed.
Sherson, Erroll. *London's Lost Theatres of the Nineteenth Century.* London. John Lane, Bodley Head 1925 William Lefanu. Eyre & Spottiswoode.1960.
Smith, Horace and James. *Rejected Addresses* http://archive.spectator.co.uk/article/20th-may-1899/24/james-and-horace-smith.
Smith, Horace and James Smith. *The Poetical Works of Horace Smith and James Smith with Portraits and a Biographical Sketch.* Ed. Epes Sargent. Mason

Brothers, New York, 1857. Kessinger Publishing Rare Reprints.
Smith, Horace and James, *Rejected Addresses: or the New Theatrum Poetarum* London 1812
Smith, Horace and James, *Rejected Addresses: or the New Theatrum Poetarum* Two vols. ed. Anthony Boyle. Constable 1929
Smith, Horace and James. *Rejected Addresses, and Other Poems.* Edited Epes Sargent. Hurd and Houghton. Boston: E.H. Dutton and Company. Reprint 1866.
Smith, Horace http://en.wikipedia.org/wiki/Horace_Smith_(poet)
Smith, James, *Memoirs, Letters, and Comic Miscellanies in Prose and Verse. 2 Vols.* Henry Colburn 1840.
Smithers, Peter *The Life of Joseph Addison* 1914
Taylor, George. *The French Revolution and the London Stage 1789-1805.* Cambridge UP 2000
Theatre Royal, Drury Lane. http://www.theatrestrust.org.uk
The British Drama: A Collection of the most approved Tragedies , Comedies, Opera, and Farces. In two volumes. Jones & co. 1824.
The Oxford Shakespeare Henry V edited by Gary Taylor OUP.
Thompson, J.M. *Napoleon Bonaparte: His Rise and Fall* 1951
Thompson, J.M. *The French Revolution.* Basil Blackwell. Oxford 1947
Thorogood, Peter. *Thomas Hood: The Progress of Cant: Caricature as Social History.* Papers in Research and Criticism. Polytechnic of Central London. 1976 (OP).
Thorogood, Peter. *Thomas Hood: Poems Comic and Serious.* Bramber Press. 1995
Thorold, Peter. *The London Rich.* Viking. Penguin Books 1999.
Thurley, Simon*, Lost Buildings of Britain.* Viking imprint from Penguin Book. 2004 Chapter 3.
Tillotson, Geoffrey *On the Poetry of Pope* OUP 1950.
Victoria County History. BIC Class. See Groot re: Drury Estate.
Wakefield, Gilbert. (DNB00)
  https://wn.wikisource.org/wiki/Wakefield,_Gilbert_(DNB00)
Walford, Edward. *Old and New London: A Narrative of its History, its People, and its Places.* Vol. III Westminster and the Western Suburbs. Cassell, Petter & Galpin. London.
Ward, Edward. *The London Spy*: See Ned Ward
Wardroper, John. *The Caricatures of George Cruikshank.* Gordon Fraser. 1977 Jonathan Cape (Random House Group) 2007.
White, Jerry. *London in the Nineteenth Century.* Jonathan Cape. 2007
Woof, Robert. *Byron: A Dangerous Romantic.* The Wordsworth Trust. 2003.
Wyatt, Benjamin. *Observations on the Principles of a Design for the Theatre Royal Drury Lane* (1813).
Wyndham-Lewis, D. B, and Charles Lee. *The Stuffed Owl: An Anthology of Bad Verse.* 1930. Ziegler.

Sources and further reading

Further websites consulted:

Booth, Barton   http://en.wikipedia.org/wiki/Barton_Booth
Boucicault, Dion http://en.wikipedia.org/wiki/Dion_Boucicault
Byron, Lord http://en.wikipedia.org/wiki/Childe_Harold's_Pilgrimage
Catnach, Jemmy http://en.wikipedia.org/wiki/Street_literature
Cobbett, William http://en.wikipedia.org/wiki/William_Cobbett
Cowley, Hannah   http://en.wikipedia.org/wiki/Hannah_Cowley
Drury Lane
  http://www.theatrestrust.org.uk/resources/theatres/show/206-drury-lane-theatre-royal
DruryLane   http://en.wikipedia.org/wiki/File:Drury_lane_interior_1808.jpg
Holland, Lady http://en.wikipedia.org/wiki/Elizabeth_Fox,_Baroness_Holland
Irving, Henry.   http://www.bradfordmidlandhotel.com 'Henry Irving and   Bram Stoker: A Working Relationship.' Michael Kilgarriff
Irving, Henry   http://elmer.hipbo.org
Irving, Henry   http://en.wikipedia.org/wiki/Henry_Irving
Irving, Henry http://www.theirvingsociety.org.uk
Johnson,Samuel
http://www.bbc.co.uk/history/historic_figures/johnson_samuel.shtml
Leno, Dan   https://en.wikipedia.org/wiki/Theatre_productions_of_Dan_Leno
Lewis, Matthew http://en.wikipedia.org/wiki/Matthew_Lewis_(writer)
MacQueen-Pope. https://en.wikipedia.org/wiki/W._J._MacQueen-Pope
Marchand, Leslie Alexis http://www.nytimes.com/1999/07/16
Moore,Thomas
  http://www.azlyrics.com/lyrics/celticwoman/thelastroseofsummer.html
Parody http://www,britannica.com/art/parody-literature
Philips, Ambrose http://en.wikipedia.org/wiki/Ambrose_Philips
Price,Stephen
   http://www.britishmuseum.org/collectionimages/AN00167/AN00167390_001_l.jpg
Smith, Horace http://en.wikipedia.org/wiki/Horace_Smith_(poet)
Spencer, William. http://en.wikipedia.org/wiki/William_Spencer_(poet)
Street Literature http://en.wikipedia.org/wiki/Street_literature
Theatre Royal, Drury Lane. http://www.theatrestrust.org.uk
Walpole, Robert https://www.rc.umd.edu/sites/default/files
Whitbread,Samuel
  http://en.wikipedia.org/wiki/Samuel_Whitbread_(1764%E2%80%931815)
Wordsworth, William http://en.wikipedia.org/wiki/The_Lucy_poems
Wordsworth, William. David Simpson http://www.jstor.org/discover
Wordsworth, William. Alison Gopnik http://www.wsj.com/articles
WordsworthWilliam. Jacqueline Banerjee
  http://www.victorianweb.org/genre/childlit/childhood1.html

SOURCES, NOTES AND REFERENCES

INTRODUCTION: Abbey Garden to 'Old Drewerie'

1. Walford, Edward. *Old and New London: A Narrative of its History, its People, and its Places.* Vol. III Westminster and the Western Suburbs, p37.
2. MacQueen-Pope, *Theatre Royal Drury Lane*. W.H. Allen 1945 p238

CHAPTER ONE: Tennis Court to Temple of the Muses

1. MacQueen-Pope, W.J. *Theatre Royal Drury Lane*. W.H. Allen. 1945 p19
2. MacQueen-Pope p20
3. MacQueen-Pope p21
4. MacQueen-Pope p36   Originally the 'Scene Room' – a retiring room for actors, later called the 'Green Room and. In Cockney rhyming slang, 'the Greengage' and eventually just 'The Green'. Cf. 'to be on the green' = the stage. An inexperienced actor was 'green' – he wasn't polished enough to play on the green.
5. Pepys *Diary* 22 August 1667.
6. Dryden *Works* p139 ll.1-8
7. Dryden Works   p139 ll. 16-19. Brian Dobbs Drury Lane: Three Centuries of the Theatre Royal 1663-1971. Cassell 1972. p51
8. Dryden *Works* p311 ll. 5-8, 13-14. Also p113 (Epil. *Wild Gallant*), p123 (Epil. *Evening's Love*), p128 (Prol. *Conquest of Granada*).
9. Cf. Thomas Hood's caricature etching, *The Progress of Cant* in which he includes an image of the Erechtheum with three female figures. Peter Thorogood Collection.
10. Dryden *Works*   p313 ll. 1-4, ll. 14-15, ll. 16-20
11. Dryden *Works* p336 ll. 335-40
12. Dryden *Works Threnody* for Charles II. p 337 ll. 364-365,ll. 368-369, ll. 383-387
13. Dryden's *Works*. References in the text: For Jubal, patron of the harp and lyre, see *Genesis* Ch4.   Saint Cecilia was patroness of musicians.   George Farquhar (1678-1707, born in Dublin, attended Trinity College,Dublin) was author of popular plays, *The Constant Couple* (1700), the recruiting Officer (1706), and *The Beaux' Stratagem*(1707. *The Fair Penitent*, by Nicholas Rowe (1674-1718), was a popular play at Lincoln's Inn Fields and Drury Lane. Rowe is known today for his edition of Shakespeare's plays, which he divided into numbered acts and scenes and modernised the spelling and punctuation. Poet Laureate 1715.
14. Dryden *Works*, as above.
15. Alexander Pope. Prologue to *The Rivals* ll 1-13
16. John Dryden. Second preface to *The Rivals*. ll 1-
17. Sir Thomas Skipwith. MacQueen-Pope records that Skipwith grew thoroughly tired of being a shareholder during Rich's dictatorship and gave his share in the Patent to a Colonel Brett, a theatre enthusiast and admirer of Cibber's periwig,' who, to make the deal legal, paid Skipwith ' a consideration of ten shillings.' Op. cit. p89, Ibid. pp111-113. Dobbs pp62 and 80.
18. Dobbs p62. MacQueen-Pope p77
19. MacQueen-Pope p88
20. MacQueen-Pope p89, pp91-2   *Apology for the Life of Colley Cibber*. Ed.

Sources and further reading

      Robert W. Lowe.
21. Dobbs p76
22. MacQueen-Pope, op cit, p120
23. Dobbs p82
24. Ibid. pp82-3 *Tatler* Nov. 1709 pp24-26
25. The subject of Matthew Arnold's advance of the Philistines in *Culture and Anarchy* (1869).
26. cf. Dunciad p92 re Greece
27. Dobbs p83 *Tatler* Nov. 1709 pp24-26
28. Dobbs p84
29. MacQueen-Pope. p123
30. Pope *Works* p93 ll. 13-18 cf. Dryden's line (Dryden *Works* p153) See Byron LJ2 p179, p210n.
31. Ibid. p95 ll. 25-26
32. Pope *Works* p93 ll. 37-38
33. Samuel Johnson *Works*.
34. Dobbs p85. Pope *Works* p93n2 re liberty, rebellion. See also Wikipedia.org/wiki/Actor Rebellion.
35. Dobbs p86
36. Ibid. p87. John Gay (1685-1732), author of the *The Beggar's Opera*. His poetry included satirical eclogues on the writings of Ambrose Philips ((1675?-1749). MacQueen-Pope p144
37. Cibert (anglicised to Cibber), Caius Gabriel, Danish sculptor, whose descent could be traced back to Pope Innocent VIII. On arrival in England via the Netherlands he settled in London and soon became prominent as a stonemason working for Sir Christopher Wren, for whom he carved the phoenix over the west door of St. Paul's Cathedral as a symbol of resurrection from the flames. He married Jane Colley, whose family were descended from the sister of William of Wykeham. The liaison accounts for much in the character of their son, Colley, the gentle, well-mannered, dignified 'angel' among the unruly miscreants of back-stage Drury politics. Many of Cibber Senior's sculptures can be seen around London today: the statue of Charles II in Soho Square, the bas reliefs for the Monument, commemorating the Great Fire of London, and other works for Trinity College Cambridge.
38. Wyndham-Lewis and Lee, *The Stuffed Owl*. See Sources and Further Reading
39. Pope *Works* p375 ll. 299-302
40. Ibid. p376 ll. 319-322 and note re Chapel Royal
41. MacQueen-Pope p152
42. Dobbs p95 Thomas Davies *Memoirs of the Life of David Garrick* (2 vols.) 1780
43. Dobbs p95 Life of James Quin 1887
44. Kane O'Hara and Intro. Note to *British Drama* pp511 and 515
45. British Drama p516
46. Intro. Note *British Drama* p511
47. *The Dunciad*. Pope *Works* p372 Macqueen Pope p162 See Dryden *Works* Prologue to *Cleomenes* ll. 1-10.
48. Dobbs pp103-4 cf. Johnson's Prologue re Mahomet. See Appendix 'A' no. 4
49. Dobbs p103 MacQueen-Pope p179
50. See MacQueen-Pope p177
51. Sheridan, *Monody* ll. 23-28

CHAPTER TWO: Richard Brinsley Sheridan - The Profligate Accountant

1. Sheridan would develop this scene more successfully in *The Critic*.
2. Dobbs p113 cf. Dryden's' travesty of *Antony and Cleopatra, All for Love*. See *Rejected Addresses*: Momus Medlar.
3. Macqueen Pope p169. Macqueen Pope p205 From the Prompter's book 3rd November 1746. Dobbs p71 and Macqueen Pope p204 re riots.
4. MacQueen-Pope p205.
5. MacQueen-Pope p212.
6. MacQueen-Pope p209. P. Zeigler, *William IV* pp76-8. Charles Matthews biography. Byron LJ3 p249 and note.
7. George Colman. Prologue to *Suicide*
8. George Terry *Rejected Addresses*. See Part Four.
9. Thomas Hood *Works*. Ed. W. Jerrold Byron W*orks* p26 re Siddons.
10. Cf. Dorothy George on caricature: *English Political Caricature* 2 vols. Oxford University Press. 1959. James Gillray (1757-1815). Caricaturist. Ridiculed habits of the Royal family, and brilliant caricatures of Pitt, Fox and Sheridan, Napoleon, Nelson, and the French Revolution. Dobbs p112. A reference to a grotesque image of Sheridan in Pizarro.
11. See Part Four *Genuine Addresses*.
12. Thomas Busby (1755-1838). Composer, journalist, parliamentary reporter. Taught music and French. Translator of Lucretius. His Drury Lane Address parodied by Byron.
13. Dobbs p128
14. Wardroper *The Caricatures of George Cruikshank*. Also Thomas Hood *Cant.*
15. Byron LJ2 p192
16. Byron LJ2 p193 See romantic Prose pp30-2
17. Byron LJ3 p272
18. Byron *Poetical Works. Monody on the Death of the Right Hon. R. B. Sheridan.* p63 ll. 11
19. Byron *Monody. Op.cit. p63 ll.1-12*
20. Byron *Monody. Op.cit*. ll. 66-79
21. Byron *Monody. Op.cit*. ll. 88-89
22. Byron *Monody Op. cit. p64* ll. 116-119

CHAPTER THREE: Prologue and Epilogue

1. Dryden *Works* p118 ll. 1-11
2. Dryden *Works* p118 ll. 16-21
3. Dryden Works p38-39. Ll. 1-8. See Part Five for Mary Russell Mitford's 'Address'.
4. Dryden *Works*. p107 ll. 22-31. Cf. p163 ('Like Hectors...').
5. Pope *Works* p92-3. Joseph Addison (1672-1719). Close association with Steele and Swift. Produced *The Spectator* with Steele.
6. Pope Works. p374, ll. 373.
7. Dryden *Works*. p417 ll.1-2
8. Shakespeare *Henry V* Act 1 ll. 23-34.
9. Dryden *Works* p34 ll.1-6 See Appendix A for the complete version
10. Dryden Works p111 ll. I-4
11. Dryden *Works* p113 ll.1-16
12. From Thomas Campbell's *Lochiel's Warning* in which the Wizard foretells the victory of the English over the Scots at Culloden in 1746. Cf. Cicero: 'Certain signs precede certain events.'
13. Dryden Works (8 lines)?

Sources and further reading

14. Dryden *Works* ll. (13 lines)?
15. *The Oxford Shakespeare*. Ed. Gary Taylor. OUP pp56-57
16. *The Princess of Cleves. The Poems of Dryden,*(1913). First printed in *Miscellanies* 1684.
17. Dryden *Works* p166 ll.1-10
18. Dryden *Works* p320 ll.21-32
19. Dryden *Works* p173 ll. 1-10
20. Dryden *Works* p178 ll 7-14
21. Dryden *Works* p448 ll. 26-31
22. Dryden *Works* ibid.
23. Byron, Poetical Works. *Monody of the Death of R. B. Sheridan*.p63 l.11
24. Op. cit. ll. 1-26
25. *Monody* p63 ll 89-90.

CHAPTER FOUR: Plagiary and Parody

1. Genuine Addresses. Anon.
2. Ibid.
3. Ibid.
4. Buckingham, George Villiers (1628-87). *The Rehearsal* (1671)
5. Isaac Watts. (*Divine Songs for Children* (1715).
6. Lewis Carroll. *Alice Adventures in Wonderland* (1865).
7. Dryden *Absalom and Achitophel.* Satire on Sir Robert Walpole.
8. See Chapter Six for Byron's devilish verbal attack on Dr. Busby's verses, *A Parenthetical Address to Dr. Plagiary.* Nov. 1812 pp434-5
9. Shakespeare parodies the pomposity of the euphuistic style of the Elizabethan playwright, John Lyly, a mannered style of English, precious, ornate and sophisticated, employing in excess a wide range of literary devices such as antithesis, alliteration, and absurd repetition. An unusual source of parody was the Scottish writer James Hogg's *The Poetic Mirror, or The Living Bards of Britain,* which was published anonymously in 1816. The work came about by chance and was never intended to be anything more than an anthology. Hogg set out to secure a poem from the principal English poets, collect them into a single volume and make his fortune. Unfortunately most of the poets ignored this request with the result that he was constrained to compose the poems himself and thus, inadvertently, created an ingenious set of parodies.
10. Francis Jeffrey, Editor of the *Edinburgh Review* Nov 1812 pp434-5
11. Norman Gillespie. 'Henry Carey', in *The New Grove Dictionary of Music and Musicians*. Vol. 15, pp127-128.
12. Pope's Works *Essay on Criticism*
13. Pope's Works *Essay on Man*
14. Ward, Thomas Humphrey, ed. *The English Poets 1880-1918* Vol. 3 *The Eighteenth Century: Addison to Blake Ibid.*
15. Ibid.
16. Published by his employer, Jacob Tonson, the bookseller, in *Miscellanies* (1709).
17. Carteret. John, 2nd Lord Carteret (c1684-1731), Member of Parliament for Hebdon, Yorkshire. Lord of the Admiralty 1721-25. Supported the Whig party but detested Walpole.
18. *Namby-Pamby* re. sentimental verse ll.23-30.
19. *Namby-Pamby* ll. 37-42
20. Scurrilous vituperation of this sort was designed to hit home with a

vengeance.

CHAPTER FIVE: The Great Literary Competition of 1811

1. Lines written out from Samuel Whitbread's own copy of Byron's Address delivered to him for comment. Holland House Papers, Department of Manuscripts, British Museum. Add. MSS 51318-52254.
2. MacQueen-Pope p225
3. Byron *Monody on the death of the Rt Hon. R B Sheridan*, spoken at Drury Lane Theatre (Byron Works).
4. Holland. *Memoirs* pp235-6.
5. *Rejected Addresses* 'Hampshire Farmer Boyle' p52
6. *Rejected Addresses* p111.
7. Byron LJ4 p254, note re. Newstead. Byron *Works* p33, ll. 137-40
8. Benjamin Dean Wyatt (1775-1850). Preface to *Observations on the Principles of a design for a Theatre* pp vii-ix. Op. cit. p x. The Wyatt family was a large one and in their profusion lies also some confusion. I have been told, though I have not attempted to verify the fact, that there were twenty-two Wyatts, most of them architects. A few of them are listed in the *Dictionary of National Biography*. Thomas Henry Wyatt (1807-1880) built a Byzantine church at Wilton, the Adelphi theatre in the Strand, the old Knightsbridge Barracks, and became President of the Royal Institute of British Architects. His brother, Sir Matthew Digby Wyatt (1820-1877), was an authority on medieval geometric mosaics and was appointed Secretary to the Executive Committee of the great Exhibition, 1851. James Wyatt (1746-1813) studied in Rome and Venice, but later was one of the principal supporters of the Gothic Revival. One of his sons, Matthew Cotes Wyatt (1777-1862), a sculptor, executed the equestrian statues to Sidney Sussex College, Cambridge and carried out the extensive restorations to Windsor castle, for which he was knighted in 1828. A sculptor cousin of Benjamin Wyatt's, Richard James Wyatt (1795-1877) settled in Rome. George Wyatt, is not listed in the DNB, and the only reference I have found to him is in connection with the Drury Lane affair.
9. *The Tatler*
10. Eventually, the Theatre had to be extended at the rear of the building to provide a deeper stage and more adequate accommodation for actors, musicians, and other theatre employees.
11. Thomas Hood gives a portrait of Samuel Beazley in *Ode to Perry* (see Jerrold *Poetical Works of Thomas Hood* p306) and gives some idea of his reactions to one of his first nights:
    > Witness how Beazley vents upon his hat
    > His nervousness, meanwhile his fate is dealt:
    > He kneads, moulds, pummels it, and sits it flat,
    > Squeezes and twists it up, until it felt
    > That went a Beaver in, comes out a Rat!
    > ll. 95-99
12. Horace and James Smith, Introduction to *Rejected Addresses* pp xxi-xxii.
13. Horace and James Smith, op. cit. p xx.
14. *The Antigallican Monitor* No. 87. 27th September 1812. p703
15. Ibid. p703. Whitbread was Foxite and as such an advocate of peace with France.
16. Ibid. No 88. 27th September 1812. P711
17. Ibid. p711
18. Ibid. p711 See *British Drama* Vol 2 p987a for Rolla's patriotic speech on home

Sources and further reading

and country.
19. MacQueen-Pope p218.
20. *The Antigallican Monitor* No 90. 11th October 1812 p728.
21. MacQueen-Pope *op. cit.* p224. Byron LJ4 re. George Henry Robins (1778-1847). Charismatic auctioneer, celebrated for his dynamic auctioneering patter and elaborate advertisements. In 1842, he sold Horace Walpole's collections at Strawberry Hill. He was frequently lampooned by Byron, Thackeray, Thomas Hood, and others. John Hamilton Reynolds refers to him in *Odes and Addresses*, 1825 p.108

> Lastly --- and thou wert built for it by nature!
> Crown'd was thy head in Drury Lane Theatre!
> Gentle George Robins saw that it was good,
> And renters cluck'd round thee in a brood.

See also Robin Myers, 'George Henry Robins, Strawberry Hill Auctioneer', *The Printing Art* Vol. I No I Spring 1973.

22. Edmund Kean (4 November 1787– 15 May 1833) was a celebrated British Shakespearean stage actor born in England, who performed in London, Belfast, New York, Quebec, and Paris among other places. He was well known for his short stature, tumultuous personal life, and controversial divorce.
23. Byron LJ2, LJ3, LJ4
24. Walter Jerrold. *'The Centenary of Parody'* in *The Fortnightly Review* No DXLVIII. New Series. August I 1912. Vol I p72
25. Lord Byron's correspondence, edited John Murray, Vol I p72. John Murray 1922.
26. Robert W Lowe. 'The Real Rejected Addresses', Blackwoods magazine DCCCCXXXI May 1893 Col CLIII.
27. Byron *Don Juan*
28. Quarterly Review, Horace Smith *Rejected Addresses* p xx
29. Many of the *Rejected Addresses* bear the initials 'J. W.' that is, James Winston, the first manager of the Garrick Club. The papers were probably in the archives of Drury Lane and came into his possession when he was assisting Elliston. Winston was a very enthusiastic collector of autograph manuscripts. He put the addresses in order, annotated them, and bound them. When his effects were sold in December 1849, the bound volumes of the genuine Rejected Addresses were acquired by the British Museum. See Robert W. Lowe, 'The Rejected Addresses', *Blackwood's Magazine*, No. DCCCCXXXI, May 1893, Vol CLIII.
30. Genuine Addresses no. 39
31. Genuine Addresses no. 50
32. Byron LJ2 p.45n, p.147, p.252, NB. Vol.4 Byron *Works* p.114
33. Genuine Addresses p iv.
34. Genuine Addresses p v. Byron *Works*. p.115, ll. 143 et seq.
35. Genuine Addresses no. 53
36. Genuine Addresses no. 53
37. Genuine Addresses no. 3 *Dryden Satires of Juvenal* 1693
38. Genuine Addresses no. 68
39. Genuine Addresses no. 47
40. Genuine Addresses no. 47
41. Genuine Addresses no. 47
42. Genuine Addresses no. 47
43. Genuine Addresses no.47! Lowe p. 746
44. Genuine Addresses no. 46a or (47?)
45. Genuine Addresses no. 78
46. Lowe p743

47. Lowe p743 Genuine Addresses No. 21.
48. Mary Russell Mitford. Genuine Addresses no. 21 cf. Pope *Works: Essay on Criticism* ll. 52, 70, 700
49. Genuine Addresses no. 21. Mary Russell Mitford.
50. See 1st draft notes, Ch. 2, n. 8
51. Genuine Addresses n. 57
52. DNB George Brewer 1st draft notes Ch. 2 n. 9
53. Rowe p744
54. Genuine Addresses n. 65 Rowe p. 744
55. Genuine Addresses n.65 See omission in 1st draft.
56. Genuine Addresses n. 65
57. Genuine Addresses no.44
58. Genuine Addresses no.44
59. Chatterton, Jerrold p.233
60. Genuine Addresses n. 104
61. Genuine Addresses no. 12
62. Genuine Addresses no. 102, Marchand p. 205n. LJ2 p.69. Competitors invoke Phoenix. 'Rhapsodising poulterer'.Byron *Works* pp. 116, 125, ll. 116-959 (?)
63. Jerrold p. 233, Byron LJ3 p. 367.
64. Lowe p. 744.
65. Genuine Addresses p. viii
66. Genuine Addresses no. 8
67. Genuine Addresses no.73 Jerrold p. 233
68. Genuine Addresses no. 30.
69. Genuine Addresses no. 112 Perhaps an echo of Byron's 'pensive eyes' Byron's *Works* p. 55

CHAPTER SIX: A Noble Lord and his Noble Critic

1. Thompson, The French Revolution, p32
2. Holland Diaries 1831-1840
3. Thompson op. cit. p37
4. Thompson op. cit. p37.
5. Holland Diaries. See Byron's remark re Lafayette LJI.
6. Cyrus Redding. Fifty Years' Recollections. (1785-1870) Journalist in London and Paris.
7. Moore's Diary
8. Lady Holland. Sent newspapers to Napoleon on Elba, which alerted him to the British plan to exile him to St. Helena.
9. Byron *Works* p86
10. Byron *Works* p85
11. Op cit. p85
12. Clubbe, John. 'Napoleon's Last Campaign and the Origins of Don Juan'. *The Byron Journal* 1997 Num. 25 pp 12-22. Taking July 1818 as 'the most fatal month of Byron's literary life,' Professor Clubbe draws a parallel between Byron exiled to the island of Venice and Napoleon to the island of St. Helena. Both Emperor and poet, mortified by 'social ostracism', one in a bold escape to fight his final battle, the other to align himself with the fight to free Greece from the Turkish yoke.
13. Byron Works. Holland Memoirs
14. Holland Memoirs pp122-3
15. Bards. Byron *Works* p116

Sources and further reading

16. Byron LJ4 p286
17. Byron *Works* pp320-1
18. Byron LJ p203 re Leigh Hunt, Byron *Works* p123.
19. Byron *Works*. Bards p122
20. Byron *Works* p867 and p125n col.1
21. Genuine Addresses, page v. 'Noble Childe' - a reference to Byron and *Childe Harold's Pilgrimage*.
22. Marchand. Op. cit.
23. Byron LJ4 pp56-7
24. Holland Diaries page xv. Byron *Works* p27 re lines on Holland's uncle Charles James Fox's death.
25. Holland Diaries p. xvii Also Cant
26. Holl. Diaries. Page xviii and p22n. Byron *Works*. Granta p11 Cant.
27. Holl. Diaries page xviii and p26n. See Romantic Prose re Burke p103. Byron *Works*
28. Holl. Memoirs p381
29. Holl. Diaries page xx
30. Ibid.
31. Lady Holland Memoir of Sidney Smith Vol. 1 p282
32. Marchand. Byron LJ
33. Bards. Byron - p126
34. Byron *Works* p197
35. Byron LJ2 p66
36. Op.cit. p66n
37. Marchand. Correspondence.
38. Byron LJ2 p165
39. Mechanism. Op.cit. p165. Mechanics Institution founded by Dr. Birkbeck in London and Glasgow 1823. Also Mechanics Magazine founded.
40. Byron LJ2 p165
41. Byron LJ2 p166
42. Romantic Prose pp118-9
43. Byron LJ p167
44. Romantic Prose p121
45. Holl. Memoirs p123
46. Byron LJ2 p168. Attributed to Pope – misquoted.
47. Op. cit. p168

CHAPTER SEVEN: The Reluctant Poet: Execution or Persecution?

1. Probably facetious ref. to Lord Holland's mentions of Byron in a missing letter re. Byron being a lover of the drama and of Drury. Ref. to asbestos: Used as safety curtain in large proscenium theatres to stop the spread of fire from stage to audience. Theatre Royal, Drury Lane was the first theatre to feature a fire (or 'iron') curtain.
2. Marchand gives 'anonymes' for 'synonymes'. Byron LJ2 p191. Also gives 'sketched' for 'hatched'.
3. MS British Museum Add. 51639. LJ4 p191
4. MS British Museum Add. 51639. Byron LJ2 pp191-2
5. Byron LJ2 p193
6. Holland Papers.
7. MS British Museum Add. 51639. LJ2 p203.
8. 'Ecco!', literally 'Behold'. In Byron's case, 'Here it is at last!' A lame apology!

373

9. Book of Common Prayer 1662. Psalm 98.7: 'with trumpets and shawms.' Also Spenser's *Faerie'Queene*: 'With shawms and trumpets and with clarions sweet.' Bk. I pp12-13.
10. Byron LJ2 p230n.
11. MS British Museum Add. 51639. LJ4 p204
12. MS British Museum Add. 51639 LJ4 p205.
13. MS British Museum Add. 51639 LJ4 p206
14. Byron LJ2 p20
15. MS British Museum Add. 51639 LJ4 p206
16. Holland *Papers.*
17. Ibid.
18. Dryden *Works. Annus Mirabilis*, a curious work which, in spite the ravage of London by plague and fire, praises God for saving the City from complete destruction and gives thanks for Charles II, the great patron of the arts and restorer of the new London. The image is further linked to the mass murder of the male population of the Greek island of Milos and the enslaving of their women and children by the invading Athenians. Home of Aphrodite and the Venus de Milo. Byron sees himself as a doomed Milotian, about to be slaughtered by a band of vicious Athenians (i.e. the rejected poets).
19. MS British Museum Add. 51639. LJ4 pp207-8
20. Holland *Papers*
21. Ibid.
22. Holland *Papers.* 2nd draft of Address ll. 11-14
23. Holland *Papers.* Comment to lines 11-14 ibid.
24. Byron *Works* ll. 11-14 p66
25. MacQueen-Pope p175
26. Op.cit. pp252-3.
27. Holland *Papers*
28. Holland. *Papers* ll. 71-76
29. Holland *Papers*
30. MacQueen-Pope pp285 and 293
31. Byron LJ2 p212n
32. Op. cit.
33. Byron LJ2 pp209-10
34. Op.cit. p180
35. Op.cit. p192
36. Op.cit. pp90 and 128
37. Byron LJ3 p206
38. Byron LJ3 p231
39. Holland *Papers*
40. Byron LJ2 p211
41. Holland *Papers* A volte-face since he had previously spoken with admiration.
42. Holland *Papers*
43. Byron LJ2 pp212-3
44. Byron LJ2 p212 and Appendix
45. Byron LJ3 p231
46. Byron LJ3 p239
47. Appointed by the joint Management Committee to organise the competition and read Address
48. Holland *Papers*
49. Epistles see Pope *Works*
50. Byron LJ2 p213
51. Byron LJ2 p213

52. Op.cit. p214
53. MS. British Museum Add. 51639. LJ4 p219
54. MS. British Museum Add. 51639. LJ4 p220
55. Op. cit.
56. Byron *Works, Parenthtical Addresses*

CHAPTER EIGHT: Phoenix Triumphant

1. Thomas Arne (1710-1778). Composer of light operas, songs and incidental music. Wrote the music for Addison's *Rosamond*, Fielding's *Tom Thumb*, Milton's *Comus*, Congreve's *Judgment of Paris*, and Shakespeare's *Twelfth night*. Appointed composer to Theatre Royal, Drury Lane, (1744). His masque, *Alfred*, included 'Rule Britannia,' which began to be regularly sung at Drury Lane on all occasions when patriotism and xenophobia were the order of the day.
2. Holland *Memoirs* p163
3. Holland House *Papers*
4. Byron *Works*
5. Holland House *Papers*. Vol. 2. 109. Not included in Leslie A. Marchand *Byron's Letters and Journals*.
6. *The Anti-Gallican* Monitor No. 87. 20 September 20 1812. P703. See Part Four re. *Genuine Addresses*.
7. LJ2 p225 and note. James Perry (1756-1821). Radical Scottish editor of the *Morning Chronicle*. Prosecuted several times for revolutionary views. Founder of the *European Magazine*. Acted on stage in his spare time.
8. Byron LJ2 p225
9. Byron LJ2 pp225-6
10. Ibid.
11. Ibid.
12. Holland Papers
13. Browning *Poems*. 'Childe Rolande to the Dark Tower Came', vs. III
14. Browning *Poems*. 'Childe Rolande to the Dark Tower Came', vs. VII
15. Byron *Works*.
16. Holland Papers
17. Isaac Bickerstaffe *The Hypocrite* Byron LJ2 p227
18. *The Antigallican Monitor* No. 91 p735 for a more detailed account of the incident. Holl. *Papers*.
19. Byron LJ2 p249 and n., 252 Byron's pun.
20. Charles Edward Horn (1786-1849). Composer of operas, oratorios and glees. Also a talented singer. His successes included the opera, *The Devil's Bridge*, but, encouraged by manager Samuel Arnold, he made his debut with *The Beehive*, a musical farce in two acts. Its popularity with Drury's audiences accounts for its choice for the opening night. He made several highly successful visits to America, eventually settling in Boston.
21. Rowe p747 Byron *Works*.
22. Rowe p748
23. Walter Jerrold. *A Centenary of* Parody. MacQueen-Pope p.218
24. *The Antigallican Monitor* No.91 p735
25. Rowe p749]
26. *Op.cit*.
27. *The Antigallican Monitor* No. 91 p735
28. *The Antigallican Monitor* No.91 p735
29. op.cit.

30. Thomas Busby. *The Age of Genius. A Satire on the Times in a Poetical Epistle to a Friend*. Printed by Harrison & Co. No. 18 Paternoster row, London. 1786.
31. *Age of Genius* ll. 9-12
32. Op.cit ll. 17-18
33. Op.cit. ll. 163-166
34. Op.cit. ll. 195-212
35. Op.cit.ll. 295-312
36. Op.cit. ll. 337-342
37. Op.cit. ll. 375-376
38. Op.cit. ll. 379-384
39. Hood. 'Ode on a Distant Prospect of Clapham Academy.' Hood *Poems* Ed. Walter Jerrold. Henry Frowde - Oxford University Press. 1906. ll. 13-18.
40. *Art of Genius* ll. 413-430
41. op.cit. 693-702.
42. In his *Journal* for 17 November 1814 (Vol 3. p210) Byron refers to Lady Oxford, who 'when that booby Busby sent his translating prospectus, she subscribed. But, the devil, prompting him to add a specimen,' on receipt of which she declined to be on the list of subscribers. I do not know on what grounds she was qualified to judge the quality of the translation.
43. Thomas Busby. *The Nature of Things, a Didascalic Poem, translated from the Latin of Titus Lucretius Carus*. J. Rodwell, (late Faulder's), White and Cochrane, and J. Hearne. 1813. p xvi. Two earlier editions – See Notes. Byron *Letters* Vol. 3 pp7, 73. Re Busby 210, 211
44. Byron *Letters* Vol. 3. Ref. *Lucretius*. op. cit Busby pp 210-211.
45. Thomas Busby, Op. cit. *Lucretius* Preface p. x
46. Op. cit. *Lucretius* Preface p viii.
47. Ibid. p. viii. Byron *Letters*.Vol 3. pp210-11.
48. *The Nature of Things*, Vol. I. Book One. pp 994-998 p63.
49. *Lucretius* Vol II. Book Four. p 1. ll. 1-2.
50. *Lucretius*. Book Five. ll. 1-4. Pope's Essay on Criticism ll. 52, and 70.
51. Busby. *Monologue for the Opening of the Drury Lane Theatre*. ll. 66-69. See Appendix A
52. *Lucretius*. Book One. ll. 966-975.
53. Busby. *Monologue*. ll. 1-17. See Appendix A.
54. Holland *Papers*. Vol. I Entry 13a. British Museum. Dept. of Prints and Drawings.
Busby's *Monologue* and anonymous criticism of it
55. Busby. *Monologue* ll. 35-6. See Appendix A
56. Lucretius *De Rerum Natura*. Book Three l. 59
57. Holland *Papers*. Vol I. Entry 11
58. Holland *Papers*. Entry 15d . Letter from Dr. Busby to daily journals defending his conduct. 23 October 1812.
59. 'vain and self- conceit'. Shakespeare: Richard II Act 3 Sc.2
60. Byron. *A Parenthetical Address by Dr. Plagiary, half stolen, with acknowledgements, to be spoken in an inarticulate voice by Master ---, at the opening of the next new theatre*. Dr. Plagiary. See Byron *Letters* Vol 2 pp227, 228n. The original MS is in the John Murray collection.
61. Samuel Arnold was the manager.
62. Holland *Papers*. Entry 18c.
63. Holland *Papers* Vol. I Entry 18g.
64. Holland *Papers*. Vol I. Entry 29.
65. Holland *Papers*. Vol. I. Entry 18e.
66. Holland *Papers*. Vol. I. Entry 18b.

Sources and further reading

67. Ziegler. p238.
68. Lucretius. *The Nature of Things.* Lord Holland's copy. British Library ref. BL 840.m.39. From an autograph letter affixed to Volume I.
69. Op. cit. Holland *Memoirs.*
70. Op. cit. Vol. I. Baron Grenville (1776-1839). Statesman. Privy counsellor. Created duke 1822. Collected rare prints.
71. *Odes and Addresses.* Thomas Hood and John Hamilton Reynolds (author of *The Fancy*) jointly published this volume. Hood married Reynolds' elder sister, Jane.
72. Byron's *volte face* here marks the beginning of a reconciliation with Busby.
73. *Lucretius. Preface* p. xi.
74. Byron wrote to Thomas Moore on 9 April 1814: 'There is a long poem, an "Anti-Byron", coming out; to prove that I have formed a conspiracy to overthrow, by rhyme, all religion and government, and have already made good progress.....I never felt myself important till I saw and heard my being such a little Voltaire as to induce such a production. Murray would not publish it; for which he was a fool, and so I told him; but some one else will, doubtless.' LJ IV. p93. Text; Moore Vol I 540-42
75. Supposedly a reference to Byron's leanings towards Atheism and Libertinism.
76. Ibid.
77. Edward Jenner (1749-1823), physician and pioneer of smallpox vaccine. Byron's remark is a topical reference here, since only a few years before (1808), the Government set up the National Vaccine Establishment. [LJ 4 p81]
78. LJ Vol 4 p81.
79. Marchand *Byron: A Portrait.* p260
80. LJ Vol 4 p81.
81. Byron had once refused to go back to school at Harrow because he had developed a precocious passion for William's daughter, Mary Chawarth.
82. Hone p4

CHAPTER NINE: The Rejected Addresses

1. Ian Jack (b 1945) Non-fiction writer, critic and journalist. See *Sir Walter Scott,* British Council 'Writers and their Work' series. Publisher: Longmans Green and Company 1958. He points out the anomaly that Scott's novel was published a few weeks after Smith's.
2. Horace managed Shelley's finances.
3. Morgan *Letters.* Brighton 23 March 1828] [A.E. Beavan *James and Horace Smith* 1899 p289.
4. Epes Sargent, *The Poetical Works of Horace and James Smith.* New York 1858. p9
5. Each inspired by Diodorus Siculus (Book I, Chapter 47), a Roman historian and contemporary of Julius Caesar. His work is now considered inaccurate. Shelley and Horace submitted their sonnets to *The Examiner.* Shelley's was published (January 11, 1818) under the pen-name. Ed. Epes Sargent. Mason Brothers, New York, 1857. New York Reprint by C.A. Alvord. For Ozymandias see http.//genius.com/Percy-bysshe-shelley-annotated .
6. See Epes Sargent, *Poetical Works of Horace and James Smith with Portraits and a Bibliographical Sketch,* 1858.
7. See Mrs Cowley re *Vers de société* [p?]
8. DNB Vol 25 p264 *Horace Smith.*
9. Beavan pp110-112.

10. *Rejected Addresses* Preface p.vi.
11. *Ibid.*
12. Beavan pp114-5.
13. Beavan p119.
14. *Edin. Rev.* November 1812 p437.
15. DNB Vol.25 p264
16. Beavan p115.
17. Hood. *New Monthly Magazine*, April 1826. JPWp412.
18. Boyle. *Rejected Addresses*. p131.
19. Byron. *English Bards and Scotch Reviewers*. ll.1-2.
20. Boyle. *Rejected Addresses*. p133
21. Boyle, *op.cit.* 24-35.
22. Boyle, *op.cit.* 24-35.
23. Fitzgerald Soldier quote
24. Fitzgerald final quote
25. *ibid.* p437
26. Edward Fitzgerald, *The Rubaiyat of Omar Khayyam,* 1859
27. Byron, *English Bards and Scotch Reviewers*
28. Rejected Addresses 1812 7th ed. p5
29. Edinburgh Review 438. See Barbara Gerlitz, The Baby's Debut: The Contemporary Reaction to Wordsworth's Poetry of Childhood. Boston University Studies: Engish 4 (1960) 85-90
30. Jeffrey Edinburgh Review 1812; Andrew Boyle Rejected Addresses 1929 p136; Blunden p203
31. Blunden p203
32. Oxford Book of English Verse 1250-1900. Ed. A. T. Quiller-Couch. 1919. ll. 1-9
33. OAEL p168n
34. Andrew Boyle p138
35. Boyle p138
36. Byron. *Letters*
37. The *Edinburgh Review* p434
38. Letter to Sir W.W. Wynn 1813. Quoted in Boyle p139
39. Letter to Francis Hodgson. LJ3 p7
40. William Walsh, *A Handy Book of Literary Curiosities* p208. 1894
41. James and Horace Smith. *Rejected Addresses* p20. 'Cui Bono?' Boyle p50
42. *Rejected Addresses* London. John Miller. 1812
43. Advice to Young Men, and (incidentally) to Young Women…in a series of Letters. B. Bensley at Andover. The Author, 1829
44. For a full account of Samuel Whitbread's life, see Roger Fulford. *Samuel Whitbread 1764 – 1815.* Macmillan 1967.
45. *Edinburgh Review.* Boyle p148
46. The Faber Book of Comic Verse. Compiled by Michael Roberts. Faber and Faber Ltd. London. 1962. p232
47. Published in *The Doctor*. 1834-47. 3 vols. 7
48. Geoffrey Cranall OUDNB 2011 re. 2011
49. Yale University. 2006
50. See http://en.wikipedia/wiki/Curse-of-Kehama for full account of the elaborate plot
51. Mohammed Kassim Harmoush: *Laureateship under the Reign of Queen Victoria*. English Language and Literature Studies, Vol. 3. No. 4, 2013. ISSN 1925-4768 E-ISSN 1925-4776. Published by Canadian Center of Science and

Sources and further reading

Education.
52. Boyle p149
53. The *Monthly Mirror,* February 1811
54. Quoted from Lionel Madden, *Robert Southey, the Critical Heritage.* Routledge, London 1972
55. *English Bards and Scotch Reviewers*
56. *The Faber Book of Comic Verse.* Compiled by Michael Roberts
57. Quoted in Bowles p205
58. Quoted in Bowles p206
59. Boyle p206
60. Boyle p142
61. Ellen Donkin, *Getting Into the Act: Women Playwrights in London 1776-1829,* 1995, Routledge
62. Quoted from Hannah More. M. G. Jones. Cambridge Uiversity Press
63. St. James's Chronicle 12-14 August 1779
64. Donkin, op. cit., p 154
65. For Ellen Donkin's informative detailed account of the controversy: 'The Paper War of Hannah Cowley and Hannah More', see Donkin, *op. cit.*
66. *The Poetry of Anna Matilda* (1788) Myers p210
67. Drabble, Margaret, ed. "Della Cruscans". *Oxford Companion to English Literature.* OUP 1985
68. Silvia Bordoni. *The Della Cruscans' Anglo-Italian Politics.* University of Nottingham. 2006
69. *The World* 29 June 1787. *The Poetry of The World.* John Bell ed. 1788. *The Della Cruscans: Survey of Criticism and resources 1956-2009.* University of Liverpool
70. *The World* 29 June 1787
71. *The World* 10 July 1787
72. *The World* 31 July 1787
73. *The World* 4 August 1787
74. Byron: English Bards ll. 59-60.
75. The Cambridge History of English and American Literature in 18 volumes (1907-21). Volume XI. *The Period of the French Revolution..* viii Southey. 23 The Della Cruscans
76. For a full account of Mary Robinson's life see websites: *Women Poets' Timeline Project: Mary Robinson: the First Modern Celebrity,* and *Mary Darby Robinson – the Poems.* Also M.J. Levy *The Mistresses of George IV.* Peter Owen, 1996
77. Shakespeare, *Hamlet* I.iii
78. *Baviad* ll. 27-28
79. Paula Byrne. *Perdita.* Random House. New York. 2004
80. Ibid.
81. Hester Davenport, *The Prince's Mistress: A Life of Mary Robinson.* Sutton Publishing, 2004
82. The Italian sonnet form was introduced into England by Sir Thomas Wyatt (1503-1542) and soon adopted by the Earl of Surrey (1516-1547). The Petrarchan sonnet adopted by Milton employed a rhyming pattern with the first and second quatrains identical, the third quatrain in alternate rhyme extended in the final couplet (thus: abba/abba/cdcdcd. Shakespeare adopted a more openly expressive tone, all three quatrains with identical rhyming pattern but changing the rhyme with each succeeding quatrain and ending with a straight rhyming couplet (thus: abab/cdcd/efef/gg.
83. Out of some 10,000 lines of Sappho's poetry, fragments of ancient papyrus. no more than 650 lines of lyrical verse remain for generations of literary critics to

theorise about down the centuries. Admired by the scholars of Alexandria, her reputation for the expression of same-sex eroticism crept surreptitiously into the thoughts of poets such as Ovid and Petrarch, onwards through 18th century with Ambrose Philips [*The Spectator* 1711], Alexander Pope, and the Della Cruscans, and thence to Byron, Tennyson, A.E. Houseman, W.H. Auden and, in America, Robert Frost.

84. T.N. Longman and O. Rees, 1799. See the recent American study by Lia A. Mandaglio: Hannah More, the Conventionalist, and Mary Robinson, the Radical: Differing Feminist Perspectives on 19th Century Women's Progress, Purity, and Power.' *Lethbridge Undergraduate Research Journal* Volume 2 Number 1. 2007.
85. Walsh p808
86. Boyle p152
87. Boyle p132; Drabble, Margaret, ed. "William Gifford". *Oxford Companion to English Literature.* OUP 1985.

CHAPTER TEN The Shape of Things to Come

1. Monroe Lippman, Head of Department of Speech and Dramatic Art. Tulane University. *Stephen Price: The American Theatre's First Commercial Manager.* Routledge. Taylor and French Group. 1 April 2009. Southern Speech Journal Vol.5 Issue 4 1940.
2. John Kenrick. *Theatre in New York County: A Brief History.* 2003/2005
3. Tracy C. Davis, *The Economics of the English Stage 1800-1941.* Cambridge University Press. 2000
4. Survey of London. Vol. 35. BM *Collection of Memoranda....The Theatre Royal, Drury Lane and the Royal Opera house, Covent Garden.* (C120 h 1 Add MS 27,831ff 110-12).
5. John Hamilton Reynolds. See Appendix A for complete poem.
6. Dobbs p146 [?]
7. Dobbs p146
8. Dobbs p147
9. *The Diaries of William Charles Macready 1833-1851.* New York 1911 p380
10. Alfred Bunn, *The Stage Before and Behind the Curtain* (3 vols. 1840)
11. Dobbs p146
12. The Complete Works of Oscar Wilde. Introduced by Vyvyan Holland, Collins 1948. New Edition 1966.
13. Dobbs p168
14. Macqueen Pope p292
15. Macqueen Pope p293
16. Violet Vanbrugh 1872-1949. ODNB Oxford University Press 2004
17. Erroll Sherson p3
18. Colley Cibber, *Lives and Characters of the most Eminent Actors and Actresses,* 1733
19. 'Dan Leno's Cricketers' *Sheffield Evening Telegraph* 20 June 1899 p4
20. Gyles Brandreth. *The Funniest Man on Earth: The Story of Dan Leno.* Hamish Hamilton London
21. Gyles Brandreth, *op. cit.,* pp85-89
22. Leno carries us out of the old 19th century traditions into a new 20th century dimension, with recordings of his monologues and 14 short films.
23. Barbara Belford, *Bram Stoker: A Biography of the Author of Dracula* p9, London: Weidenfeld and Nicolson, 1996; Paul Davis, *From Castle Rackrent to*

Castle Dracula Ch.8.
24. Madeleine Bingham. *Henry Irving and the Victorian Theatre* 1978.
25. Hugh Lamb. 'Erckmann-Chatrian'. Penguin *Encyclopedia of Horror and the Supernatural*. Viking. New York 1986. Much admired by M.R. James.
26. From a review in *Over the Footlights* 1871.
27. Eric Jones-Evans (editor). Henry Irving and 'The Bells': Irving's Personal Script to the Play. Manchester University University Press (1980) p6
28. George Rowell *Theatre in the Age of Irving*. Oxford. Basil Blackwell 1981.
29. Richard Findlater *The Player Kings* London. Weidenfeld and Nicolson. 1971
30. Alan Hughes: *Henry Irving, Shakespearean*. Cambridge, Cambridge UP 1981.
31. William Archer *Study and Stage: a yearbook of Criticism.* London. Grant Richards 1899
32. George Bernard Shaw *Plays Pleasant and Unpleasant* I:xxv 1898

Index of Persons

Abington, Frances 45-6, 51
Adam, Robert and James 8
Addington, Henry 154
Addison, Joseph 28ff, 74, 104, 107, 186, 217, 23, 318-9, 327
Arne, Susanna 45
Arne, Thomas 45
Arnold, Samuel James 122, 222,
Astley, Philip 315, 321
Austen, Jane 101, 221

Baddeley, Robert 45
Balfe, Michael William 306, 308
Barbon, Nicholas 6
Barry, Elizabeth 8, 41, 45n
Barry, Sir Charles 9
Barry, Spranger 52, 54, 179-180
Beaumont and Fletcher 15, 18, 313
Beazley, Samuel 118
Bellamy, George Anne 45, 52
Betterton, Thomas 16, 18, 21-2, 24, 31n, 41, 63
Betty, William 7, 9, 66-7, 187, 249
Bickerstaffe, Isaac 198
Bolingbroke, Robert 31
Booth, Barton 31ff, 104, 318,
Boucicault, Dion 308ff
Bowles, William Lisle 157
Bradshaw, Augustus Cavendish 122
Brougham, Henry, Lord 151, 155n, 206, 222
Browne, Isaac Hawkins 102
Buckhurst, Lord 7
Bunn, Alfred 123, 306-8
Burdett, Sir Francis 154, 159, 222
Busby, Dr Thomas 87, 99, 199, 202-3, 206ff, 214-5, 219, 221, 223, 225-6, 229, 327
Busby, George Frederick 65, 199-200, 207, 222
Busby, Richard 207
Butt, Alfred 325
Byron, Lord 67-8, 74, 88, 93, 99, 114, 116, 122-4, 126, 138-9, 142ff, 171ff, 192ff, 202-3, 211, 214ff, 222ff, 236, 239, 241, 243, 245, 253ff, 260-1, 264, 275, 277, 283, 285, 303, 306, 315, 327

Campbell, Herbert 313, 319
Campbell, Thomas 126, 183, 222

Canning, George 142, 151
Carey, Henry 103-4, 108ff, 302
Carlo the Dog 63, 65
Carroll, Lewis 99-100, 111
Centlivre, Susanna 46-7
Charles I 12-3
Charles II 8, 13-4, 18-9, 57, 88, 104, 233, 243, 326
Chatterton, Thomas 101, 135
Cibber, Colley 17, 21ff, 32ff, 65, 104, 318
Cibber, Mrs 52, 54
Cibber, Theophilus 32, 38, 45
Cibert, Caius Gabriel 34
Cobbett, William 243, 257ff
Coleridge, Samuel Taylor 138, 150, 222, 241, 252-3, 265, 267-8, 286, 290
Collier, William 25ff, 32, 86
Collins, Arthur 313-4
Colman, George 47, 58-60, 204, 218, 241
Congreve, William 22, 69, 80, 85, 134, 172
Corneille, Pierre 16
Cowley, Abraham 88
Cowley, Hannah 279ff, 286, 292, 294
Crawford, Ann 52
Cromwell, Oliver 12, 103, 111, 267
Cruikshank, George 229, 232, 304

Daly, Richard 55-6
Daniel, George 132
Davenant, Alexander 21
Davenant, Charles 21
Davenant, Sir William 12-3, 19, 21, 32, 38, 40, 104, 239, 326
Dibdin, Thomas 125
Dickens, Charles 5
Doggett, Thomas 25, 27-8, 32, 318
Drury, Sir Richard 3
Drury, Sir William 3
Dryden, John 14ff, 38, 40, 72ff, 85-6, 88, 92, 96-7, 101, 111, 128, 155, 160, 176, 197, 207, 209, 303, 311
Duke of Bedford 6, 13, 57, 221, 313
Duke of Cambridge 219, 221
Duke of Clarence 56
Duke of Cumberland 219, 221
Duke of Kent 219, 221
Duke of Marlborough 31, 80, 137
Duke of Sussex 219-221
Duke of York 66, 221

Dyer, George 208

Earl Marshall 12
Earl of Aberdeen - see George Hamilton Gordon
Earl of Anglesey 14
Earl of Rochester 8, 41n
Elgin, Lord 156-7
Ellenborough, Lord 5
Elliston, Robert 123, 137, 167, 171, 174, 183, 185, 187, 189, 192, 194-6, 218, 222, 303, 306, 315, 327
Erckmann-Chatrian 322

Farquhar, George 19, 22, 85, 304
Farren, Elizabeth, Countess of Derby 59
Fielding, Henry 5, 34, 38, 40, 101, 104
Fitzgerald, William Thomas 223, 242-5
Fitzherbert, Mrs xv
Fitzpatrick, Richard 54, 97, 142n
Fleetwood, Charles 36ff
Foote, Samuel 45
Forbes-Robertson, Sir Johnstone 325
Ford, Dr James 50, 56
Fox, Charles James 142, 154
Frederick Howard, Earl of Carlisle 151-2, 156, 227

Garrick, David 8-9, 35ff, 50ff, 57, 63, 66, 78, 83, 86, 98, 101, 134-5, 166, 169, 174, 179-181, 184, 188, 192-3, 195, 233, 279-80, 288, 304, 319, 324-7
Gaunt, John of 2
Gay, John 33-4, 107-08
George I 32, 103
George II 37
George III 65, 87, 277
Gifford, William 87, 155, 222, 281
Gillray, James 63
Girondistes 144
Goldsmith, Lewis 119-121, 195
Gordon, George Hamilton 146, 157
Gray, Thomas 120n, 175
Grenville, William Wyndham 159, 220-1
Grimaldi, Joseph 62-3, 65, 308, 315
Gwynne, Nell 7, 14, 292, 319, 326

Hadfield, James 66
Hallam, Henry 148n
Hallam, Thomas 37

Hammond, W H 308
Handel, George Frederick 37, 45
Harley, Edward 31
Harris, Sir Augustus 310ff, 318
Harris, Thomas 57
Hart, Charles 13-4, 18
Heatherington, Henry 317
Herbert, Sir Henry 13
Hewat, Sir Thomas 33
Highmore, John 36
Hill, Rowland 16, 222
Hobhouse, John Cam 143, 155-7
Hogarth, William 8, 37
Holland, Henry 56-7, 59-60, 326
Holland, Lady 145-8, 152-4, 175, 182-3, 188, 195, 197, 227, 229, 327
Holland, Lord 67, 116, 122, 124, 138-9, 142ff, 164ff, 192ff, 202, 253, 327
Home, John 52
Hone, William 229, 232
Hood, Thomas xiv, 14, 16, 57, 61-2, 88, 126, 155-6, 206, 222, 232-3, 236, 243, 252, 259, 266, 321
Hume, Joseph 125-6

Inwood, William xiv-xv, 8
Irving, Edward 16, 233
Irving, Henry xvi, 9, 44, 310, 312, 315, 318, 320, 321ff

James I 5
Jeffrey, Francis 102, 240-241, 245-6, 261, 273, 300
Jersey, Lady xv, 164, 188
Johnson, Samuel 37, 42, 46, 64, 78ff, 92, 96, 101, 172-3, 176, 178, 181ff, 197, 205, 233, 239, 326-7
Jonson, Ben 12, 42, 69, 80ff, 92n, 101, 136n
Jordan, Dorothy 9, 56, 61-2, 279

Kean, Edmund 9, 44, 86, 123, 180, 302ff
Kemble, John Philip 44, 55-6, 61, 64-5, 86, 180, 204, 222, 279, 302-3, 307
Killigrew, Thomas 12ff, 57-8, 72, 326
Kotzebue, Auguste von 61, 92, 303

Lacy, James 41, 44, 50, 57
Lacy, John 13, 53
Lafayette, Marquis de 142-4
Lamb, Caroline, Lady 67, 153, 164, 182, 228-9
Lamb, Charles 126, 246
Lamb, George 126, 183

Index

Lansdowne, Lord 148n, 185, 188
Lardner, Dionysius 309
Lefanu, Alicia 125
Leigh, Augusta 229
Leno, Dan xvi, 9, 311, 318ff
Lewis, Matthew Gregory ('Monk') 145, 241, 322
Linley, William 125, 133-4
Lisle, Thomas 13, 22
Lord Chamberlain 22, 25, 32, 41, 103-4
Loutherbourg, Philippe-Jacques 46
Lucretius 87, 99, 203, 207ff, 213, 216ff
Ludd, Ned 158

Macklin, Charles 36ff, 44, 54, 320
Macready, William 9, 44, 305ff
Madame Vestris 9, 61, 306, 309, 315
Marlowe, Christopher 100, 285
Martineau, Philip 134
Medbourne, Matthew 35
Melbourne, Lady 67, 124, 153, 164-5, 182, 196
Merry, Robert 282-3
Milbanke, Annabella 153, 223, 225, 228
Mirabeau, Comte de 144
Mitford, Mary Russell 131
Mohun, Michael 13
Moliere 35
Moore, Thomas xvi, 93, 145, 222, 239, 261ff, 276-7
More, Hannah 205, 280, 292, 361
Murray, John 150, 171, 223, 225-6, 240, 255, 264

Napoleon xvi, 92, 94, 120-1, 142, 146-8, 154, 175, 221, 227, 233, 242, 244, 256-7, 277, 327
Nash, John 9, 118
Nelson, Lord xvi, 80, 87, 93, 137, 221, 242, 267
Novello, Ivor 326

Oldfield, Anne 22, 25, 35
Otway, Thomas 53, 61, 85, 172

Page, Anne 131
Palmer, John 33
Patterson, W 135
Pepys, Samuel 14
Petty-Fitzmaurice, Henry see Lansdowne
Philips, Ambrose 31n, 105ff

Piozzi 282
Pitt, William 67, 82, 134, 159
Pope, Alexander 29-30, 34-5, 37, 41, 46, 74, 78, 82, 85-6, 88, 92, 96, 105-7, 110, 146, 155, 167, 176, 182, 186, 197, 205, 209, 252-3, 291, 294
Pope, Jane 46, 51
Price, Stephen 123, 303-4, 325
Prince Regent xv, 4, 6, 9, 44, 57, 87, 118, 219-21, 229
Pritchard, Hannah 41, 45

Queen Anne 28, 32, 58, 104
Queen Mary 3n, 22
Quin, James 36-8, 54

Raleigh, Cecil 312-3
Raleigh, Walter 94, 100
Raymond, George 167, 199, 201-2
Redding, Cyrus 145
Reynolds, Frederick 63
Rich, Christopher 21ff, 32, 40, 57, 320
Rich, John 32-3, 41n, 51
Robinson, Mary xv, 44, 87, 286ff
Rogers, Samuel 126, 138, 149, 151, 158

Sappho 291, 299
Scott, Walter 9, 60, 120, 123, 126, 138, 221, 236, 239, 241
Sedley, Sir Charles 7
Shakespeare, William 14, 18, 23, 44, 46, 75, 78, 82ff, 94, 96, 101, 105, 129, 134-135, 137, 180, 181, 184, 187, 233, 291, 303, 305, 308, 311, 320-1, 324-5, 327
Shelley, Percy Bysshe 236-8, 277
Sheridan, Richard Brinsley xvi, 39, 44, 46, 48, 49ff, 85, 88-9, 92, 94, 99, 101, 114-6, 121-2, 125, 132-3, 136-7, 145, 155, 159, 166, 174, 184, 186, 195, 200, 204, 218, 238-9, 257, 261, 279-80, 304, 307, 309, 327
Siddons, Sarah xv, 9, 52-3, 55-6, 58, 61-2, 64-6, 86, 98, 134, 166, 169, 172, 187-8, 193, 195, 292
Skipwith, Sir Thomas 21
Smith, Horace and James 87, 236ff, 246, 253, 257, 261, 264, 277, 295, 300
Southerne, Thomas 53, 80
Southey, Robert xvi, 106, 120, 123, 126, 138, 221, 241, 256, 264ff
Steele, Sir Richard 28, 32
Stoker, Bram 321-2, 324
Swiney, Owen 25

Talleyrand, Charles Maurice de 142-4, 146
Tate, Nahum 23, 82
The Harlot's House 8
Tickell, Thomas 107

Index

Twiss, Horace 124, 164

Vanbrugh, John 22, 25, 51, 69, 80, 85
Vassall, Elizabeth 145
Vassall-Fox, Henry - see Lord Holland

Wade, J 129-30
Walpole, Robert 37-8, 40, 104, 108-9
Ward, Charles 126, 130, 238-9, 257
Warton, Thomas 102
Watts, Isaac 99-100, 251
Webber, Andrew Lloyd 326-327
Wellington, Duke of xvi, 80, 87, 92-3, 137-8, 242, 244
West, Sarah 87
Whitbread, Samuel 114ff, 126, 130, 135-7, 154, 173-4, 178, 183-4, 187, 192, 222, 257, 260, 274-5, 327
Whitefield, Rev George 38
Wilks, Robert 25, 27, 32, 35-6, 104
William and Mary 20
Wilmot, John 8
Woffington, Peg 41, 45
Wordsworth, William 138, 150, 239, 245ff, 254, 265, 276, 293
Wren, Christopher xiv, 16-7, 56
Wyatt, Benjamin xiv, xvii, 114, 117-8, 122, 127, 129, 175, 189, 222, 233, 244, 248-9, 315, 321, 326
Wyatt, George 117

Yates, Mary Ann 52
Yates, Richard 44
Young Roscius - see Betty, William
Younge, Elizabeth 46

Subject Index

Adelphi Terrace 8
An Address without a Phoenix by STP 252
Antigallican Monitor 195, 201, 364

Baby's Debut, The by WW 245-6
Baviad, The (Gifford) 87, 185, 222, 281
Bedlam 45, 66, 176
Beggar's Opera, The (John Gay) 33, 107, 184
Bells, The (Erckmann-Chatrian) 322-3
Bloomsbury 6, 13
Bow Street 7, 33, 201
Brunswick Theatre 9, 60
Brydges Street 14
Button's coffee house 107

Cataract of Lodore, The (Southey) 265
Cato (Addison) 28ff, 74, 86, 104, 182, 318, 331-2
Chelsea 2, 57n
Childe Harold (Byron) 93, 147, 153, 157, 160, 197, 223, 228, 254-6
Cockpit Theatre 12
Covent Garden 2, 4, 6, 9, 13, 24, 33, 37-8, 41, 51-3, 56, 61, 64ff, 94, 114, 179-181, 184, 189, 217-8, 239, 280, 307ff, 313, 316
Critic, The (Sheridan) xvi, 14, 39-40, 52, 69, 92-4, 97, 101, 132
Cui Bono? By Lord B 254, 256, 283

De Rerum Natura 203, 207-209, 217, 219, 221, 223, 226
Della Cruscans 281ff, 291, 293-4
Dorset Gardens 8, 16, 18, 21
Drury House 3
Drury Lane - Rotunda 6, 118
Drury Lane Addresses xv, 19, 26, 34, 51, 59, 74, 78, 80, 86, 93, 96, 198-9, 205, 214, 223, 327
Drury's Dirge by LM 279ff
Duke's House - see Dorset Gardens
Dunciad, The (Pope) 34-5, 41, 86, 97, 105, 155

Edinburgh Review 102, 149, 151, 240, 253, 261, 268, 300
English Bards and Scotch Reviewers (Byron) 148-9, 155, 160, 227
English Opera House 9, 61, 321
Epilogues see Prologues

390

Index

Fire of 1672 15, 58, 296
Fire of 1809 xvi, 69, 114, 123, 326
Frame-breakers 153, 160, 260

Genuine Addresses xvi, xvii, 6, 30, 64, 80, 92, 233, 239-240, 327
Gibbon's Tennis Court 13
Globe Theatre 14,75
Goodmans's Fields 3, 38, 40, 44-5
Goths and Vandals 26
Great Fire 4, 6
Green Room, The 14, 37, 45, 53
Grub Street 104,124,148n, 165, 220

Hampshire Farmer's Address by WC 257ff
Harlequin 25, 44, 51, 65, 86, 104, 133, 211-2, 215, 275, 319
Harlot's House, The (Hogarth} 8
Haymarket Theatre 9, 38, 60, 122n, 302, 316
Holland House Papers 181

Idler, The 101

Jacobins 144,261
Jacobites 35, 44, 50

King's Theatre - see Haymarket Theatre
King's House 13, 14, 18

Lincoln's Inn Fields 2, 4, 13, 15, 22, 24, 32, 37
Lisle's Tennis Court 22
Living Lustres, The by TM 261ff
London Magazine 126, 236
London Spy, The 3
Long Acre 2, 4
Love for Love (Congreve) 22
Loyal Effusion by WTF 242ff

MacQueen-Pope 27
Maeviad, The (Gifford) 87, 155
Monody 48, 86ff, 188, 327, 329
Monthly Magazine 236
Morning Chronicle 195, 245
Muses, The 11, 26, 50-1, 58, 80, 85-6, 93, 120-1, 178, 195, 197, 233, 296, 318, 327
Musicals 325-6
Namby-Pamby 110-1, 212

Old Drury 14, 16, 64, 135-6, 156, 197, 216-7, 243, 299
Old Price' riots 24, 189
On the Nature of Things see De Rerum Natura

Palace of Whitehall 2
Pantomime 32, 44, 51, 62-3, 84, 86, 104, 124, 133, 137, 180, 302, 307-8, 310-1, 318, 320, 324
Parliament Hill Fields 8
Parody xvi, 39-40, 69, 72, 86, 91ff, 99ff, 132, 135, 186, 215, 217, 236, 239, 242ff,
Parthenon xiv, xv, 156, 157n
Patriotism 31, 77, 103, 212, 204, 229
Phoenix, The 12, 18, 19, 34, 93, 121, 136-8, 174, 195, 233, 242-3, 252, 257, 297, 302, 313, 318, 326-7
Pizarro (Sheridan) 67, 92, 121, 303
poetaster 92, 94, 120-1, 126, 174, 178, 185-6, 212, 283
Pop goes the Weasel 316
Progress of Cant, The xiv,16, 57, 155, 157, 206, 232,
Prologues (Dryden) xv, 20, 72ff, 85ff, 136, 176, 182, 186, 198, 242, 273, 326
Punch magazine 101

Queen of Bohemia 3

Rambler, The 101
Rebuilding,The by RS 264ff
Regent Street 4, 9, 118
Rejected Addresses xvi, 87, 102, 116, 123, 135, 138, 146, 150, 195, 235ff, 318, 327
Riots 24, 41, 54, 56, 189, 317
Rivalries xvi, 33, 103
Rivals, The (Sheridan) 20, 200
Rolliad, The 87, 97n, 142n, 255
Roscius' 36, 38, 65ff
Royalty Theatre 9, 33, 60, 307, 324
Rural Rides (Cobbett) 259

Scandal xvi, 14, 19, 44, 98, 103, 117, 132, 145, 148, 282, 287-8, 314
School for Scandal 46, 51, 184
Sir Fretful Plagiary 94, 96, 176, 202, 215
Sneer, Dangle and Puff 14, 73, 92, 94-5, 138
Somerset House 3
Spanish Armada, The (Augustus Harris) 311
Spanish Wars 51, 92, 94, 103, 115, 222, 233, 311, 327
St James's Chronicle 214, 280
St Paul's Cathedral xiv, 34, 37
St. Clement Danes 3-4
St. Giles Church 4, 184

St. Pancras New Church xiv, 233
Stabbing Act 5
Strand(e), The 2-4, 8, 315
Tartuffe (Moliere) 35, 199n
Tatler, The 26, 28
Temple of the Muses 11, 50, 58, 80, 86, 121, 195, 197, 296
Theatre Royal Drury Lane xvi, 9, 18, 21, 25-6, 29, 32ff, 46, 50-1, 57, 60-1, 65, 72, 86, 93, 98ff, 104, 114, 116-7, 123, 142, 153, 160, 164, 179, 192, 199, 203, 207, 213, 232-3, 248, 288, 302, 315, 318, 321, 325-6
Theatre Royal Drury Lane: Fire of 1809 - see Fire of 1809
Three Bears, The (Southey) 266
Times, The 101, 195, 198
Tom Thumb 38-40

Utrecht, Treaty of 31

Way of the World, The (Congreve) 22
West Mynstre 2
Westminster 2, 6, 37, 114, 232, 315, 324
Westminster School 32, 207, 269,
Whigs 28ff, 37ff, 104, 115, 122, 143-4, 154, 158, 227, 260
Wyche Street (Aldwych) 3

Milton Keynes UK
Ingram Content Group UK Ltd.
UKHW050922290823
427498UK00006BA/107/J